Penguin Education

Kinship

Editology Readings

Editor
Tom Burns

Advisory Board
Fredrik Barth
Michel Crozier
Ralf Dahrendorf
Erving Goffman
Alvin Gouldner
Edmund Leach
David Lockwood
Gianfranco Poggi
Hans Peter Widmaier
Peter Worsley

Kinship

Selected Readings
Edited by Jack Goody

Penguin Books

Penguin Books Ltd, Harmondsworth,
Middlesex, England
Penguin Books Inc., 7110 Ambassador Road,
Baltimore, Md 21207, U.S.A.
Penguin Books Australia Ltd,
Ringwood, Victoria, Australia

First published 1971
This selection copyright © Jack Goody, 1971
Introduction and notes copyright © Jack Goody, 1971

Made and printed in Great Britain by
Cox & Wyman Ltd, London, Reading and Fakenham
Set in Monotype Times

This book is sold subject to the condition that
it shall not, by way of trade or otherwise, be lent,
re-sold, hired out, or otherwise circulated without
the publisher's prior consent in any form of
binding or cover other than that in which it is
published and without a similar condition
including this condition being imposed on the
subsequent purchaser

Contents

Introduction 9

Note on Abbreviations 15

Part One **The Family** 17

1 R. N. Adams (1960) 19
The Nature of the Family

2 B. Malinowski (1930) 38
The Principle of Legitimacy

3 B. Malinowski (1927) 42
The Family Complex in Patrilineal and Matrilineal Societies

Part Two **Incest and Sex** 45

4 C. Lévi-Strauss (1949) 47
The Principles of Kinship

5 J. Goody (1956) 64
Incest and Adultery

Part Three **The Developmental Cycle** 83

6 M. Fortes (1958) 85
The Developmental Cycle in Domestic Groups

Part Four **Joking and Avoidance** 99

7 A. R. Radcliffe-Brown (1952) 101
Joking Relationships

Part Five **Marriage Transactions** 117

8 A. R. Radcliffe-Brown (1950) 119
Dowry and Bridewealth

9 E. Friedl (1962) 134
Dowry, Inheritance and Land-Tenure

10 J. Hajnal (1965) 140
European Marriage Patterns in Perspective

Part Six Plural Marriage 149

11 E. R. Leach (1955) 151
Polyandry, Inheritance and the Definition of Marriage

12 R. Clignet (1970) 163
Determinants of African Polygyny

Part Seven Marriage and Alliance 181

13 L. Dumont (1957) 183
The Marriage Alliance

14 D. Maybury-Lewis (1965) 199
Prescriptive Marriage Systems

Part Eight Divorce and Marriage Stability 225

15 M. Gluckman (1950) 227
Marriage Payments and Social Structure among the Lozi and Zulu

16 J. C. Mitchell (1961) 248
Social Change and the Stability of Marriage in Northern Rhodesia

Part Nine Kin Groups 261

17 M. Fortes (1953) 263
The Structure of Unilineal Descent Groups

18 A. I. Richards (1950) 276
Matrilineal Systems

19 R. N. Pehrson (1964) 290
Bilateral Kin Groupings

Part Ten Kin Terms 297

20 J. Goody (1970) 299
The Analysis of Kin Terms

21 A. R. Radcliffe-Brown (1930) 307
Kin Terms and Kin Behaviour

22 E. A. Hammel (1965) 317
Formal Semantic Analysis

Part Eleven **Ritual and Fictive Kinship** 329

23 E. N. Goody (1970) 331
Forms of Pro-Parenthood: The Sharing and Substitution of Parental Roles

24 S. W. Mintz and E. R. Wolf (1950) 346
Ritual Co-Parenthood (compadrazgo)

Part Twelve **Changing Patterns of Kinship** 363

25 W. J. Goode (1963) 365
World Changes in Family Patterns

Further Reading 384

Acknowledgements 391

Author Index 393

Subject Index 397

Introduction

In this book I have tried to set the study of kinship in as wide a framework as possible. Social anthropologists have been primarily concerned with studies of other cultures, while sociologists have dwelt very much upon the part of the world in which they live. Hence the rough division of labour between this Volume of Readings and its parallel on the family (Anderson, 1971) is between other cultures and Western society. This division is far from satisfactory and not one that should be perpetuated. The alternative split between close (familial) and distant (kin) relationships is equally objectionable, especially when it gives rise to the idea that complex societies have the family and simpler ones have kinship.

To try to dissolve the boundaries, I have included some sections that refer to European kinship, especially those by Friedl, Hajnal and Goode (Readings 9, 10 and 25). But as important as extending the scope of studies of other cultures in a geographical or sociological sense is the job of extending their theoretical and technical range. In the early days of anthropology, large-scale, long-run hypotheses were subjected to wide-ranging discussions; E. B. Tylor's essay (1889) on marriage and descent is perhaps the most remarkable. Since that time, the range of topics considered has in many ways grown smaller. In recent years, interest has been concentrated on three main fields, the role of kin groups (see Readings 6, 17 and 18), the role of marriage as alliance (see Readings 4, 13 and 14), and the componential analysis of kin terms. In all of these fields, stress has been placed upon 'formal' analysis, a tendency which can lead to a severe restriction in the number of variables considered. Such theoretical model building has its uses in letting us see how systems of limited possibility might work, but it is often at a disadvantage in showing us how they actually do work. The alternative view, which holds that these models apply to how the actors see them work, is usually backed by insufficient evidence; 'ideological models' are in any case no substitute for 'working models'.

In this book, then, I have included important contributions to the main developments in the study of kinship, and especially articles which attempted to sum up the state of play. But there are also sections on important subjects which have had too little attention given to them in recent years, at any rate on the general level. In this category of neglected topic I would include the analysis of marriage transactions (except in the limited context of divorce), as well as the study of joking and avoidance relations, and, indeed, that kind of depth analysis of intra-familial relationships with which Malinowski was much concerned (Fortes (1949) provides a notable exception). I have also included sections upon two other aspects of kinship which have never received sufficient attention. The first is the influence of 'demographic' factors. The work of Hajnal (Reading 10), among others, has emphasized how important for the social system are variables like the age of marriage (for particular studies see Tait (1961), Hart and Pilling (1960)); the excerpt from the work of Clignet (Reading 12) examines the effects of widespread plural marriage in Africa. Significantly, these two authors also analyse problems of social change; Hajnal discusses the emergence as well as the effects of the 'European marriage pattern' (characterized by a late age of marriage for men and women and the large proportion of spinsters and bachelors), and Clignet looks at the part played by polygyny in the processes of urbanization and development in contemporary West Africa. The study of changing kinship systems has inevitably played a smaller part in field studies, whose duration is limited to a restricted period. But it is a necessary part of the total picture of those institutions and one that has received an intelligent treatment in the work of Goode (Reading 25).

The study of kinship goes back about a century to the work of the American lawyer, Lewis Henry Morgan (1818–81), whose major books included an account of the matrilineal society of the Iroquois (1851), a worldwide analysis of kin terms (1871) and an important essay on the history of the human family (1877). Morgan's work had much influence on Marx, whose notes were written up by Engels as *The Origin of the Family, Private Property and the State* (1884). Apart from Morgan, the most significant figures of the nineteenth century writing on social anthropology were J. J. Bachofen (1861), Sir Henry Maine (1861), and J. F. McLennan (1865); the first of these claimed the primacy of matriarchy, the second stressed the significance of early patriarchy. Maine also insisted upon the importance of the kinship corporation, the clan or lineage. It was McLennan, a supporter of theories of early matriarchy, who introduced the terms exogamy (the rule of out-marriage) and endogamy (the rule of in-marriage) into the technical vocabulary.

A book of this kind cannot go into these early discussions of kinship. Indeed there is insufficient space even for what is perhaps the most seminal paper ever written on kinship institutions: the article of E. B. Tylor (1889) to which I have already referred. This contribution provided the starting point for much of the exchange theory of incest and marriage (see Lévi-Strauss and Goody (Readings 4 and 5)); in it the author describes early marriage as a 'family transaction' and introduces the term 'cross-cousin marriage' (see Reading 14). But it is also the first example of the systematic application of numerical techniques to the comparison of human societies, and pioneered the cross-cultural method continued by Hobhouse, Wheeler and Ginsberg (1930) and later developed by G. P. Murdock (1949; see also Marsh, 1967). Tylor was fortunate in having as the chairman of the meeting at which he gave his paper the statistician, Francis Galton, who raised a number of points in discussion about the possible effects of diffusion (often referred to as 'Galton's problem'), which have been given much thought in the revival of interest in cross-cultural studies over the past decade (Naroll, 1965).

In the same essay, Tylor discussed a number of institutions such as the levirate (by which he meant the inheritance of the widow by the husband's brother or other close kinsman), the sororate (the replacement of a dead wife by her sister or close kinswoman), the couvade ('the father, on the birth of his child, makes a ceremonial pretence of being the mother'), and marriage 'by capture'. Like other writers of the later nineteenth century he was concerned to present long-term schemes of unilineal development, which turned largely upon changes in the major systems of descent (matrilineal and patrilineal), and in the main forms of marriage (polyandry, marriage by capture, etc.). However, his paper was a turning point in that it stressed correlational studies: the relations of institutions existing side by side with one another.

A turning point of yet greater importance was the shift to intensive analysis encouraged by the development of professional fieldwork, notably by A. R. Radcliffe-Brown and B. Malinowski. Because of their sociological bent towards functional analysis and their experience in the field, they were able to bring a new dimension to the study of kinship, not only in the analysis in depth of particular societies (in which many of their students excelled) but also in the more general fields of kinship: Radcliffe-Brown's paper on Australia (1930) and his introduction to *African Systems of Kinship and Marriage* (1950) remain the best general statements on a number of aspects of kinship, although much more work has been done on studies of particular societies and on specific topics such as cross-cousin marriage, lineage systems and the formal analysis of kin terms.

What about the future of kinship studies? With so broad a subject, there is an equally broad range of possibilities. We can look forward to growing numbers of analyses in depth of particular societies, especially as more scholars from developing countries study their own or neighbouring cultures. The study of one's own culture has some disadvantages; but one clear gain is in the command one has in matters of communication, a command that can help to avoid some of the superficiality to which the outside scholar is likely to fall victim. In this way, the qualitative data on inter-personal relations should greatly improve. Secondly, the advent of computers is already making itself felt in another way, that is, in the formalization, categorization and measurement of data for constructing models that attempt to simulate social processes. Thirdly, the division between the 'family studies' of 'industrial societies' and the 'kinship studies' of 'pre-industrial' ones is inevitably becoming blurred. This shift is taking place partly as a result of recognizing the greater differentiation in the pre-industrial sphere. For example, the lumping together of Australian, Chinese and South Indian systems as 'elementary structures' would appear to overlook the radical effects of economic factors on kinship; there are many features of Chinese kinship that link it to the peasants of Europe rather than to the hunters of Australia. This change in emphasis is also affected by a recognition of greater differentiation within and between industrial societies themselves (for example, the matrifocal tendencies among the urban working class as contrasted with the landed aristocracy), especially in those societies that are in the process of 'modernization,' namely, the countries of the Third World. These factors are blurring the old lines of division between the family and kinship, between sociology and anthropology, and hence raising more questions and leading to more adequate answers.

In making this selection I have tried to cover a range of topics in the field and to give preferences to articles which summarize a number of alternative approaches as well as making a theoretical point. In some cases I have been unable to find a suitable article that dealt generally with the field (outside the pages of an encyclopedia); in these cases (Readings 20 and 23), contributions have been prepared specially for this volume. In two other cases (Readings 15 and 22) Professors Gluckman and Hammel have kindly made additions to their original articles. Finally, I would like to thank Esther Goody, Sarah Cattermole and Joan Buckley for their help with this volume.

References

ANDERSON, M. (ed.) (1971), *Sociology of the Family*, Penguin.
BACHOFEN, J. J. (1861), *Das Mutterrecht*, von Krais & Hoffman.
FORTES, M. (1949), *The Web of Kinship among the Tallensi*, Oxford University Press.
ENGELS, F. (1884), *The Origin of the Family, Private Property and the State*, Höttingen.
HART, C. W. M., and PILLING, A. R. (1960), *The Tiwi of North Australia*, Holt, Rinehart & Winston.
HOBHOUSE, L. T., WHEELER, G. C., and GINSBERG, M. (1930), *The Material Culture and Social Institutions of the Simpler Peoples*, London School of Economics.
McLENNAN, J. F. (1865), *Primitive Marriage*, Black.
MAINE, H. (1861), *Ancient Law*, Murray.
MARSH, R. M. (1967), *Comparative Sociology*, Harcourt Brace & World.
MORGAN, L. H. (1851), *The League of the Iroquois*, Sage & Brother.
MORGAN, L. H. (1871), *Systems of Consanguinity and Affinity of the Human Family*, Smithsonian Institution.
MORGAN, L. H. (1877), *Ancient Society*, Macmillan Co.
MURDOCK, G. P. (1949), *Social Structure*, Macmillan Co.
NAROLL, R. (1965), 'Galton's problem: the logic of cross-cultural analysis', *Soc. Res.*, vol. 32, pp. 428–51.

RADCLIFFE-BROWN, A. R. (1930), 'Social organization of Australian tribes', *Oceania*, monogr. no. 1.

RADCLIFFE-BROWN, A. R. (1950), 'Introduction', *African Systems of Kinship and Marriage*, Oxford University Press.

TAIT, D. (1961), '*The Konkomba of Northern Ghana*, Oxford University Press.

TYLOR, E. B. (1889), 'On a method of investigating the development of institutions: applied to laws of marriage and descent', *J. anthropol. Inst.*, vol. 18, pp. 245–72.

Note on Abbreviations

The following abbreviations occur in this book:
FS   Father's son
MS   Mother's son
FBS Father's brother's son
FBD Father's brother's daughter
MZS Mother's sister's son
MZD Mother's sister's daughter
FZS Father's sister's son
FZD Father's sister's daughter

Part One The Family

The study of the family began with a long controversy about whether non-Western societies had such an institution at all. Its extensive, if not universal, distribution (the answer depends upon one's definition) was established by the investigations of E. A. Westermarck (1891) and by a fellow member of the London School of Economics, Bronislaw Malinowski (1913). The nature and necessity of the nuclear (or elementary) family, found to have such a widespread distribution, has been subject to extensive discussion which has recently been reviewed by Adams (Reading 1). There follow two short excerpts from Malinowski, one dealing with the importance of parent-child ties in the process of socialization, and the other specifically discussing the Freudian hypothesis about the universality of the Oedipus Complex. From his experience among the matrilineal Trobiands, he argues that different family systems will give rise to different kinds of 'nuclear complex' (Reading 3). While Malinowski's treatment of kinship has contributed little to later attempts in the direction of its formal analysis, his approach has been important in the study of the character of specific relationships, especially insofar as these are associated with different systems of inheritance and descent.

References

MALINOWSKI, B. (1913), *The Family among the Australian Aborigines: A Sociological Study*, University of London Monographs in Sociology, no. 2.

WESTERMARCK, E. A. (1891), *The History of Human Marriage*, Macmillan.

1 R. N. Adams

The Nature of the Family

Excerpts from R. N. Adams, 'An inquiry into the nature of the family', in G. E. Dole and R. L. Carneiro (eds.), *Essays in the Science of Culture*, Crowell, 1960, pp. 30–49.

Literature on the human family appearing during the past decade has taken a decided swing away from the earlier simple classificatory goals of identifying lineality, locality, descent groups and formal kin structures. The new direction, as has been noted by many persons active in the movement, has been towards examining the phenomenon within wider dimensions. No longer, for example, is it possible to speak simply and securely of matrilocality or of patrilocality without extensive and adequate analysis of the precise configurations standing behind the activities of the members of the particular society concerned (Fortes, 1949; Goodenough, 1956). In a very real sense many of the formerly analytic terms have become heuristic and descriptive.

With respect to the form of the nuclear family, however, there has been little evidence of increased interest in fundamentals. Concern here is as ancient as any in the field of social organization, but treatments of it continue to be predominantly expressions of profound convictions, buttressed by more or less convincing logical arguments stemming from a variety of theoretical premises. A recent example of this may be found in LaBarre's (1954) absorbing and provocative though unconvincing argument for the absolute necessity and inevitability of a continuing nuclear family. A more rigorous argument with the same conclusion but based on different kinds of evidence is contained in Murdock (1949). Murdock claims, on the basis of an examination of 250 societies, that there are no cases where the nuclear family is not the fundamental unit or cell upon which all further familial and kin elaborations are based. Both before and after Murdock's study, exceptions to this picture were cited, specifically the Nayar of Malabar (Linton, 1936; Gough, 1952; Cappannari, 1953), but in principle Murdock's judgement has met with general approval. Even an examination of the *kibbutz* led Spiro (1954) to conclude that whereas the *kibbutz* may have eliminated the nuclear family, it did so only through converting the entire community into a single large *gemeinschaft*.

The purpose of the present essay is to question whether some arguments in support of this general view are satisfactory, and to do so through a review of selected cases in which the nuclear family is manifestly only one type of basic form. This is in accord with, but varies in focus from, the interest expressed by Levy (1955) when he asked whether the nuclear family was 'institutionalized' in all societies. Levy pointed out that even though the statuses of father, mother, spouse, sister and brother may be present, they may not function as a nuclear family unit. He gave as an example the case of the traditional Chinese family. In the present paper the position is taken that social organization is flexible enough to permit different forms of the family to exist simultaneously. These different forms may not even take care of the same general functional needs of the total society, and in many cases certain of the standard nuclear family statuses (that is, mother-wife, father-husband, unmarried children) may not function at all. So far as present evidence indicates, there is no question but that these statuses are present in the society; rather it is a question of how they are filled and how they function. The flexibility of social organization permitting the appearance of different family forms rests on the fact that there are more elemental forms of the family than the nuclear, and that different forms may function in relation to different aspects or characteristics of the total social structure.

The cases to be discussed are taken from contemporary Central and South America. We are intentionally treating only this material (and omitting the Nayar and similar cases) because it better illuminates the propositions we wish to explore. Studies in Latin America have increasingly indicated that while most contemporary family systems of that region reckon descent bilaterally, there are many instances where family forms other than the nuclear are operative. The nuclear family is generally replaced in these circumstances by a group based on what we will call the maternal dyad, a residential unit composed of a mother and one or more children. As is the case in many nuclear family residences, these dyad households may also have a variety of other members present, both kin and non-kin.

Our interest will focus on two dyad forms: the maternal dyad, just described; and an adult dyad, composed of a man and woman, which we shall clumsily call the sexual or conjugal dyad. This dyad may be based simply on the sexual act, or may be further sanctioned by marriage. There is a third dyad, the paternal (composed of father and one or more children) which we will not treat here. It is with no intent of minimizing the importance of this dyad in the world at large that it is minimized here, but simply because it does not appear in significant numbers apart from the nuclear family in our data.[1] The identification of the maternal dyad, as distinct from the nuclear family, is made on the basis of the fact that there is no husband-father regularly resident. The cases used here are based on a distinction made between households with a woman head and those with a man head. This identification in terms of the sex of household heads stems from the nature of census data from which much of the information is derived. While having both theoretical and practical disadvantages, it serves sufficiently well for present purposes. The presence of woman-headed households (in these bilateral societies) is being used here as an index to the prevalence of the maternal dyad family form, and man-headed households as an index to the prevalence of the nuclear family form. While some woman-headed households are doubtless due to widowhood, the percentage of widows seldom exceeds 5 per cent of the women in the society, and, of course, many widows are not heads of households. While some man-headed households may be paternal dyads and not nuclear families, the number is not significant in all cases where specific information is available.

Some cases from Latin America

In his recent monograph on the community of Villa Recôncavo, Bahia, Brazil, Harry W. Hutchinson (1957) defines an entire

[1] It would perhaps be well to note at this point that not only the paternal dyad, but many other forms both of family elements and artificial or pseudo-kin relationships are pertinent to the discussion as it progresses. In the interests of brevity, I am raising these principles for discussion, and am intentionally not pursuing here all the lines of exploration they suggest.

social class segment of his community in terms of the fact that it is composed of women-headed households. Ninety (31 per cent) of the 290 households in the community were reported to be of this type in the 1950 census. Although Hutchinson says (1957, p. 151) that, 'The composition of these households almost defies classification', he promptly notes that 55 of them (19 per cent of the total number of families, and 61 per cent of the 90) are 'composed of mothers and children, with the addition in some cases of relatives and an *agregado* as well as boarders'. The other households in this class, Hutchinson describes as 'left-overs' from other families or marital unions. Although Hutchinson evidently feels that these families offer the scientist nothing but confusion, the fact that they were sufficiently distinct to move him to the extreme of categorizing them as an entirely separate 'social class', and the fact that they do manifest a considerable consistency with respect to the presence of the dyad family indicate that they do not defy classification.

The Services, in their report on Tobatí, Paraguay (1954), indicate that what they call 'incomplete' families form a prominent part of the community. Of a total of 292 families, only 133 (45·5 per cent) are complete nuclear families (with or without additional members); of the remainder, 113 (38·8 per cent of the total) are woman-headed households. This detailed report gives a somewhat higher woman-headed household rate than Emma Reh's earlier study (1947) of the Paraguayan community of Piribebuy where she estimated that 60 per cent of the families were complete and 33 per cent were headed by women. Since there are almost as many woman-headed households as man-headed households in Tobatí, there is little doubt that the maternal dyad is the basis of a highly significant portion of the household units.

Although national statistics for Brazil and Paraguay were not available to the writer, there is evidence from other areas that the presence of maternal dyad families is not a matter of limited or local significance. In Central America, 1950 census data are available for four countries concerning the relative number of families recorded as having women as heads of households: see page 23.

[. . .] The presence of woman heads of households in Central America is not a confused and random situation but is definitely associated with the Ladino population, as opposed to the Indian

Country	Number of families	Per cent of families with woman heads
Guatemala	561,944	16·8
El Salvador	366,199	25·5
Nicaragua	175,462	26·0
Costa Rica	143,167	17·2

population, is concentrated in certain regions, and is probably more commonly associated with town dwellers than with rural populations (Adams, 1957).

Another region from which there has been an increasing number of reports of dyad families is the Caribbean and the Guianas. Of the studies that have appeared in recent years one in particular has addressed itself to this issue and should concern us here. Raymond T. Smith (1956) studied three Negro towns in British Guiana in which the percentage of woman heads of households was as follows:

Town	Number of households	Per cent of households with woman heads
August Town	275	37·1
Perseverance	103	16·5
Better Hope	74	29·2

Many accounts of West Indian societies have indicated the presence of these families (as in the work of Herskovits, Campbell, Simey, and Henriquez) but for present purposes we will restrict ourselves to the work of Smith.

These cases from Paraguay, Brazil, Central America and British Guiana give ample evidence that in contemporary populations with bilateral descent systems woman-headed households are quite common. We infer, especially from those cases which have been described in some detail, that this is an index to an almost equally high incidence of families that have the maternal dyad as their basic unit.

The universal functions approach

The problem now is to arrive at a theoretical framework that will make these data intelligible. As literature on the family is extensive, we will restrict ourselves to a limited number of theories concerning the status of the nuclear family. The writers of particular interest to us here are Murdock, Parsons and R. T. Smith.

Murdock's multiple-function approach

Murdock's major reasons for seeing the nuclear family as a universal and inevitable phenomenon are that it was present in all the societies in his original sample for *Social Structure* (1949), and that logically it seemed to him that the family fulfilled a number of functions better than any other conceivable agency. The four functions he regards as primary (although he would doubtless allow others for any specific society) are 'fundamental to human social life – the sexual, the economic, the reproductive, and the educational'. Murdock is quite explicit in saying that 'Agencies or relationships outside of the family may, to be sure, share in the fulfillment of any of these functions, but they never supplant the family' (1949, p. 10). The immediate issue that arises from Murdock's propositions is whether in fact other agencies have not frequently taken over the functions that he regards as being uniquely served by the nuclear family. In reading Murdock, one gathers that he is referring not only to the presence of a nuclear family in all societies, but also to its pervasiveness among household groups in all societies. The implication is that its absence is considered by him to be an abnormal situation. When he says that 'no society . . . has succeeded in finding an adequate substitute for the nuclear family, to which it might transfer these functions', one cannot help concluding that almost everyone in all societies must therefore rely on the nuclear family to fulfill these functions.

The cases cited earlier make it clear that large segments of some contemporary societies do not have functioning nuclear families, and that the non-nuclear family segments cannot fruitfully be cast aside as 'abnormal' or 'disorganized', but are regular, viable, family units in a regular, functioning society. With respect to the four functions listed by Murdock, we simply find that other social agents do in fact take over the functions for extended periods; precisely who may do it varies from one society to another. The educational function may be taken care of by the mother, other relatives, chums, schools, and so on. The rationale that a male child must have a resident father in order to learn to be a man does not hold in fact. The economic function may be handled by the mother and the children as they grow older; to this can be added grandparents, brothers and other relatives who help either regularly or periodically. And, of course, the sexual function is handled well by other married men, boarders, visitors, friends, and so forth. The reproductive function does not need the father's presence; a midwife is more useful. While there is no denying the social necessity of the functions that Murdock has delineated, there is evidence that some families can achieve them without the presence of someone identified as a 'father-husband'.

Parsons's dual-function approach

In a recent collection of papers Talcott Parsons (1955) has expressed the opinion that the multiple-functions approach is not adequate to explain the basic necessity of the nuclear family. In its place, he offers another functional explanation. There are, he feels, two functions, and two functions only, that are necessary everywhere and account for the universal presence of the nuclear family. One of these concerns, which Murdock calls the 'educational', is namely the necessity of providing socialization of the child. The other (not on Murdock's list, but again he probably would not deny its potential importance) consists of the constant development and balancing of the adult personality which is achieved because of the constant interaction between spouses. Parsons singles out this second function as being of particular importance in explaining the restrengthening of the American (USA) nuclear family today.

Since Parsons proposes these two functions as being essential everywhere, any documented instance in which they are not operative should be sufficient to cast doubt on his thesis. Such an instance is provided by R. T. Smith's detailed study of the British Guiana Negro family. While Smith would hold that the nuclear family does have universality in the sense that all the statuses therein are recognized, he makes it clear in his study that some households remain with women as heads for extended periods, often for the greater part of the adult life of the woman concerned. He adds, furthermore, that even when men are attached to the household, it is precisely during this period that the 'men spend a considerable amount of time working away from home and they do not take any significant part in the daily life of the household. ... There are no tasks allotted to a man in his role as husband-father beyond seeing that the house is kept in good repair, and providing food and clothing for his spouse and the children' (1956, pp. 112–13). The function of socio-psychological integration assigned by Parsons to the husband-wife relationship would have considerable difficulty operating if the husband were absent most of the time. The specific functions that Smith assigns to the husband-father are economic. Parsons's argument for the universality of the nuclear family is basically no stronger than that of Murdock since the functions delineated by both can be taken care of by other agents in the society, or by other members of the family.

The fundamental weakness in Murdock's and Parsons's points of view is that they take functions that may be 'imperatives', 'universal functions', or 'basic prerequisites' for a society, and try to correlate them with functions that are fulfilled by the nuclear family. Since it is mistakenly believed that the nuclear family form is found everywhere, that is, a universal, it must therefore be correlated with some universal requirement of human society. It is correct that there are social prerequisites, and that the nuclear family has numerous functions; but to correlate the two is a deduction that is not empirically supported.

A structural approach

Another approach to the problem of the significance of the woman-headed household and maternal-dyad families is taken up in Smith's study (1956). Following the lead of his mentor, Meyer Fortes, Smith regards the family as something to be studied empirically and within a temporal as well as spatial framework (Fortes, 1949) and not a hardshelled cell that forms the building unit of all kin-based social structure. Unlike Murdock and Parsons, Smith has approached the family from the point of view of the ethnographer and not the ethnologist or comparative sociologist, and studied a society where the dyad family and woman-headed households are normal. Much of Smith's work is of interest, but we will concentrate here on some major propositions referring to the woman-headed households.

Smith reports that the woman-headed household in British

Guiana Negro society almost always goes through a stage during which there is a man attached to it.[2] A family starts in a nuclear form, and later develops into the maternal dyad form when the man leaves. Smith goes on to propose that there is a basic 'matrifocal' quality in the familial relations so that it is relatively easy for a family to be reduced to the maternal dyad type; the husband-wife relationship and the father-child relationship are much less important than is the mother-child relationship. The weak character of the husband-father role is related to a situation in the general social structure in British Guiana. General social status is conferred through ascribed membership in an ethnic-class group. The specific occupation of the husband, in the lower class, confers no prestige, and hence the children have nothing to gain from their fathers in this matter. This is made more obvious by comparing the lower class Negroes with members of the higher class. In the latter, the occupation of the father is of importance for the general social status of the entire family, and the father is considered an indispensable part of the family. Smith correlates the presence of the woman-headed household with a social status system in which the father can achieve no superior status.

Smith's work provides an important structural analysis of the significance of the woman-headed household and shows that the maternal dyad can and does exist effectively in spite of the theoretical positions of Murdock and Parsons. Parsons, who had access to Smith's study prior to the preparation of his own paper, failed to see the full implications of the Guiana material (Parsons, 1955, pp. 13 ff.). The fact that the Guiana family may include a man long enough to get a household institutionalized in the local society and to undertake the procreation of children, does not mean that the man is present to fulfill either of the functions that

2. This temporal difference was also noted in a survey of El Salvador in terms of residence pattern: 'even though the patterned residence at the time of marriage or beginning to live together may be neo-local, the subsequent departure of the man of the family leaves it a domestic establishment based on the fact that the woman lives there. It is, if you like, matrilocality by default.' And further: 'The solidarity of the Salvadorean nuclear family was reported in some places (Texistepeque and Chinameca) to be increased after the birth of children. This does not, however, seem to hold in all cases in view of the numerous cases in which the woman has retained her children and the man has gone elsewhere' (Adams, 1957, pp. 460–61).

Parsons tries to hold as being 'root functions' that 'must be found wherever there is a family or kinship system at all ...'.

The elemental family units: dyads and nucleus

In rejecting the propositions advanced by Parsons and Murdock in favour of a structural approach, their position concerning the elemental importance of the nuclear family is also cast into doubt. If 'functions' do not explain the absence of the nuclear family in some situations, they can hardly be called upon to support the claim of universality for that form. No matter how fruitful this position has been in reference to other problems in social structure, we must seek an alternative view here.

The nuclear family comprises three sets of relationship that are identifiable as dyads. There is the relationship based on coitus between a man and a woman, and which may be identified as the sexual dyad until or unless it is recognized as a marital union, in which case it becomes a conjugal dyad. There is, second, the maternal dyad, composed of mother and child, that presumably begins at the time of conception but is not of great social significance as a dyad until parturition. And third, there is the paternal dyad, between father and child, that is identified specifically because of the relationship established by the sexual or conjugal dyad. Both the sexual and conjugal dyad, on the one hand, and the maternal on the other, have clear cut correlates in biological activity. The paternal does not. So no matter what importance it may hold in a given society, at the present level of analysis it must be looked upon as a dyadic relationship of a different order; it exists not by virtue of a biological correlate, but by virtue of other dyads. Once given these dyads (all three: the sexual-conjugal, maternal and paternal) there are important economic functions that may be assigned them. Infant dependency through nursing is, after all, an economic relationship as well as a biological one. But the economic cooperation and interdependency that may be assigned beyond this level is clearly a socially defined activity with no immediate biological correlates.

If we reject the idea that the nuclear family is the fundamental 'atom' in the social 'molecule', or the irreducible unit of human kin organization, and take initially the two dyads with biological correlates as two distinct components which must each be present at certain times, but not necessarily always or simultaneously, we will be approaching a view of the elements of social organization which is less biased by contemporary social system philosophy. If we allow that the nuclear family is not the minimum model for the building of subsequent structures, then we can see that it is basically, as Lowie partially suggested (1948, p. 215), an unstable combination of two simpler elements, each of which is also unstable and temporal. This allows us to look at more complex forms without the bias of assuming the nuclear family always to be present, and to seek excuses for its absence. There is a significance to be attached to the nuclear as well as the dyad forms, but it is distinctive. The conjugal or sexual dyad is particularly significant because it is the reproductive unit of the society; the maternal dyad is the temporal link between successive generations of adult dyads. While theoretically the two kinds of dyads can operate independently at all times, the society would be a sadly disjointed affair were they to do so. Their combination into a nuclear family provides generational relationships for all concerned. Since such combinations can be a short-lived activity for the individuals involved, and actually may occupy only a limited time, most people are theoretically available most of the time to focus on the dyadic relationships.

The reason that human societies have supported the nuclear family in such abundance can be found at the level of social analysis. Like all animals, human beings live not only in families, but in larger aggregates which, following general usage, can generically be called *communities*. A community cannot maintain stability and continuity solely with such unstable and temporal forms as dyads for elemental units. Seen from this point of view, the nuclear family becomes one combination that, if on nothing more than a random basis, must inevitably occur from time to time. It is the simplest way of joining the two dyads. Since the mother is the only adult in the maternal dyad, and the wife is the only female in the sexual dyad, they can be joined most readily by identifying the wife with the mother. Once this identification is made, the nuclear unit is created and can fulfill many potential functions. But while its occurrence is inevitable, its continuation is by no means inevitable because each of the dyads alone can also fulfill some functions, and there are, in addition, presumably other societal agents that can also fulfill them. The nuclear family therefore becomes only *one of the ways* the community maintains itself. For some functions and under some circumstances, individuals may be effective agents; for others the elemental dyads are more efficient; for yet others the nuclear family may serve, and still others find other kinds of groups more useful. There are, in short, *alternative* ways in which the basic kin units can be used and combined for continued maintenance of the community.

The social universals of human society are not, then, as has been held by many students, the nuclear family and the community, but rather the community and the two dyads. The nuclear family is, in a sense, a structural by-product of the nature of the dyads, but one which is almost inevitable, even if for the briefest period. However, beyond these, the dyads may be subject to a variety of combinations to further the continuity of the community. The case described by Spiro (1954) as existing in the *kibbutz* and the details of the woman-headed households of the British Guiana Negroes described by Smith should not be interpreted as being exceptions to a principle of nuclear family universality, but as positive illustrations of how dyads may and do operate outside of the nuclear family. [...]

It should not be thought that the concept of the dyad in social structure has gone unnoticed in social anthropology. Its significance, however, has usually been in descriptive terms rather than as an analytical tool. A. R. Radcliffe-Brown, certainly a pioneer in structural studies, pointed out on a number of occasions that the basic elements of social structure were dyadic:

I regard as a part of the social structure all social relations of person to person. For example, the kinship structure of any society consists of a number of such dyadic relations, as between a father and son, or a mother's brother and his sister's son. In an Australian tribe the whole social structure is based on a network of such relations of person to person, established through genealogical connections (1952a, p. 191; see also 1952b, pp. 52–3).

But Radcliffe-Brown's view was somewhat different from that proposed here, as he also held that, 'The unit of structure from which a kinship system is built up is the group which I call an "elementary family", consisting of a man and his wife and their child or children, whether they are living together or not' (1952b

p. 51). The nuclear family, as a constellation of statuses, served as the central block although, unlike Murdock and Parsons, Radcliffe-Brown did not hold that this unit must everywhere exist.

While Radcliffe-Brown saw in the 'elementary family' three kinds of social relationships, 'that between parent and child, that between children of the same parents (siblings), and that between husband and wife as parents of the same child or children' (1952b, p. 51), he did not expressly project these as potential analytical units that could themselves be examined apart from the nuclear family context and considered as distinctive building blocks. On the other hand, Radcliffe-Brown did, in his principles of 'the unity of the sibling group' and 'the unity of the lineage', recognize the theoretical significance of a society's placing emphasis upon a given set of relationships that, in terms of the present discussion, we would see as a 'sibling dyad' and either the maternal or paternal dyad. He did not carry it farther at the time of the essay in question to include the husband-wife dyad as also being a potential centre of emphasis, nor did he distinguish between other maternal and paternal relations.

The woman-headed household and the total society

The thesis presented by Smith concerning the reasons for the appearance of the woman-headed household provides an analysis that on the surface fits well into the present argument. Over a single life cycle of Guiana Negroes the sexual or conjugal dyad tends to come into play strongly only at limited periods – for procreation and for support of the woman with infant. As a woman becomes free of dependent infants, the conjugal relation can and often does disappear or change its character. This dyad is weak because the members are part of an ethnically distinct, lower class community in which there is no status differentiation possible between males, and hence, little that one man can offer a family or son over what another can offer. According to this analysis we would expect to find similar developments in other similar situations. However, the data from Latin America do not support the extension of the analysis. Three examples will indicate the nature of the variations.

The first involves a comparison of the Guatemalan Indians and neighbouring Ladinos. The former have predominantly nuclear families while the latter have a significantly high proportion of woman-headed households. The populations involved hold comparable positions within the total social structure, but the Indians in particular are similar to the Guiana Negroes in being a lower class ethnic group within which the status of the father does not necessarily give status to the son. There is some variation in this matter, and a situation comparable to that of the Guiana Negroes is to be found less among the more traditional Indians than among the more acculturated ones. Among both Indians and Ladinos some segments of the population work on plantations, some live in independent villages, and some are part-time subsistence farmers and part-time labourers. Both have the same general concept of land tenure, and both live within the same general national context. But, it will be remembered, in the predominantly Indian departments the percentage of households with women as heads is considerably lower than that of the Ladino departments.

Although Indians and Ladinos live under similar conditions, the Ladino family is much closer to the model Smith sets up for the British Guiana Negroes than is the Mayan Indian family. The difference lies in what Smith has referred to in the Guiana situation as the 'marginal nature of the husband-father role' that gives rise to a 'matrifocal system of domestic relations and household groupings'. Shifting the theoretical focus from the structure of the family to the values associated with it is in one sense a shorthand method of indicating that somewhere the structure, in spite of overtly similar conditions, is different. Thus, presumably the Indians have within the structure of their total community certain features which stress the father-husband role, but they are not necessarily the same features whose absence causes the weak role in the Guiana Negro situation.

Smith reports another case in a later paper (n.d.) in which he says that the East Indian residents of British Guiana (like the Guatemalan Mayan Indians) have retained a strong father-husband role in spite of the similarity to the Negroes in their general circumstances. 'Quite apart from their historical derivation the ideal patterns of [East] Indian culture and family life have themselves become an object of value in distinguishing Indians from their nearest neighbours in the ethnic status system, the Negroes.' If Smith is interpreting his Guiana data and I my Guatemalan material correctly, the reasons behind women-headed households among the Guiana Negroes are relative to the structure of the particular society. Values associated with one phase or aspect of the social structural system may in fact conflict with or contradict values stemming from or associated with other aspects. Thus in many Guatemalan Indian situations, where the population works on coffee plantations, the nuclear family is not sustained through variable social status derived from the father, but is important economically. During the five or six months of harvest, the wife also brings in a significant income through picking coffee. This means that a man with a wife has access to a larger income than one without a wife.

Societies, in which families exist, offer many faces, and the form a specific family takes must integrate with as much of the total system as possible. Total systems are complex and seldom completely self-integrated, so some aspects will be more significant for the family form of some parts of the population, while other aspects prove to be more important for others. There is thus room for variation in the form a family may take simply because different families may be answering to different structural features.

The last case involves the Guiana Negroes and the Ladinos themselves, both societies in which two distinctive forms of the family appear within similar total structural situations. Smith reported, and the censuses for Central America show, that within these populations there are variations in the degree to which the woman-headed household occurs. If Smith's argument with respect to the relation between the dyadic Negro household and the total system is valid, we must then account for the presence of some continuous nuclear families. The answer here is probably the same as that just discussed. Within the total structure, there is room for variation, and we must assume that in spite of the structural features appearing to be the same, we are not identifying those features which the different family forms are answering to.

The evidence from the present cases does not provide us with a clear enough picture to delineate with precision why some families go one way and some go another. It is here that we must rest our case simply by preferring to place our confidence in the structural approach to solve the issue as over and against the 'universal functions' preferred by other writers. We need to seek out facts pertaining to a number of situations:

1. We need to delineate the types of structural aspects which can differentially affect family forms within a single class or ethnic societal group, or both.
2. Given this, we need then to establish the principles which will hold for such relationships within any society.

Summary and conclusions

The preceding discussion has been exploratory, working on the hypothesis-building level. The following summary remarks are made in the light of the same approach.

1. The concept of 'functions' as being activities necessary to the maintenance of the species, society, or individual personality is one which is not satisfactory to explain the various forms that the family may have in a given society. The economic, sexual, reproductive and educational functions as outlined by Murdock, or the socialization and adult-personality-maintaining functions of Parsons, may be taken care of by the nuclear family under some circumstances and not under others. We cannot agree with Parsons that there are 'root functions' everywhere associated with the nuclear family. If there are such things, they would probably be better identified in terms of the community and the dyads. The search for universal functions has unfortunately become an activity not unlike the continuing search for human instincts: it is not that there are none, but that it is misleading unless it is correlated with structure.

2. A theoretical analysis of the human family must not start with the assumption that the nuclear family is a basic cell or atom, but rather that there are two distinct dyadic relations that go into the formation of the nuclear family as well as into other family forms. While the concept of the nuclear family is doubtless useful for many kinds of social analysis, the fact that it fails in analysing some family forms means we must look further. A full understanding of family form requires an analysis beginning with dyads. With this kind of approach, it may well prove that the nuclear family has not had the extensive ramifications which have

been attributed to it heretofore. By adding other dyads, we are in a position to re-analyse kin and family structure as well as to pursue more analytically the nature of intrafamilial and other interpersonal relationships. It has been recognized that the nuclear family, as found among apes and men, is essentially a very primitive form. It is not surprising to find that man's culture elaborates on the dyadic possibilities of the family and produces forms intricate and fantastic.

3. Smith's work among the British Guiana Negroes gives us a most important insight into the structural correlates of the woman-headed household in that society. It leads us to the next step, which is to seek the structural correlates which will explain why woman-headed households sometimes appear and sometimes do not within apparently a single structural system. One step in this explanation is to have recourse to the theoretical position that the other aspects of the total social structure may be working adversely to those which are producing a nuclear or a dyadic emphasis. The emphasis thus placed, however, must have structural correlates, even if they are merely reflective of some structural aspect that is about to disappear. In this case we need more research into the exact nature of form and structure relationships, both in a synchronic and a diachronic context.

4. The final general position to be derived from the preceding discussion is that it is neither necessary nor valid to attempt to find a single normal structural form for the family within a society. That there *may* be only one is possible; but the assumption that there *can* be only one is unfruitful. The conviction that there is only one right way is older than social science, but it continues to make itself felt today. Many sociologists and anthropologists have regarded the woman-headed household as an abnormal, incomplete or disorganized form of the family. This has contributed to the argument that the nuclear family is an indispensable, basic, stable, family type, and that its absence must therefore represent a breakdown. If we accept the notion, however, that the basic relational elements of the family are dyadic, and that the nuclear family is a more complex arrangement but one which is probably even less significant temporally than its dyad components, then we are in a position to see women-headed

households as alternative or secondary norms rather than forms of disorganization. The assertion that the nuclear family successfully fulfills certain functions is perfectly valid. But the reverse assertion that other social forms can never suitably fulfill these functions is both empirically and theoretically invalid.

The denial of this reverse assertion is also important for our approach to other cultural forms. The search for a fundamental cell or building block of kin organization leads not only to a misplaced emphasis on the nuclear family, but towards a biased approach in the study of the entire family system. As Goodenough (1956) has pointed out with respect to residence, there are ethnographic ways of seeing things, and there are ethnological ways of seeing the same things. Just as the desire to discover cross-cultural regularities has led to forcing an ethnological strait jacket on a society's residence rules, so it has led to misleading assumptions concerning the identification of the nuclear family as the minimum structural form of family organization. If we look into other aspects of culture, it seems likely that we should assume that all cultural forms are alternatives (in the Lintonian sense) until a given form can be demonstrated to be universal by the ethnographers. To assume that a form, because it is a variant, is abnormal, is to evade the task before us. The first job of science is, after all, to study what *is*, not what might, or could, or should be.[3]

3. I am indebted to William Davenport, Iwao Ishino, Raymond T. Smith, Nancie Solien de González, John Useem, Gertrude E. Dole and Robert L. Carneiro for critical readings of earlier drafts of this paper.

References

ADAMS, R. N. (1957), 'Culture surveys of Panama – Nicaragua – Guatemala – El Salvador – Honduras', *Panamerican Sanitary Bureau, Scientific Publications*, no. 33.

CAPPANNARI, S. C. (1953), 'Marriage in Malabar', *Southwestern J. Anthropol.*, vol. 9, pp. 263–7.

FORTES, M. (1949), 'Time and social structure: An Ashanti case study', in M. Fortes (ed.), *Social Structure: Studies Presented to A. R. Radcliffe-Brown*, Clarendon Press, pp. 54–84.

FRAZIER, E. F. (1939), *The Negro Family in the United States*, University of Chicago Press.

GOODENOUGH, W. H. (1956), 'Residence rules', *Southwestern J. Anthropol.*, vol. 12, pp. 22–37.

GOUGH, E. K. (1952), 'Changing kinship usages in the setting of political and economic change among the Nayar of Malabar', *J. roy. anthropol. Inst.*, vol. 82, pp. 71–88.

HUTCHINSON, H. W. (1957), *Village and Plantation Life in Northeastern Brazil*, American Ethnological Society, University of Washington Press.

LABARRE, W. (1954), *The Human Animal*, University of Chicago Press.

LÉVI-STRAUSS, C. (1956), 'The family', in H. L. Shapiro (ed.), *Man, Culture, and Society*, Oxford University Press, pp. 261–85.

LEVY, M. J., JNR (1955), 'Some questions about Parsons' treatment of the incest problem', *Brit J. Sociol.*, vol. 6, pp. 277–85.

LINTON, R. (1936), *The Study of Man*, Appleton-Century-Crofts.

LOWIE, R. H. (1948), *Social Organization*, Holt, Rinehart & Winston.

MURDOCK, G. P. (1949), *Social Structure*, Macmillan Co.

PARSONS, T. (1955), 'The American family: Its relations to personality and to the social structure', in T. Parsons and R. F. Bales, *Family, Socialization and Interaction Process*, Free Press, pp. 3–33.

RADCLIFFE-BROWN, A. R. (1952a), 'On social structure', in A. R. Radcliffe-Brown, *Structure and Function in Primitive Society*, Cohen & West, pp. 188–204.

RADCLIFFE-BROWN, A. R. (1952b), 'The study of kinship systems', in A. R. Radcliffe-Brown, *Structure and Function in Primitive Society*, Cohen & West, pp. 49–89.

REH, E. (1946), *Paraguayan Rural Life*, Institute of Inter-American Affairs.

SERVICE, E. R., and SERVICE, H. S. (1954), *Tobatí: Paraguayan Town*, University of Chicago Press.

SMITH, R. T. (1956), *The Negro Family in British Guiana: Family Structure and Social Status in the Villages*, Routledge & Kegan Paul.

SMITH, R. T. (1957), 'Family structure and plantation systems in the New World', paper presented at the seminar on Plantation Systems of the New World, San Juan, Puerto Rico.

SPIRO, M. E. (1954), 'Is the family universal?' *Amer. Anthropol.*, vol. 56, pp. 839–46.

2 B. Malinowski

The Principle of Legitimacy

Excerpt from B. Malinowski, 'Parenthood – the basis of social structure', in V. F. Calverton and S. D. Schmalhausen (eds.), *The New Generation*, Allen & Unwin, 1930, pp. 113–68.

We can say that motherhood is always individual. It is never allowed to remain a mere biological fact. Social and cultural influences always endorse and emphasize the original individuality of the biological fact. These influences are so strong that in the case of adoption they may override the biological tie and substitute a cultural one for it. But statistically speaking, the biological ties are almost invariably merely reinforced, redetermined and remolded by the cultural ones. This remolding makes motherhood in each culture a relationship specific to that culture, different from all other motherhoods, and correlated to the whole social structure of the community. This means that the problem of maternity cannot be dismissed as a zoological fact, that it should be studied by every field-worker in his own area, and that the theory of cultural motherhood should have been made the foundation of the general theory of kinship.

What about the father? As far as his biological role is concerned he might well be treated as a drone. His task is to impregnate the female and then to disappear. And yet in all human societies the father is regarded by tradition as indispensable. The woman has to be married before she is allowed legitimately to conceive. Roughly speaking, an unmarried mother is under a ban, a fatherless child is a bastard. This is by no means only a European or Christian prejudice; it is the attitude found amongst most barbarous and savage peoples as well. Where the unmarried mother is at a premium and her offspring a desirable possession, the father is forced upon them by positive instead of negative sanctions.

Let us put it in more precise and abstract terms. Among the conditions which define conception as a sociologically legitimate fact there is one of fundamental importance. The most important moral and legal rule concerning the physiological side of kinship is that no child should be brought into the world without a man – and one man at that – assuming the role of sociological father, that is, guardian and protector, the male link between the child and the rest of the community.

I think that this generalization amounts to a universal sociological law and as such I have called it in some of my previous writings *The Principle of Legitimacy*.[1] The form which the principle of legitimacy assumes varies according to the laxity or stringency which obtains regarding prenuptial intercourse; according to the value set upon virginity or the contempt for it; according to the ideas held by the natives as to the mechanism of procreation; above all, according as to whether the child is a burden or an asset to its parents. Which means according as to whether the unmarried mother is more attractive because of her offspring or else degraded and ostracized on that account.

Yet through all these variations there runs the rule that the father is indispensable for the full sociological status of the child as well as of its mother, that the group consisting of a woman and her offspring is sociologically incomplete and illegitimate. The father, in other words, is necessary for the full legal status of the family.

In order to understand the nature and importance of the principle of legitimacy it is necessary to discuss the two aspects of procreation which are linked together biologically and culturally, yet linked by nature and culture so differently that many difficulties and puzzles have arisen for the anthropologists. Sex and parenthood are obviously linked biologically. Sexual intercourse leads at times to conception. Conception always means pregnancy and pregnancy at times means childbirth. We see that in the chain there are at least two possibilities of a hiatus; sexual intercourse by no means always leads to conception, and pregnancy can be interrupted by abortion and thus not lead to childbirth.

1. Compare article entitled 'Kinship' in the *Encyclopedia Britannica*, 14th edn.; also *Sex and Repression in Savage Society*, Routledge & Kegan Paul (1927), and *The Family Among the Australian Aborigines*, Schoken (1913), ch. 6. In this latter the relevant facts are presented though the term is not used.

The moral, customary and legal rules of most human communities step in, taking advantage of the two weak links in the chain, and in a most remarkable manner dissociate the two sides of procreation, that is sex and parenthood. Broadly speaking, it may be said that freedom of intercourse though not universally is yet generally prevalent in human societies. Freedom of conception, outside marriage is, however, never allowed, or at least in extremely few communities and under very exceptional circumstances.

Briefly to substantiate this statement: it is clear that in those societies, primitive or civilized, where prenuptial intercourse is regarded as immoral and illegitimate, marriage is the *conditio sine qua non* of legitimate children – that is children having full social status in the community.

In the second place, in most communities which regard prenuptial intercourse as perfectly legitimate, marriage is still regarded as essential to equip the child with a full tribal position. This is very often achieved without any punitive sanctions, by the mere fact that as soon as pregnancy sets in a girl and her lover have to marry. Often in fact pregnancy is a prerequisite of marriage or the final legal symptom of its conclusion.

There are tribes, again, where an unmarried mother is definitely penalized and so are her children. What is done under such conditions by lovers who want to live together sexually and yet not to produce children is difficult to say. Having had in my own field-work to deal with the case in point, I was yet unable to arrive at a satisfactory solution. Contraceptives, I am firmly convinced, do not exist in Melanesia, and abortion is not sufficiently frequent to account for the great scarcity of illegitimate children. As a hypothesis, I venture to submit that promiscuous intercourse, while it lasts, reduces the fertility of woman. If this side of the whole question still remains a puzzle it only proves that more research, both physiological and sociological, must be done in order fully to throw light upon the principle of legitimacy.

There is still one type of social mechanism through which the principle of legitimacy operates, and that is under conditions where a child is an asset. There an unmarried mother need not trouble about her sociological status, because the fact of having children only makes her the more desirable, and she speedily acquires a husband. He will not trouble whether the child is the result of his love-making or not. But whether the male is primed to assume his paternity, or whether child and mother are penalized, the principle of legitimacy obtains throughout mankind; the group of mother and child is incomplete and the sociological position of the father is regarded universally as indispensable.

3 B. Malinowski

The Family Complex in Patrilineal and Matrilineal Societies

Excerpts from B. Malinowski, *Sex and Repression in Savage Society*, Routledge & Kegan Paul, 1927, pp. 79–262.

The repressing and molding forces in Melanesia are twofold – the submission to matriarchal tribal law, and the prohibitions of exogamy. The first is brought about by the influence of the mother's brother, who, in appealing to the child's sense of honour, pride and ambition, comes to stand to him in a relation in many respects analogous to that of the father among us. On the other hand, both the efforts which he demands and the rivalry between successor and succeeded introduce the negative elements of jealousy and resentment. Thus an 'ambivalent' attitude is formed in which veneration assumes the acknowledged dominant place, while a repressed hatred manifests itself only indirectly.

The second taboo, the prohibition of incest, surrounds the sister and to a lesser degree other female relatives on the maternal side, as well as clanswomen, with a veil of sexual mystery. Of all this class of women, the sister is the representative to whom the taboo applies most stringently. We noted that this severing taboo, entering the boy's life in infancy, cuts short the incipient tenderness towards his sister which is the natural impulse of a child. This taboo also, since it makes even an accidental contact in sexual matters a crime, causes the thought of the sister to be always present, as well as consistently repressed.

Comparing the two systems of family attitudes briefly, we see that in a patriarchal society, the infantile rivalries and the later social functions introduce into the attitude of father and son, besides mutual attachment, also a certain amount of resentment and dislike. Between mother and son, on the other hand, the premature separation in infancy leaves a deep, unsatisfied craving which, later on, when sexual interests come in, is mixed up in memory with the new bodily longings, and assumes often an erotic character which comes up in dreams and other fantasies. In the Trobriands there is no friction between father and son, and all the infantile craving of the child for its mother is allowed gradually to spend itself in a natural, spontaneous manner. The ambivalent attitude of veneration and dislike is felt between a man and his mother's brother, while the repressed sexual attitude of incestuous temptation can be formed only towards his sister. Applying to each society a terse, though somewhat crude formula, we might say that in the Oedipus complex there is the repressed desire to kill the father and marry the mother, while in the matrilineal society of the Trobriands the wish is to marry the sister and to kill the maternal uncle. [. . .]

Cultural training is not merely the gradual development of innate faculties. Besides an instruction in arts and knowledge, this training also implies the building up of sentimental attitudes, the inculcation of laws and customs, the development of morality. And all this implies one element which we have found already in the relation between child and mother, the element of taboo, repression, of negative imperatives. Education consists in the last instance in the building up of complex and artificial habit responses, of the organization of emotions into sentiments.

As we know, this building up takes place through the various manifestations of public opinion and of moral feeling, by the constant influence of the moral pressure to which the growing child is exposed. Above all it is determined by the influence of that framework of tribal life which is made up of material elements and within which the child gradually grows up, to have its impulses molded into a number of sentiment patterns. This process, however, requires a background of effective personal authority, and here again the child comes to distinguish between the female side of social life and the male side. The women who look after him represent the nearer and more familiar influence, domestic tenderness, the help, the rest and the solace to which the child can always turn. The male aspect becomes gradually the principle of force, of distance, of pursuit of ambition and of authority. This distinction obviously develops only after the earlier period of infancy, in which, as we have seen, the father and the mother play a similar part. Later on, though the mother, side by side with the father, has to train and teach the child, she still continues the tradition of tenderness, while the father in most cases has to supply at least a minimum of authority within the family.

At a certain age, however, there comes the time at which the male child becomes detached from the family and launches into the world. In communities where there are initiation ceremonies this is done by an elaborate and special institution, in which the new order of law and morality is expounded to the novice, the existence of authority displayed, tribal conditions taught and very often hammered into the body by a system of privations and ordeals. From the sociological point of view, the initiations consist in the weaning of the boy from the domestic shelter and submitting him to tribal authority. In cultures where there is no initiation the process is gradual and diffused, but its elements are never absent. The boy is gradually allowed or encouraged to leave the house or to work himself loose from the household influences, he is instructed in tribal tradition and submitted to male authority.

But the male authority is not necessarily that of the father. [...] In societies where the authority is placed in the hands of the maternal uncle the father can remain the domestic helpmate and friend of his sons. The father to son sentiment can develop simply and directly. The early infantile attitudes gradually and continually ripen with the interests of boyhood and maturity. The father in later life plays a role not entirely dissimilar to that at the threshold of existence. Authority, tribal ambition, repressive elements and coercive measures are associated with another sentiment, centring round the person of the maternal uncle and building up along entirely different lines. [...]

There is only one way of avoiding the dangers which surround the paternal relation and this is to associate the typical elements which enter into the paternal relation with two different people. This is the configuration which we find under mother-right.

Part Two Incest and Sex

The role of prohibitions on sex between close kin ('the incest taboo') in the development of human society was the theme of Freud's study *Totem and Taboo* (1913). Like Malinowski, Freud attempted to relate these taboos to the requirements of family structure, and particularly to the process of socialization. Another line of thought, which was set in train by E. B. Tylor in a famous essay (1889), linked incest with exogamy, that is, with the rule of out-marriage by which lines of communication are established and maintained between adjacent social groups. This view was developed by Lévi-Strauss in his book, *The Elementary Structures of Kinship* (1949), an excerpt from which is included in this section. The article by Goody attempts to reconcile these two approaches and to suggest that they can each be seen as applying to different aspects of the taboo, that is, to parent-child and sibling incest respectively.

References

FREUD, S. (1913), *Totem and Taboo*, Routledge & Kegan Paul.
LÉVI-STRAUSS, C. (1969), *The Elementary Structures of Kinship*, Eyre & Spottiswoode.
TYLOR, E. B. (1889), 'On a method of investigating the development of institutions: applied to laws of marriage and descent', *J. anthropol. Inst.*, vol. 18, pp. 245-72.

4 C. Lévi-Strauss

The Principles of Kinship

Excerpt from C. Lévi-Strauss, *The Elementary Structures of Kinship*, Eyre & Spottiswoode, 1969, pp. 478–90. First published in 1949.

It is always a system of exchange that we find at the origin of rules of marriage, even of those of which the apparent singularity would seem to allow only a special and arbitrary interpretation. In the course of this work, we have seen the notion of exchange become complicated and diversified; it has constantly appeared to us in different forms. Sometimes exchange appears as direct (the case of marriage with the bilateral cousin), sometimes as indirect (and in this case it can comply with two formulas, one continuous, the other discontinuous, corresponding to two different rules of marriage with the unilateral cousin). Sometimes it functions within a total system (this is the theoretically common characteristic of bilateral marriage and of matrilateral marriage), and at others it instigates the formation of an unlimited number of special systems and short cycles, unconnected among themselves (and in this form it represents a permanent threat to moiety systems, and as an inevitable weakness attacks patrilateral systems). Sometimes exchange appears as a cash or short-term transaction (with the exchange of sisters and daughters, and avuncular marriage), and at other times more as a long-term transaction (as in the case where the prohibited degrees include first, and occasionally second, cousins). Sometimes the exchange is explicit and at other times it is implicit (as seen in the example of so-called marriage by purchase). Sometimes the exchange is closed (when marriage must satisfy a special rule of alliance between marriage classes or a special rule for the observance of preferential degrees), while sometimes it is open (when the rule of exogamy is merely a collection of negative stipulations, which, beyond the prohibited degrees, leaves a free choice). Sometimes it is secured by a sort of mortgage on reserved categories (classes or degrees); sometimes (as in the case of the simple prohibition of incest, as found in our society) it rests on a wider fiduciary guarantee, viz., the theoretical freedom to claim any woman of the group, in return for the renunciation of certain designated women in the family circle, a freedom ensured by the extension of a prohibition, similar to that affecting each man in particular, to all men in general. But no matter what form it takes, whether direct or indirect, general or special, immediate or deferred, explicit or implicit, closed or open, concrete or symbolic, it is exchange, always exchange, that emerges as the fundamental and common basis of all modalities of the institution of marriage. If these modalities can be subsumed under the general term of exogamy (for endogamy is not opposed to exogamy, but presupposes it), this is conditional upon the apperception, behind the superficially negative expression of the rule of exogamy, of the final principle which, through the prohibition of marriage within prohibited degrees, tends to ensure the total and continuous circulation of the group's most important assets, its wives and its daughters.

The functional value of exogamy, defined in its widest sense, has been specified and brought out in the preceding chapters. This value is in the first place negative. Exogamy provides the only means of maintaining the group as a group, of avoiding the indefinite fission and segmentation which the practice of consanguineous marriages would bring about. If these consanguineous marriages were resorted to persistently, or even overfrequently, they would not take long to 'fragment' the social group into a multitude of families, forming so many closed systems or sealed monads which no pre-established harmony could prevent from proliferating or from coming into conflict. The rule of exogamy, applied in its simplest forms, is not entirely sufficient to the task of warding off this mortal danger to the group. Such is the case with dual organization. With it there is no doubt that the risk of seeing a biological family become established as a closed system is definitely eliminated; the biological group can no longer stand apart, and the bond of alliance with another family ensures the dominance of the social over the biological, and of the cultural over the natural. But there immediately appears another risk, that of seeing two families, or rather two lineages, isolate themselves from the social continuum to form a bi-polar system, an indefinitely self-sufficient pair, closely united by a succession of intermarriages. The rule of exogamy, which determines the modalities for forming such pairs, gives them a definite social and cultural character, but this social character is no sooner given than it is disintegrated. This is the danger which is avoided by the more complex forms of exogamy, such as the principle of generalized exchange, or the subdivision of moieties into sections and subsections in which more and more numerous local groups constitute indefinitely more complex systems. It is thus the same with women as with the currency the name of which they often bear, and which, according to the admirable native saying, 'depicts the action of the needle for sewing roofs, which, weaving in and out, leads backwards and forwards the same liana, holding the straw together' (Leenhardt, 1930, pp. 48, 54). Even when there are no such procedures, dual organization is not itself ineffective. We have seen how the intervention of preferred degrees of kinship within the moiety, e.g. the predilection for the real cross-cousin, and even for a certain type of real cross-cousin, as among the Kariera, provides the means of palliating the risks of an over-automatic functioning of the classes. As opposed to endogamy and its tendency to set a limit to the group, and then to discriminate within the group, exogamy represents a continuous pull towards a greater cohesion, a more efficacious solidarity, and a more supple articulation.

This is because the value of exchange is not simply that of the goods exchanged. Exchange – and consequently the rule of exogamy which expresses it – has in itself a social value. It provides the means of binding men together, and of superimposing upon the natural links of kinship the henceforth artificial links – artificial in the sense that they are removed from chance encounters of the promiscuity of family life – of alliance governed by rule. In this connection, marriage serves as model for that artificial and temporary 'conjugality' between young people of the same sex in some schools and on which Balzac makes the profound remark that it is never superimposed upon blood ties but replaces them: 'It is strange, but never in my time did I know brothers who were "Activists". If man lives only by his feelings, he thinks perhaps that he will make his life the poorer if he merges an affection of his own choosing in a natural tie.'[1]

On this level, certain theories of exogamy which were criticized at the beginning of this work find a new value and significance. If, as we have suggested, exogamy and the prohibition of incest have a permanent functional value, co-extensive with all social groups, surely all the widely differing interpretations which have been given for them must contain an atom of truth? Thus the theories of McLennan, Spencer and Lubbock have, at least, a symbolical meaning. It will be recalled that McLennan believed that exogamy had its origin in tribes practising female infanticide, and which were consequently obliged to seek wives for their sons from outside. Similarly, Spencer suggested that exogamy began among warrior tribes who carried off women from neighbouring groups. Lubbock proposed a primitive opposition between two forms of marriage, viz., an endogamous marriage in which the women were regarded as the communal property of the men of the group, and an exogamous marriage, which reckoned captured women as the private property of their captor, thus giving rise to modern individual marriage. The concrete detail may be disputed, but the fundamental idea is sound, viz., that exogamy has a value less negative than positive, that it asserts the social existence of other people, and that it prohibits endogamous marriage only in order to introduce, and to prescribe, marriage with a group other than the biological family, certainly not because a biological danger is attached to consanguineous marriage, but because exogamous marriage results in a social benefit.

Consequently, exogamy should be recognized as an important element – doubtless by far the most important element – in that solemn collection of manifestations which, continually or periodically, ensures the integration of partial units within the total group, and demands the collaboration of outside groups. Such are the banquets, feasts and ceremonies of various kinds which form the web of social life. But exogamy is not merely one manifestation among many others. The feasts and ceremonies are periodic, and for the most part have limited functions. The law

1. 'The conjugal regard that united us as boys, and which we used to express by calling ourselves "Activists" ...' (Balzac, 1937, vol. 10, pp. 366, 382).

of exogamy, by contrast, is omnipresent, acting permanently and continually; moreover, it applies to valuables – viz., women – valuables *par excellence* from both the biological and the social points of view, without which life is impossible, or, at best, is reduced to the worst forms of abjection. It is no exaggeration, then, to say that exogamy is the archetype of all other manifestations based upon reciprocity, and that it provides the fundamental and immutable rule ensuring the existence of the group as a group. For example, among the Maori, Best tells us:

Female children of rank, as also male children of that status, were given in marriage to persons of important, powerful tribes, possibly of a quite unrelated people, as a means of procuring assistance from such tribes in time of war. In this connection we can see the application of the following saying of older times: '*He taura taonga e motu, he taura tangata e kore e motu*' ('A gift connection may be severed, but not so a human link'). Two peoples may meet in friendship and exchange gifts and yet quarrel and fight in later times, but intermarriage connects them in a permanent manner (Best, 1929, p. 34).

And, further on, he quotes another proverb: '*He hono tangata e kore e motu, kapa he taura waka, e motu*', 'A human joining is inseverable, but not so a canoe-painter, which can be severed' (p. 36). The philosophy contained in these remarks is the more significant because the Maori were by no means insensible to the advantages of marriage within the group. If both families quarrelled and insulted each other, they said, this would not be serious, but merely a family affair, and war would be avoided (Best, 1924, vol. 1, p. 447).

The prohibition of incest is less a rule prohibiting marriage with the mother, sister or daughter, than a rule obliging the mother, sister or daughter to be given to others. It is the supreme rule of the gift, and it is clearly this aspect, too often unrecognized, which allows its nature to be understood. All the errors in interpreting the prohibition of incest arise from a tendency to see marriage as a discontinuous process which derives its own limits and possibilities from within itself in each individual case.

Thus it is that the reasons why marriage with the mother, daughter or sister can be prevented are sought in a quality intrinsic to these women. One is therefore drawn infallibly towards biological considerations, since it is only from a biological, certainly not a social, point of view that motherhood, sisterhood or daughterhood are properties of the individuals considered. However, from a social viewpoint, these terms cannot be regarded as defining isolated individuals, but relationships between these individuals and everyone else. Motherhood is not only a mother's relationship to her children, but her relationship to other members of the group, not as a mother, but as a sister, wife, cousin or simply a stranger as far as kinship is concerned. It is the same for all family relationships, which are defined not only by the individuals they involve, but also by all those they exclude. This is true to the extent that observers have often been struck by the impossibility for natives of conceiving a neutral relationship, or more exactly, no relationship. We have the feeling – which, moreover, is illusory – that the absence of definite kinship gives rise to such a state in our consciousness. But the supposition that this might be the case in primitive thought does not stand up to examination. Every family relationship defines a certain group of rights and duties, while the lack of family relationship does not define anything; it defines enmity:

If you wish to live among the Nuer you must do so on their terms, which means that you must treat them as a kind of kinsman and they will then treat you as a kind of kinsman. Rights, privileges and obligations are determined by kinship. Either a man is a kinsman, actually or by fiction, or he is a person to whom you have no reciprocal obligations and whom you treat as a potential enemy (Evans-Pritchard, 1940, p. 183).

The Australian aboriginal group is defined in exactly the same terms:

When a stranger comes to a camp that he has never visited before, he does not enter the camp, but remains at some distance. A few of the older men, after a while, approach him, and the first thing they proceed to do is to find out who the stranger is. The commonest question that is put to him is 'Who is your *maeli* (father's father)?' The discussion proceeds on genealogical lines until all parties are satisfied of the exact relation of the stranger to each of the natives present in the camp. When this point is reached, the stranger can be admitted to the camp, and the different men and women are pointed out to him and their relation to him defined ... If I am a blackfellow and meet another blackfellow that other must be either my relative or my enemy. If he is my enemy I shall take the first opportunity of killing him, for fear he will kill me. This, before the white man came, was the aboriginal view of one's duty towards one's neighbour ... (Radcliffe-Brown, 1913, p. 151).

Through their striking parallelism, these two examples merely confirm a universal situation:

Throughout a considerable period, and in a large number of societies, men met in a curious frame of mind, with exaggerated fear and an equally exaggerated generosity which appear stupid in no one's eyes but our own. In all the societies which immediately preceded our own and which still surround us, and even in many usages of popular morality, there is no middle path. There is either complete trust or complete mistrust. One lays down one's arms, renounces magic, and gives everything away, from casual hospitality to one's daughter or one's property (Mauss, 1925, p. 138).

There is no barbarism or, properly speaking, even archaism in this attitude. It merely represents the systematization, pushed to the limit, of characteristics inherent in social relationships.

No relationship can be arbitrarily isolated from all other relationships. It is likewise impossible to remain on this or that side of the world of relationships. The social environment should not be conceived of as an empty framework within which beings and things can be linked, or simply juxtaposed. It is inseparable from the things which people it. Together they constitute a field of gravitation in which the weights and distances form a coordinated whole, and in which a change in any element produces a change in the total equilibrium of the system. We have given a partial illustration at least of this principle in our analysis of cross-cousin marriage. However, it can be seen how its field of application must be extended to all the rules of kinship, and above all, to that universal and fundamental rule, the prohibition of incest. Every kinship system (and no human society is without one) has a total character, and it is because of this that the mother, sister and daughter are perpetually coupled, as it were, with elements of the system which, in relation to them, are neither son, nor brother, nor father, because the latter are themselves coupled with other women, or other classes of women, or feminine elements defined by a relationship of a different order. Because marriage is exchange, because marriage is the archetype of exchange, the analysis of exchange can help in the understanding of the solidarity which unites the gift and the counter-gift, and one marriage with other marriages.

It is true that Seligman disputes that the woman is the sole or predominant instrument of the alliance. She cites the institution of blood brotherhood, as expressed by the *henamo* relationship among the natives of New Guinea (1935, pp. 75–93). The establishment of blood brotherhood does indeed create a bond of alliance between individuals, but by making them brothers it entails a prohibition on marriage with the sister. It is far from our mind to claim that the exchange or gift of women is the only way to establish an alliance in primitive societies. We have shown elsewhere how, among certain native groups of Brazil, the community could be expressed by the terms for 'brother-in-law' and 'brother'. The brother-in-law is ally, collaborator and friend; it is the term given to adult males belonging to the band with which an alliance has been contracted. In the same band, the potential brother-in-law, i.e. the cross-cousin, is the one with whom, as an adolescent, one indulges in homosexual activities which will always leave their mark in the mutually affectionate behaviour of the adults (Lévi-Strauss, 1948a). However, as well as the brother-in-law relationship, the Nambikwara also rely on the notion of brotherhood: 'Savage, you are no longer my brother!' is the cry uttered during a quarrel with a non-kinsman. Furthermore, objects found in a series, such as hut posts, the pipes of a Pan-pipe, etc. are said to be 'brothers', or are called 'others', in their respective relationships, a terminological detail which is worth comparing with Montaigne's observation that the Brazilian Indians whom he met at Rouen called men the 'halves' of one another, just as we say 'our fellow men' (1962, vol. 1, ch. 31). However, the whole difference between the two types of bond can also be seen, a sufficiently clear definition being that one of them expresses a mechanical solidarity (brother), while the other involves an organic solidarity (brother-in-law, or god-father). Brothers are closely related to one another, but they are so in terms of their similarity, as are the post or the reeds of the Pan-pipe. By contrast, brothers-in-law are solidary because they complement each other and have a functional efficacy for one another, whether they play the role of the opposite sex in the erotic games of childhood, or whether their masculine alliance as adults is confirmed by each providing the other with what he does not have – a wife – through their simultaneous renunciation of what they both do have – a sister. The first form of solidarity adds nothing and unites nothing; it is based upon a cultural limit, satisfied by the reproduction of a type of connection the model for which is provided by nature. The other brings about an integration of the group on a new plane.

Linton's observation on blood-brotherhood in the Marquesas helps to place the two institutions (blood-brotherhood and intermarriage) in their reciprocal perspectives. Blood-brothers are called *enoa*: 'When one was *enoa* with a man, one had equal rights to his property and stood in the same relation to his relatives as he did' (Linton, 1945, p. 149). However, it emerges very clearly from the context that the *enoa* system is merely an individual solution acting as a substitute, while the real and effective solution of the relations between the groups, i.e. the collective and organic solution of intermarriages, with the consequent fusion of the tribes, is made impossible by the international situation. Although vendettas may be in progress, the institution of *enoa*, a purely individual affair, is able to ensure a minimum of liaison and collaboration, even when marriage, which is a group affair, cannot be contracted.

Native theory confirms our conception even more directly. Mead's Arapesh informants had difficulty at first in answering her questions on possible infringements of the marriage prohibitions. However, when they eventually did express a comment the source of the misunderstanding was clearly revealed: they do not conceive of the prohibition as such, i.e. in its negative aspect; the prohibition is merely the reverse or counterpart of a positive obligation, which alone is present and active in the consciousness. Does a man ever sleep with his sister? The question is absurd. Certainly not, they reply: 'No, we don't sleep with our sisters. We give our sisters to other men, and other men give us their sisters' (1935, p. 84). The ethnographer pressed the point, asking what they would think or say if, through some impossibility, this eventuality managed to occur. Informants had difficulty placing themselves in this situation, for it was scarcely conceivable: 'What, you would like to marry your sister!

What is the matter with you anyway? Don't you want a brother-in-law? Don't you realize that if you marry another man's sister and another man marries your sister, you will have at least two brothers-in-law, while if you marry your own sister you will have none? With whom will you hunt, with whom will you garden, whom will you go to visit?' (1935, p. 84).

Doubtless, this is all a little suspect, because it was provoked, but the native aphorisms collected by Mead, and quoted as the motto to the first part of this work, were not provoked, and their meaning is the same. Other evidence corroborates the same thesis. For the Chukchee, a 'bad family' is defined as an isolated family, 'brotherless and cousinless' (Bogoras, 1904-9, p. 542). Moreover, the necessity to provoke the comment (the content of which, in any case, is spontaneous), and the difficulty in obtaining it, reveal the misunderstanding inherent in the problem of marriage prohibitions. The latter are prohibitions only secondarily and derivatively. Rather than a prohibition on a certain category of persons, they are a prescription directed towards another category. In this regard, how much more penetrating is native theory than are so many modern commentaries! There is nothing in the sister, mother or daughter which disqualifies them as such. Incest is socially absurd before it is morally culpable. The incredulous exclamation from the informant: 'So you do not want to have a brother-in-law?' provides the veritable golden rule for the state of society.

There is thus no possible solution to the problem of incest within the biological family, even supposing this family to be already in a cultural context which imposes its specific demands upon it. The cultural context does not consist of a collection of abstract conditions. It results from a very simple fact which expresses it entirely, namely, that the biological family is no longer alone, and that it must ally itself with other families in order to endure. Malinowski supported a different idea, namely, that the prohibition of incest results from an internal contradiction, within the biological family, between mutually incompatible feelings such as the emotions attached to sexual relationships and parental love, or 'the sentiments which form naturally between brothers and sisters' (1934, p. lxvi). These sentiments nevertheless only become incompatible because of the cultural role which the biological family is called upon to play. The man should teach his children, and this social vocation, practised naturally within the family group, is irremediably compromised if emotions of another type develop and upset the discipline indispensable to the maintenance of a stable order between the generations: 'Incest would mean the upsetting of age distinctions, the mixing up of generations, the disorganization of sentiments and a violent exchange of roles at a time when the family is the most important educational medium. No society could exist under such conditions' (Malinowski, 1927, p. 251).

It is unfortunate for this thesis that there is practically no primitive society which does not flagrantly contradict it on every point. The primitive family fulfils its educative function sooner than ours, and from puberty onwards – and often even before – it transfers the charge of adolescents to the group, with the handing over of their preparation to bachelor houses or initiation groups. Initiation rituals confirm this emancipation of the young man or girl from the family cell and their definitive incorporation within the social group. To achieve this end, these rituals rely on precisely the processes which Malinowski cites as a possibility solely in order to expose their mortal dangers, viz., affective disorganization and the violent exchange of roles, sometimes going as far as the practice, on the initiate's very person, of most unfamilial usages by near relatives. Finally, different types of classificatory system are very little concerned to maintain a clear distinction between ages and generations. However, it is just as difficult for a Hopi child to learn to call an old man 'my son', or any other assimilation of the same order, as it would be for one of ours (Simmons, 1942, p. 68). The supposedly disastrous situation that Malinowski depicts in order to justify the prohibition of incest, is, on the whole, no more than a very banal picture of any society, envisaged from another point of view than its own.

This naïve egocentrism is so far from being new or original that Durkheim made a decisive criticism of it years before Malinowski gave it a temporary revival in popularity. Incestuous relationships only appear contradictory to family sentiments because we have conceived of the latter as irreducibly excluding the former. But if a long and ancient tradition allowed men to marry their near relatives, our conception of marriage would be quite different. Sexual life would not have become what it is. It would have a less personal character, and would leave less room for the free play of the imagination, dreams and the spontaneities of desire. Sexual feeling would be tempered and deadened, but by this very fact it would compare closely with domestic feelings, with which it would have no difficulty in being reconciled. To conclude this paraphrase with a quotation: 'Certainly, the question does not pose itself once it is assumed that incest is prohibited; for the conjugal order, being henceforth outside the domestic order, must necessarily develop in a divergent direction. This prohibition clearly cannot be explained in terms of ideas which obviously derive from it' (Durkheim, 1898, p. 63).

Must we not go even further? On the very occasion of marriage, numerous societies practise the confusion of generations, the mingling of ages, the reversal of roles, and the identification of what we regard as incompatible relationships. As these customs seem to such societies to be in perfect harmony with a prohibition of incest, sometimes conceived of very rigorously, it can be concluded, on the one hand, that none of these practices is exclusive of family life, and, on the other hand, that the prohibition must be defined by different characteristics, common to it throughout its multiple modalities. Among the Chukchee, for example:

the age of women thus exchanged is hardly considered at all. For instance, on the Oloi River, a man named QI'mIqai married his young son five years old to a girl of twenty. In exchange he gave his niece, who was twelve years of age, and she was married to a young man more than twenty years old. The wife of the boy acted as his nurse, fed him with her own hands and put him to sleep (Bogoras, 1904-9, p. 578).

The writer also cites the case of a woman who, married to a two-year-old baby and having a child by 'a marriage companion', i.e. an official and temporary lover, shared her attentions between the two babies: 'When she was nursing her own child, she also nursed her infant husband. ... In this case the husband also readily took the breast of his wife. When I asked for the reason of the wife's conduct, the Chukchee replied, "Who knows? Perhaps it is a kind of incantation to insure the love of her young husband in the future"' (Bogoras, 1904–9, p. 578). At all events, it is certain that these apparently inconceivable unions are compatible with a highly romantic folklore, full of devouring passions, Prince Charmings and Sleeping Beauties, shy heroines and triumphant loves (Bogoras, 1904–9, pp. 578–83). We know of similar facts in South America (Means, 1931, p. 360).

However unusual these examples may appear, they are not unique, and Egyptian-style incest probably represents only the limit. They have their parallel among the Arapesh in New Guinea, among whom infant betrothals are frequent, the two children growing up as brother and sister. But this time the age difference is on the side of the husband:

An Arapesh boy grows his wife. As a father's claim to his child is not that he has begotten it but rather that he has fed it, so also a man's claim to his wife's attention and devotion is not that he has paid a bride-price for her, or that she is legally his property, but that he has actually contributed the food which has become flesh and bone of her body (Mead, 1935, p. 80).

Here again, this type of apparently abnormal relationship provides the psychological model for regular marriage: 'The whole organization of society is based upon the analogy between children and wives as representing a group who are younger, less responsible, than the men, and therefore to be guided. Wives by definition stand in this child-relationship ... to all of the older men of the clan into which they marry' (Mead, 1935, pp. 80–81).

Likewise, among the Tapirapé of central Brazil, depopulation has brought about a system of marriage with young girls. The 'husband' lives with his parents-in-law and the 'wife's' mother is responsible for woman's work (Wagley, 1940, p. 12). The Mohave husband carries the little girl that he has married on his shoulders, busies himself with household duties, and generally speaking acts both as husband and *in loco parentis*. The Mohave comment upon the situation cynically, and ask, sometimes even when the person concerned is present, whether he has married his own daughter: '"Whom are you carrying around on your back? Is that your daughter?" they ask him. When such marriages break up, the husband often has a manic attack' (Devereux, 1939, p. 519).

I myself have been present, among the Tupi-Cawahib of the upper Madeira, in central Brazil, at the betrothal of a man about thirty years old with a scarcely two-year-old baby, still in its mother's arms. Nothing was more touching than the excitement with which the future husband followed the childish frolics of his fiancée. He did not tire of admiring her, and of sharing his feelings with the onlookers. For some years his thoughts would be filled with the prospect of setting up house. He would feel strengthened by the certainty, growing alongside him in strength and beauty, of one day escaping the curse of bachelorhood. Henceforth, his budding tenderness is expressed in innocent gifts. According to our standards, this love is torn between three irreducible categories, viz., paternal, fraternal and marital, but in an appropriate context it reveals no element of disquiet or defect, endangering the future welfare of the couple, let alone the whole social order.

We must decide against Malinowski and those of his followers who vainly attempt to support an outmoded position (Seligman, 1931–2, pp. 250–76), in favour of those, like Fortune and Williams, who, following Tylor, found the origin of the incest prohibition in its positive implications (Fortune, 1932, pp. 620–2; Williams, 1936, p. 169; Tylor, 1889). As one observer rightly puts it: 'An incestuous couple as well as a stingy family automatically detaches itself from the give-and-take pattern of tribal existence; it is a foreign body – or at least an inactive one – in the body social' (Devereux, 1939, p. 529).

No marriage can thus be isolated from all the other marriages, past or future, which have occurred or which will occur within the group. Each marriage is the end of a movement which, as soon as this point has been reached, should be reversed and develop in a new direction. If the movement ceases, the whole system of reciprocity will be disturbed. Since marriage is the condition upon which reciprocity is realized, it follows that marriage constantly ventures the existence of reciprocity. What would happen if a wife were received without a daughter or a sister being given? This risk must be taken, however, if society is to survive. To safeguard the social perpetuity of alliance, one must compromise oneself with the chances of descent (i.e. in short, with man's biological substructure). However, the social recognition of marriage (i.e. the transformation of the sexual encounter, with its basis in promiscuity, into a contract, ceremony or sacrament) is always an anxious venture, and we can understand how it is that society should have attempted to provide against the risks involved by the continual and almost maniacal imposition of its mark. The Hehe, says Brown, practise cross-cousin marriage, but not without hesitation, for if cross-cousin marriage allows the clan-line to be maintained, it risks it in the case of a bad marriage, and informants report: 'Thus some forbid their children to marry a cousin' (1934, p. 28). The ambivalent attitude of the Hehe towards a special form of marriage is the pre-eminent social attitude towards marriage in any of its forms. By recognizing and sanctioning the union of the sexes and reproduction, society influences the natural order, but at the same time it gives the natural order its chance, and one might say of any culture of the world what an observer has noted of one of them: 'Perhaps the most fundamental religious conception relates to the difference between the sexes. Each sex is perfectly all right in its own way, but contact is fraught with danger for both' (Hogbin, 1935, p. 330).

Marriage is thus a dramatic encounter between nature and culture, between alliance and kinship. 'Who has given the bride?' chants the Hindu hymn of marriage: 'To whom then is she given? It is love that has given her; it is to love that she has been given. Love has given; love has received. Love has filled the ocean. With love I accept her. Love! let her be yours' (Banerjee, 1896, p. 91).[2] Thus, marriage is an arbitration between two loves, parental and conjugal. Nevertheless, they are both forms of love, and the instant the marriage takes place, considered in isolation, the two meet and merge; 'love has filled the ocean'. Their meeting is doubtless merely a prelude to their substitution for one another, the performance of a sort of *chassé-croisé*. But to intercross they must at least momentarily be joined, and it is this

2. As to marriage considered as bordering upon incest, compare the following, written in a completely different spirit: 'Profound sentiment [between husband and wife] would have seemed odd and even "ridiculous", in any event unbecoming; it would have been as unacceptable as an earnest "aside" in the general current of light conversation. Each has a duty to all, and for a couple to entertain each other is isolation; in company there exists no right of the *tête-à-tête*' (Taine, 1876, p. 133).

which in all social thought makes marriage a sacred mystery. At this moment, all marriage verges on incest. More than that, it is incest, at least social incest, if it is true that incest, in the broadest sense of the word, consists in obtaining by oneself, and for oneself, instead of by another, and for another.

However, since one must yield to nature in order that the species may perpetuate itself, and concomitantly for social alliance to endure, the very least one must do is to deny it while yielding to it, and to accompany the gesture made towards it with one restricting it. This compromise between nature and culture comes about in two ways, since there are two cases, one in which nature must be introduced, since society can do everything, the other in which nature must be excluded, since it rules from the first – before descent and its assertion of the unilineal principle, and before alliance, with its establishment of prohibited degrees.

References

DE BALZAC, H. (1937), *Louis Lambert, Oeuvres Complètes*, vol. 10, Paris.

BANERJEE, G. N. (1896), *The Hindu Law of Marriage and Stridhana*, Calcutta.

BEST, E. (1924), 'The Maori', *Mem. Polynesian Soc.* no 5.

BEST, E. (1929), 'The Whare Kohanga (the "Nest House") and its lore', *Dominion Mus. Bull.*, no. 13, pp. 1–72.

BOGORAS, W. (1904–9), 'The Chukchee', *Mem. Amer. Mus. nat. Hist.*, no. 11, pp. 1–733.

BROWN, G. G. (1934), 'Hehe cross-cousin marriage', in E. E. Evans-Pritchard, *et al.* (eds.), *Essays Presented to C. G. Seligman*, Routledge & Kegan Paul.

DEVEREUX, G. (1939), 'The social and cultural implications of incest among the Mohave Indians', *Psychoanal. Q.*, vol. 8, pp. 510–33.

DURKHEIM, E. (1898), 'La prohibition de l'inceste et ses origines', *Ann. sociol.*, vol. 1, pp. 1–70.

EVANS-PRITCHARD, E. E. (1940), *The Nuer*, Clarendon Press.

FORTUNE, R. F. (1932), *Sorcerers of Dobu*, Routledge & Kegan Paul.

HOGBIN, H. I. (1935), 'Native culture in Wogeo: report of field work in New Guinea', *Oceania*, vol. 5, pp. 308–37.

LEENHARDT, M. (1930), 'Notes d'ethnologie néo-calédonniene', *Travaux Mém. Inst. Ethnol.*, vol. 8.

LÉVI-STRAUSS, C. (1948), 'La vie familiale et sociale des Indiens Nambikwara', *J. Soc. Amer.* vol. 37.

LINTON, R. (1945), 'Marquesan culture', in A. Kardiner (ed.) *The Individual and his Society*, Columbia University Press.

MALINOWSKI, B. (1927), *Sex and Repression in Savage Society*, Routledge & Kegan Paul.

MALINOWSKI, B. (1934), 'Introduction', in H. I. Hogbin, *Law and Order in Polynesia*, Allen & Unwin.

MAUSS, M. (1925), 'Essai sur le don', *Ann. sociol.*, vol. 1, pp. 30–186.

MEAD, M. (1935), *Sex and Temperament in Three Primitive Societies*, Apollo.

MEANS, P. A. (1931), *Ancient Civilizations of the Andes*, Gordion.

DE MONTAIGNE, M. (1962), *Essais*, Garnier Frères. First published 1580.

RADCLIFFE-BROWN, A. R. (1913), 'Three tribes of western Australia', *J. roy. anthropol. Inst.*, vol. 43, pp. 143–70.

SELIGMAN, B. Z. (1931–2), 'The incest barrier: its role in social organisation', *Br. J. Psychol.*, vol. 22, pp. 250–76.

SELIGMAN, B. Z. (1935), 'The incest taboo as a social regulation', *Sociol. Rev.*, vol. 27, pp. 75–93.

SIMMONS, L. W. (ed.) (1942), *Sun Chief*, New Haven.

TAINE, H. A. (1876), *Les Origines de la France Contemporaine*, Hachette.

TYLOR, E. B. (1889), 'On a method of investigating the development of institutions: applied to laws of marriage and descent', *J. anthropol. Inst.*, vol. 18, pp. 245–72.

WAGLEY, C. (1940), 'The effects of depopulation upon social organisation as illustrated by the Tapirapé Indians', *Trans. New York Acad. Sci.*, vol. 3, pp, 12–16.

WILLIAMS, F. E. (1936), *Papuans of the Trans-Fly*, Oxford University Press.

5 J. Goody

Incest and Adultery

Excerpts from J. Goody, 'A comparative approach to incest and adultery', *British Journal of Sociology*, vol. 7, 1956, pp. 286–305. Reprinted in J. Goody, *Comparative Studies in Kinship*, Routledge & Kegan Paul, 1969, pp. 13–38.

... The continuous analysis in depth of different societies calls for more precise conceptual discriminations than were previously required. The terms often employed by social scientists are those which we use as members of a particular society to refer to our own institutions. Such concepts may turn out to be quite inappropriate for the purpose of cross-cultural analysis. The English 'family' is an obvious case in point. From the sociological point of view, the term has at least four analytically separable meanings. A statement of the kind, 'the family is a universal institution among all human societies', is meaningless without further elaboration.

A refinement of concepts is a product of onward-going research; it proceeds hand in hand with it. The depth analysis of societies through long periods of residence by trained observers is a necessary concomitant of the sharpening of concepts for cross-cultural studies.

The particular concept in which I am interested here is that of 'incest'. I want also to mention the related ones of adultery and fornication, as I shall later be concerned with them as categories of heterosexual offence. The everyday meanings given by the *Concise Oxford Dictionary* are as follows:

Incest Sexual commerce of near kindred.
Adultery Voluntary sexual intercourse of married person with one of the opposite sex, married (double adultery) or not (single adultery).
Fornication Voluntary sexual intercourse between man (sometimes restricted to unmarried man) and unmarried woman.

These particular definitions are by no means standardized. For instance, the *Encyclopaedia Britannica* (Eleventh Edition) and *Webster's Dictionary* both define incest as 'sexual intercourse between persons so related by marriage or affinity that legal marriage cannot take place between them', a formula which assumes an identical range in prohibitions on heterosexual intercourse and prohibitions on marriage.

It is these everyday usages which have formed the basis of the anthropological concepts. Malinowski, for example, appeared to treat the incest taboo (the prohibition on sexual intercourse) and exogamy (the prohibition on marriage) as being but two sides of a single coin.

Murdock, on the other hand, adheres more closely to the *Concise Oxford Dictionary* when he defines incest and adultery:

When it (heterosexual intercourse) takes place outside of marriage between two persons of whom at least one is married to another person, it is called *adultery*. If its participants are related to one another by a real, assumed, or artificial bond of kinship which is culturally regarded as a bar to sex relations, it is classed as *incest* (1949, p. 261).

Radcliffe-Brown, while retaining the criterion of kinship, offers a more restricted definition of incest. He writes, 'Incest is properly speaking the sin or crime of sexual intimacy between immediate relatives within the family, father and daughter, mother and son, brother and sister' (1950, p. 69).

Such extensive controversies have raged around the 'incest taboo' that it may perhaps appear impertinent to raise the question as to whether all these writers are in fact discussing the same range of phenomena or looking for explanations of the same set of prohibitions. But when we put the definitions of Murdock and Radcliffe-Brown side by side it is obvious that such doubts are not altogether misplaced. It is clear for instance that in terms of Radcliffe-Brown's definition, Murdock's 'second factual conclusion . . . that incest taboos do not apply universally to any relative of opposite sex outside of the nuclear family' (1949, p. 285) is tautologous. Equally, on the basis of Murdock's formula, it is difficult to decide whether sexual intimacy with the father's wives other than one's own mother would constitute incest or adultery, particularly in societies like the Tiv or Bedouin where kinship is universal. The difference between the two definitions is this, that though both apparently see the regulations as 'grounded in the constitution of the nuclear family' (1949, p. 284), Radcliffe-Brown attempts to limit the application of the term to the elementary family itself, while Murdock prefers to include all kin-based prohibitions, seeing these as 'extensions' of the primary taboo. Murdock's emphasis is in line with Malinowski's stress upon the elementary family and with his dogma of 'extension of sentiments'. Both definitions are clearly based upon the institutions of our own society, where prohibitions on intercourse, like prohibitions on marriage, are bilaterally organized within limited ranges of kin. But are these necessarily adequate for the analysis of non-European societies?

In order to answer this question, let us examine the evidence from two societies characterized by unilineal descent, one by matrilineal, the other patrilineal descent. I have selected for this purpose the Ashanti and Tallensi of Ghana, for which the main sources on incest are Rattray (1929) and Fortes (1936, 1949) respectively. These societies were chosen partly because of the high standard of the available reports and partly because of my own familiarity with the area. The Trobriand and the Nuer material will be used as a check upon the results obtained from an analysis of the examples from Ghana. In each case I want to examine both the explicit verbal categories of the actors themselves and the classifications implicit in the system of sanctions. These will be compared with the concepts employed by the observers.

The matrilineal case

In his treatment of sexual offences among the Ashanti, Rattray distinguished what he calls sins or tribal offences (*oman akyiwadie*) from household offences (*efiesem*). The former demanded the intervention of the central authority and the execution of the guilty party, although in some instances compensation was allowed. The latter 'were settled by the persons directly concerned or were decided by argument before any Elder, without reference to the "house-father", who stood entirely aloof' (1929, p. 287). The offences falling under these two categories were discussed separately.

Among the Ashanti sexual offences can be categorized in two ways, firstly according to the different names used by the Ashanti themselves, and, secondly, according to the different sanctions employed. I shall consider first the classification according to the nature of the sanctions.

This reveals three classes of offence. In the first class falls *mogyadie*, intercourse with a woman of the same clan, punishable by death; this includes intercourse with full siblings and maternal half-siblings and with the mother; it excludes intercourse of father with daughter. But there is another type of offence, which though not given the same name, is also punishable by death; this is *atwebenefie*, intercourse with a member of the same patrilineal sub-group, which of course includes that between father and daughter. Terminologically this constitutes a different category, but in respect of the nature of the sanction it must be associated with *mogyadie*. Both are cases of intercourse with members of the same descent group. The terminological distinction indicates that it is intercourse within the matriclan which is the major prohibition here, while that within the patrilineal sub-group is subsidiary. This is consistent with the nature of double clanship among the Ashanti.

The second class of offence consists basically of intercourse not with members of the same descent group but with the wives of fellow members, as well as with other classificatory wives. It also includes some prohibitions on intercourse with affines which might tend to confuse the social position of the wife herself. The punishment for this class of offence varies. It is never death, but consists of some variant of the adultery payment.

The third class of sexual offence is with wives of other men, and the sanction here is the simple adultery payment.

The threefold typology on the basis of sanctions is an indication of the weight placed by the society on these various offences. The first class brings together offences relating to the structure of descent groups, both matrilineal and patrilineal, offences relating to the hierarchical organization and 'ritual' offences relating to the cult of the Earth and to the fertility of women.

When we look at the terms used by the Ashanti themselves, we find there is another threefold typology, if we exclude the category *baratwe*, which represents a different method of classifying these offences. Intercourse within the matriclan is sharply differentiated terminologically from intercourse within the patriclan, the latter falling into the same category as intercourse with the *wives* of members of the matriclan and of other social groups. In this way it is assimilated to what I wish to call group-wife offences to distinguish them from intra-group offences. This is clearly related to the overwhelmingly greater importance of the matriclans in the social system. The third category is residual in that it consists essentially in sexual intercourse with people other than the members or wives of members of the descent groups, and of a few other quasi-kin groups such as guilds and military companies. Thus the concepts of the Ashanti themselves concerning heterosexual offences closely reflect the system of social groups. Intercourse with a daughter falls into a different category from intercourse with a sister, although for us both would be classified as 'incest'.

Now let us turn to Rattray's own use of the terms 'incest' and 'adultery' to see how he meets this situation. 'Incest' he uses simply to translate *mogyadie*, 'eating of one's own blood', that is, sexual intercourse with a matriclanswoman. He applies the term to none of the other offences, even those also punishable by death. The term 'adultery' he uses to translate all the household offences, 'eating a man's wife' (*di obi yere*) and *atwebenefie* – 'a vagina near to the dwelling-house'. He also uses it to translate those offences called *di obi yere* which fall under tribal jurisdiction and are therefore punishable by death. This consists of two offences only, intercourse with a chief's wife, and the worst type of sexual sin against the Earth, the rape of a married woman in the bush. His difficulty arises with *atwebenefie*. In his original list of offences, he translates this neutrally as 'sexual intercourse with certain individuals other than those related by "blood"' (p. 304) – i.e. females of the same matriclan. On the following page he writes:

Atwe-bene-fie means literally (having sexual intercourse with) 'a vagina that is near to the dwelling-house', and the offence, as the title implies, consisted in committing adultery with the wives of certain persons with whom the existing *ménage* necessarily compelled close social intercourse or constant physical proximity ... (p. 305).

The term 'adultery' has now replaced the neutral circumlocution previously used. However, when we examine the list of *atwebenefie* offences we find that those included under 'tribal sins' are not defined by the affinal relationship to ego. The women are forbidden not because they are someone's wives but because they are female members of the same patrilineal sub-group. For such an offence adultery seems a misleading translation.

The point at issue is this. In English usage the term 'adultery' is defined in relation to the marital status of one or both participants and is in effect residual to the category 'incest'. The term 'incest' is defined bilaterally, in keeping with other aspects of the social system. Heterosexual offences among the Ashanti do not fall into these categories, and in trying to translate these simply by the English words 'incest' and 'adultery', Rattray was faced with an impossible task. The English concept 'incest' refers to heterosexual intercourse with persons within a particular range of kin, whether they fall within that range by birth or by marriage. When a male ego marries, the immediate female kin of his wife are assimilated to his own kinship chart by becoming sisters- or mothers-in-law. Intercourse with affines is defined as incestuous, and placed in the same conceptual category as intercourse with consanguineous kin.

Thus, whereas the Ashanti differentiate between intra-group offences and group-wife offences, the European system does not have to do this because at marriage the spouses are assimilated, for many social purposes, into each other's natal groups. There is no distinction, in the context of heterosexual offences, between group-member and group-spouse.

This interpretation is strikingly confirmed in another matrilineal case, that of the Trobriands. Malinowski discusses incest in considerable detail in his book *The Sexual Life of Savages* (1929). First let us ask what Malinowski means by incest. 'Incest within the family and breach of exogamy', he says, is the meaning of the Trobriand word *suvasova* (p. 389). As the family is bilateral, the term *suvasova* should therefore cover the intercourse of a man with his mother, his sister, or his daughter.

When we look at the Trobriand concepts themselves we find that this is not the meaning of the word *suvasova*. Malinowski himself makes this apparent in another context, although he continues to assume an equivalence.

It must be clearly understood that, although father to daughter incest is regarded as bad, it is not described by the word *suvasova* (clan exogamy or incest), nor does any disease follow upon it; and, as we know, the whole ideology underlying this taboo is different from that of *suvasova* (p. 447).

Suvasova corresponds precisely to the Ashanti concept *mogyadie*. It is the name for what I have called intra-group offences (intercourse or marriage), and has to be distinguished from intercourse with wives of members of the matriclan, such as brother's wife, which to judge from the example Malinowski gives (p. 98) is not heavily sanctioned. The category *suvasova* includes intercourse with the mother, the daughter and the sister, the last being considered the most heinous, possibly because this was felt to be the most likely. The worst heterosexual offences in the Trobriands, as among the Ashanti, in each case distinguished terminologically, are those committed with members of the same matriclan. Malinowski repeatedly insists that it is the brother-sister prohibition which is the basis of the 'incest' taboo in Trobriand society.

The patrilineal case

Let us now consider a patrilineal case, the Tallensi. According to Fortes (1949) the Tallensi have no word for incest. There is a term *poγamboon* which might be translated literally 'matters concerning women'. Fortes himself translates this as 'adultery', but on the basis of my own experience among the LoDagaa I would suggest that it covers a wider range of heterosexual offences than is usually indicated by this term.

If the Tallensi have no specific word for incest, what range of phenomena does Fortes include under this term and how does he differentiate this from other types of offence? Looking at his analysis, we find that incest consists in sexual relations within the 'expanded family', that is, the family group based upon the inner lineage (1949, p. 111). Thus, in the absence of an indigenous concept, Fortes has introduced what is essentially a bilateral classification, one that includes in the same category offences with a paternal aunt, a sister or a daughter (intra-group offences) as well as offences with the wife of a father, brother or a son (group-wife offences). But though he calls both of these offences 'incest' he emphasizes that they are differently thought of by the Tallensi. For the first category of offence is merely 'disreputable', while the latter is viewed with the horror usually taken as being characteristic of incest. Outside the inner (or medial) lineage this dichotomy becomes even more obvious, for a lover relationship with a female lineage member is in fact permitted, while intercourse with the *wife* of a lineage or even a clan member is still considered a wrong. Fortes claims that this latter offence is not incest, but 'the most reprehensible form of adultery. It does not bear the same moral stigma as the corresponding form of incest, nor does it carry religious penalties for the adulterer' (1949, p. 116). For Fortes, therefore, incest consists in sexual intercourse with female members of the inner lineage and with the wives of its male members, while adultery consists in intercourse with the wives of male members outside that range as well as with wives of non-clansmen.

There is then no Tallensi term for heterosexual offences other than one for 'matters concerning women'. Fortes uses the English terms 'incest' and 'adultery' to divide up this category. The way in which he does so is bilaterally oriented. 'Incest' is the offence of sexual intercourse within the 'expanded family', 'adultery' the offence of sexual intercourse with any married woman outside it.

An alternative method of treating this problem is to infer the implicit classification of offences among the Tallensi from the nature of their reaction to any breach. This in effect is what Fortes does when he insists that 'incest' with a sister or daughter falls in a different category of sexual acts from 'incest' with a wife of the lineage (1949, p. 114). This standardized procedure for the investigation of moral, ritual or legal norms gives the following threefold division:

1. Sexual intercourse with a member of the same patriclan (up to the inner lineage only).
2. Sexual intercourse with the wife of a member of the same patriclan.
3. Sexual intercourse with the wife of a non-clansman.

I suggest that this classification has more inherent probability for three reasons. Firstly, it appears to fit better with the Tallensi emphasis on unilineal descent. Secondly, it corresponds to the classification I found among the LoDagaa of the same general area who are culturally similar to the Tallensi in very many ways. Thirdly, it is analogous to the classification which we have found among the Ashanti. Thus in both the matrilineal and patrilineal cases prohibitions on sexual intercourse are grouped together, depending upon whether they were:

1. With a member of the same descent group (intra-group sexual prohibition).
2. With the wife of a member (group-wife prohibition).
3. With another married woman (extra-group prohibition).

I suggest that a similar typology will be found in most societies characterized by unilineal descent, but has been obscured in anthropological reports because of the ethnocentric bias of the observers towards bilateral classifications. It is only possible to rectify this in the case of the Tallensi and Ashanti because of the excellence of the reporting and the fact that the authors have provided us with the terms used by the actors themselves. If we accept these three basic categories for heterosexual prohibitions and offences in societies characterized by unilineal descent groups, it would be reasonable to refer to the last as adultery, or more specifically non-group adultery. But what about the other two types of offence? Which of these should be called 'incest'?

The classification of heterosexual offences

The whole lengthy discussion of incest has turned on the supposition that it is a type of illicit sexual intercourse which is characterized by a particular horror. In the Western European system it is true that the entire range of offences included under the category incest is so regarded. But in many other societies, this is not so. Even within the minimal domestic units, heterosexual offences may be differently classified both terminologically and with regard to the organized sanctions with which they are met. Furthermore, they are also distinguished by diffuse sanctions, by the reactions which they arouse in the other members of the community. Among the Tallensi, offences between brother and sister (intra-group offences) are merely 'disreputable', while group-wife offences are met with 'horror'. On the other hand, and this is a point of fundamental theoretical interest, among the

Ashanti the reverse is the case. It is the intra-group offences which are dealt with by death, while the group-wife offences are treated as a heightened form of extra-clan adultery. I would claim that it is a mistake in either of these societies to class both these types of offence together as 'incest', because they are treated in such markedly different ways in terms of the sanctions employed, and, among the Ashanti, in terms of the actor categories themselves. Equally it would be difficult to classify either the first or the second types as incest on the basis of the internal reaction to them, as this varies so markedly in the two societies. I suggest that the word incest be retained for the category of offences inside the group and that it be divorced from the criterion of 'horror'. The group-spouse category should be associated with adultery rather than incest, for at the core of the prohibition lies the fact that the woman is *married* into the group; the taboo depends upon her married status. If she were not married, intercourse with her would be neither incest nor adultery but rather fornication, an act which may not be negatively sanctioned at all. For the group-wife category I therefore suggest the somewhat clumsy phrase, 'group-wife adultery'. Let me now schematize the threefold categorization of offences which we found among the Ashanti and the Tallensi. The terminology I suggest seems to me more appropriate for the cross-cultural analysis of heterosexual acts outside marriage (see Table 1). [...]

Table 1 The Classification of Heterosexual Offences

Offences that are	Offences with	
	Unmarried person	Married person
Intra-group	Incest	Incestuous adultery
Extra-group	Fornication	i. Spouse of group (group-spouse adultery)
		ii. Other married person (non-group adultery)

A further variable has been introduced into this table, that of marital status. I have already explained why this is essential in considering extra-group offences. But it may also be relevant in the case of intercourse with a fellow-member of the group. For instance, the LoDagaa of northern Ghana, among whom I worked, and who are in many ways very similar to the Tallensi, regarded intercourse with a clanswoman before her marriage, that is, before her sexuality had been alienated to a member of another clan, as being of very minor importance. But intercourse with the same woman after her marriage, what I have called 'incestuous adultery', is more severely treated.

For the comprehensive analysis of heterosexual offences, it is essential to introduce another variable, not shown in the table, that of generation. Social relationships with a member of the same or alternate generation are usually characterized by relative equality and those between adjacent generations by super or sub-ordination. This fact is likely to affect the severity with which the offence is treated. It will tend to be more severely treated where the relationship is characterized by authority, and especially where the male offender is of junior generation, for example, in the event of intercourse of a man with his father's wife. The same is true of other unequal statuses.

The incidence of horror

By breaking down the categories of incest and adultery in this manner, it is possible to offer not only a more adequate analysis of heterosexual offences in any one particular society, but also to begin to examine these offences on a cross-cultural basis. I have already called attention to the different incidence of 'horror' among the Tallensi and the Ashanti. In the former case it was offences with clan wives that were considered most heinous, whereas among the latter it was with the clan females themselves. The category heavily sanctioned among the Ashanti was relatively lightly treated among the Tallensi and vice versa. Why should the Tallensi represent the 'mirror image' of the Ashanti in this respect?

I suggest the following is the explanation of this remarkable reversal. The Tallensi are patrilineal; their classification of offences resembles that of many other patrilineal peoples. The category 'wives' is of fundamental importance to the descent group because it is through them that the continuity of the clan is obtained. Hence illegal intercourse with the wife of another member of the group is treated most severely.

The Ashanti are matrilineal. Social reproduction, as distinct from physiological reproduction, is obtained not through wives but through 'sisters', the female members of the clan. Hence it is interference with *their* sexuality that constitutes the most heinous heterosexual offence. An interesting aspect of this explanation is that it accounts for the differential treatment of father-daughter and mother-son offences. In neither the patrilineal Tallensi nor in matrilineal Ashanti does the father-daughter relationship fall into the most heinous category, while in both societies the mother-son relationship does. In the Tallensi the mother is the closest *wife* of a clansman of *senior* generation, while in the Ashanti she is the closest *female clan member* of *senior* generation. This I suggest forms a more satisfactory explanation of the different treatment of these offences than the usual 'biological' one.

To put this difference in another way, in patrilineal societies the rights over a woman that are transferred at marriage include rights to her reproductive capacities as well as rights to her sexual services, whereas in matrilineal societies it is only the latter that are transferred. Indeed among the Ashanti, a male only acquires exclusive sexual rights by the payment of a special sum, known as the *tiri-nsa*, which is not intrinsic to the 'marriage' itself.

The rights over the sexual services of women are customarily vested in one man, except in the rare cases of polyandrous systems. But the degree of this exclusiveness varies. For example, the LoDagaa, like the Tallensi, regard intercourse with the wife of a patriclansman as being the worst form of heterosexual offence. Yet the junior of a pair of male twins, if unmarried, is said to have access to the wife of his elder brother. In this case, the social identification of the siblings is such that it overrules the individualization of rights to the sexual services of the wife. There is always an incipient contradiction in patrilineal societies centring around the fact that while rights to the sexual services of women are in general acquired by individuals, rights to their procreative capacities are to some extent vested in the clan as a whole. An offspring of a particular union is an offspring of the entire clan. This contradiction is differently resolved in various societies. In

Brahmin groups, for example, rights over women are so highly individualized that a widowed woman may not marry again. Among the Tallensi a man's exclusive rights in a woman cease at his death, and by the institution of widow inheritance are taken over by another member of the same patriclan. Fraternal polyandry, or polycoity, represents the extreme case of corporate rights over the sexual services of women, at the opposite pole as it were to the individualization of Brahmin society. The problem of plural access is different from, but not unrelated to, that of plural marriage. [...]

Explanations of incest

Once the distinction between intra-group and group-wife sexual offences has been understood the problems of the 'explanation' of incest, and of the relationship between incest and exogamy, can be seen in a new light. Explanations of incest fall into three categories. Firstly, there are those framed in terms of the internal relations of the group. These are associated with writers who have concentrated their attention on sexual prohibitions within the elementary family: Freud, Radcliffe-Brown, Malinowski, Brenda Seligman, Murdock, Parsons and others. Secondly, there are those framed in terms of the external relations of the group, which are associated principally with Tylor, Fortune, and Lévi-Strauss. In the third category fall the biological, psychological-genetic variety. With this last I am not concerned here, although I am aware that they find their way into the formulations of some of the writers mentioned above. I take the two sociological hypotheses as my starting point not because I automatically assume that they will serve as complete explanations, but because for heuristic purposes it seems to me desirable to see how far one can get with these before employing theories which from the sociologist's standpoint are residual.

The two sociological theories are normally viewed as alternatives and a considerable literature has accrued as to their relative merits. Brenda Seligman has already summarized this discussion, herself coming down on the side of internal relations. Her argument is worth presenting not only because it gives some idea of how the discussion has developed but also because it deals fairly with both points of view. She writes:

Dr R. W. Fortune ... considers that the barrier itself is adopted not because of its internal value to the family, but because the external value of the marriage alliance is essential to social structure (1950, p. 313).

She distinguishes two types of incest. 'One is the union of parent and child, the other is of siblings of opposite sex' (p. 306). And she maintains that, while the marriage alliance might account for the brother-sister taboo, it cannot possibly explain the parent-child prohibition. Therefore, she concludes, it is the internal value of the arrangement which is the most important aspect of incest. 'With the prohibition of incest within the elementary family, the foundation of social structure is laid' (p. 307). Thus she succeeds in categorizing heterosexual offences on generation lines and perceives that different explanations might be appropriate to each. But she fails to dichotomize either in terms of group members and group wives, or in terms of the structure of unilineal descent groups. The reason for this appears to be her commitment to the Malinowskian stress on the elementary family. If this is seen as the primary unit in relation to which the incest taboo functions, then the only possible breakdown of incest is by generation. The point elaborated in this paper is that, in the analysis of 'descent societies', a further breakdown is necessary, and exists within the actor frame of reference either in the terms used or in the sanctions employed. But the breakdown is made according to whether the prohibition is on intercourse with a group member or with a group wife; and the groups in question are in general based upon unilineal descent. It is from this point of view that explanations of incest and exogamy must be considered.

Incest and exogamy are usually analysed as related prohibitions, the one on intercourse, the other on marriage. For example, Evans-Pritchard in his study of the Nuer maintains that the former is derived from the latter. Malinowski sometimes speaks of incest and exogamy as if they were entirely complementary. This point of view arises from a failure to make the distinction discussed above. For while the rule prohibiting marriage inside the group (exogamy) may be associated with the prohibition on intercourse within the group (intra-group prohibition), it cannot possibly be related, in any direct manner, to the prohibition on intercourse with the wives of the group, for these women must of necessity fall within the general category of permitted spouse. They cannot possibly be excluded by any marriage rule.

Exogamy, then, can only be related to the prohibition on intra-group intercourse. But as Fortes has shown, there need be no complete overlap even here. The Tallensi allow sexual intercourse with distant clansmen where they do not allow marriage. The reason is clear. Marriage affects the alignment of relationships between groups; it has to be publicly validated by overt transactions and it provides a precedent for similar arrangements in the future. Sexual intercourse in itself does none of this, and therefore when carried on in semi-secrecy requires no realignment of social relations. And indeed, as Fortes has also shown, under certain conditions there may be advantages for the individuals concerned if the lover is forbidden as a spouse, for then these relationships are necessarily of limited duration. Within groups of more restricted span, however, intercourse between members can render other social relations difficult. This is especially true where the relationship is characterized by superordination, as for example between members of adjacent generations.

Although there is no inevitable overlap between the prohibition of intra-group intercourse and the prohibition of intra-group marriage, there is nevertheless a strong tendency for such an overlap to occur. Exogamy is frequently phrased in terms of kinship. ... 'We cannot marry our "sisters".' So is the intra-group sexual taboo. ... 'We cannot sleep with our "sisters".' It is true that the classificatory reference of the term 'sister' may not be the same in the two cases. This is so with the Tallensi. In the first instance 'sister' refers to clan females as a whole, in the second, to those belonging to the inner or medial lineage. But the principle of structural congruence acts in favour of the same referent in both cases. And indeed the prohibition on temporary sexual relations and the prohibition on semi-permanent sexual relations are patently not unrelated.

If therefore the rule of exogamy is to be related to the external value of the marriage alliance, as Tylor and others have suggested, I think correctly, then the intra-group prohibition on intercourse cannot be dissociated from it. The rejection of temporary sexuality within the group is in part a reflection of the rejection of permanent sexuality, and the latter is related to the importance of establishing inter-group relationships by the exchange of rights in women.

Let us now turn to the prohibition on intercourse with those who have married members of the descent group. This is spoken of by Seligman, Fortes and many others as incest. Yet clearly the explanations of Fortune, Lévi-Strauss and others concerning marriage alliances have no bearing at all upon this phenomenon, because it is not intercourse with the women as such that is forbidden, but intercourse with them as wives of group members. Rights over their sexual services have been pre-empted by other males with whom one has prior relationships. These women are not necessarily consanguineal kin at all, with the exception of ego's mother; they are affines. Moreover, when the specific relationship with the member of the descent group ceases, then they may be legitimate sexual partners. In many cases one is in fact obliged to marry them when their husband dies, because of one's relationship with the dead man. Now this type of prohibition has nothing directly to do with marriage alliances, but rather with the other explanation which has been put forward, namely, the necessity of preserving the structure, not merely of the 'family', for there would then be no need for a rule of any extensive application, but rather of the descent group. For where rights of sexual access are individualized, conflict over females may be a cause of internecine dispute, and this prohibition renders such disputes less likely. It is indeed closely related to the taboo, found among the Tallensi and among many other African peoples, against more than one clansman having sexual relationships with one woman during the same period.

Conclusions

The current sociological explanations of incest are not, then, alternatives. Explanations in terms of external relations are relevant to the prohibitions on intra-group intercourse, while those in terms of internal relations are primarily relevant to the group-wife prohibition, although they also bear upon the intra-group taboo. Exogamy can be related to the former, but not to the latter.

This paper has attempted to establish a typology of heterosexual prohibitions to facilitate both cross-cultural studies and the depth analysis of particular societies. The typology depends in the first place upon a distinction between women who are considered to belong to the group and women who are married to its male members. In the societies with which the discussion has been mainly concerned, the reference group is the unilineal descent group rather than the elementary family. It is impossible to relate the concepts 'incest' and 'exogamy' when one term is held to refer to a bilateral group, the family, and the other to a unilineal one, the clan or lineage. It is impossible to account for the different sanctions placed upon these acts among the patrilineal Tallensi and the matrilineal Ashanti unless one introduces the system of descent as a variable. For the 'grisly horror of incest' is not a universal characteristic of all heterosexual offences with kinswomen and the wives of kinsmen. The reactions to a breach vary within and between societies. This is a fact which psychologists venturing into the cross-cultural field have often forgotten. Indeed, so concerned have they been with their own findings that they have tended, even more than anthropologists, to impose the categories derived from their own institutions upon the other societies with which they have been concerned. This is noticeable even in the type cases which psychologists have taken from classical Greek mythology. The nature of early Greek society makes it possible that their system of classification was closer to the patrilineal societies of Africa than the bilateral ones of modern Europe.

Like anthropologists, sociologists and psychologists dealing with our own society have patently failed to realize the ethnocentric nature of their categories. They have tended to treat 'incest' as an isolate instead of examining the system of prohibitions as a whole in relation to the social structure. Thus there is a quite disproportionate amount of literature devoted to 'incest' as compared to 'adultery', yet from the stand-point of social problems the latter would seem to deserve the greater attention. But the lure of the exotic has overcome the attraction of the mundane.

The study of 'incest' in any society must be related not merely to the analysis of marriage prohibitions or preferences, but also to 'adultery', so that it can be seen within the total constellation of sexual offences within that society. And this can only be done by accepting a breakdown of the monolithic category 'incest' into concepts more closely related to the structure of the society in question.

References

FORTES, M. (1936), 'Kinship, incest and exogamy of the Northern Territories of the Gold Coast', in L. H. D. Buxton (ed.), *Custom is King*, Hutchinson.

FORTES, M. (1949), *The Web of Kinship among the Tallensi*, Oxford University Press.

MALINOWSKI, B. (1929), *The Sexual Life of Savages*, Routledge & Kegan Paul.

MURDOCK, G. P. (1949), *Social Structure*, Macmillan Co.

MURDOCK, G. P. (1955), 'Changing emphases in social structure', *Southwestern J. Anthropol.*, vol. 11, pp. 361–70.

RADCLIFFE-BROWN, A. R. (1950), 'Introduction', in A. R. Radcliffe-Brown and D. Forde (eds.), *African Systems of Kinship and Marriage*, Oxford University Press.

RATTRAY, R. S. (1929), *Ashanti Law and Constitution*, Oxford University Press.

SELIGMAN, B. (1950), 'Incest and exogamy: A reconsideration', *Amer. Anthropol.*, vol. 52, pp. 305–16.

Part Three The Developmental Cycle

One way of approaching the study of 'the family', the domestic aspect of kinship, is through the analysis of the various types of group – productive, reproductive, residential and consuming – around which domestic activities revolve. Such groups are dynamic systems. Their structure may be changing over the long term, due to external or internal forces. But there is also a cyclical movement of growth and decline, fission and fusion, as members marry, set up on their own, bear children and die. In pre-industrial society, this pattern of growth may be complicated by the fact that the groups formed on the basis of these activities do not necessarily overlap, so that more sensitive concepts are required for the process of building up a comparative sociology of kinship and the family. The analysis of the developmental cycle has been developed by Fortes and his colleagues, who have used it to shed light on patterns of residence, divorce and other more general aspects of kinship. In this volume we present Fortes' introduction to a series of studies on this theme, which has influenced much sociological thinking (e.g. Stacey, 1969).

Reference

STACEY, M. (ed.) (1969), 'Family and Household', *Comparability in Social Research*, Heinemann.

6 M. Fortes

The Developmental Cycle in Domestic Groups

Excerpts from M. Fortes, 'Introduction', in J. Goody (ed.), *The Developmental Cycle in Domestic Groups*, Cambridge University Press, 1958, pp. 1–14.

The most promising advance in recent research on the social structures of homogeneous societies has been the endeavour to isolate and conceptualize the time factor. By this I do not mean the amorphous subject matter usually labelled 'culture change' or 'social change'. I mean the more fundamental and difficult problems involved in the truism that the idea of society, the notion of a social system or a social structure, necessarily implies extension through a stretch of time. A social system, by definition, has a life. It is a social system, that particular social system, only so long as its elements and components are maintained and adequately replaced; and the replacement process is the crucial one because the human organism has a limited life span. Maintenance and replacement are temporal phenomena. It is the processes by which they are ensured that concern us when we study the time factor in social structure.

These processes have biological determinants. One is the life span of the individual; the other is the physical replacement of every generation by the next in the succession of death and birth. We must leave to physiology, genetics and demography the exact study of these determinants. It is enough to remind ourselves that a social system will not persist if the average life span of its members is too short for them to have offspring and to rear them to the age when they in turn can have offspring, or, in demographic terms, if the balance of births and deaths does not yield a net reproduction rate of unity or more. From the anthropological point of view, the important thing is that the physical growth and development of the individual is embodied in the social system through his education in the culture of his society, and the succession of the generations through their incorporation in the social structure. The facts of physical continuity and replacement are thus converted into the process of social reproduction.

These generalities can be put in another way. For a social system to maintain itself its two vital resources must be maintained at an adequate level by continuous use and replacement. These two resources are its human capital and its social capital, and it is the latter that specially concerns the anthropologist. It consists of the total body of knowledge and skill, values and beliefs, laws and morals, embodied in the customs and institutions of a society and of the utilities made available for supporting the livelihood of its members through the application of the cultural outfit to natural resources. The process of social reproduction, in broad terms, includes all those institutional mechanisms and customary activities and norms which serve to maintain, replenish and transmit the social capital from generation to generation.

Of course generalizations of this sort are not susceptible of investigation by observation and experiment, nor do they lend themselves to profitable theoretical discussion. They are useful only as a step in the task of giving empirical content to the study of the time factor in social structure. They lead us to ask what are the institutional mechanisms and customary activities of social reproduction in a particular society and how do they operate? The nodal mechanism is well known. In all human societies, the workshop, so to speak, of social reproduction, is the domestic group. It is this group which must remain in operation over a stretch of time long enough to rear offspring to the stage of physical and social reproductivity if a society is to maintain itself. This is a cyclical process. The domestic group goes through a cycle of development analogous to the growth cycle of a living organism. The group as a unit retains the same form, but its members, and the activities which unite them, go through a regular sequence of changes during the cycle which culminates in the dissolution of the original unit and its replacement by one or more units of the same kind.

I shall later explain why it is useful to distinguish between the *domestic group* and the *family*, in the strict sense. Here I am interested in a different distinction. It is now commonly agreed that it is necessary, for analytical purposes, to distinguish between the domestic field of social relations, institutions and activities, viewed from within as an internal system, and the politico-jural field, regarded as an external system. A significant feature of the developmental cycle of the domestic group is that it is at one and the same time a process within the internal field and a movement governed by its relations to the external field.

To investigate this process in a given society we must first establish what the domestic group is in that society. The conventional ethnographic method is to give a generalized description derived from the observation of casually selected examples and couched in terms of stereotyped persons and institutions. This is like the amateur demography of travellers and colonial officials in the days before rigorous census methods were introduced. To find out what the average family size was in a primitive community, one rounded up twenty or thirty women at random and questioned them about their children. One then divided the total number of living children recorded by the total number of women and so obtained an 'average'. Such data are now regarded as useless, owing partly to the faulty sampling method, but chiefly to the failure to take into account age differences among the women questioned. Similarly, if we wish to determine reliably the structure and boundaries of the domestic group in a given society, it is essential to use a reliable and representative sample of domestic groups, and more particularly, to take into account their 'age-specific' characters – that is, the stages of the developmental cycle. A domestic group comprising only two successive generations is at a different stage from one made up of three generations; and so is one in which all the filial generation are pre-adolescent as compared with one with some or all the children at marriageable ages. The developmental factor is intrinsic to domestic organization and to ignore it leads to serious misinterpretation of the descriptive facts.

Residence patterns illustrate this very well. We know that they provide a basic index of the boundaries of the internal structure of domestic groups. But they are not a primary factor of social structure of the order of kinship, descent, marriage and citizenship. The alignments of residence are determined by the economic, affective, and jural relations that spring from these primary factors, and it is fallacious to analyse them in terms of ostensibly discrete rules or types that come into effect at marriage. There are numerous examples in the descriptive literature of kinship, but a timely and particularly pertinent one is a recent paper by Goodenough (1956).

There are, as he notes, several distinct questions involved. First, there is the question of the normal residential composition of the domestic group in the society. He shows how two investigators can arrive at totally discrepant conclusions about the incidence of different 'types' of residence in the same community though they use what seem to be the same census methods. In fact the source of the apparent discrepancies is the neglect by both investigators of the developmental dimension. [...] Residence patterns are the crystallization, at a given time, of the development process.

Secondly, there is quite a different problem when we consider residential alignments from the point of view of the person rather than from that of the domestic group as a unit. Genetical analysis then needs to be supplemented by the numerical and conceptual isolation of the structural and cultural variables involved. Marriage is certainly a crucial element in determining choice of residence by or for a person. In developmental terms, the reason for this is because marriage leads to an actual or incipient split in one or both of the spouses' natal families and domestic groups, and fission in the domestic group is always translated into spatial representation in the residence arrangements. In analytical terms, this developmental moment is the starting point of a redistribution of control over productive and reproductive resources associated with a change in the jural status of the spouses. Other things being equal, a wife will reside with her husband if he, or whoever has jural authority over him, has unrestricted rights over her sexual and economic services and her reproductive powers, and children will reside with those who have similar powers over, and the concomitant responsibilities towards, them. Only numerical analysis can show what 'degree of freedom', if any, exists.[...]

We can set up a paradigm distinguishing three main stages or phases in the developmental cycle of the domestic group. First there is a phase of expansion that lasts from the marriage of two people until the completion of their family of procreation. The biological limiting factor here is the duration of the wife's (or wives') fertility. In structural terms it corresponds to the period during which all the offspring of the parents are economically, affectively and jurally dependent on them. Secondly, and often overlapping the first phase in time (hence my preference for the term 'phase' instead of 'stage'), there is the phase of dispersion or fission. This begins with the marriage of the oldest child and continues until all the children are married. Where the custom by which the youngest child remains to take over the family estate is found, this commonly marks the beginning of the final phase. This is the phase of replacement, which ends with the death of the parents and the replacement in the social structure of the family they founded by the families of their children, more specifically, by the family of the father's heir amongst the children. [...]

Mutatis mutandis this paradigm can be applied to all social systems. The birth of a couple's first child, so frequently picked out by special ritual observances, which initiates the phase of expansion, and the marriage of their oldest child, which precipitates the eventual dissolution and replacement of their domestic group, are always critical episodes in the developmental cycle. But they are not, of course, the only critical turning points. The initiation, retirement, or death of a member of the group may be equally important.

In short, by the structural and cultural variables involved in the developmental cycle I mean all the forces generated by the social structure, and all the customs and institutions through which these forces and the values they reflect are manifested. Biological laws ensure that children inexorably grow up if they are not cut off by death. Growing up requires a minimum time span, at least fifteen years for the attainment of physiological maturity, and often rather longer for the attainment of social maturity. The complex and fundamental tasks of child-rearing imposed on the domestic group by this fact generates critical forces for its cycle of development.

The most important of these forces is the opposition between successive generations focused in the incest taboos. This is not a static condition. The opposition develops in intensity and may change in its customary forms of expression during the time that the filial generation is growing up. It is a factor in the partial or complete secession of offspring at marriage; for the essential stake is the right to use and dispose of the productive and reproductive resources which every generation must gain possession of when it reaches maturity. Among the Fulani we see very clearly how growing up, for a boy, is projected into the social structure through his increasing skill and responsibility in cattle husbandry and the corresponding extension of his rights in herd ownership, and culminates, after his marriage and achievement of fatherhood, in the dispossession and virtual expulsion of his father from the productive and reproductive organization of the domestic group. In general, the allocation by gift, prestation, inheritance and succession of rights over property, persons and office on the one hand, and of rights over the fertility of women on the other, is a major, if not the most significant, factor in the developmental cycle of the domestic group.

Now the opposition between successive generations operates primarily within the internal structure of the domestic group. But it is legitimized and kept within bounds through being allowed customary expression in forms sanctioned by the total society. Marriage, inheritance, succession, and so forth, are events in the internal system, or, to be more specific, domain of the domestic group; but they are simultaneously events in the external domain, where the domestic group is integrated into the total social structure in its political, jural and ritual aspects. The interests involved are those of society at large as well as those of the domestic group *per se*. This is shown in many customary forms, e.g. in the conjunction of rules of exogamy with rules of incest in the regulation of marriage, in the obligatory participation of extra-domestic kin and of political authorities in funeral ceremonies and in decisions about inheritance and succession, in initiation ceremonies, and so on. That is to say, it is through political, jural and ritual institutions and customs which derive their force from society at large that the interests of the total social system, as opposed to those specific to the domestic domain, are brought to bear on the latter. Classificatory kinship institutions, unilineal descent corporations, age sets, and the great variety of institutions and organizations through the medium of which citizenship is exercised, are the structural links between the two domains. We now have a number of excellent studies showing how the domestic group and the unilineal descent group are interlocked. The former is the source from which the latter is continually replenished. This is not just a matter of physical recruitment. There is a 'feeding in' process by which the differentiation of persons in the domestic domain by generation, filiation, and descent, is projected into the structure of the unilineal descent group to generate the modes of collocation and segmentation so characteristic of lineage systems. It is a continuous process that goes on as long as a lineage endures.

But there is a feature of this process that can easily be overlooked. It is true that fission in the domestic group can be regarded as the model and starting point of segmentation in the lineage, if we are concerned with the internal growing points of the lineage as a temporal system. But if we look at lineage systems from the point of view of their place in the external politico-jural domain and consider their connection with the domestic domain from that angle, we can see that differentiation and fission in the domestic group are reciprocally determined by norms and rules derived from the external domain. The classical example is descent rules. [. . .]

In primitive societies the domain of domestic relations is commonly organized around a nucleus consisting of a mother and her children. Where the conjugal relationship and patrifiliation are jurally or ritually effective in establishing a child's jural status, the husband-father becomes a critical link between the matricentral cell and the domestic domain as a whole. In this case the elementary family may be regarded as the nucleus. This is the reproductive nucleus of the domestic domain. It consists of two, and only two, successive generations bound together by the primary dependence of the child on its parents for nurture and love and of the parents on the child as the link between them and their reproductive fulfilment. The domestic group, on the other hand, often includes three successive generations as well as members collaterally, or otherwise, linked with the nucleus of the group. In this domain, kinship, descent and other jural and affectional bonds (e.g. of adoption or slavery) enter into the constitution of the group, whereas the nucleus is formed purely by the direct bonds of marriage, filiation and siblingship. The domestic group is essentially a householding and housekeeping unit organized to provide the material and cultural resources needed to maintain and bring up its members. The distinction, as I have said before, is an analytical one. The actual composition of the nuclear family and the domestic group may be identical, as it generally is in our own society; but the strictly reproductive functions, in the sense given to our concept of social reproduction, are distinguishable from the activities concerned with the production of food and shelter and the non-material means for ensuring continuity with society at large. One might put it that the domestic domain is the system of social relations through which the reproductive nucleus is integrated with the environment and with the structure of the total society.

If we consider a person's life cycle in the context of the domestic group and its development, we can distinguish four major phases in the period between his birth and his attainment of jural adulthood. In the first he is wholly contained within the matricentral cell. He is virtually merged with his mother, being no more than an appendage to her in the social and affective as well as the physiological sense. He is related to the total society only through her. This phase may last for only the few days of postpartum seclusion and may be ritually terminated, or it may merge imperceptibly into the second phase. In this the child is accepted into the patricentral nuclear family unit and his father assumes responsibility for him in relation to society and to spiritual powers. Or rather, the husband-father assumes responsibility for the mother-and-child as a unit. Presently, in the paradigmatic case, after weaning and with the acquisition of the ability to walk, he enters the third phase. He now moves into the domain of the domestic group. The spatial correlate of this phase is that the child is no longer confined to his mother's quarters but has the freedom of the whole dwelling house. He now comes under the jural and ritual care of the head of the domestic group, who may or may not be his own parent. This is the phase of childhood proper and may last for some years. During the whole of it he has no autonomous rights over property or productive resources, not even his own developing skills, no independent access to ritual institutions, and no political or jural standing in his own right. Finally he is admitted to the politico-jural domain. This confers on him actual or potential autonomy in the control of some productive resources, the elements of jural independence, rights of access to ritual powers and institutions, and some rights and duties of citizenship, as in warfare or feud. It is common for this phase to be legitimized by *rites de passage*, and to have a spatial correlate, as with the Trobriand boy who takes up residence with his maternal uncle. The culmination of the fourth phase is marriage and the actual or incipient fission of the natal domestic group.

What I am stressing in this paradigm is the changing structural relationships that make up the framework of a person's lifecycle. The stages of physiological maturation that accompany this development are of secondary significance. They are chiefly important as signs of readiness for a shift from one phase to the next. For each phase has its appropriate norms and activities connected with the basic psycho-physical capacities and needs. In the first phase a child is wholly dependent on the mother's breast for food and her arms for shelter and love. In the next phase he usually eats with his mother, sleeps in her room, and learns from her the fundamental self-oriented skills and values involved in walking, talking, feeding and cleanliness. He is regarded as sexually neutral and morally irresponsible. This pattern persists through the second phase. In the third phase the sexual division of roles and activities becomes effective. Boys are attached to their fathers and girls to their mothers. A boy commonly eats with his father or older brothers, sleeps with them, and learns objectively oriented social and economic skills and values from them. Moral responsibility is demanded of both sexes. They have to learn to control their affective attitudes to conform to customary norms of conduct and, in particular, they become subject to the incest taboos. In the next phase boys and girls eat and sleep with their like-sex age mates or peers. They are expected to take a responsible part in the performance of economic, military, jural and ritual duties for the benefit of the total society. They become answerable, to a greater or lesser degree, for moral and jural misdemeanours. Above all, they are now permitted to enter into relationships which involve adult sexuality for procreative ends, as opposed to childish sexuality for pleasurable ends. They are subject not only to the incest rules, which belong to the domestic domain, but also to the marriage regulations, which emanate from the politico-jural domain. *Rites de passage* often serve to dramatize this fact.

Though these phases do not invariably conform to stages of physiological growth, in relatively homogeneous social systems there is a close parallelism between them. For in such societies the basic educational tasks required to produce an adult person capable of playing a full part in maintaining and transmitting the social capital seem to be complete at about the same time as the attainment of physical and sexual maturity and therewith the capacity for replacing the parental generation in productive and reproductive activities. But what I want particularly to emphasize is that the maturation of the individual and his proper passage through the life cycle is of paramount concern to society at large. This is shown in the widespread occurrence of institutionalized procedures for legitimizing each step in it, and especially for terminating the period of jural infancy, whether it ends with adolescence or extends into the stage of physical adulthood.

Initiation, puberty and nubility ceremonies are the most dramatic instances of such procedures. In these ceremonies the domestic group's task of social reproduction is terminated. Having bred, reared and educated the child, it hands over the finished product to the total society. It is a transaction in which the power and authority of the politico-jural order as the final arbiter over the human and social capital of society are asserted. It is a situation in which the distinctive interests of the domestic group and those of the total society are liable to clash. In their capacity as citizens, parents wish their children to be admitted to the politico-jural domain and to have the rights of jural adulthood conferred on them. But as parents they may fear and resent having to relinquish their children to the superior and impersonal powers of society at large. Their resistance may be strengthened by the knowledge that initiation is the thin end of the wedge that will ultimately split the family. The children for their part, however mature they are and however much they value admission to adulthood, may hesitate to step out of the protective circle of the home. It may be particularly hard to renounce the bond of primal dependency on the mother which goes back to the first phase of the life cycle. If there is a marked cleavage between the domestic domain and the politico-jural domain these resistances may be institutionalized and the more difficult to overcome. Hence society may have to use harsh and abrupt rites to tear the new citizen away from his natal family and to assert its right to incorporate him as an adult. Citizenship may need a drastic reorientation of moral values and of social and economic roles in the new recruit. Shock tactics may be the readiest way to bring this about. Furthermore, the stamp of legitimacy must be publicly and incontrovertibly set upon the new rights (notably those of jural autonomy and procreative sexuality) – and corresponding duties (notably those defending the social order against dangers from within, such as crime, and against the external dangers of war and feud) – which are conferred by citizenship.

I am not here concerned with the theory of initiation ceremonies and further discussion of them would be out of place. I have referred to them merely in order to illustrate what I mean by a movement or transaction between the two domains of social structure we have been analysing. There are many societies in which the movement is not legitimized by means of initiation or other ceremonies. The reason may be that the two domains are not, analytically speaking, separated by a decisive cleavage. In any case, the movement does take place. There is a phase in the life cycle when jural infancy draws to an end and jural adulthood begins. It may be initiated, as has already been suggested, by marriage or by the birth of a couple's first child. Initiation ceremonies, in the strict sense, are often regarded as the prelude to marriage, if they do not actually end in marriage. In general, what finally terminates jural infancy is the emergence of the family nucleus for the new domestic group that is destined to replace that of the parents. Initiation ceremonies are sometimes spread over months or years, the preliminary rites serving, as it were, to apprentice the new recruit to the politico-jural domain and the later ones serving to make him free of that domain when he has proved worthy. Analogously, institutions like the shift of residence at adolescence from the father's to the maternal uncle's house may be regarded as the first steps in a longer process of jural emancipation which ends with marriage.

One consideration that must not be lost sight of is the reciprocal relationship between the two domains. Every member of a society is simultaneously a person in the domestic domain and in the politico-jural domain. His status in the former receives definition and sanction from the latter. Jural infancy is structurally located in the domestic domain, but its character is defined by norms validated in the politico-jural domain. Take the extreme case of an Ashanti infant which is defined as being non-human, that is, not a potential member of society, if it dies before the naming ceremony on the eighth day after its birth. This jural status derives from the politico-jural domain. The parents are obliged to accept the definition whatever their private emotions may be.

This has a direct bearing on the internal structure of the domestic group. The differentials in this structure are in part inherent in the procreative relationship and spring from the requirements of child rearing. But their character is also decisively regulated by politico-jural norms. The gap between successive generations can be large or small, varying with the kind and degree of authority and power vested in the parental generation; solidarity can be stressed more than rivalry in the sibling group, as in lineage systems, or vice versa, as among the Iban. These are differences of magnitude and of precedence related to the balance that is struck in a particular social system between the variables that combine together in the organization of the domestic domain. They are expressed in customs, beliefs and institutions that are the collective possessions of the whole society not the private culture of each domestic group.

The classical illustration is the contrast in the relationships of fathers and children in patrilineal and in matrilineal descent systems. It is because the father is not vested with jural authority over his son and the son has no title to the inheritance of his father's properties or to succession to his offices and rank, that matrilineal fathers and sons have an affectionate, non-competitive relationship. Conversely, it is because maternal uncles have jurally sanctioned rights over their nephews and the latter have jurally sanctioned claims on their uncles that there is tension in their relationship. And the pattern is reversed in patrilineal systems because the locus of rights and claims is jurally reversed.

Matrilineal fatherhood is defined as primarily a domestic relationship with only a minimal function in the politico-jural domain. Hence its focus is the task of bringing up and educating a child and fathers must rely on moral and affectional sanctions to fulfil it. In the last resort society will stand behind them to prevent trespass on their prerogative but gives them no support in the enforcement of their will on their children. We can contrast this with the juridical support society gives to the matrilineal husband in enforcing his rights to the sexual services of his wife. A patrilineal father, on the other hand, has not only the domestic and parental roles of provider and educator. He also has rights enforceable by juridical sanctions over and towards them and they have corresponding claims on him. He represents the power of society as a force within the domestic group in a way that the matrilineal father does not. And this analysis could be carried further if we were to take into consideration a third domain of social structure, that of ritual institutions. I have made allusions to this domain but it is not directly pertinent to our inquiries.

This formulation enables us to see why numerical data are essential for the analysis of the developmental cycle of the domestic group. Each phase of the cycle can be thought of as the outcome of a set of 'pushes' and 'pulls', antecedent and contemporaneous. They come in part from within the domestic domain and in part from the external structure of society. Numerical data provide a means of assessing the relative strength of these forces and of describing their configuration at a given phase. Let us take a case such as we find in a society like the Tallensi, with their rigorous patrilineal descent system. During the expansion phase of the domestic group all forces converge on supporting the paramountcy of the father in the domestic domain. He controls all the productive resources required to provide for his wife and children and he is vested with jural authority over them. Neither his wife nor his children have jural status, economic rights or ritual standing except through him. Consistently with this a man's wife, and his children during their jural infancy, can be expected to live with him, and numerical data show that they invariably do so. In the dispersion phase, however, a son's rights to some measure of jural, economic and ritual independence become operative, and he may set up his own dwelling group.

But whether he moves out of the parental home altogether to farm on his own or remains residentially attached to his father's homestead depends on factors internal to the domestic group. If he is the only son he will be less likely to move away than if he has brothers and if he is the oldest son he will be more likely to do so than if he is a younger son. Moreover the move may take place by stages and will not be complete until he has young children of his own. Numerical data are essential to assess the relative weight of these factors; and it has now become an established practice among social anthropologists to use such data in the analysis of social structure.

Reference

GOODENOUGH, W. H. (1956), 'Residence rules', *Southwestern J. Anthropol.*, vol. 12, pp. 22–37.

Part Four Joking and Avoidance

The fact that, in Western societies, the widespread custom of avoidance of the wife's mother has provided the substance of so many music-hall jokes indicates one of its functions: the preservation of social distance when two persons with conflicting interests in a third person are brought into direct confrontation. Somewhat crudely, formalized behaviour between persons in kin relationships can be seen as varying on a continuum between avoidance and familiarity, with piety, respect, joking and friendship lying in between. The subject was discussed by E. B. Tylor (1889) and later pursued in much field research. An important step forward in systematizing ideas about such behaviour was taken by Radcliffe-Brown (Reading 7). To do justice to the many facets of even the standardized behaviour between kin would require a great deal more space than we have at our disposal; meanwhile the present essay must stand as representative of a wide field of interest.

Reference

TYLOR, E. B. (1889), 'On a method of investigating the development of institutions: applied to laws of marriage and descent', *J. anthropol. Inst.*, vol. 18, pp. 245–72.

7 A. R. Radcliffe-Brown

Joking Relationships[1]

A. R. Radcliffe-Brown, 'On joking relationships', *Africa*, vol. 13, 1940, pp. 195–210. Reprinted in A. R. Radcliffe-Brown, *Structure and Function in Primitive Society*, Cohen & West, 1952, pp. 90–104.

What is meant by the term 'joking relationship' is a relation between two persons in which one is by custom permitted, and in some instances required, to tease or make fun of the other, who in turn is required to take no offence. It is important to distinguish two main varieties. In one the relation is symmetrical; each of the two persons teases or makes fun of the other. In the other variety the relation is asymmetrical; A jokes at the expense of B and B accepts the teasing good humouredly but without retaliating; or A teases B as much as he pleases and B in return teases A only a little. There are many varieties in the form of this relationship in different societies. In some instances the joking or teasing is only verbal, in others it includes horseplay; in some the joking includes elements of obscenity, in others not.

Standardized social relationships of this kind are extremely widespread, not only in Africa but also in Asia, Oceania and North America. To arrive at a scientific understanding of the phenomenon it is necessary to make a wide comparative study. Some material for this now exists in anthropological literature, though by no means all that could be desired, since it is unfortunately still only rarely that such relationships are observed and described as exactly as they might be.

The joking relationship is a peculiar combination of friendliness and antagonism. The behaviour is such that in any other social context it would express and arouse hostility; but it is not meant seriously and must not be taken seriously. There is a pretence of hostility and a real friendliness. To put it in another

[1]. Professor Marcel Mauss has published a brief theoretical discussion of the subject (1927–8). It is also dealt with by Dr F. Eggan (1937).

way, the relationship is one of permitted disrespect. Thus any complete theory of it must be part of, or consistent with, a theory of the place of respect in social relations and in social life generally. But this is a very wide and very important sociological problem; for it is evident that the whole maintenance of a social order depends upon the appropriate kind and degree of respect being shown towards certain persons, things and ideas or symbols.

Examples of joking relationships between relatives by marriage are very commonly found in Africa and in other parts of the world. Thus Mademoiselle Paulme (1939) records that among the Dogon a man stands in a joking relationship to his wife's sisters and their daughters. Frequently the relationship holds between a man and both the brothers and sisters of his wife. But in some instances there is a distinction whereby a man is on joking terms with his wife's younger brothers and sisters but not with those who are older than she is. This joking with the wife's brothers and sisters is usually associated with a custom requiring extreme respect, often partial or complete avoidance, between a son-in-law and his wife's parents.[2]

The kind of structural situation in which the associated customs of joking and avoidance are found may be described as follows. A marriage involves a readjustment of the social structure whereby the woman's relations with her family are greatly modified and she enters into a new and very close relation with her husband. The latter is at the same time brought into a special relation with his wife's family, to which, however, he is an outsider. For the sake of brevity, though at the risk of over-simplification, we will consider only the husband's relation to his wife's family. The relation can be described as involving both attachment and separation, both social conjunction and social disjunction, if I may use the terms. The man has his own definite position in the social structure, determined for him by his birth into a certain family, lineage or clan. The great body of his rights and duties and the interests and activities that he shares with others are the result of his position. Before the marriage his wife's family are outsiders for him as he is an outsider for

2. Those who are not familiar with these widespread customs will find descriptions in Junod (1927) and in F. Eggan (1937).

them. This constitutes a social disjunction which is not destroyed by the marriage. The social conjunction results from the continuance, though in altered form, of the wife's relation to her family, their continued interest in her and in her children. If the wife were really bought and paid for, as ignorant persons say that she is in Africa, there would be no place for any permanent close relation of a man with his wife's family. But though slaves can be bought, wives cannot.

Social disjunction implies divergence of interests and therefore the possibility of conflict and hostility, while conjunction requires the avoidance of strife. How can a relation which combines the two be given a stable, ordered form? There are two ways of doing this. One is to maintain between two persons so related an extreme mutual respect and a limitation of direct personal contact. This is exhibited in the very formal relations that are, in so many societies, characteristic of the behaviour of a son-in-law on the one side and his wife's father and mother on the other. In its most extreme form there is complete avoidance of any social contact between a man and his mother-in-law.

This avoidance must not be mistaken for a sign of hostility. One does, of course, if one is wise, avoid having too much to do with one's enemies, but that is quite a different matter. I once asked an Australian native why he had to avoid his mother-in-law, and his reply was, 'Because she is my best friend in the world; she has given me my wife'. The mutual respect between son-in-law and parents-in-law is a mode of friendship. It prevents conflict that might arise through divergence of interest.

The alternative to this relation of extreme mutual respect and restraint is the joking relationship, one, that is, of mutual disrespect and licence. Any serious hostility is prevented by the playful antagonism of teasing, and this in its regular repetition is a constant expression or reminder of that social disjunction which is one of the essential components of the relation, while the social conjunction is maintained by the friendliness that takes no offence at insult.

The discrimination within the wife's family between those who have to be treated with extreme respect and those with whom it is a duty to be disrespectful is made on the basis of generation and sometimes of seniority within the generation. The usual respected relatives are those of the first ascending generation, the wife's mother and her sisters, the wife's father and his brothers, sometimes the wife's mother's brother. The joking relatives are those of a person's own generation; but very frequently a distinction of seniority within the generation is made; a wife's older sister or brother may be respected while those younger will be teased.

In certain societies a man may be said to have relatives by marriage long before he marries and indeed as soon as he is born into the world. This is provided by the institution of the required or preferential marriage. We will, for the sake of brevity, consider only one kind of such organizations. In many societies it is regarded as preferable that a man should marry the daughter of his mother's brother; this is a form of the custom known as cross-cousin marriage. Thus his female cousins of this kind, or all those women whom by the classificatory system he classifies as such, are potential wives for him, and their brothers are his potential brothers-in-law. Among the Ojibwa Indians of North America, the Chiga of Uganda, and in Fiji and New Caledonia, as well as elsewhere, this form of marriage is found and is accompanied by a joking relationship between a man and the sons and daughters of his mother's brother. To quote one instance of these, the following is recorded for the Ojibwa.

When cross-cousins meet they must try to embarrass one another. They 'joke' one another, making the most vulgar allegations, by their standards as well as ours. But being 'kind' relations, no one can take offence. Cross-cousins who do not joke in this way are considered boorish, as not playing the social game (Landes, 1937, p. 103).

The joking relationship here is of fundamentally the same kind as that already discussed. It is established before marriage and is continued, after marriage, with the brothers- and sisters-in-law.

In some parts of Africa there are joking relationships that have nothing to do with marriage. Mr Pedler's note (1940) refers to a joking relationship between two distinct tribes, the Sukuma and the Zaramu, and in the evidence it was stated that there was a similar relation between the Sukuma and the Zigua and between the Ngoni and the Bemba. The woman's evidence suggests that this custom of rough teasing exists in the Sukuma tribe between persons related by marriage, as it does in so many other African tribes.[3]

While a joking relationship between two tribes is apparently rare, and certainly deserves, as Mr Pedler suggests, to be carefully investigated, a similar relationship between clans has been observed in other parts of Africa. It is described by Professor Labouret (1929) and Mademoiselle Paulme (1939) in the articles previously mentioned, and amongst the Tallensi it has been studied by Dr Fortes (1945).

The two clans are not, in these instances, specially connected by intermarriage. The relation between them is an alliance involving real friendliness and mutual aid combined with an appearance of hostility.

The general structural situation in these instances seems to be as follows. The individual is a member of a certain defined group, a clan, for example, within which his relations to others are defined by a complex set of rights and duties, referring to all the major aspects of social life, and supported by definite sanctions. There may be another group outside his own which is so linked with his as to be the field of extension of jural and moral relations of the same general kind. Thus, in East Africa, as we learn from Mr Pedler's note, the Zigua and the Zaramu do not joke with one another because a yet closer bond exists between them since they are *ndugu* (brothers). But beyond the field within which social relations are thus defined there lie other groups with which, since they are outsiders to the individual's own group, the relation involves possible or actual hostility. In any fixed relations between the members of two such groups the separateness of the

3. Incidentally it may be said that it was hardly satisfactory for the magistrate to establish a precedent whereby the man, who was observing what was a permitted and may even have been an obligatory custom, was declared guilty of common assault, even with extenuating circumstances. It seems quite possible that the man may have committed a breach of etiquette in teasing the woman in the presence of her mother's brother, for in many parts of the world it is regarded as improper for two persons in a joking relationship to tease one another (particularly if any obscenity is involved) in the presence of certain relatives of either of them. But the breach of etiquette would still not make it an assault. A little knowledge of anthropology would have enabled the magistrate, by putting the appropriate questions to the witnesses, to have obtained a fuller understanding of the case and all that was involved in it.

groups must be recognized. It is precisely this separateness which is not merely recognized but emphasized when a joking relationship is established. The show of hostility, the perpetual disrespect, is a continual expression of that social disjunction which is an essential part of the whole structural situation, but over which, without destroying or even weakening it, there is provided the social conjunction of friendliness and mutual aid.

The theory here put forward, therefore, is that both the joking relationship which constitutes an alliance between clans or tribes and that between relatives by marriage are modes of organizing a definite and stable system of social behaviour in which conjunctive and disjunctive components, as I have called them, are maintained and combined.

To provide the full evidence for this theory by following out its implications and examining in detail its application to different instances would take a book rather than a short article. But some confirmation can perhaps be offered by a consideration of the way in which respect and disrespect appear in various kinship relations, even though nothing more can be attempted than a very brief indication of a few significant points.

In studying a kinship system it is possible to distinguish the different relatives by reference to the kind and degree of respect that is paid to them (see Eggan, 1937; Mead, 1934). Although kinship systems vary very much in their details there are certain principles which are found to be very widespread. One of them is that by which a person is required to show a marked respect to relatives belonging to the generation immediately preceding his own. In a majority of societies the father is a relative to whom marked respect must be shown. This is so even in many so-called matrilineal societies, i.e. those which are organized into matrilineal clans or lineages. One can very frequently observe a tendency to extend this attitude of respect to all relatives of the first ascending generation and, further, to persons who are not relatives. Thus in those tribes of East Africa that are organized into age-sets a man is required to show special respect to all men of his father's age-set and to their wives.

The social function of this is obvious. The social tradition is handed down from one generation to the next. For the tradition to be maintained it must have authority behind it. The authority is therefore normally recognized as possessed by members of the preceding generation and it is they who exercise discipline. As a result of this the relation between persons of the two generations usually contains an element of inequality, the parents and those of their generation being in a position of superiority over the children who are subordinate to them. The unequal relation between a father and his son is maintained by requiring the latter to show respect to the former. The relation is asymmetrical.

When we turn to the relation of an individual to his grandparents and their brothers and sisters we find that in the majority of human societies relatives of the second ascending generation are treated with very much less respect than those of the first ascending generation, and instead of a marked inequality there is a tendency to approximate to a friendly equality.

Considerations of space forbid any full discussion of this feature of social structure, which is one of very great importance. There are many instances in which the grandparents and their grandchildren are grouped together in the social structure in opposition to their children and parents. An important clue to the understanding of the subject is the fact that in the flow of social life through time, in which men are born, become mature and die, the grandchildren replace their grandparents.

In many societies there is an actual joking relationship, usually of a relatively mild kind, between relatives of alternate generations. Grandchildren make fun of their grandparents and of those who are called grandfather and grandmother by the classificatory system of terminology, and these reply in kind.

Grandparents and grandchildren are united by kinship; they are separated by age and by the social difference that results from the fact that as the grandchildren are in process of entering into full participation in the social life of the community the grandparents are gradually retiring from it. Important duties towards his relatives in his own and even more in his parents' generation impose upon an individual many restraints; but with those of the second ascending generation, his grandparents and collateral relatives, there can be established, and usually is, a relationship of simple friendliness relatively free from restraint. In this instance also, it is suggested, the joking relationship is a method of ordering a relation which combines social conjunction and disjunction.

This thesis could, I believe, be strongly supported if not demonstrated by considering the details of these relationships. There is space for only one illustrative point. A very common form of joke in this connection is for the grandchild to pretend that he wishes to marry the grandfather's wife, or that he intends to do so when his grandfather dies, or to treat her as already being his wife. Alternatively the grandfather may pretend that the wife of his grandchild is, or might be, his wife (see Labouret, 1931, p. 248; Roy, 1915, pp. 352–4). The point of the joke is the pretence at ignoring the difference of age between the grandparent and the grandchild.

In various parts of the world there are societies in which a sister's son teases and otherwise behaves disrespectfully towards his mother's brother. In these instances the joking relationship seems generally to be asymmetrical. For example the nephew may take his uncle's property but not vice versa; or, as amongst the Nama Hottentots, the nephew may take a fine beast from his uncle's herd and the uncle in return takes a wretched beast from that of the nephew (Hoernlé, 1925).

The kind of social structure in which this custom of privileged disrespect to the mother's brother occurs in its most marked forms, for example the Thonga of South-East Africa, Fiji and Tonga in the Pacific and the Central Siouan tribes of North America, is characterized by emphasis on patrilineal lineage and a marked distinction between relatives through the father and relatives through the mother.

In a former publication (1924) I offered an interpretation of this custom of privileged familiarity towards the mother's brother. Briefly it is as follows. For the continuance of a social system children require to be cared for and to be trained. Their care demands affectionate and unselfish devotion; their training requires that they shall be subjected to discipline. In the societies with which we are concerned there is something of a division of function between the parents and other relatives on the two sides. The control and discipline are exercised chiefly by the father and his brothers and generally also by his sisters; these are relatives who must be respected and obeyed. It is the mother who is primarily responsible for the affectionate care; the mother and her brothers and sisters are therefore relatives who can be looked to for assistance and indulgence. The mother's brother is called 'male mother' in Tonga and in some South African tribes.

I believe that this interpretation of the special position of the mother's brother in these societies has been confirmed by further field work since I wrote the article referred to. But I was quite aware at the time it was written that the discussion and interpretation needed to be supplemented so as to bring them into line with a general theory of the social functions of respect and disrespect.

The joking relationship with the mother's brother seems to fit well with the general theory of such relationships here outlined. A person's most important duties and rights attach him to his paternal relatives, living and dead. It is to his patrilineal lineage or clan that he belongs. For the members of his mother's lineage he is an outsider, though one in whom they have a very special and tender interest. Thus here again there is a relation in which there is both attachment or conjunction, and separation or disjunction, between the two persons concerned.

But let us remember that in this instance the relation is asymmetrical.[4] The nephew is disrespectful and the uncle accepts the disrespect. There is inequality and the nephew is the superior. This is recognized by the natives themselves. Thus in Tonga it is said that the sister's son is a 'chief' (*eiki*) to his mother's brother, and Junod (1927, p. 255) quotes a Thonga native as saying 'The uterine nephew is a chief! He takes any liberty he likes with his maternal uncle'. Thus the joking relationship with the uncle does not merely annul the usual relation between the two generations, it reverses it. But while the superiority of the father and the father's sister is exhibited in the respect that is shown to them, the nephew's superiority to his mother's brother takes the opposite form of permitted disrespect.

It has been mentioned that there is a widespread tendency to feel that a man should show respect towards, and treat as social superiors, his relatives in the generation preceding his own, and

4. There are some societies in which the relation between a mother's brother and a sister's son is approximately symmetrical, and therefore one of equality. This seems to be so in the Western Islands of Torres Straits, but we have no information as to any teasing or joking, though it is said that each of the two relatives may take the property of the other.

the custom of joking with, and at the expense of, the maternal uncle clearly conflicts with this tendency. This conflict between principles of behaviour helps us to understand what seems at first sight a very extraordinary feature of the kinship terminology of the Thonga tribe and the VaNdau tribe in South-East Africa. Amongst the Thonga, although there is a term *malume* (= male mother) for the mother's brother, this relative is also, and perhaps more frequently, referred to as a grandfather (*kokwana*) and he refers to his sister's son as his grandchild (*ntukulu*). In the VaNdau tribe the mother's brother and also the mother's brother's son are called 'grandfather' (*tetekulu*, literally 'great father') and their wives are called 'grandmother' (*mbiya*), while the sister's son and the father's sister's son are called 'grandchild' (*muzukulu*).

This apparently fantastic way of classifying relatives can be interpreted as a sort of legal fiction whereby the male relatives of the mother's lineage are grouped together as all standing towards an individual in the same general relation. Since this relation is one of privileged familiarity on the one side, and solicitude and indulgence on the other, it is conceived as being basically the one appropriate for a grandchild and a grandfather. This is indeed in the majority of human societies the relationship in which this pattern of behaviour most frequently occurs. By this legal fiction the mother's brother ceases to belong to the first ascending generation, of which it is felt that the members ought to be respected.

It may be worth while to justify this interpretation by considering another of the legal fictions of the VaNdau terminology. In all these south-eastern Bantu tribes both the father's sister and the sister, particularly the elder sister, are persons who must be treated with great respect. They are also both of them members of a man's own patrilineal lineage. Amongst the VaNdau the father's sister is called 'female father' (*tetadji*) and so also is the sister (see Boas, 1922). Thus by the fiction of terminological classification the sister is placed in the father's generation, the one that appropriately includes persons to whom one must exhibit marked respect.

In the south-eastern Bantu tribes there is assimilation of two kinds of joking relatives, the grandfather and the mother's brother. It may help our understanding of this to consider an example in which the grandfather and the brother-in-law are similarly grouped together. The Cherokee Indians of North America, probably numbering at one time about 20,000, were divided into seven matrilineal clans (Gilbert, 1937). A man could not marry a woman of his own clan or of his father's clan. Common membership of the same clan connects him with his brothers and his mother's brothers. Towards his father and all his relatives in his father's clan of his own or his father's generation he is required by custom to show a marked respect. He applies the kinship term for 'father' not only to his father's brothers but also to the sons of his father's sisters. Here is another example of the same kind of fiction as described above; the relatives of his own generation whom he is required to respect and who belong to his father's matrilineal lineage are spoken of as though they belonged to the generation of his parents. The body of his immediate kindred is included in these two clans, that of his mother and his father. To the other clans of the tribe he is in a sense an outsider. But with two of them he is connected, namely with the clans of his two grandfathers, his father's father and his mother's father. He speaks of all the members of these two clans, of whatever age, as 'grandfathers' and 'grandmothers'. He stands in a joking relationship with all of them. When a man marries he must respect his wife's parents but jokes with her brothers and sisters.

The interesting and critical feature is that it is regarded as particularly appropriate that a man should marry a woman whom he calls 'grandmother', i.e. a member of his father's father's clan or his mother's father's clan. If this happens his wife's brothers and sisters, whom he continues to tease, are amongst those whom he previously teased as his 'grandfathers' and 'grandmothers'. This is analogous to the widely spread organization in which a man has a joking relationship with the children of his mother's brother and is expected to marry one of the daughters.

It ought perhaps to be mentioned that the Cherokee also have a one-sided joking relationship in which a man teases his father's sister's husband. The same custom is found in Mota of the Bank Islands. In both instances we have a society organized on a matrilineal basis in which the mother's brother is respected, the father's sister's son is called 'father' (so that the father's sister's husband is the father of a 'father'), and there is a special term for the father's sister's husband. Further observation of the societies in which this custom occurs is required before we can be sure of its interpretation. I do not remember that it has been reported from any part of Africa.

What has been attempted in this paper is to define in the most general and abstract terms the kind of structural situation in which we may expect to find well-marked joking relationships. We have been dealing with societies in which the basic social structure is provided by kinship. By reason of his birth or adoption into a certain position in the social structure an individual is connected with a large number of other persons. With some of them he finds himself in a definite and specific jural relation, i.e. one which can be defined in terms of rights and duties. Who these persons will be and what will be the rights and duties depend on the form taken by the social structure. As an example of such a specific jural relation we may take that which normally exists between a father and son, or an elder brother and a younger brother. Relations of the same general type may be extended over a considerable range to all the members of a lineage or a clan or an age-set. Beside these specific jural relations which are defined not only negatively but also positively, i.e. in terms of things that must be done as well as things that must not, there are general jural relations which are expressed almost entirely in terms of prohibitions and which extend throughout the whole political society. It is forbidden to kill or wound other persons or to take or destroy their property. Besides these two classes of social relations there is another, including many very diverse varieties, which can perhaps be called relations of alliance or consociation. For example, there is a form of alliance of very great importance in many societies, in which two persons or two groups are connected by an exchange of gifts or services (Mauss, 1927–8). Another example is provided by the institution of blood-brotherhood which is so widespread in Africa.

The argument of this paper has been intended to show that the joking relationship is one special form of alliance in this sense. An alliance by exchange of goods and services may be associated with a joking relationship, as in the instance recorded by Professor Labouret (1929, p. 245). Or it may be combined with the custom of avoidance. Thus in the Andaman Islands the parents of a man and the parents of his wife avoid all contact with each other and do not speak; at the same time it is the custom that they should frequently exchange presents through the medium of the younger married couple. But the exchange of gifts may also exist without either joking or avoidance, as in Samoa, in the exchange of gifts between the family of a man and the family of the woman he marries or the very similar exchange between a chief and his 'talking chief'.

So also in an alliance by blood-brotherhood there may be a joking relationship as amongst the Zande (Evans-Pritchard, 1933); and in the somewhat similar alliance formed by exchange of names there may also be mutual teasing. But in alliances of this kind there may be a relation of extreme respect and even of avoidance. Thus in the Yaralde and neighbouring tribes of South Australia two boys belonging to communities distant from one another, and therefore more or less hostile, are brought into an alliance by the exchange of their respective umbilical cords. The relationship thus established is a sacred one; the two boys may never speak to one another. But when they grow up they enter upon a regular exchange of gifts, which provides the machinery for a sort of commerce between the two groups to which they belong.

Thus the four modes of alliance or consociation, (1) through intermarriage, (2) by exchange of goods or services, (3) by blood-brotherhood or exchanges of names or sacra, and (4) by the joking relationship, may exist separately or combined in several different ways. The comparative study of these combinations presents a number of interesting but complex problems. The facts recorded from West Africa by Professor Labouret and Mademoiselle Paulme afford us valuable material. But a good deal more intensive field research is needed before these problems of social structure can be satisfactorily dealt with.

What I have called relations by alliance need to be compared with true contractual relations. The latter are specific jural relations entered into by two persons or two groups, in which either party has definite positive obligations towards the other, and failure to carry out the obligations is subject to a legal sanction. In an alliance by blood-brotherhood there are general obligations of mutual aid, and the sanction for the carrying out of these, as shown by Dr Evans-Pritchard, is of a kind that can be called magical or ritual. In the alliance by exchange of gifts failure to fulfil the obligation to make an equivalent return for a gift received breaks the alliance and substitutes a state of hostility and may also cause a loss of prestige for the defaulting party. Professor Mauss (1923-4) has argued that in this kind of alliance also there is a magical sanction, but it is very doubtful if such is always present, and even when it is it may often be of secondary importance.

The joking relationship is in some ways the exact opposite of a contractual relation. Instead of specific duties to be fulfilled there is privileged disrespect and freedom or even licence, and the only obligation is not to take offence at the disrespect so long as it is kept within certain bounds defined by custom, and not to go beyond those bounds. Any default in the relationship is like a breach of the rules of etiquette; the person concerned is regarded as not knowing how to behave himself.

In a true contractual relationship the two parties are conjoined by a definite common interest in reference to which each of them accepts specific obligations. It makes no difference that in other matters their interests may be divergent. In the joking relationship and in some avoidance relationships, such as that between a man and his wife's mother, one basic determinant is that the social structure separates them in such a way as to make many of their interests divergent, so that conflict or hostility might result. The alliance by extreme respect, by partial or complete avoidance, prevents such conflict but keeps the parties conjoined. The alliance by joking does the same thing in a different way.

All that has been, or could be, attempted in this paper is to show the place of the joking relationship in a general comparative study of social structure. What I have called, provisionally, relations of consociation or alliance are distinguished from the relations set up by common membership of a political society which are defined in terms of general obligations, of etiquette, or morals, or of law. They are distinguished also from the true contractual relations, defined by some specific obligation for each contracting party, into which the individual enters of his own volition. They are further to be distinguished from the relations set up by common membership of a domestic group, a lineage or a clan, each of which has to be defined in terms of a whole set of socially recognized rights and duties. Relations of consociation can only exist between individuals or groups which are in some way socially separated.

This paper deals only with formalized or standardized joking relations. Teasing or making fun of other persons is of course a common mode of behaviour in any human society. It tends to occur in certain kinds of social situations. Thus I have observed in certain classes in English-speaking countries the occurrence of horse-play between young men and women as a preliminary to courtship, very similar to the way in which a Cherokee Indian jokes with his 'grandmothers'. Certainly these unformalized modes of behaviour need to be studied by the sociologist. For the purpose of this paper it is sufficient to note that teasing is always a compound of friendliness and antagonism.

The scientific explanation of the institution in the particular form in which it occurs in a given society can only be reached by an intensive study which enables us to see it as a particular example of a widespread phenomenon of a definite class. This means that the whole social structure has to be thoroughly examined in order that the particular form and incidence of joking relationships can be understood as part of a consistent system. If it be asked why that society has the structure that it does have, the only possible answer would lie in its history. When the history is unrecorded, as it is for the native societies of Africa, we can only indulge in conjecture, and conjecture gives us neither scientific nor historical knowledge.[5]

References

BOAS, F. (1922), 'Das Verwandtschaftssystem der Vandau', *Zeits. Ethnolog.*, vols. 53–4.

EGGAN, F. (ed.) (1937), *Social Anthropology of North American Tribes*, University of Chicago Press.

5. The general theory outlined in this paper is one that I have presented in lectures at various universities since 1909 as part of the general study of the forms of social structure. In arriving at the present formulation of it I have been helped by discussions with Dr Meyer Fortes.

EVANS-PRITCHARD, E. E. (1933), 'Zande blood-brotherhood', *Africa*, vol. 6, pp. 369–401.

FORTES, M. (1945), *The Dynamics of Clanship among the Tallensi*, Oxford University Press.

GILBERT, W. H. (1937), 'Eastern Cherokee social organisation', in F. Eggan (ed.), *Social Anthropology of North American Tribes*, University of Chicago Press, pp. 285–338.

HOERNLÉ, A. W. (1925), 'Social organisation of the Nama Hottentot', *Amer. Anthropol.*, vol. 27, pp. 1–24.

JUNOD, H. (1927), *The Life of a South African Tribe*, vol. 1, Macmillan. 2nd rev. edn.

LABOURET, H. (1929), 'La parenté a plaisanteries en Afrique occidentale', *Africa*, vol. 2, pp. 244 ff.

LABOURET, H. (1931), *Les Tribus du Rameau Lobi*, Institut d'Ethnologie, Paris.

LANDES, R. (1937), 'The Ojibwa of Canada', in M. Mead (ed.), *Co-operation and Competition among Primitive Peoples*, McGraw-Hill, pp. 87–126.

MAUSS, M. (1923–4), 'Essai sur le don', *Ann. sociol.*, vol. 1, pp. 30–186.

MAUSS, M. (1927–8), *Ann. École pratique hautes Études: Section Sci. relig.*

MEAD, M. (1934), 'Kinship in the Admiralty Islands', *Anthropol. Papers Amer. Mus. nat. Hist.*, vol. 34, pp. 181–358.

PAULME, D. (1939), 'Parenté à plaisanteries et alliance par le sang en Afrique occidentale', *Africa*, vol. 12, pp. 433–44.

PEDLER, F. J. (1940), 'Joking relationships in East Africa', *Africa*, vol. 13, pp. 170 ff.

RADCLIFFE-BROWN, A. R. (1924), 'The mother's brother in South Africa', *South Africa J. Sci.*, vol. 21, pp. 542–55.

ROY, S. C. (1915), *The Oraons of Chota Nagpur*, Ranchi.

Part Five **Marriage Transactions**

The study of marriage transactions revolves around the major distinction between bridewealth and dowry, though bride-service, sister exchange and token gifts provide alternative general forms. The typology is crude but the distinction is important, as Radcliffe-Brown indicates (Reading 8). Bridewealth is particularly characteristic of Africa, while dowry is found, in varying forms, in all the major cultures in Europe and Asia. While bridewealth tends to be associated with the possibility of marrying more than one wife (polygyny), dowry is linked with monogamy. Moreover, while bridewealth circulates wealth throughout the society, in the exchange of rights over property for rights over women, dowry is a kind of anticipated inheritance whereby the bride receives her 'lot' or portion of the familial estate at her marriage. The operation of the system of dowry, which extends from Japan to Ireland, is well illustrated in Friedl's account of the Greek village of Vasilika. In many parts of Europe, especially in Ireland, the dowry system is linked to a late age of marriage and a low proportion of persons who never get married. As Hajnal (Reading 10) points out in his study of European marriage patterns, these features were widely distributed in Western Europe.

8 A. R. Radcliffe-Brown

Dowry and Bridewealth

Excerpt from A. R. Radcliffe-Brown, 'Introduction', in A. R. Radcliffe-Brown and D. Forde (eds.), *African Systems of Kinship and Marriage*, Oxford University Press for the International African Institute, 1950, pp. 1–85.

In order to understand the African customs relating to marriage we have to bear in mind that a marriage is essentially a rearrangement of social structure. What is meant by social structure is any arrangement of persons in institutionalized relationships. By a marriage certain existing relationships, particularly, in most societies, those of the bride to her family, are changed. New social relations are created, not only between the husband and the wife, and between the husband and the wife's relatives on the one side and between the wife and the husband's relatives on the other, but also, in a great many societies, between the relatives of the husband and those of the wife, who, on the two sides, are interested in the marriage and in the children that are expected to result from it. Marriages, like births, deaths, or initiations at puberty, are rearrangements of structure that are constantly recurring in any society; they are moments of the continuing social process regulated by custom; there are institutionalized ways of dealing with such events.

We tend, unless we are anthropologists, to judge other people's customs by reference to our own. To understand African marriage we must remember that the modern English idea of marriage is recent and decidedly unusual, the product of a particular social development. We think of a marriage as an event that concerns primarily the man and woman who are forming a union and the State, which gives that union its legality and alone can dissolve it by divorce. The consent of parents is, strictly, only required for minors. Religion still plays some part, but a religious ceremony is not essential.

We may compare English marriage with the following account of a 'wedding' in early England.

If people want to wed a maid or a wife and this is agreeable to her and to her kinsmen, then it is right that the bridegroom should first swear according to God's right and secular law and should wage [pledge himself] to those who are her forspeakers, that he wishes to have her in such a way as he should hold her by God's right as his wife – and his kinsmen will stand pledge for him.

Then it is to be settled to whom the price for upfostering her belongs, and for this the kinsmen should pledge themselves.

Then let the bridegroom declare what present he will make her for granting his desire, and what he will give if she lives longer than he does.

If it is settled in this way, then it is right that she should enjoy half the property, and all if they have a child, unless she marries another man.

All this the bridegroom must corroborate by giving a gage, and his kinsmen stand to pledge for him.

If they are agreed in all this, then let the kinsmen of the bride accept and wed their kinswoman to wife and to right life to him who desires her, and let him take the pledge who rules over the wedding.

If she is taken out of the land into another lord's land, then it is advisable that her kinsmen get a promise that no violence will be done to her and that if she has to pay a fine they ought to be next to help her to pay, if she has not enough to pay herself.[1]

The marriage here is not any concern of the State or political authorities; it is a compact between two bodies of persons, the kin of the woman who agree to wed their daughter to the man, and his kinsmen who pledge themselves that the terms of the agreement will be carried out. The bridegroom and his kinsmen must promise to make a payment (the 'marriage payment') to her father or other legal guardian. He must also state what present he will give to his bride for permitting the physical consummation of the marriage; this was the so-called 'morning-gift' to be paid after the bridal night. There was further an agreement as to the amount of the dowry, the portion of the husband's wealth of which the wife should have the use during her lifetime

---

1. Quoted by Vinogradoff, *Outlines of Historical Jurisprudence*, vol. 1, p. 252, from Liebermann, *Gesetze der Angelsachsen*, vol. 1, p. 442. The 'wedding' was the agreement or contract entered into by the kinsfolk of bride and bridegroom, equivalent to the Roman *sponsalia*, not the ceremony of handing over the bride (the Roman *traditio puellae*).

if her husband died before her. The agreement is concluded by giving of the *wed*, the symbolic payment made by the bridegroom and his kin to the woman's kinsmen.

In modern England the pledge or gage, in the form of a 'wedding' ring, is given, not to the bride's kinsmen when the marriage arrangement is made, but to the bride herself at the wedding ceremony. The change in custom is highly significant. The 'giving away' of the bride is a survival of something which at one time was the most important feature of the ceremonial of marriage.

Thus in Anglo-Saxon England a marriage, the legal union of man and wife, was a compact entered into by two bodies of kin. As the Church steadily increased in power and in control of social life, marriage became the concern of the Church and was regulated by canon law. There was a new conception that in marriage the man and woman entered into a compact with God (or with His Church) that they would remain united till parted by death. The marriage was under the control of the Church; matrimonial cases were dealt with in the ecclesiastical courts.

At the end of the Middle Ages there came the struggle for power between Church and State in which the State was, in Protestant countries, victorious. Marriage then came under State control. At the present day to legalize a union of man and wife the marriage, whether there is or is not a religious ceremony must be registered by someone licensed by the State and a fee must be paid. It is the State that decides on what conditions the marriage may be brought to an end by a divorce granted by a court which is an organ of the State.

A most important factor in the development of the modern English (and American) conception of marriage was the idea of romantic love, a theme that was elaborated in the nineteenth century in novel and drama and has now become the mainstay of the cinema industry. In its early development romantic love was conceived as not within but outside marriage, witness the troubadours and their courts of love and Dante and Petrarch. In the eighteenth century Adam Smith could write: 'Love, which was formerly a ridiculous passion, became more grave and respectable. As a proof of this it is worth our observation that no ancient tragedy turned on love, whereas it is now more respectable and influences all the public entertainments.' The idea that marriage should be a union based on romantic love leads logically to the view that if the husband and wife find they do not love one another they should be permitted to dissolve the marriage. This is the Hollywood practice, but conflicts with the control of marriage by the Church or by the State.

Another very important factor has been the change in the social and economic position of women during the nineteenth and twentieth centuries. A married woman may now hold property in her own right; she may take employment that has no connection with her family life but takes her away from it. In the marriage ceremony many women now refuse to promise that they will obey their husbands.

Not only are marriage and ideas about marriage in England and America the product of a recent, special and complex development, but there is good evidence that they are still changing. The demand for greater freedom of divorce is one indication of this. Yet it is clear that despite all this some people take twentieth-century English marriage as a standard of 'civilized' marriage with which to compare African marriage.

The African does not think of marriage as a union based on romantic love although beauty as well as character and health are sought in the choice of a wife. The strong affection that normally exists after some years of successful marriage is the product of the marriage itself conceived as a process, resulting from living together and cooperating in many activities and particularly in the rearing of children.

An African marriage is in certain respects similar to the early English marriage described above. The dowry or dower does not exist in Africa, though writers who do not know, or do not care about, the meanings of words use the term 'dowry' quite inappropriately to refer to the 'marriage payment'.[2] There is also in Africa nothing exactly corresponding to the English 'morning-gift' regarded as a payment for accepting sexual embraces, though it is usual for the bridegroom to give gifts to his bride. The two other features of the early English marriage

2. Belgian and some French writers make a similar misuse of the term 'dot', which is a woman's marriage portion of which the annual income is under her husband's control.

are normally found in African marriages. Firstly, the marriage is not the concern of the political authorities but is established by a compact between two bodies of persons, the kin of the man and the kin of the woman. The marriage is an alliance between the two bodies of kin based on their common interest in the marriage itself and its continuance, and in the offspring of the union, who will be, of course, kin of both the two kin-groups. The understanding of the nature of this alliance is essential to any understanding of African kinship systems. Secondly, in Africa generally, as in early England, and in a great number of societies in ancient and modern times in all parts of the world, a marriage involves the making of a payment by the bridegroom or his kin to the father or guardian of the bride. Africans distinguish, as we do, between a 'legal' marriage and an irregular union. In modern England a marriage is legal if it is registered by a person licensed by the State. Only children born of such a union are legitimate. But in Africa the State or political authority is not concerned with a marriage. How then, are we to distinguish a legal marriage? The answer is that a legal marriage, by which the children who will be born are given definite 'legitimate' status in the society, requires a series of transactions and formalities in which the two bodies of kin, those of the husband and those of the wife, are involved. In most African marriages, as in the early English marriage, the making of a payment of goods or services by the bridegroom to the bride's kin is an essential part of the establishment of 'legality'.

Some people regard payments of this kind as being a 'purchase' of a wife in the sense in which in England today a man may purchase a horse or a motor-car. In South Africa it was at one time held officially that a marriage by native custom with the payment of cattle (*lobola*) was 'an immoral transaction' and not a valid marriage. The Supreme Court of Kenya in 1917 decided that 'a so-called marriage by the native custom of wife-purchase is not a marriage'. The idea that an African buys a wife in the way that an English farmer buys cattle is the result of ignorance, which may once have been excusable but is so no longer, or of blind prejudice, which is never excusable in those responsible for governing an African people.

A marriage in many, perhaps most, African societies involves a whole series of prestations[3] (payments, gifts, or services), and while the most important of these are from the husband and his kin to the wife's kin, there are frequently, one might say usually, some in the other direction. One of the best accounts of the whole procedure is that given by Father Hulstaert for the Nkundo of the Belgian Congo (1938). The procedure begins with the presentation, on the part of the future husband, of the *ikula*, at one time an arrow, now two copper rings. The acceptance of this by the woman and her kin constitutes a formal betrothal. The marriage, i.e. the 'tradition' of the bride, may take place before any further payment. At the marriage, gifts are made to the bride by the parents of the bridegroom, by others of his relatives, and by the bridegroom himself. The next step is the formal prestation of the *ndanga*, formerly a knife, to the bride's father. It signifies that the husband thereafter becomes responsible for accidents that might befall his wife. In return there is a prestation from the bride's family to the husband and his family. This is part of the *nkomi*, the payment that is made to the bridegroom by the wife's family. The marriage is not fully established until the husband pays his father-in-law the *walo*, a substantial payment consisting chiefly of objects of metal. After this the woman becomes fully the man's wife. When the *walo* is handed over the woman's family make a return payment (*nkomi*) and give a present of food to the husband's family. The husband must also make a special payment to his wife's mother and must give a considerable number of presents to the father, mother, brothers and other relatives of the bride. The relatives of the husband then demand and receive presents from the wife's family. The final payment to be made by the husband is the *bosongo*, formerly a slave, now a quantity of copper rings.

There is, of course, an immense diversity in the particulars of prestations connected with betrothal and marriage in different societies and in each case they have to be studied, with regard to their meanings and functions, in relation to the society in which

3. 'Prestation' is defined in the *Oxford Dictionary* as 'the act of paying, in money or service, what is due by law or custom'. The prestations with which we are here concerned are all those gifts and payments of goods or services which are required by custom in the process of establishing a valid marriage.

they are found. For general theory, however, we have to look for general similarities. In the first place it is necessary to recognize that whatever economic importance some of these transactions may have, it is their symbolic aspect that we chiefly have to consider. This may be made clear by the English customs of the engagement ring, the wedding ring and the wedding presents. Though an engagement ring may have considerable value (more than many Africans 'pay' for their wives), the giving of it is not regarded as an economic or at least not as a business transaction. It is symbolic.

In what follows the term 'marriage payment' will be used for the major payment or payments made by the bridegroom to the wife's kin. Where there is a payment from the wife's kin to the husband (as in the Nkundo) this will be called the 'counter-payment'. The rule in many African societies is that if there is a divorce the marriage payment and the counter-payment must be returned. There are qualifications of this; for example, in some tribes where on divorce there are children and they belong to the father the marriage payment may be not returnable, or returnable only in part. Also, there are tribes in Africa in which, instead of a payment in goods, the bridegroom must serve for his wife, by working for her kin, just as Jacob served his mother's brother Laban seven years for each of the two sisters, Leah and Rachel, his cousins, whom he married (Genesis, ch. 29). This service, the equivalent of the marriage payment or of part thereof, is of course not returnable if there is a divorce.

Let us return to the early English marriage. In the formulary quoted above the marriage payment was called 'the price of upfostering' and was thus interpreted as a return to the father or guardian of the expense of rearing a daughter. But in somewhat earlier times the payment was differently interpreted. It was a payment for the transfer of the woman's *mund* from the father or guardian to the husband, whereby the latter gained and the former lost certain rights. The term for a legitimately married wife in Old Norse law was *mundi kjöbt*, meaning one whose *mund* has been purchased. In Sweden the transfer of *mund* was not by purchase but by gift, and the expression for marriage was *giftarmal*. In Roman law the marriage by *coemptio*, sometimes called 'marriage by purchase', was not the sale of a woman but the legal transfer of *manus* to her husband, and *mund* and *manus* are roughly equivalent terms. In these Roman and Teutonic marriages the important point is that to legalize the union of a man and a woman, so that it is really a marriage, legal power over his daughter must be surrendered by the father and acquired by the husband, whether the transfer be by gift or by payment. The early English marriage was of this type.

In Africa an unmarried woman is in a position of dependence. She lives under the control and authority of her kin, and it is they who afford her protection. Commonly, if she is killed or injured her guardian or her kinsfolk can claim an indemnity. At marriage she passes to a greater or less extent, which is often very considerable, under the control of her husband (and his kin), and it is he (and they) who undertake to afford her protection. (Note the *ndanga* payment amongst the Nkundo, by which the bridegroom accepts responsibility for accidents that may befall the bride.) The woman's kin, however, retain the right to protect her against ill treatment by her husband. If she is killed or injured by third parties it is now the husband and his kin who can claim an indemnity. It is this transfer of *mund*, to use the Old English term, that is the central feature of the marriage transaction.

To understand African marriage we must think of it not as an event or a condition but as a developing process. The first step is usually a formal betrothal, though this may have been preceded by a period of courtship or, in some instances in some regions, by an elopement. The betrothal is the contract or agreement between the two families. The marriage may proceed by stages, as in the instance of the Nkundo mentioned above. A most important stage in the development of the marriage is the birth of the first child. It is through the children that the husband and wife are united and the two families are also united by having descendents in common.

We may consider African marriage in three of its most important aspects. First, the marriage involves some modification or partial rupture of the relations between the bride and her immediate kin. This is least marked when the future husband comes to live with and work for his future parents-in-law while his betrothed is still a girl not old enough for marriage. It is most marked when, as in most African societies, the woman when she marries leaves her family and goes to live with her husband and his family. Her own family suffers a loss. It would be a gross error to think of this as an economic loss.[4] It is the loss of a person who has been a member of a group, a breach of the family solidarity. This aspect of marriage is very frequently given symbolic expression in the simulated hostility between the two bodies of kin at the marriage ceremony, or by the pretence of taking the bride by force (the so-called 'capture' of the bride). Either the bride herself or her kin, or both, are expected to make a show of resistance at her removal.

Customs of this kind are extremely widespread not only in Africa but all over the world, and the only explanation that fits the various instances is that they are the ritual or symbolic expression of the recognition that marriage entails the breaking of the solidarity that unites a woman to the family in which she has been born and grown up. Ethnographical literature affords innumerable instances. One example may be given here. In Basutoland, or at least in some parts of it, on the day fixed for the marriage the young men of the bridegroom's group drive the cattle that are to constitute the marriage payment to the home of the bride. When they draw near, the women of the bride's party gather in front of the entrance to the cattle kraal. As the bridegroom's party try to drive the cattle into the kraal the women, with sticks and shouts, drive them away so that they scatter over the veld and have to be collected together again and a new attempt made to drive them into the kraal. This goes on for some time until at last the cattle are successfully driven into the kraal. The women of the group make a show of resistance at the delivery of the cattle which will have as its consequence the loss of the bride. The proper interpretation of these customs is that they are symbolic expressions of the recognition of the structural change that is brought about by the marriage.

When this aspect of marriage is considered the marriage payment can be regarded as an indemnity or compensation given by the bridegroom to the bride's kin for the loss of their daughter.

4. This is the view of modern English law. If an unmarried woman is seduced her father can recover damages for the loss of her 'services'; as though the only value attached to a daughter is as a servant.

This is, however, only one side of a many sided institution and in some kinship systems is of minor importance. In societies in which the marriage payment is of considerable value it is commonly used to replace the daughter by obtaining a wife for some other member of the family, usually a brother of the woman who has been lost. A daughter is replaced by a daughter-in-law, a sister by a wife or sister-in-law. The family is compensated for its loss.

A second important aspect of legal marriage is that it gives the husband and his kin certain rights in relation to his wife and the children she bears. The rights so acquired are different in different systems. Some of these are rights of the husband to the performance of duties by the wife (rights *in personam*) and he accepts corresponding duties towards her. He has, for example, rights to the services of his wife in his household. But the husband usually acquires rights *in rem* over his wife. If anyone kills or injures her, or commits adultery with her, he may claim to be indemnified for the injury to his rights.

The husband acquires his rights through an action by the wife's kin in which they surrender certain of the rights they have previously had. The marriage payment may be regarded in this aspect as a kind of 'consideration' by means of which the transfer is formally and 'legally' made. It is the objective instrument of the 'legal' transaction of the transfer of rights. Once the payment, or some specific portion of it, has been made the bride's family have no right to fetch their daughter back, and in most tribes, if the union is broken by divorce at the instance of the husband, the payment has to be returned and the woman's family recover the rights they surrendered.

The rights obtained by a husband and his kin are different in some respects in different systems. The most important difference is in the matter of rights over the children the wife bears. An African marries because he wants children – *liberorum quaerendorum gratia*. The most important part of the 'value' of a woman is her child-bearing capacity. Therefore, if the woman proves to be barren, in many tribes her kin either return the marriage payment or provide another woman to bear children.

In a system of father-right, such as the Roman *patria potestas*, the rights of the father and his kin over the children of a marriage are so preponderant as to be nearly absolute and exclude any rights on the part of the mother's kin. On the other hand, in a system of mother-right such as that formerly existing amongst the Nayars of southern India, the father has no legal rights at all: the children belong to the mother and her kin. This does not, of course, exclude a relationship of affection between father and child. Both father-right and mother-right are exceptional conditions; most societies have systems which come between these extremes and might be called systems of joint right or divided right. The system of division varies and there may be an approximation either to father-right or to mother-right.

Some societies in Sumatra and other parts of the Malay Archipelago have two kinds of marriage. If a full marriage payment is made the children belong to the father; we may call this a father-right marriage. But if no payment is made the children belong to the mother and her kin, the marriage being one of mother-right.

The same sort of thing is reported from some parts of Africa, for example from Brass in Southern Nigeria (Talbot, 1926, pp. 437–40). The father-right marriage, with a substantial marriage payment, is the usual form, but if only a small payment is made the children belong to the mother's kin. The most definite example is from the Nyamwezi. In the *kukwa* form of marriage there is a payment (*nsabo*) made by the bridegroom to the father or guardian of the bride; children of such a marriage fall into the possession of the husband and his agnatic kin. In the *butende* form of marriage there is no payment and the children belong to the mother and her kin.

There is another aspect of marriage that must be taken into account. In Africa a marriage is not simply a union of a man and a woman; it is an alliance between two families or bodies of kin. We must consider the marriage payments in this connection also.

In so-called primitive societies the exchange of valuables is a common method of establishing or maintaining a friendly relation between separate groups or between individuals belonging to separate groups. Where material goods are exchanged it is common to speak of gift-exchange. But the exchange may be of services, particularly those of a ritual character. There are societies in which there is an exchange of women, each group (family, lineage or clan) providing a wife for a man of the other. The rule governing transactions of this kind is that for whatever is received a return must be made. By such exchanges, even by a single act of exchange, two persons or two groups are linked together in a more or less lasting relation of alliance (Mauss, 1923–4).

There are societies in some parts of the world in which the marriage payment and the counter-payment are equal or approximately equal in value. We may regard this as an exchange of gifts to establish friendship between two families, of which the son of one is to marry a daughter of the other. The kind, and to some extent the amount of the gifts is fixed by custom. But where the marriage payment is considerable in amount and there is a much smaller counter-payment, or none at all, we must interpret this as meaning that the bride's family is conferring a specific benefit on the bridegroom by giving him their daughter in marriage, a benefit that is shared by his kin, and that the marriage payment is a return for this. The transaction can still be regarded as a form of 'gift-exchange' and as such establishes a relation (of alliance) between the parties.

It is characteristic of a transaction of purchase and sale that once it has been completed it leaves behind no obligations on either the buyer or the seller. (This does not, of course, exclude claims based on warranty.) In an African marriage the position is very different. For one thing the marriage payment may in certain circumstances have to be repaid. In some tribes where the payment consists of cattle it is the same cattle with all their increase that should be returned. Further, in some African societies the family that has made the marriage payment continues to have an interest in the cattle or other goods of which it consists. The payment received for a woman's marriage may be used to obtain a wife for a member of her family, usually her brother. This sets up a number of important relations between the persons involved.

$$A = b \quad B = c \quad C = d$$

B and b are brother and sister, and so are C and c. A marries b and makes a marriage payment which is used to obtain a wife (c) for B. In various tribes the marriage payment establishes a series of special personal relations between *b* and *B*, between *A* and *B*, between *b* and *c*, and between *A* and *c*. These are defined differently in different tribes. We may briefly consider three varieties.

It is usual to speak of *B* and *b* as 'linked' brother and sister, and *B* is the 'linked' mother's brother of the children of *A* and *b*, while *b* is the 'linked' father's sister of *B*'s children. In the Shangana-Tonga tribes there is a very special relation between *A* and his 'great *mukonwana*' *c*, the wife that *B* married with the payment provided by *A*. *A* can claim in marriage a daughter of *c*, particularly if his wife *b* dies and there is no younger sister to take her place (Junod, 1927, pp. 231 ff.).

In the Lovedu the relations between the families of *A*, *B* and *C* ought to be continued in the next and succeeding generations. A son of *A* should marry a daughter of *B* and a son of *B* should marry a daughter of *C*. There is thus established a chain of connected families. The *B* family (or lineage) gives brides to and receives cattle from the *A* family and gives cattle to and receives brides from *C*. The linked sister *b* is said to have 'built the house for her brother' *B*, and she 'has a gate' by which she may enter the house. She has the right to demand a daughter of the house to come as her daughter-in-law, to marry her son and be her helper. Thus, in this tribe, cross-cousin marriage is systematized in terms of marriage payments, and a complex set of relations between persons and between families is created (Krige and Krige, 1943; J. D. Krige, 1939). In the Shangana-Tonga tribes *b* can demand a daughter of *c* as her co-wife or 'helper', the wife of her husband, not as her daughter-in-law (Earthy, 1933).

Amongst the Nkundo the relationships are given a different form. There is a special relation of *b* to *c*, the wife of her linked brother whose marriage was provided for by her marriage payment. The sister *b* is the *nkolo* of *c*, who is her *nkita*. The *nkolo* (*b*) stands in a position of superiority to the *nkita* (*c*). This relation is continued in the succeeding generations; the children of *b* (the *nkolo*) are in a position of superiority to the children of *c*. This is connected with a peculiar ordering of relations amongst the Nkundo by which the relation between cross-cousins is an asymmetrical one in which they are treated as if they belonged to different generations. The children of the father's sister are 'fathers', male and female (*baise*), to their cousins, the children of the mother's brother who are their 'children' (*bana*). The 'children' must show respect to their 'fathers' and help them. As a consequence a man regards the son of his father's sister's son as his 'brother' and uses that term for him (Hulstaert, 1938, pp. 164 ff.).

It should now be evident that the marriage payment is a complex institution having many varieties in form and function. In any given society it has to be interpreted by reference to the whole system of which it is a part. Nevertheless, there are certain general statements that seem to be well grounded. In Africa the marriage payment, whether it be small or large, is the objective instrument by which a 'legal' marriage is established. In some instances it is a compensation or indemnity to the woman's family for the loss of a member. This is particularly so where the marriage payment is considerable and is used to obtain a wife for the woman's brother. The payment may in some instances be regarded as part of an exchange of a kind that is used in many parts of the world to establish a friendly alliance between two groups. In some societies of South Africa and the Nilotic region it is the derivation of the cattle used in the marriage payment that fixes the social position of the children born of the union. Where the same cattle or other goods are used in two or more successive marriages this is in some tribes held to establish a special relation between the families thus formed. Where cattle are sacred in the sense that the cattle of a lineage are the material link between the living and their ancestors (having been received from those ancestors and being used for sacrifices to them), the use of cattle in marriage payments has a significance which a transfer of other goods would not have. This is not intended as a complete survey, which would be impossible within the limits of this essay. It is only an indication of how this institution, which is the procedure by which a husband acquires those rights which characterize a legal marriage (rights that vary in different societies), may be elaborated in different ways.

References

EARTHY, E. D. (1933), *Valenge Women*, Oxford University Press.
HULSTAERT, R. P. G. (1938), *Le Mariage des Nkundo*, Inst. roy. colon. belg., *Mémoires*, vol. 8, ch. 2.
JUNOD, H. (1927), *The Life of a South African Tribe*, Macmillan. Second rev. edn.

KRIGE, J. D. (1939), 'The significance of cattle exchanges in Lovedu social structure', *Africa*, vol. 12, pp. 393–424.

KRIGE, E. J., and KRIGE, J. D. (1943), *The Realm of a Rain Queen*, Oxford University Press.

MAUSS, M. (1923–4), 'Essai sur le don', *Ann. sociol.*, vol. 1, pp. 30–186.

TALBOT, P. A. (1926), *The Peoples of Southern Nigeria*, vol. 3., Oxford University Press.

9 E. Friedl

Dowry, Inheritance and Land-Tenure

Excerpt from E. Friedl, *Vasilika: A Village in Modern Greece*, Holt, Rinehart & Winston, 1962, pp. 64–8.

The discussion of the dowry as a mechanism of inheritance for children of farmers who remain farmers may now be summarized. The dowry is part of a system in which children receive property through the parents of both their fathers and their mothers. Property from two sources merges in each generation and is redistributed in the next generation. Although patrilineally inherited lands (those passed from a father to his sons in each generation) have some continuity in space and have some continuity of ownership in the male line, such lands always constitute only one part of the total holdings of any particular elementary family. Therefore, in Vasilika and its vicinity, the pattern of land and money circulation through inheritance has two facets: one portion that is patrilineally inherited straight down the line of males; a second, distributed at marriage, that eventually circulates among unrelated elementary families. The system cannot be described as one in which women inherit from women, in spite of the legal residual control of a woman over her dower properties, because brothers have equal rights with their sisters to their mother's dower lands. In Vasilika, at least, there is neither an explicit nor an implicit pattern of giving daughters only dower property and sons only patrilineally inherited lands.

The combination of practices including the function of the dowry as inheritance, land as a major form of property, and village exogamy have some further consequences for the relation of property to groups of kinsmen in the Boeotian countryside. In spite of patrilocal residence and some patrilineally inherited land, the descendants of a male line are not associated with any particular landed estates. Since no man owns or farms exactly the same holdings as his father farmed before him, nor the same holdings his brothers have, and since he himself will expect to work different lands in different communities even in the course of his own adult life, the permanent association of certain estates with certain lineages is obstructed (Friedl, 1959a.) Moreover, since dowries move down the generations and not across to a man of one's own generation who might use the property to marry off one of his daughters, there is no economic advantage to brother-and-sister exchange marriages. This situation is congruent with both the Greek Orthodox Church's and the Civil Code's (Section 1357) prohibitions on marriages between sisters and brothers-in-law and between cousins to the third degree. This rule, as well as the bilateral reckoning of kin in Greece (Section 1356), prevents the transfer of property at marriage from resulting in either a series of equal exchanges between two sets of kin groups or in a regular pattern of circulation through several generations among particular sets of such groups. The control of property establishes social links between a man and his wife's relatives not only in the ways we have mentioned, but because his wife's parents and brothers and sisters have a legal and customary right to be consulted before the final alienation of dower property (Section 1418). These links last only one generation, however, so that in each generation a new network of relations between elementary families in the neighborhood develops, clustering around the management of dower properties. These matters are important because they reveal some of the economic and social structure of Vasilika and its neighborhood that is congruent with the type of relationships people, both kin and non-kin, have with each other.

One other situation occurs frequently enough in Vasilika to be worth mentioning. When a farmer has no sons to inherit his land and his house, but has a daughter, the father may acquire a man's assistance on the farm by importing a son-in-law. Such a man is called a *soghambros* in Vasilika; he is a husband who moves into his wife's household instead of vice versa. The importation of a *soghambros* is also a solution to the problem of a young widow who has no grown sons to run the farm left by her husband and arranges a second marriage for herself with a man who is willing to work her first husband's holdings and her original dower lands. Since a *soghambros* is always a manager of, and laborer on, property belonging to others and is expected to bring no property of his own with him, there is a slight social stigma attached to the status in

Vasilika. The villagers say also that a *soghambros* is not 'master in his own house'. Certainly, the lot of a man who is not a master in his own house and comes as a stranger to a village where most of the other men have known each other all their lives is not a happy one. But a *soghambros* is not really dishonored by his position; the villagers, in this situation, as in so many others, recognize the practical necessities which brought about the arrangement and do not strongly condemn a man for making the best of his difficulties.

The dowry in Vasilika enters into the life of the villagers in other ways besides inheritance at marriage. It has long served as a means of upward social mobility for girls. Since the marriage of a daughter is among the most important obligations of parents, the dowry comes into the consciousness of the villagers more often as a property requirement for marrying off their daughters than as a means of transmitting inheritance. When, in addition, the high value placed on upward social mobility is translated into an effort to find urban sons-in-law for one's daughters, the dowry emerges as a mechanism for increasing the social prestige of the family. Farmers are willing to give larger dowries in exchange for the great satisfaction they derive from having town sons-in-law. In Vasilika, the education of some sons has released land to add to the girls' dowries. Improved agricultural income has also enabled the farmers to give larger dowries. In the decade ending in 1959, every marriage of a Vasilika daughter whose father was in the upper half of the village's income range has been one with a man of respectable occupation who lived in a provincial town or in Athens. The husbands are tailors, small retail store owners, or civil service workers. One young man is a photographer, another is a gymnasium professor who has become the principal of his gymnasium. In 1961, however, the son of a rather prosperous village farmer became attracted to a daughter of another Vasilika farmer with good land holdings. The young man asked his father to arrange the marriage for him, and, since all the conditions were entirely suitable, the young couple were engaged.

The trend in favor of town husbands prevails, however, among most of those who can afford it. Once a few girls had married urban men, the rivalry between village families led to greater efforts to secure town husbands for the others. Consequently, there has been an inflation in dowries which is alarming the villagers themselves.

In the early 1950s, a *prika* worth $3000 was enough for a town husband of no special prestige; by the late 1950s, the same kind of man was asking for one worth $4500.

The inflation has had several consequences. Often the value of the dowry can no longer be limited to the share of the inheritance to which a girl is entitled. Farming sons are willing to give up some portion of their shares so that their sisters can 'live well', as they put it. The brothers gain also from the added prestige and influence of the family. These in turn may make it possible for them to find a girl with a larger dowry than their property qualifications might warrant. A farmer so situated may make higher demands on the ground that his and his wife's children will have an urban aunt and uncle. The town sister might provide board for her nephews and nieces (girls are increasingly being sent to gymnasium) while they are in school and can also be expected to help them find jobs.

Another consequence of the dowry inflation is the increasingly late age of marriage for the village girls and the town men. It takes farmers longer to accumulate the larger amounts of cash for the dowry, and the prospective grooms longer to attain a position or income at least partially commensurate. Vasilika's girls who marry town men are usually between twenty-five and thirty. Those whose fathers have few land holdings, and consequently can offer only small dowries, have been marrying farmers from other villages or within Vasilika itself and have been in their early twenties at the time of the engagement.

Now let us consider the disposition of the dowry which goes with a girl marrying a town husband. First, if he accepts land as part of the dowry, he will of necessity have it worked by his wife's male relatives. In time, however, often by the end of the first decade of the marriage, the son-in-law may wish to expand his shop, or may wish to start building a house for himself or for his daughter's dowry, or may hear of a good investment opportunity. He will want money for these purposes, and so he begins, with his wife's consent and after consultation with her father, to arrange for the sale of dowry lands. Since the 1950s, prospective town grooms have been less willing to take land which they know they will eventually want to sell, and have been asking for cash or for a house in town. Anticipating this situation, several of Vasilika's farmers who have small daughters have begun to use their savings and even to sell a little land in order to build houses in Athens or in a provincial town so that by the time their daughters are ready to marry, the houses will provide the main portion of the dowry. Rents are high and earnings relatively low in cities so that houses are a good investment. However, since building materials must be bought, and contractors paid, in cash, the houses may take many years to build. The young couple may then move into the habitable shell, and the rest of the dwelling will be completed out of the farmer's then current income. This kind of dowry-on-the-installment-plan becomes part of the marriage contract. It is often a source not only of continuing long-term discussions between a farmer and his town son-in-law, but also a source of quarrels – what in Greece are called *fasaries*.

The rate of movement of farmers' daughters into the towns and cities has been accelerating in the last decade, but marriages to urban husbands are not a new phenomenon. Between 1930 and 1950, at least five of Vasilika's women married 'into Athens'.

This type of marriage, like those discussed above in which both bride and groom are members of farm families, accelerates land sales and exchanges. The network of association which develops between Vasilika's residents and their relatives in Athens and the towns, is, however, perhaps the most important consequence of the urban marriages of village women (Friedl, 1959). In addition to the economic reasons for continuing relationships, there are several customary patterns which increase the frequency of contacts between the two groups. Lonely village mothers are grateful for visits from their married daughters and their grandchildren, and the midsummer season not uncommonly finds city women with their children back in the village for Easter, sometimes for most of the Holy Week as well, is a well-known pattern in Greece. *Paniyiri* in one's *patridha* (home village) is another occasion for visiting.

Journeys in the opposite direction also occur with some frequency. Village men and women, when ill, may enter hospitals in a town in which they have sons or daughters, or brothers or sisters. Village men visit their town brothers and bring their children; occasionally a child spends a summer with his town aunt or uncle. Visits to the village or to the town usually last several days. They are made possible by still another congruent pattern of Greek culture. Neither the villagers nor their town relatives seem to have any strong need for personal privacy. Visiting relatives are bedded down on pallets when there are not enough regular beds, and it is not considered either indecent or especially uncomfortable for one or even two families to sleep in the same room. It is through this inter-visiting process that so many urban traits of culture are introduced to the villagers and, indeed, that some village patterns are conserved in urban areas.

An additional consequence of the town marriages of village girls is that rural wealth derived from land flows into the cities. This wealth is an addition to what the productivity of land normally contributes to urban centers in the form of food, taxes and the export of rural produce. A portion of the farmer's profits, through the dowry, is being used, it would seem, directly to support a part of the urban population. When the dowries are invested in housing or in small commercial enterprises, many low-salaried employees, civil service workers, or economically marginal entrepreneurs find it possible to support themselves and their families in the town and cities. Without the aid of dower wealth, they might not be able to do so.

References

FRIEDL, E. (1959), 'The role of kinship in the transmission of national culture to rural villages in mainland Greece', *Amer. Anthropol.* vol. 61, pp. 30–38.

FRIEDL, E. (1959a), 'Dowry and inheritance in modern Greece', *Trans. New York Acad. Sci.* vol. 22, pp. 49–54.

10 J. Hajnal

European Marriage Patterns in Perspective

Excerpt from J. Hajnal, 'European marriage patterns in perspective', in D. V. Glass and D. E. C. Eversley (eds.), *Population in History*, Edward Arnold, 1965, pp. 101-43.

The main theme of this paper is not new. It is one of the main topics of Malthus' *Essay* (1970) and indeed implicit in its very structure (especially in the revised version of the second edition). Malthus devoted Book I of his *Essay* to 'the checks to population in the less civilized parts of the world and in past times', and Book II to 'the different states of modern Europe'. In Europe he traces again and again the workings of the 'preventive checks of moral restraint' which implies 'principally delay of the marriage union' and he contrasts the condition of Europe with that of the peoples described in Book I.

Was Malthus right in thinking that late marriage in Europe resulted in lower birth rates, and hence lower death rates, than obtained among non-European populations? Whatever the nature of the causal connection, his notions about the levels of birth and death rates gain some support from modern research. European birth rates, so far as we can tell, were rarely over 38 before the spread of birth control; in underdeveloped countries, they are almost always over 40 and often over 45. So far as mortality is concerned, the contrast is less clear cut, but there seems no record in European experience since the eighteenth century of conditions such as those in India or Formosa in the initial decades of the twentieth century.

The way in which a non-European marriage pattern goes with non-European birth and death rates may be illustrated by a recent study by Csoscán (1959) of the parish registers for three Hungarian villages in the eighteenth century. This population is not in 'Europe' as defined for this paper. The distribution of marriages by age of bride in 1770–1800 was quite definitely 'non-European', as the following figures show:

Age group	Per cent distribution[1] of Bridegrooms	Brides
Under 20	11	52
20–24	48	25
25–29	14	9
30–39	15	9
40 and over	12	5
Total	100	100

In the same period (1770–1800) the crude birth rate in these Hungarian villages was 52 per 1,000 and the death rate was 43 per 1,000. This may be compared, for example, with the following figures for the French village of Crulai given in the study by Gautier and Henry (1958):

Period	Birth rate	Death rate
1675–1749	36	31
1750–89	31	28

The marriage data for Crulai are, of course, quite clearly 'European'. The eighteenth-century Hungarian villages are thus non-European in all three respects (age at marriage, birth rate, death rate) in contrast with the European levels of Crulai's vital rates, as well as its marriage patterns.

There was a widespread conviction among eighteenth-century authors that European conditions were fundamentally different not only in marriage, birth and death rates, but above all in standards of living, from those obtaining elsewhere in the world. Europeans, a large proportion of them, not just the rich, had better housing, better clothing, a greater variety of food, more furniture and utensils, than people elsewhere. This uniqueness of Europe, so evident to contemporaries, has been largely ignored in recent discussions of economic development; all that is pre-industrial, including eighteenth-century Europe, is often lumped together in

1. These percentages are based on 440 cases for men and 442 for women. The number of marriages in which the age was not recorded was, surprisingly for this period, very small. The figures are from p. 106 of Csoscán's paper. Remarriages are included and they form a high proportion of the total.

generalizations about 'agricultural' or 'peasant' or 'underdeveloped' societies.

Presumably the uniqueness of Europe in standards of living and in death rates did not extend back beyond the seventeenth century (except in limited regions). But if European death rates were as high as in other parts of the world, could birth rates have been lower? And if the European birth rate before the seventeenth century was as high as elsewhere, does this not imply that European women must have married young as in other populations of high fertility? These large and vague questions need to be broken up and investigated by careful calculations on the interrelationships between marriage, birth and death rates. Even the relation between marriage patterns and crude birth rates is not nearly as obvious as is often supposed and it is not independent of mortality.

An inquiry into the origins of the European marriage pattern will inevitably take one into fundamental issues of economic and social history. This is so not only because of the connections just discussed between marriages and births and deaths. There are other links. A marriage almost by definition requires the establishment of an economic basis for the life of the couple and their children. The arrangements current in a society for achieving this must fit in with the marriage pattern: they will shape it and will be in turn influenced by it. Unmarried men and women must be attached to households in some way, or form independent households. The structure and size of households and the rate of formation of new households and disappearance of old ones, therefore, depend on the marriage pattern. In societies where the household is the principal unit of economic production as well as consumption, all this means that the marriage pattern is tied in very intimately with the performance of the economy as a whole. The emotional content of marriage, the relation between the couple and other relatives, the methods of choosing or allocating marriage partners – all this and many other things cannot be the same in a society where a bride is usually a girl of sixteen and one in which she is typically a woman of twenty-four. These things are perhaps obvious, but they have not been much explored, at least not in histories which trace the emergence of modern Europe. A full explanation of the background of European marriage patterns would probably lead into such topics as the rise of capitalism and the protestant ethic.

The economic system influences the marriage pattern through the arrangements by which the economic basis for the support of a couple and their children is established. It is equally true that the marriage pattern influences the economic system. The traditional argument, that late marriage retarded population growth, has already been mentioned but other possible effects need to be explored. In the European pattern a person would usually have some years of adult life before marriage; for women especially this period would be much larger than outside Europe. It is a period of maximum productive capacity without responsibility for children; a period during which saving would be easy. These savings (e.g. by means of the accumulation of household goods in preparation of marriage) might add substantially to the demand for goods other than the food etc. required for immediate survival. In this respect delayed marriage may be similar to income inequality in stimulating the diversion of resources to ends other than those of minimum subsistence; but when later marriage is the norm the total volume of demand generated might be much larger than that which can be caused by a small class of wealthy families in a population at subsistence level.[2] Could this effect, which was uniquely European, help to explain how the groundwork was laid for the uniquely European 'take-off' into modern economic growth?

If late marriage brings about wealth, wealth may equally cause late marriage. It was suggested in the eighteenth century (for example by Cantillon) that people married late because they insisted on a certain standard of living (a standard varying with the social position of the individual) as a prerequisite of marriage. More simply, men marry late because they cannot 'afford' to marry young; they have to wait until they have a livelihood, a farmer till he acquires land, an apprentice till he finishes his apprenticeship and so on.

It is tempting to see in this feature a key to the uniqueness of the European marriage pattern. In Europe it has been necessary for a

2. The mere presence in the labour force of a large number of adult women not involved in child bearing or rearing must have been a considerable advantage to the eighteenth-century European economies.

man to defer marriage until he could establish an independent livelihood adequate to support a family; in other societies the young couple could be incorporated in a larger economic unit, such as a joint family.[3] This, presumably, is more easily achieved and does not require such a long postponement of marriage. This line of argument seems especially convincing if the larger economic unit is such that extra labour is often felt to be an economic asset. A system of large estates with large households as in Eastern Europe might thus be conducive to a non-European marriage pattern, while small holdings occupied by a single family and passed on to a single heir would result in a European pattern. If this reasoning has substance, the uniqueness of the European marriage pattern must be ascribed to the European 'stem-family'.[4] (The term 'stem-family' was coined by Le Play in describing the type of family organization in which land descends to a single heir, the other sons going elsewhere.) This explanation calls attention to a force which may have helped to bring about the European marriage pattern, if it did not exist in the Middle Ages. If men had to wait till land became available, presumably a delay in the death of the holders of land resulting from declining death rates would tend to raise the age at marriage. Whether there was, in fact, a decline in mortality over the relevant period is a

---

3. The young Duc de la Rochefoucauld, on his visit to England, makes a similar point: 'Perhaps another reason for this [i.e. late marriage in England] is because it is usual to set up house immediately after marriage. The young couple never stay with their parents and they must be sensible enough to avoid extravagance both in their conduct and in their expenditure.'

4. The extent to which generalizations can justifiably be made about the family system in parts of Europe at particular times (let alone about the whole of Europe or all non-European societies) is totally beyond my competence. There have been large estates and joint families in some regions of Western Europe in the Middle Ages and beyond. Presumably it would be possible to have a system in which each couple is in principle an independent economic unit, but in which early marriage is made possible by arrangements to provide for the couple until they achieve complete independence. The study by Katz (1959) mentions such arrangements among Jews in Eastern Europe. Joint families can perhaps be regarded as fulfilling the function of such transitional arrangements. In countries where in theory joint families prevail the average size of household is not large. Households consisting of several nuclear families may not remain long in this condition, but this arrangement makes it possible for young couples to be part of a larger unit at the beginning of marriage for some years.

dubious point (the decline in question must have occurred before the eighteenth century); but this is certainly a hypothesis that merits study.

The connection between the death of the holder of land and its availability for the founding of a new family is, however, rather an indirect one. Under the mortality conditions of the Middle Ages fathers often died while their children were very young; interim arrangements had to be made till the son was old enough to take over. Even if the father survived to old age, it does not follow that a young family could not be set up on the holding until he died. Homans (1941) in his book on thirteenth-century England describes many instances where a father made over the land to his son while he lived, thus permitting the latter to get married. He also mentions instances where a father, while he lived, turned over his holding to be shared between two sons, where a man transferred his holding to someone other than his son, etc. To understand the effect on the frequency of marriage and age of marriage of a rule that a man must acquire land before marrying we should have to know the frequency of the various arrangements by which land was passed on. The rate at which land became available for the founding of new families may have been controlled not so much by death as by social arrangements. It is not at all clear *a priori* how a rule that a man must have a livelihood before marrying would operate to produce just such a postponement as is in fact observed. Even if we understood how the age at marriage of men was determined at a given period it would still need to be explained how women's age at marriage was affected. The uniqueness of the European pattern lies primarily in the high age at marriage of women (often with a relatively small difference between the age of husband and wife), rather than in a high age at marriage for men.

There is no space for further speculation in the causes or consequences of the European marriage pattern. The primary concern of this account has been the mere existence of the pattern. This aspect should be kept distinct from the search for explanations. It has been shown (1) that the distinctively European pattern can be traced back with fair confidence as far as the seventeenth century in the general population; (2) that its origins lie somewhere about the sixteenth century in several of the special upper class groups available for study and in none of these groups was the pattern European before the sixteenth century; (3) the little fragmentary evidence which exists for the Middle Ages suggests a non-European pattern, as do scraps of information for the ancient world.

Some at least of the data presented have probably been misinterpreted. In dealing with sources of a type of which one has no experience coming from remote periods of whose historical background one is ignorant, one is very likely to make mistakes. In an effort to survey so great a variety of materials, some of them could only be looked at superficially. Even if individual pieces of information have been soundly interpreted, there remains the problem how far generalizations can properly be based on isolated demographic facts. This is a basic problem of much of historical demography. We wish to draw conclusions about the demography of large groups. The terms in which questions are posed (like the distinction between European and non-European marriage patterns) are based on modern statistics for whole countries; but the historical data often relate to small groups such as one village. To what extent are conclusions from such data to larger units justified? How far are statistics of particular groups likely to deviate from those of larger populations of which they form a part (aside from sample fluctuations)? Are data likely to be systematically misleading because they do not relate to a closed population?

In spite of these and other difficulties, there seem to be good prospects of obtaining substantial further information on the origins and spread of the European marriage pattern. The distinction between European and non-European patterns is substantial so that no very refined measuring instrument is required for its detection. There is probably a good deal of material for the seventeenth and even the sixteenth century. The parish registers offer a large mine of information waiting to be exploited. If it were indeed to prove the case that in the Middle Ages the marriage pattern of Europe was entirely 'non-European', traces of the transition should be visible in some of the early parish register materials. Even for the Middle Ages there seems hope that various types of records (for example manorial extents[5]) if carefully

5. The recent study by Hallam (1958), which came to my attention after this paper was written, suggests that promising material may be awaiting analysis.

handled may yield useful information. If the recent rate of output of studies in historical statistics is maintained, and if those who engage in such work keep their eyes open for information on marriage, the mystery of the origins of European marriage patterns may be cleared up.

References

CSOSCÁN, J. (1959), 'Három Pest megyei falu népesedése a XVIII század második felében', *Történelmi Statisztikai Közlemények*, vol. 3, nos. 1–2, pp. 58–107. 'Demographic changes in three villages in the county of Pest in the second half of the 18th century', *Publications of Historical Statistics*, Budapest.

GAUTIER, É., and HENRY, L. (1958), *La Population de Crulai, Paroisse Normande*, Institut National d'Études Démographiques: Travaux et Documents, Cahier no. 33.

HALLAM, H. E. (1958), 'Some thirteenth century censuses', *Econ. Hist. Rev.*, vol. 10, no. 3, pp. 340–61.

HOMANS, G. C. (1941), *English Villagers of the Thirteenth Century*, Harvard University Press.

KATZ, J. (1959), 'Family kinship and marriage among Ashkenazim in the sixteenth to eighteenth centuries', *Jewish J. Sociol.*, vol. 1, no. 1, pp. 3–22.

MALTHUS, T. R. (1970), *An Essay on the Principle of Population*, Penguin. First published 1798.

Part Six Plural Marriage

Plural marriage may take a variety of forms, depending on whether it is the husband (polygyny) or wife (polyandry) who has more than one spouse, and depending too upon whether the marriage is plural in a simultaneous or in a consecutive sense. Frequent divorce establishes a kind of serial polygyny. But here we are concerned with the two main kinds of plural marriage, namely, polyandry, which was virtually limited to a small area of India and Tibet, and polygyny, which is most widely practised in Africa (in bridewealth and non-bridewealth societies alike). In Reading 11 Leach reconsiders some of the main characteristics of polyandrous marriages and relates these to the type of inheritance, as Friedl does with dowry (see Reading 9). In Reading 12 Clignet reports on some general features of African polygyny.

11 E. R. Leach

Polyandry, Inheritance and the Definition of Marriage

E. R. Leach, 'Polyandry, inheritance and the definition of marriage', *Man*, vol. 55, 1955, pp. 182–6. Reprinted in E. R. Leach, *Rethinking Anthropology*, Athlone Press, pp. 105–13.

Although polyandry has been an important topic of anthropological discussion for almost a century the definition of the concept remains strikingly unsatisfactory.[1] This is sufficiently indicated by the fact that Fischer (1952) maintains that adelphic polyandry, regarded as a form of polygamy, is non-existent, while HRH Prince Peter of Greece and Denmark (1955), ignoring Fischer, continues to discuss adelphic polyandry as a species of polygamy.

At first sight the issue seems a simple one with the logic all on Fischer's side. The *Notes and Queries* (1951) definition of marriage is: 'Marriage is a union between a man and a woman such that children born to the woman are recognized legitimate offspring of both partners'. Now certainly, in many cases of polyandry, the legal status of the children is similar to that described by Caesar for the ancient Britons (Fischer, 1952, p. 114): 'Wives are shared between groups of ten or twelve men, especially between brothers and between fathers and sons; but the offspring of these unions are counted as the children of those to whom the maid was conducted first.' This clearly is not a condition of polygamy; the children have only one legal father and the woman has only one legal husband. The other 'husbands' have tolerated sexual access to the woman, but she is not married to them in terms of the *Notes and Queries* definition. The situation is one of plural mating, or, as Fischer would call it, 'polykoity'.

More specifically, Fischer argues that we should reserve the concept of polygamy for situations in which the polygamous spouse goes through a succession of marriage rites with different partners. In adelphic polyandry 'the woman does not contract

1. This paper is based in part upon fieldwork carried out in Ceylon in 1954.

different successive marriages. There is no reason for this, since the social position of her children is guaranteed completely by the fact that she is married' (Fischer, 1952, p. 114).

Fischer agrees that an institution of polyandrous polygamy is a possibility. For example a woman might be mated to several men in such a way that each of them in turn assumed the role of social father in respect to her successive children. This very approximately seems to be the state of affairs among the Todas, and Fischer concedes that it 'approaches very closely to that of polygamy'. The institution of secondary marriage as described by Smith (1953) is also polyandrous polygamy in Fischer's sense. In both these cases every child has one, and only one, clearly defined social father.

But is it really so certain that the role of social father cannot be vested simultaneously in several different individuals? Is it not possible that in some societies social fatherhood is not an attribute of individuals at all but of a collective corporation which may include several brothers or even fathers and sons?

When Radcliffe-Brown (1941) argued that adelphic polyandry is to be 'interpreted in the light of the structural principle of the solidarity of the sibling group', he presumably had in mind that social fatherhood might sometimes be vested in a collective corporation of this kind, and Prince Peter sought to demonstrate that this is in fact the case. Does this mean that the notion of group marriage is once again respectable?

There is certainly one well attested case of 'corporate polyandry' of this kind, namely that of the Iravas (Aiyappan, 1945, pp. 98–103). Although Aiyappan states that on the occasion of a marriage 'the common practice is for the eldest brother alone to go to the bride's house to fetch her', it is plain, from the further details that he gives, that the eldest brother is here acting as representative of the group of brothers considered as a corporation. Even so, it is not entirely clear what rights this corporation possesses. It is Aiyappan's thesis that *all* marital rights are completely merged in the corporation – that the sexual rights of the individual husbands and the property rights of the individual children are alike indistinguishable. Nevertheless one would welcome more detailed evidence on these points.

There is another way of looking at the problem. Instead of

arguing pedantically about whether adelphic polyandry does or does not constitute plural marriage, let us consider whether a definition of marriage solely in terms of legitimacy (*Notes and Queries*, p. 111; Fischer, p. 108) is altogether adequate. There are other definitions of marriage with respectable backing, e.g. 'a physical, legal, and moral union between a man and a woman in complete community of life for the establishment of a family' (Ranasinha, 1950, p. 192). Is the *Notes and Queries* definition any less question-begging than this? What, for example, does the phrase 'legitimate offspring' really connote?

Prince Peter, in the lecture under discussion, seemed to assume that, of the various forms of heterosexual mating recognized and tolerated in any society, there is always one which may properly be described as 'marriage' in the anthropological sense. Yet if we adhere rigidly to our *Notes and Queries* definition this is not the case.

Thus traditionally among the matrilineal Nayar of South India (Gough, 1952; 1955) a woman had a ritual husband in her *enangar* lineage and also various 'recognized lovers' (*sambandham*), who lacked ritual status; but all of these men were excluded from any legal rights in respect to the woman's children. There was here then no marriage in the strict sense of the term but only a 'relationship of perpetual affinity' between linked lineages (Gough, 1955). The woman's children, however they might be begotten, were simply recruits to the woman's own matrilineage.

Yet as Gough has shown, even in this system, certain *elements* of a normal marriage institution are present.

The notion of fatherhood is lacking. The child uses a term of address meaning 'lord' or 'leader' towards *all* its mother's lovers, but the use of this term does not carry with it any connotation of paternity, either legal or biological. On the other hand the notion of affinity is present, as evidenced by the fact that a woman must observe pollution at her ritual husband's death (Gough, 1955).

Both Gough (1952) and Prince Peter have described the Nayar as having a system of polyandrous marriage. I do not wish to insist that this is a misnomer, but we need to be clear that *if* we agree that the Nayar practise polyandrous marriage then we are using the term 'marriage' in a sense different from that employed by Fischer and by *Notes and Queries*.

My personal view is that the *Notes and Queries* definition of marriage is too limited and that it is desirable to include under the category 'marriage' several distinguishable sub-types of institution.

The institutions commonly classed as marriage are concerned with the allocation of a number of distinguishable classes of rights. In particular a marriage may serve:

1. To establish the legal father of a woman's children.
2. To establish the legal mother of a man's children.
3. To give the husband a monopoly in the wife's sexuality.[2]
4. To give the wife a monopoly in the husband's sexuality.
5. To give the husband partial or monopolistic rights to the wife's domestic and other labour services.
6. To give the wife partial or monopolistic rights to the husband's labour services.
7. To give the husband partial or total rights over property belonging or potentially accruing to the wife.
8. To give the wife partial or total rights over property belonging or potentially accruing to the husband.
9. To establish a joint fund of property – a partnership – for the benefit of the children of the marriage.
10. To establish a socially significant 'relationship of affinity' between the husband and his wife's brothers.

One might perhaps considerably extend this list, but the point I would make is that in no single society can marriage serve to establish all these types of right simultaneously; nor is there any one of these rights which is invariably established by marriage in every known society. We need to recognize then that the institutions commonly described as marriage do not all have the same legal and social concomitants.

If we attempt a typology of marriage on these lines it is at once obvious that the nature of the marriage institution is partially correlated with principles of descent and rules of residence. Thus in a society structured into patrilineal patrilocal lineages we commonly find that right 1 is far and away the most important element,

2. I use the term 'monopoly' advisedly. I consider that this right 3 is to be regarded as a monopoly control over the disposal of the wife's sexuality rather than an exclusive right to the use thereof. In discussing adelphic polyandry this distinction is important.

whereas among the matrilineal matrilocal Nayar, as we have seen, right 10 is the only marriage characteristic that is present at all. Or again, in the matrilineal virilocal structure of the Trobriands, right 7 assumes prior, though not altogether unique, importance in the form of *urigubu* (Malinowski, 1932, pp. 69–75).

Although the early writers on polyandry (e.g. McLennan, 1865) supposed that it was an institution closely associated with matriliny, Prince Peter has pointed out that the best-established cases of adelphic polyandry occur in societies which express patrilineal ideals. This was true of the Kandyan Sinhalese (D'Oyly, 1929); it is true of the patrilineal Iravas of Madras (Aiyappan, 1945) and of the Tibetans (Bell, 1928, p. 88). But it is also the case that the patriliny in these societies is of an ambiguous and rather uncertain type. The position in each case is that while the people concerned profess a preference for patrilocal marriage and the inheritance of landed property through males only, matrilocal marriage and inheritance through females is not at all uncommon (Aiyappan, 1945; Li An-Che, 1947; D'Oyly, 1929, p. 110). Moreover although women who marry patrilocally surrender their claims on their own ancestral land, they receive a dowry of movable goods in lieu.

This aspect of adelphic polyandry, namely that it is intimately associated with an institution of dowry, has previously received inadequate attention. In patrilineal systems of the more extreme type *all* significant property rights are vested in males so that, from the inheritance point of view, marriage does no more than establish the rights of a woman's sons in her husband's property (right 1 above). Fission of the patrimonial inheritance group does of course occur, and when it occurs it is very likely that individual marriages will be cited (retrospectively) as a justification for such a split; the model given by Fortes (1945, p. 199) is typical in this respect. Yet, in such cases, marriage, as such, does not create an independent partible estate.

But when property in land and saleable valuables is vested in women as well as in men, a very different state of affairs prevails; for each marriage then establishes a distinct parcel of property rights and the children of any one marriage have, of necessity, a different total inheritance potential from the children of any other marriage.

E. R. Leach 155

Systems of inheritance in which both men and women have property endowment are very general in Southern India, Ceylon and throughout South-East Asia. Such systems are found in association with patrilineal, matrilineal and cognatic descent structures. The general pattern is that the nuclear family, as a unit, possesses three categories of property, namely the entailed inheritance of the father, the entailed inheritance of the mother and the 'acquired property' – that is, the property owned jointly by the parents by virtue of their operations as a business partnership during the period of the marriage. The children of the marriage are heirs to all three categories of property, but the categories are not merged.

Now it is quite obvious that an inheritance principle whereby women as well as men can be endowed with property conflicts with the ideal that landed property should be maintained intact in the hands of the male heirs. Yet it is a fact that there are many societies which manage to maintain both principles simultaneously. There are a variety of customary behaviours which can best be understood if they are regarded as partial solutions to the dilemma that arises from maintaining these contradictory ideals.

Let us be clear what the dilemma is. On the one hand there is the ideal that the patrimonial inheritance ought to be maintained intact. Full brothers and the sons of full brothers *ought* to remain together in the ancestral home and work the ancestral land. On the other hand, since the wives of these men, when they join the household, bring with them property which will be inherited by their own children but not by their husbands' nephews and nieces, each new marriage creates a separate block of property interests which is in conflict with the ideal of maintaining the economic solidarity of male siblings.

One way out of the difficulty was that adopted in the Jaffna Tamil code of Thesawalamai (Tambiah, 1954, p. 36): the sons inherited the hereditary property of their father, and the acquired property of both spouses was inherited by the sons and the undowered daughters. The dowries to the daughters were given out of the mother's dowry. Systems of double unilineal descent such as that described by Forde for the Yakö operate in a somewhat comparable way (Forde, 1950, p. 306), though the distinction here is between property passed to men through men (the patrilineal inheritance of land rights) and property passed to men through women (the matrilineal inheritance of movables).

The Moslem preference for patrilineage endogamy likewise resolves the conflict between female rights of inheritance and a patrilineal principle of descent. A declared preference for reciprocal or patrilateral cross-cousin marriage may sometimes have similar implications. Indeed, marriage preferences of this latter type seem to be more or less confined to societies in which a substantial proportion of the inheritance rights are transmitted through women (cf. Homans and Schneider, 1955).

Adelphic polyandry, I would suggest, is to be understood as yet another variation on the same theme. If two brothers share one wife so that the only heirs of the brothers are the children born of that wife, then, from an economic point of view, the marriage will tend to cement the solidarity of the sibling pair rather than tear it apart, whereas, if the two brothers have separate wives, their children will have separate economic interests, and maintenance of the patrimonial inheritance in one piece is likely to prove impossible. If the ethnographical evidence is to be believed, polyandrous institutions, where they occur, are deemed highly virtuous and tend to eliminate rather than heighten sexual jealousies (Aiyappan, 1937).

In the lecture under discussion, Prince Peter referred repeatedly to contemporary polyandry among the Kandyan Sinhalese. It seems important that we should be clear what the word 'polyandry' means in this case. Sinhalese law does not recognize the existence of polyandrous marriage and it is not possible for any individual to maintain in a law court that he or she is 'the recognized offspring' of two different fathers, nor can a woman bear 'legitimate offspring' to two different husbands, without an intermediate registration of divorce. Thus, strictly speaking, polyandry in Ceylon is not a variety of marriage, if marriage be narrowly defined. On the other hand it is certainly the case that there are parts of Ceylon where two brothers often share a common domestic household with one 'wife', these arrangements being permanent, amicable and socially respectable.[3]

3. It is difficult to accept Prince Peter's claim that in the Ratnapura District of Ceylon polyandry is so common as to be the norm. The *Census* (1946, vol. I, pt 2) includes figures for 'customary marriages' as well as

Polyandrous households of this type contrast rather strikingly with the more normal pattern in which two or more brothers live together in a single compound each with his separate 'wife'. This latter situation is characterized by marked restraint between the brothers and even complete avoidance between a man and his 'sister-in-law'.

The 'wives' in such cases may or may not be married according to Sinhalese law. In a high proportion of cases they are not so married. In law the children of these unions are then illegitimate. The children, however, have birth certificates and these certificates give the name not only of the mother but also of the acknowledged father, a circumstance which provides the child with a potential claim to a share of the heritable property of each of its parents.[4] The child therefore, although not the *legitimate offspring* of both its parents, is nevertheless a *legitimate heir* of both its parents. If then the principle of legitimacy be here defined in terms of property rights rather than descent it seems quite proper that Sinhalese customary unions should be regarded as marriages.

Is it then possible in this case to have a polyandrous *marriage*?

---

registered marriages'. The Census enumerators were required to enter as 'married' anyone who 'claimed to be married according to custom or repute' and there seems no reason why they should have excluded 'polyandrous husbands'. However, in all districts, the overall total of 'married' males is roughly equal to the overall total of 'married' females, which does not suggest that the frequency of polyandry can be numerically significant. For Ceylon as a whole the Census gave 389,846 women as 'married by custom' and 843,493 as 'legally married by registration'. While this is evidence that the strict definition of legitimate marriage is unrealistic, it does not follow that the anthropologist must accept the *Census* enumerators' notions of what constitutes customary marriage.

4. *The Report of the Kandyan Law Commission* (1935, paragraphs 199–210) recommends that all children born of non-registered marriages shall be deemed illegitimate and shall be excluded from any share in the entailed property of the father. The *Report* recognizes that this conflicts with the customary law of the pre-British period which did not restrict entailed (*paraveni*) property to the offspring of formal marriages. Ranasinha (1950, vol. I, pt 1, p. 192) ignores this *Report* and asserts that the highest authorities have held that 'registration was not essential to the validity of a marriage in Ceylon, and the marriage relation could be presumed on adequate evidence of cohabitation and repute'. Certainly in many parts of Ceylon today the children of non-registered 'marriages' are treated as having full inheritance rights in their father's property, but whether this right could now be sustained in a Court of Law I am uncertain.

Legally, no. Since a birth certificate certainly cannot show more than one father, no child possesses the basis for establishing a legal claim to the property of a polyandrous corporation. All the same, it seems probable that in polyandrous households the children do ordinarily inherit jointly the undivided property of the two fathers and that Sinhalese custom recognizes their right to do so. Provided that we are not too pedantic about what we mean by 'legitimate' it does appear that we are dealing here with something that an anthropologist can properly call polyandrous marriage. Even so the issue is by no means clear-cut.

Aiyappan (1945, p. 103), in commenting on the refusal of an English judge to admit the possibility of a woman being simultaneously married to two brothers at the same time, treats the issue as being simply one of a conflict between English law and customary Irava law. But so far as the Sinhalese are concerned the issue is not so simple.

The classical formulation of the former Sinhalese law regarding polyandry appears in Sawers's *Digest* (see D'Oyly, 1929, p. 129):

Polygamy as well as polyandry is allowed without limitation as to the number of wives or husbands – but the wife cannot take a second associated husband without the consent of the first – though the husband can take a second wife into the same house as his first wife without her consent. The wife, however, has the power of refusing to admit a second associated husband at the request of her first husband, even should he be the brother of the first. And should the proposed second associated husband not be a brother of the first, the consent of the wife's family to the double connection is required.

It is clear that two separate rights are here distinguished. First, there is the right in the wife's sexuality which marriage serves to vest partly, but not completely, in the person of the first husband. The sexual rights of the other husbands are exercised, not by virtue of the marriage, but through the individual consent of the first husband and the joint wife. On the other hand, the ritual of patrilocal marriage – the essence of which is that a man conducts his bride from her father's house to his own (*Report*, 1935, paragraph 168) – serves to establish a relation of affinity between the wife's family as a whole and the husband's family as a whole. The wife's family have no interest in what sexual arrangements pertain unless it is proposed to extend the rights of sexual access beyond the limits of the husband's sibling group.

It is notable that, in this formulation of Sawers, the rights of the children are not mentioned; the ritual procedures of Sinhalese marriage are not concerned with the rights of the potential children. The marriage rite disposes of the woman's sexuality to her first husband; it also has the effect of making a public pronouncement that the woman has been properly endowered so that she has no further claims on her parental property. The status of children arises from quite a different source.

In Sinhalese customary law it was (and is) the rule that if a man and a woman are publicly known to have cohabited together and the woman bears a child, then the woman has a claim on the man for the support of the child (D'Oyly, 1929, p. 84). In ordinary rural practice, all of a man's acknowledged children are equally his heirs whether or not he has at any time gone through a ritual of marriage with the children's mother. Likewise all of a woman's children have equal claims on her inheritance.

My conclusion is that in the Sinhalese case, and very probably in other analogous cases, we are dealing with two different institutions both of which resemble marriage as ordinarily understood, but which need to be carefully distinguished. Neither institution corresponds precisely to the ideal type of marriage as defined in *Notes and Queries*.

On the one hand we have a formal and legal arrangement, by which, so far as Ceylon is concerned, a woman can only be married to one man at a time. 'Marriage' in this sense establishes a relationship of affinity between the family of the bride and the family of the first husband, and it gives the disposal of the bride's sexuality to the first husband, subject to the bride's personal consent. On the other hand we have another institution of 'marriage', which is entered into quite informally but which nevertheless, by virtue of its public recognition, serves to provide the children with claims upon the patrimonial property of the men with whom the woman cohabits and publicly resides. This second form of 'marriage', although it establishes the inheritance rights of the children, does not establish their permanent status as member of a corporate descent group, and Sinhalese children, as they grow up, have wide choice as to where they finally align themselves for the purposes of affiliation.

If we accept this second institution as a form of 'marriage', then polyandry in Ceylon is a form of polygamy. If we confine the term 'marriage' to the first institution, polyandry in Ceylon is a form of polykoity. These niceties of definition are worth making because it is important that anthropologists should distinguish the various classes of right that are involved in marriage institutions.

Of greater importance is my hypothesis that adelphic polyandry is consistently associated with systems in which women as well as men are the bearers of property rights. Polyandry exists in Ceylon because, in a society where both men and women inherit property, polyandrous arrangements serve, both in theory and practice, to reduce the potential hostility between sibling brothers.

References

AIYAPPAN, A. (1937), 'Polyandry and sexual jealousy', *Man*, art. no. 130.
AIYAPPAN, A. (1945), 'Iravas and Culture Change', *Bull. Madras Govt. Mus.*, General Section, vol. 5, no. 1.
BELL, Sir C. (1928), *The People of Tibet*, Oxford University Press.
D'OYLY, J. (1929), *A Sketch of the Constitution of the Kandyan Kingdom (Ceylon)*, Colombo.
FISCHER, H. (1952), 'Polyandry', *Int. Arch. Ethnog.*, vol. 46, pp. 106–15.
FORDE, D. (1950), 'Double descent among the Yakö', in A. R. Radcliffe, Brown and D. Forde (eds), *African Systems of Kinship and Marriage*, Oxford University Press.
FORTES, M. (1945), *The Dynamics of Clanship among the Tallensi*, Oxford University Press.
GOUGH, K. (1952), 'Changing kinship usages in the setting of political and economic change among the Nayars of Malabar', *J. roy. anthropol. Inst.*, vol. 82, pp. 71–88.
GOUGH, K. (1955), 'The traditional lineage and kinship systems of the Nayar', unpublished manuscript in the Haddon Library, Cambridge.
LI AN-CHE (1947), 'Dege: A study of Tibetan population', *Southwestern J. Anthropol.*, vol. 3, pp. 279–93.
MALINOWSKI, B. (1932), *The Sexual Life of Savages*, Routledge & Kegan Paul.
MCLENNAN, J. F. (1865), *Primitive Marriage*, Black.
Notes and Queries in Anthropology, 1951, Royal Anthropological Institute, 6th edn.
PETER, H. R. H. Prince of Greece and Denmark (1955), 'Polyandry and the kinship group', lecture delivered to the Royal Anthropological Institute, 8 December. Summarized in *Man*, 1955, no. 198.
RADCLIFFE-BROWN, A. R. (1941), 'The study of kinship systems', *J. roy. anthropol. Inst.*, vol. 71, pp. 1–18.

Ranasinha, A. G. (1946), *Census of Ceylon*, vol. 1, pt 1, Colombo.
Report of the Kandyan Law Commission (1935), Sessional Paper 24, Colombo (Govt. Press).
Smith, M. G. (1953), 'Secondary marriage in northern Nigeria', *Africa*, vol. 23, pp. 298–333.
Tambiah, H. W. (1954), *The Laws and Customs of the Tamils of Ceylon*, Colombo.

12 R. Clignet

Determinants of African Polygyny

Excerpt from R. Clignet, *Many Wives, Many Powers*, Northwestern University Press, 1970, pp. 16–34.

Our purpose here is to demonstrate that there are variations in (1) the distribution of plural marriage among African cultures, (2) the principles underlying the recruitment of additional co-wives, (3) the social, economic and political characteristics of African societies which practise plural marriage, and (4) the individual motivations which underlie this particular form of familial arrangement. In a last section, we will show how social change affects these various dimensions.

The distribution of polygyny in Africa

The distribution of polygyny in a given population presents two characteristics relevant to our analysis: its incidence and its intensity (Dorjahn, 1959). *Incidence* is measured by the number of married women per hundred married males or, alternatively, by the number of males married to more than one wife. For the first measure to be useful, however, the communities investigated should be demographically stable. The first indicator of incidence is misleading in urban centers, where the relative excess of men over women and the uneven incidence of singles among the male and female segments of the population prevents distributions of married men and women from being really matched. *Intensity*, on the other hand, refers to the number of married women per hundred polygynous men or, alternatively, to the number of polygynous males with more than two wives.

An examination of the Human Relations Area Files gives us a first approximation of the significance of plural marriage in Africa.[1] Approximately three-fourths of the 136 peoples included

1. For all criteria used in the first section of this Reading, see Murdock (1957), quoted in Moore (1961).

in these files are characterized by general polygyny – that is, by both an incidence of polygynous families in excess of 20 per cent, and an absence of special restrictions on the recruitment of additional co-wives. Of the entire world sample, Africa has the lowest percentage of monogamous cultures; hence, we can see the importance of an analysis of the dominant behavior patterns in African polygynous institutions.

For all sub-Saharan countries, the mean number of wives per hundred married males is 150, but the variance is extremely large (Moore, 1961). Maximal ratios are found in Ghana and Sierra Leone, and the lowest percentages in the southeastern parts of

Table 1 Incidence and Intensity of Polygyny in selected African Countries

Countries	Date	Married women per 100 married men	Married women per 100 polygynous men
Basutoland	1936	114	218
Bechuanaland	1946	112	201
Swasiland	1936	168	307
South Africa	1921	112	216
Northern Rhodesia	1947	122	211
Tanganyika	1934	117	219
Kenya	1951	236	283
Sudan	1945	199	253
Congo	1947–48	131–44	224–73
Portuguese Guinea	1950	159	245
French Equatorial Africa	1952	145	?
French Cameroon	1942	152	?
Togo	1931	131–57	?
Upper Volta	1951	190	233
Nigeria	1950	155	237
Gold Coast	1909–39	190–218	?
	1945	160	252
Sierra Leone	1945	304	325
Gambia	1951	184	276

Derived from Dorjahn (1954, pp. 134–6)

the continent. Intensity has an equally large variance and ranges from a minimal level of 201 for Bechuanaland to a maximal value of 325 for Sierra Leone, as shown in Table 1.

More important, these two dimensions have remained stable throughout time. The figures obtained from adjacent territories at different points in time are comparable. In the specific case of the former Gold Coast, the incidence of polygyny has apparently increased throughout time.

Finally, Table 1 indicates that there is no clear-cut relationship between incidence and intensity of polygyny. It would be tempting to assume *a priori* that the number of women per polygynous family declines as the institution spreads among a greater variety of social levels (Dorjahn, 1954, ch. 1).[2] This is obviously not the case.

Principles of recruitment of co-wives

Both the incidence and the intensity of plural marriage should reflect the principles underlying the recruitment of additional co-wives. Polygyny should be more frequent wherever there are few boundaries in the definition of the field of eligible additional spouses. Thus, in some societies, polygyny is at least partially due to *levirate*, or 'inheritance of widows' – that is, the transmission to the inheritor of all the rights that the deceased testator had in his wife or wives. In contrast, the field of eligible co-wives may be narrowly defined; in some societies, for example, *sororal polygyny*, in which a man marries two or more sisters, is the only form of plural marriage socially allowed. This type of plural marriage tends to prevent the multiplication of polygynous arrangements. It also tends to erase the incompatibilities between the functions of polygyny, more specifically, the division of the loyalties of each co-wife between her affinal group and her family of origin. The common background of co-wives, as it exists in this case, should help to lower potential tensions between familial actors. This leads us to predict that variations in the number and the form of restrictions imposed on plural marriage will be accompanied by

2. In fact, it has been demonstrated that there was a positive relationship ($r = 0.85$) between incidence and intensity of plural marriage among the twenty-six districts of the Congo. See Brass *et al.* (1968, p. 215).

similar variations in the types of relationships prevailing both within and between polygynous families.

Only 8 per cent of the African societies included in the Human Relations Area Files practice sororal polygyny exclusively and they are concentrated in the cluster of Bantu subcultures.[3]

Characteristics of polygynous societies

Since the incidence and intensity of polygyny are higher in some parts of Africa than in others, it is necessary to determine whether African cultures that are characterized by similar distributions of plural marriage also present certain common traits in their economic, political and social organizations. The absence of such regularities should lead us to suspect that variations in type of marriage reflect a number of factors, and that, accordingly, the organization of polygynous families is not stable throughout time or space. Conversely, the identification of certain recurrent patterns in the distributions of plural marriage across African cultures would not necessarily exclude the possibility of observing marked disparities in the functioning of these families.

Interestingly enough, although monogamous familes are characteristic of modern, highly industrialized nations, they also tend to be frequently found in African social systems whose subsistence patterns are predominantly gathering and hunting. In these societies, the proportion of resources available to an individual declines as the population density increases.[4] Associated with a high density, polygyny would lead to starvation. On the other hand, general polygyny tends to prevail in societies where subsistence is based upon the cultivation of roots and tubers and upon arboriculture. This type of economic organization encourages the maintenance of large-sized households and also

3. Twenty-two out of forty Bantu cultures are characterized by general polygyny; in the southern cluster of these people, five out of ten cultures indulge in sororal polygyny.

4. See Zelditch, Jr. (1964). For a more exhaustive discussion of the correlates of marriage type, see Osmond (1965), who demonstrates on a world-wide basis that the relationship between monogamy and societal complexity is curvilinear in nature; see also Sawyer and LeVine (1966). It is quite clear that the correlations between polygyny and other variables remain quite low when the investigation deals with a world-wide sample.

constitutes a necessary condition to the emergence of any form of social differentiation. It is to this point that we will turn our attention first.

The existence of politically or socially stratified divisions in the population, associated with the transmission of land or other resources, which ensures that a man's children will remain grouped around his own place of residence, favors the emergence of polygynous households. In fact, the relationship between the incidence of polygyny and social stratification is curvilinear in nature. Rare among societies characterized by a lack of social stratification or, alternatively, by a large number of social levels, plural marriage is most frequent among societies divided into age grades or in which a hereditary aristocracy is separated from the bulk of the population (Table 2).

A stabilized mode of agricultural production, however, is not only conducive to the emergence of certain forms of social

Table 2 Relationship between Social Stratification and Marriage Practices among selected African Cultures (percentages)

Type of stratification	Monogamy	Limited polygyny[a]	General polygyny[a]
Complex stratification	22	8	17
Hereditary aristocracy	0	25	27
Wealth distinction	11	8	10
Age grades	11	13	14
No social stratification	56	42	28
Unascertained	0	4	4
Total	100	100	100
N	9	24	103

[a] Limited polygyny means that the incidence is below 20 per cent, whereas general polygyny refers to all societies where this threshold is exceeded. Variations in the form of polygyny have been disregarded.

Computed from Murdock (1957). The Horn, Ethiopia and Moslem Sudan have been added to African samples.

stratification, but it also tends to encourage the maintenance of large households and to accentuate the division of labor among individual actors of the family group. In contrast to monogamous cultures, polygynous social systems are characterized by principles of division of labor leading women to carry out a substantial part of the agricultural activities of the household (Table 3). In effect, the incidence of polygyny is positively related to the productive value of the female members of a group. It might have been assumed

Table 3 Relationship between Division of Agricultural Labor and Plural Marriage (percentages)

Division of labor in agricultural work	Monogamy	Limited polygyny	General polygyny
Division of labor equal along sex lines	11	50	49
Female share of the work greater	0	12	21
Male share of the work greater	56	4	20
No agricultural activity	33	17	8
Work performed by slaves	0	0	1
Not ascertained	0	17	1
Total	100	100	100
N	9	24	103

that plural marriage would decline with the development of cash economies and that successful individuals would be anxious to invest their surpluses of cash income in assets more readily negotiable than women, but this does not appear to have happened. In societies where subsistence depends upon agricultural production and where such production depends heavily on the manpower available, particularly so on the productive value of women, each family group tends to use its surplus income to increase its labor force – and, more specifically, the number of its polygynous units as well as the number of its co-wives. In short, polygyny is most tenacious in cultures where economic rights to women can be acquired and have a high significance (Bohannan 1963, p. 109).

The productive value of a woman in turn influences the brideprice, that is, the goods and services which either the bridegroom or his family must pay to the bride's family as a compensation for the emotional, social and economic loss resulting from her marriage. Since polygyny is most frequent among cultures which invest high values in their female members, it is not surprising that the institution of brideprice is more often found in polygynous than in monogamous African societies.[5]

Finally, the incidence of plural marriage depends on the rules of residence followed by each culture. Where 84 per cent of African peoples with widespread polygyny are patrilocal, this is true of only two-thirds of the societies with a limited rate of polygyny, and of 54 per cent of the cultures which practise monogamy. Influenced by the productive value of women, polygyny is also associated with a predominance of male orientations because patrilocal rules of residence tend to reinforce the loyalties and obligations of a husband toward his own family.

Having determined some relationships between the incidence of polygyny and some features most typical of the African cultures under study, it would be useful to examine the extent to which these features are associated with one or another form of polygyny. Unfortunately, the number of African cultures practising sororal polygyny is too small to enable us to do so. Analysis of a world-wide sample of matrilineal descent groups, however, has led to the assumption that sororal polygyny is most likely to be found in societies with matrilocal residence combined with a weak descent group that is not permanently attached to stable, scarce cultivation sites. Under these circumstances, ties between sisters and their offspring are easily maintained, the interests of co-resident husbands are more easily harmonized, and the com-

5. Of African monogamous societies, 22 per cent are characterized by an absence of any significant matrimonial compensation in marriage. This percentage drops to 16·6 among cultures with a limited incidence of polygyny. Regardless of the form of polygyny that they practise, none of the remaining societies presents this feature.

mitment of these husbands to their respective conjugal groups is increased (see Gough, 1961, pp. 623–4).

Thus far, we have determined the limits within which the incidence and the intensity of plural marriage vary. We have also examined those traits in the economic and social organization of a given culture which tend to facilitate or impede plural marriage. More specifically, we have isolated two functions of polygyny. On the one hand, plural marriage is associated with social differentiation and makes significant distinctions between certain categories of 'have' and 'have not' of the particular ethnic groups investigated. On the other hand, this institution may also constitute a basic mechanism indispensable for economic survival. In the first context, additional co-wives are mainly liabilities, but in the second they are additional assets. It remains of course to determine the extent to which these two types are mutually exclusive.

However, the most necessary condition to the emergence of polygynous families in a given society is, of course, an imbalance in its sex ratio; it may be said that polygyny constitutes a most rational solution to the problem of absorbing an actual surplus of females. Our initial task, therefore, is to assess the sex ratio of the populations of African countries.

A high sex ratio may result from an insufficient gross or net reproduction rate;[6] it may reflect discrepancies in the distribution of mortality rates by sex at various points in the age pyramid. For example, male fetuses may be more vulnerable to miscarriage than female; or males may be more susceptible to death in childhood or in early or late adulthood. As a matter of fact, the sparse information available on these points in various parts of the world leads us to believe that miscarriage occurs less frequently to male than to female fetuses. While it is a fact that the number of male children born is consistently greater than the number of female births, this unbalanced character of the sex ratio tends to disappear later on since male children are inclined to be more vulnerable to fatal diseases than females (Dorjahn, 1954, pp. 310–70). In addition, the hunting, military and commercial enterprises of males also

6. For definitions of these terms, see Winch (1964), pp. 186–7. These rates answer the question of how many female children the average woman in a hypothetical cohort of females will bear.

increase their exposure to death. To rebut this, many scientists argue that only women are involved in the most hazardous of all activities – childbearing – and that this offsets any increased male exposure to death (Bohannan, 1963, p. 109).

Data available on the overall population of African countries indicate that the sex ratio tends to be roughly equal (Table 4). For the Gold Coast, Table 4 establishes that, between the turn of the century and 1948, while polygyny increased slightly, the rate of female births declined. In short, plural marriage cannot be explained by disparities in the natural distribution of male and female populations. Such disparities, however, might still be the product of cultural or social factors. For example, massive urbanization of males of a given rural society will skew the distribution of that segment of the population which remains at home. Migrations facilitate polygyny, not only for the stable male elements of the rural society but also for the mobile members of the populations who, with an increased cash income, are able to

Table 4 Sex Ratio in selected African Countries

Country	Date	Number of females per 100 males
Southern Rhodesia	1948	101·0
Tanganyika	1948	108·4
Kenya	1948	102·6
Uganda	1948	100·0
Portuguese Guinea	1950	103·0
French Equatorial Africa	1948	104·0
Ruanda Urundi	1951	114·4
Gold Coast	1891	118·0
Gold Coast	1948	98·0

Derived from Dorjahn (1954, p. 267).

support two households and two wives – one in the city and one in the village of origin.[7]

If male migrations can facilitate polygyny, so also can female migration, most especially the importing of marriageable women.

7. Africans are not the only ones to follow this practice. The film *The Captain's Paradise* explains the *de facto* polygyny of some sailors and the difficulties which result from this state of affairs.

For example, in a tribal or inter-village war, the women of a weaker society may be captured and taken home by victorious males, who thus artificially augment the female population of their own village. On the other hand, marked inequalities in the amount of brideprice required by neighboring societies may foster variations in the number of eligible women available to men in both groups. The males of the wealthier society will be able to invade the field of potential brides of the poorer society. Similarly, the differential rates of mobility of African males and females are also likely to affect the sex ratio of the marriageable populations derived from distinctive subparts of a given territory or region. For example, the adult population of Upper Volta probably comprises a larger proportion of women than the eastern zones of the Ivory Coast, which attract a considerable number of male migrants. The influence of such factors on polygyny depends, however, on the degree of ethnocentrism prevalent in the societies in question. The extent of this ethnocentrism varies naturally with the various patterns of interaction investigated. Evidence concerning patterns of interethnic marriage and the distribution of the relevant motivations remains unfortunately scarce. In Dakar, it has been established that in 1954 the incidence of interethnic marriages increased with socioeconomic status and, more important, was higher among polygynous than monogamous families (Mercier, 1955, p. 553). It is difficult, however, to derive long-term generalizations from this evidence, which is limited both in time and space.

It might be interesting to speculate that polygyny reflects a difference in the incidence of marriage for each sex. A large percentage of celibate males certainly increases the number of available marriageable women and thus increases polygyny. But it has been authoritatively estimated that the proportion of adult single males in African populations does not exceed 28 per cent, while that of unmarried adult females is still lower (22 per cent) (Dorjahn, 1954, pp. 269–309). Neither the low percentage among males nor the limited difference in the occurrence of male and female celibacy can account for polygynous marriages.

A more satisfactory explanation lies in the age characteristics of conjugal partners. An excess of marriageable women can be the result of the difference in mean age at first marriage in both sexes, as well as of the specific mean ages of the people who marry. Assuming that (1) the incidence of singles is equally low among both sexes, (2) there is little variation in the average age at marriage of male and female populations, and (3) the size of various age groups is equally uneven for the two sexes, it is possible to evaluate the surplus of marriageable women. Thus, Dorjahn has established that if, for example, the first-marriage age of women is sixteen and that of men twenty-five, there will be a surplus of 26 per cent of marriageable women. If the first-marriage age of women is twenty-four and that of men thirty-three, there will be a 33 per cent surplus of marriageable females. Yet inequalities in the number of marriageable men and women may also result from differences in the relative number and duration of their respective matrimonial experiences. The imposition of differing limitations upon male and female divorcees or widows concerning their remarriage is likely to affect the overall number of potential partners.[8]

In summary, inequalities in the distribution of polygyny throughout Africa mainly reflect the variety of cultural norms pertaining to age at marriage and to the respective matrimonial experiences of male and female actors.

Polygyny and individual motivations

African informants frequently indicate that polygyny constitutes the most efficacious way of maintaining a high birth rate in their societies. This proposition has been critically examined by various observers and social scientists; but the discussion has sometimes been obscured by religious and political considerations which generally lead to a formal condemnation of plural marriage. Thus the belief that modernization of a country necessitates a constant increase of population is often accompanied by the opinion that modernization is incompatible with the maintenance of poly-

8. (Dorjahn, 1954, p. 299). The additional comments presented here result from private communications with R. Cohen. In this context, we must note a highly significant correlation ($r = 0.80$) among Congo districts between number of married women per 100 married men and difference in mean age at marriage between the sexes. There is, alternatively, a negative correlation ($r = -0.45$) between this indicator of polygyny and the proportion of widowed and divorced among women fifteen to forty-five years old. See Brass *et al.* (1968, pp. 220–21).

gynous families. The organization of such families, it is deemed, does not meet the requirements of an industrial system and also has negative effects on the desired growth of the population. It is possible to demonstrate, for example, that fertility of monogamously married women is one-third higher than that of women in polygynous families.[9]

Sterility of his senior co-wife often leads a man to acquire an additional wife. This necessarily affects the distribution of children born in polygynous households. Further, since polygyny presupposes a certain order in sexual relationships between a man and his spouses, it can be argued that the frequency of sexual intercourse per woman decreases, leading to a corresponding decline of fertility.[10] In addition, all African societies are subject to various sexual taboos; and it is obvious that such taboos are more likely to be enforced with greater frequency and for longer periods of time by women who are polygynously married. Given the fact that there is a significant relationship between polygyny and the severity of post-partum taboos, the nature of this relationship remains to be explored. It might be argued that the severity of this taboo leads married males to contract plural marriage. Alternatively, however, plural marriage may lead to the formulation of universal prescriptions regarding the appropriate behavior of new mothers.

The effects of all these factors are convergent and account for the lower number of children born to polygynous wives. Perceived by all Africans as the most effective way to insure a numerous posterity, is polygyny nevertheless destined to maintain fertility below a certain threshold? A proper answer to this question depends on the level of analysis selected. A decline in the number of children born of a given category of women does not necessarily imply a corresponding decline in the number of children of a male individual. In fact, a decline in fertility may be compensated for by an increase in the number of potentially child-bearing women.

9. For a general discussion of the factors affecting fertility, see Blake and Davis (1956, p. 211–14). More specifically on the problem of fertility and plural marriage, see Whiting (1964, pp. 511 ff.).

10. See Muhsam (1956). Yet distinctions should be made between senior and junior co-wives in this respect, and it is, for example, necessary to control the ages of the women analysed.

A second justification of polygyny offered by Africans concerns the complexity of female roles in the society. The obligations of a woman to her husband and his family do not cancel her duties to the members of her own family. For example, in many African cultures a married woman is required to visit her kin group at regular intervals and on special occasions, such as funerals. These prescribed absences lead to the often-voiced complaint of African husbands that to have one wife is to have none, intimating that wives spend more time in their households of origin than in their own.[11] Furthermore, this situation might impose on husbands the performance of domestic chores, such as cooking and fetching water and wood, which are considered female tasks and therefore incompatible with male dignity. Regardless of these strains, females are expected to fill plural roles and, as in many societies, the significance of a wife for the hearth can be contrasted with the importance of a wife for the heart.

Besides economic and symbolic properties attached to female roles, Africans cite other social and psychological factors which influence the size of a family group. If there is no difference between having only one wife and having none, as African husbands say, then males with two wives only are not much better off. The positive effects of an additional wife are too often mitigated by the husband's obligation to mediate in the conflicts and jealousies which arise between the women. Since three is conducive to the formation of coalitions, four is generally considered the optimal number of co-wives for a man to have (Joseph, 1913, p. 595).

Social change and polygyny

Having established that, on the whole, both the incidence and intensity of polygyny have not varied throughout time, can we then infer that there has been no alteration in the motivations which support it? Let us examine the effects of social change.

Social change implies differential access of the male population to modern residential, educational and occupational structures and is accompanied by a modification of the criteria on which the social hierarchy is based. Education, occupation and experience

11. See also Serere proverb, quoted by Monteil (1964): 'With one wife, a man has only one eye.'

in urban centers increasingly differentiate the positions occupied by males within the social structure. Yet changes in the degree of social stratification and in the routes leading to higher status do not necessarily imply corresponding shifts in the symbolic qualities attached to the various positions in the status system. Indeed, with one notable exception, many observers of the contemporary African scene agree that the incidence of polygyny in cities tends to increase with the length of time spent there and with the higher levels of occupation achieved.[12]

Social change implies a restructuring of ideology. The persistence of polygyny has been reinforced by the diffusion of Islam, which on this very point converged with the principles of social organization prevalent in traditional African cultures. It should be pointed out, however, that Islamic teaching is not always equated with male domination over women. Koranic laws provide a legal status for women which is often refused them by traditional African customs (Monteil, 1964). Likewise, in spite of its missionary success, Catholicism has failed to eliminate this type of family deemed incompatible with Christian principles.

Even though, during most of the colonial period, efforts of the Christian missionaries to end polygyny have been supported by administrative authority, the institution has survived. In French territories few women have taken advantage of the right to protest their traditional matrimonial status. Theoretically, French citizenship was reserved to African individuals who were monogamously married. Yet this provision has too often conflicted with other sections of the law which accorded citizenship to the most educated and most economically successfully segments of the population, within which many polygynists were to be found. In addition, in the early 1950s the French government decided to extend to African workers in both public and private sectors certain fringe benefits already existing in metropolitan France, among which was an allotment of money to individuals with many

12. For a discussion of the diffusion of polygyny in Senegalese urban areas, see, for instance, Masse (1955). See also Mercier (1960) and Thore (1964). For the diffusion of polygyny in the Belgian Congo, see Clement (1955). For Dahomey, see Tardits (1958), pp. 47–9 and 63–5). For English-speaking Africa, see Little (1959, pp. 72–3). For Sierra Leone, see Gamble (1963, pp. 75–84). Against these views, see Banton (1957, pp. 207ff.). See also Bird (1963, pp. 59–74).

children. The purpose of the decision was both to stimulate a natural increase in the population and to satisfy the demands of local politicians and union leaders to be treated as 'Black Frenchmen'. This lagniappe had the unexpected effect of reinforcing polygyny among the already privileged wage-earners in urban areas. Introduction of this legislation in Africa is an illustration of the inconsistencies which characterize a colonial policy based on 'assimilationist' principles that appear to favor at the same time both the emergence of new patterns of action and the persistence of traditional ways of life.[13]

Of all manifestations of social change, schooling of the female population is the only one which has had a negative effect on polygyny and has, thus, tended to contribute to the disruption of the overall functioning of traditional family structures. Not only have educated women refused to belong to polygynous families, even as senior co-wives, but they have frequently been in a position to force males to change their domestic attitudes and behavior. For example, educated women have repudiated mealtime etiquette which obliges them to eat, in another room, leftovers from meals taken by men. They have challenged the principle on which the payment of a brideprice is based, and they have become increasingly eager to marry mates of their own choosing.[14] Hence, there is a certain amount of ambivalence on the part of both males and older females toward educated women. Male domination is too ancient a phenomenon to be easily eroded, and elder women tend to perceive formal education as a devious way of dissociating oneself from traditional duties. The first generation of educated women is therefore necessarily marginal, and many of them seem doomed to remain single or to marry at a late age.

Summary and conclusions

In a polygynous culture, co-wives may be perceived as direct (through their work) and indirect (through their offspring) sources of increased income and prestige. In other words, the functions ascribed to polygyny may be instrumental in character.

13. On the general effects of laws on changes in familial organization, see Baker and Bird (1959).
14. For a description of the African educated woman, see Desanti, (1962).

Yet, although they augment the family's social and economic resources, additional co-wives are also a privilege reserved to individuals who initially hold higher than average positions. In other words, the functions ascribed to plural marriage may also be symbolic and closely related to social differentiation.

The recruitment of co-wives, the size of the surplus of marriageable women, the instrumental or symbolic nature of polygyny and the variety of motivations experienced by individual actors – all these factors should affect the functioning of polygynous families and introduce variations both within and among distinctive cultures in the style of interaction of a senior co-wife with her husband, her family of origin, the other spouses of her husband and her own children.

References

BAKER, T., and BIRD, M. (1959), 'Urbanization and the position of women', *Sociol. Rev.*, vol. 7, pp. 110 ff.

BANTON M. (1957), *A Study of Tribal Life in Freetown*, Oxford University Press.

BIRD, M. (1963), 'Urbanization, family, and marriage in Western Nigeria', in *Urbanization in African Social Change*, Proc. Inaugural Seminar in Centre of African Studies, University of Edinburgh, pp. 59–74.

BLAKE, J., and DAVIS, K. (1956), 'Social structure and fertility: an analytic framework', *Econ. Devel. Cultural Change*, vol. 4, pp 211–35.

BOHANNAN, D. (1963), *Social Anthropology*, Holt, Rinehart & Winston.

BRASS, W. et al. (eds.) (1968), *The Demography of Tropical Africa*, Princeton University Press.

CLEMENT, P. (1955), 'Social patterns of urban life' in D. Forde (ed.), *Social Implications of Industrialization and Urbanization in Africa South of the Sahara*, UNESCO, pp. 393–469.

DESANTI, D. (1962), 'Quand l'Africain revient d'Europe', in *Le Dossier Afrique*, Marabout Université, pp. 156–63.

DORJAHN, V. (1954) *The Demographic Aspects of African Polygymy*, doctoral thesis, Northwestern University.

DORJAHN, V. (1959), 'The factor of polygamy in African demography', in M. Herskovits and W. Bascom (eds.), *Continuity and Change in African Cultures*, University of Chicago Press, pp. 87–112.

GAMBLE, D. (1963), 'Family organization in new towns in Sierra Leone', in *Urbanization inAfrican Social Change*, Proc. Inaugural Seminar in Centre of African Studies, University of Edinburgh, pp. 75–84.

GOUGH, K. (1961), 'Preferential marriage forms', in D. Schneider and K. Gough (eds.), *Matrilineal Kinship*, University of California Press.

Joseph, G. (1913), 'La condition de la femme en Côté d'Ivoire', *Bull. soc. Anthropol. de Paris*, vol. 4 pp. 585–9.

Kobben, A. (1956), 'Le planteur noir', *Études éburnéennes*, vol. 5, Centre IFAN.

Little, K. (1959), 'Some patterns of marriage and domesticity in West Africa', *Sociol. Rev.*, vol. 7, pp. 65–81.

Masse, L. (1955), 'Preliminary results of demographic surveys in the urban centres of Senegal', in D. Forde (ed.), *Social Implications of Industrialization and Urbanization in Africa South of the Sahara*, UNESCO, pp. 523–35.

Mercier, P. (1955), 'An experiment investigation into occupational and social categories in Dakar', in D. Forde (ed.), *Social Implications of Industrialization and Urbanization in Africa South of the Sahara*, UNESCO, pp. 510–23.

Mercier, P. (1960), 'Étude du mariage et enquête urbaine', *Cahiers d'études africaines*, vol. 1, pp. 28–43.

Moore, F. (ed.) (1961), *Readings in Cross-Cultural Methodology*, Human Relations Area Files Press, pp. 193–216.

Monteil, V. (1964), *L'Islam Noir*, Le Seuil.

Muhsam, H. V. (1956), 'Fertility of polygynous marriages', *Pop. Stud.*, vol. 10, pp. 3–16.

Murdock, G. P. (1957), 'World ethnographic sample', *Amer. Anthropol.*, vol. 69, pp. 664–87.

Osmond, M. (1965), 'Correlates of types of marriage', *Soc. Forces*, vol. 44, pp. 8–16.

Sawyer, J., and LeVine, R. (1966), 'Cultural dimensions: factor analysis of the *World Ethnographic Sample*', *Amer. Anthropol.*, vol. 68, pp. 708–31.

Tardits, C. (1958), *Les Nouvelles Générations Africaines entre leurs Traditions et l'Occident*, Mouton.

Thore, L. (1964), 'Monogamie et polygamie en Afrique noire', *Rev. action pop.*, pp. 807–21.

Whiting, J. (1964), 'Effects of climate on certain cultural practices', in W. Goodenough (ed.), *Explorations in Cultural Anthropology*, McGraw-Hill.

Winch, R. (1964), *The Modern Family*, Holt, Rinehart & Winston.

Zelditch, M. Jr (1964), 'Cross-cultural analysis of family structures', in H. Christensen (ed.), *Handbook of Marriage and the Family*, Rand McNally.

Part Seven Marriage and Alliance

The marriage of cross-cousins (that is, children of parents' siblings of opposite sex) has been a major focus of inquiry since the topic was studied by J. G. Frazer and E. B. Tylor. It was the subject of Lévi-Strauss's work, *The Elementary Structures of Kinship* (1969), a study much influenced in its general orientation by Durkheim and Mauss. In it he examined the various types of marriage exchange found in Western Asia and in Australia. The approach behind this study, with its emphasis upon the distinction between the ties created by marriage (alliance, affinity) and those created by birth (descent, filiation), was applied to South Indian societies by Louis Dumont in his monograph, *Une Sous-caste de l'Inde du Sud* (1957), and in a general paper, 'Hierarchy and marriage alliance in South Indian kinship', from which Reading 11 is taken. The discussion of cross-cousin marriage has been mainly concerned with those systems that can be described as 'prescriptive', where the category of spouse (e.g. mother's brother's daughter) is unambiguously laid down. In his paper on 'Prescriptive Marriage Systems', Maybury-Lewis summarizes the recent discussions on this subject, pointing out that we must see cross-cousin marriage as one type of a more general category of systems of prescriptive marriage, which are characterized by the marriage alliance.

References

DUMONT, L. (1957), *Une Sous-Caste de l'Inde du Sud: Organisation Sociale et Religion des Pramalai Kallar*, Mouton.

LÉVI-STRAUSS, C. (1969), *The Elementary Structures of Kinship*, Eyre & Spottiswoode. First published 1949.

13 L. Dumont

The Marriage Alliance

Excerpt from L. Dumont, 'Hierarchy and marriage alliance in South Indian kinship', Occasional Paper no. 12, 1957, Royal Anthropological Institute.

To introduce an institution which is shared by all groups referred to here and, I believe, by many others, some criticism of current anthropological categories is first necessary.

Marriage regulations and affinity

A (positive) marriage regulation like 'a man should marry his mother's brother's daughter' might be a native statement indicating whom a given individual should marry. But, in anthropological thought, it takes on a slightly different meaning. There it appears as a rule for deriving a man's marriage from a relationship excluding any idea of marriage or affinity, i.e. from a relationship of consanguinity. It is implied that consanguinity is pre-existent to the marriage, since I must be born before I marry. The marriage regulation is in fact used as a tool for deducing a secondary category (a certain marriage) from a primary category (a certain relationship of consanguinity). After marriage is so introduced, it brings with it relationships of a secondary kind (affinal relationships) which are never considered as full kinship relationships, because they are individual and above all temporary – they disappear with the married person and are not transmitted to his or her descendants but under the form of a consanguinity relationship.

I submit that all this is wrong and needs revision for the following reasons: (1) it rests only on undue generalization of our commonsense categories, and does not do justice to the facts because in our societies marriage is an individual affair, not positively regulated; (2) it is contradictory for, as I shall show, the very existence of the marriage regulation implies that affinity is transmitted from one generation to the next just as consanguinity ties are. We have thus to give a proper definition of marriage regulation on the one hand and to widen our concept of affinity on the other.

First, it is almost unnecessary to recall that marriage cannot in general be considered as a secondary product of other institutions such as descent, which are then taken as being primary; there is rather an interrelation in the complete make-up. Still less it is possible to reduce the content of the marriage regulation to the codification of an individual affair, which marriage is not. Consequently, the regulation should not be considered as consisting of a relation between consanguineous ties and affinity, but as a feature of affinity itself. It is possible to do so, by pointing out that the regulation determines one's marriage by reference to one's ascendants' marriages: in a patrilineal, patrilocal society, marrying the matrilateral cross-cousin means reproducing the marriage of one's father, while in the patrilateral formula one reproduces one's grandfather's marriage, and so on. In general, the regulation determines a cycle of repetition of a marriage of a certain sort. If we say that 'one marries one's cross-cousin', we merely state a condition to be observed in order to maintain a certain pattern of intermarriage.

In other words, the regulation causes marriage to be transmitted much as membership in the descent group is transmitted. With it, marriage acquires a diachronic dimension, it becomes an institution enduring from generation to generation, which I therefore call 'marriage alliance', or simply 'alliance'.

In the matter of affinity, we generally admit too readily that, while the relationship between a man and his brother-in-law is affinal, the relationship between their sons (cross-cousins) has no longer any affinal content, but is a mere consanguineous relationship. This is certainly not so in South India, where to call E and A cross-cousins – as in Figure 1 (b) – instead of 'sons of affines' – as in Figure 1 (a) – is quite deceptive. Being sons of affines, they are *ipso facto* affines, at least in a virtual or rather a general sense, before or without becoming so individually, as when E marries A's sister. We are now out of the vicious circle and we can look at it with amusement: 'marrying a cross-cousin',[1] is nothing but

1. Briffault (1927, vol. 1, pp. 563 ff.) rightly uses the Tamil term for 'cross-cousin', *machuna* (for *maccuNaN*) to stress the affinal content of the category; he speaks of a 'marriage agreement between two groups'. Aiyappan (1944, p. 68) classifies the sister's son among the *bandhukkal* or affines, but contradicts it in a footnote.

marrying an affine, i.e. the person who is the closest affine by virtue of the transmission of affinity ties from one generation to the next.

I submit that, in societies where there are (positive) marriage regulations: (1) marriage should be considered as a part of a marriage alliance institution running through generations; (2) the concept of affinity should be extended so as to include not only

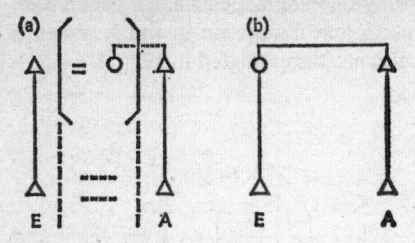

Figure 1 Cross-cousins or affines
(a) A as an 'affine' of E
(b) A as a 'cross-cousin' of E

immediate, individual relationships (affines in the ordinary sense) but also the people who inherit such a relationship from their parents, those who share it as siblings of the individual affines, etc.; (3) there is likely to be an affinal content in terms which are generally considered to connote consanguinity or 'genealogical' relationships (such as 'mother's brother' etc.). This is obviously so when there are no special terms for affines, for otherwise we should have to admit that in such cases affinity is not expressed at all.

Terminological dichotomy: kin and affines
Structure of terminology

All our groups share with many others a structurally identical terminology which in its broad features has been recorded from all four written Dravidian languages. Here I shall summarize a separate study (Dumont, 1953a; see also Radcliffe-Brown, 1953; Dumont 1953b).

The two sexes should be taken separately. With certain exceptions there is one term for all males in the grandfather's generation, but two terms in the father's generation. The latter terms, generally translated as 'father' and 'mother's brother', denote two classes, the members of which are respectively brothers-in-law to one another. Or, if we call 'alliance relationship' this relationship between two persons of the same sex, and represent it by $\Delta[=]\Delta$, standing for $\Delta = \overline{\delta\Delta}$ as well as for $\overline{\Delta\delta} = \Delta$ etc., the relation between the two classes is $\Delta[=]\Delta$. This is true also in Ego's generation (for older and younger relatives), whereas the distinction does not fully operate in Ego's son's generation, where a mere prefix is used, and disappears in the grandson's generation. Terms for males are recapitulated in Figure 2 (a).

(a)

generations	terms
grandfather	Δ
father	$\Delta[=]\Delta$
ego $\begin{cases} >e \\ <e \end{cases}$	$\Delta[=]\Delta$ $\Delta[=]\Delta$
son	$\triangle\!\triangle$
grandson	Δ

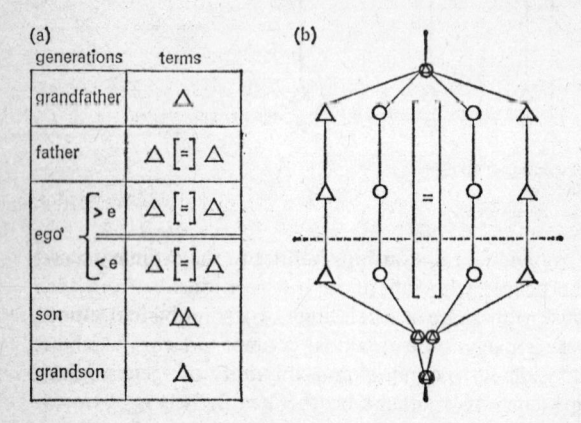

(b)

Figure 2 Structure of the system of kinship terms.
(a) terms for males only, five generations; (b) terms for both sexes, five generations. The superposition of signs shows identity of terms, apart from word-endings

Among females, the 'mother' and the 'father's sister' may be distinguished exactly as above. Now if we remark (1) that the terms for grandmother and grand-daughter are not distinct, except for the ending, from those for grandfather and grandson, and that the same root is used for all in the son's generation; and (2) that the principle of distinction is the same for males and for females, we can represent the whole by a symmetrical scheme in which the identity of terms is expressed by superpositions of signs – see Figure 2 (b). One sees that the distinction of sex and the alliance distinction go together, and that the system might be called 'bifurcate-merging' in a new sense, that is, bifurcate in the central and

186 Marriage and Alliance

merging in the extreme generations. One sees also how simple and regular the system looks once one ceases to remove alliance artificially from the content of kinship terms. It consists in distinguishing, in three generations or age groups, two kinds of relatives of each sex: those related to Ego by a link excluding alliance, or 'kin link' (Figure 2 (a)), and those related to the first by alliance (Figure 2 (b)). From the basic structure of the system we have on one side the 'fathers', on the other the 'fathers' affines', and on one side the 'mothers', on the other the 'mothers' affines'; and nowhere such beings as mother's brother or father's sister, who are just particular cases of fathers' affines and mothers' affines. Obviously, too, the system implies a marriage regulation, namely that one marries an affine in one's generation, the nearest of these in terms of individual relationship being a cross-cousin.

Definitions

The whole of the kinship terminology is split into two halves, 'kin' terms and 'alliance' or 'affinity' terms. By thus stating that kinship = kin + affinity, we escape an ambiguity found in anthropological writings, where 'kin' or 'kinship' is sometimes opposed to affinity and sometimes taken as embracing it. We prefer to speak of kin and affines rather than of parallel and cross-relatives. We should not however forget that these are only categories abstracted by us from the form of the terminological system. To avoid any confusion when actual kinship configurations are studied, we should designate them as 'terminological kin' and 'terminological affines'. Moreover, as the latter expression has been obtained by extending the meaning of the word 'affine', we should distinguish between (a) immediate or synchronic affines, i.e. affines in the ordinary sense, in-laws, and (b) genealogical or diachronic affines, who inherit, so to speak, an affinal tie which originated in an upper generation (e.g. mother's brother). When the marriage regulation is observed, the two categories (a) and (b) merge, and a person is at the same time a genealogical and an immediate affine, what might be called a perfect affine.

How the terminology is applied

The system as analysed hitherto is no more than an abstract frame of reference, no doubt pointing to alliance as a fundamental institution, but one to which each social group will give a particular concrete form according to its particular institutions. (We may imagine, for instance, that in a matrilineal matrilocal society the kin link is with the mother's brother while the father is an affine; then their ordinary positions in the system would be reversed, without the structure being altered.) Among our groups, the actual relationship with the father's sister may vary, but there will always be found as a common background the fact that she is different from a 'mother', first of all in the sense that Ego may marry her daughter even if she is not the preferred mate, while he may not marry a 'mother's' daughter.

Again, within one and the same terminological class the distinction of particular relatives, whether expressed or not in the language, may differ from one group to another. The broad opposition between kin and affines suggested by the terminology will itself be unequally realized for different relatives: among the terminological kin, a part is singled out as really or fully kin, and the same happens among terminological affines. The choice varies, but all the different choices fit into the general terminological frame, no doubt because they fit into a common alliance pattern. Another general difference is found in the degree to which relationships are extended from the groups of siblings to extensive socio-political groups. A comparison will show how the terminological categories are given different shapes by different institutions.

The Pramalai Kallar are patrilineal and patrilocal. In one locality there is as a rule only one or a few patrilineages. Hence:

1. The category of 'brothers' is split into two: on the one hand all my paternal 'brothers' (sons of my father's brothers etc.) are members of my local descent group, on the other hand my maternal 'brothers' (sons of my mother's sisters etc.) are spread over different groups and places. On the paternal side each individual link is made to endure through generations by becoming an element among all other similar elements in the continuous fabric of the local group, clearly defined as against others by the exogamic rule. On the maternal side, each individual relationship, being isolated – see however (2) below – is liable to be rapidly forgotten. While the paternal half is stressed to the point of becoming almost equivalent to the whole, the maternal half

appears, except in special cases, as temporary, subsidiary, almost conventional.

2. The opposition between kin and affines takes on a spatial aspect; there are kin places and affinal places, and as one marries mostly in the neighbourhood, this might be represented ideally in the form of concentric circles, a territorial unit made up of kin, A, being surrounded by affinal places, B. As these in their turn intermarry with other places, there arises a third circle, C, made up of people who are affines to B, and hence 'brothers' to A, as the affine of my affine is kin to me. (In these C places will be found some of the maternal brothers mentioned above.) The matter is of course not so simple in fact, but on the whole, when seen from one point, there is a picture of the division of the not-too-far-removed localities into the two fundamental categories. It will be readily grasped that this apparent dichotomy in space results from the working of the organization and has nothing to do with a systematic division or a dual organization of the society. Nevertheless it represents a maximum in the extension to groups of the basic terminological categories.

3. Let us now compare the position of the mother's brother with that of the father's sister. The mother's brother is not only terminologically opposed to the father, who is here kin *par excellence*, but he also lives in an affinal place. He is an affine pure and simple, in fact the closest, at least until one marries. On the contrary, the father's sister, born in one's local descent group, becomes only with her marriage a member of an affinal group, just as the mother, born in an affinal group, has become kin first as mother, at the same time thrusting, so to speak, the father's sister into the affinal category. The terminology here directs us to look at the father's sister as already married and as mother of affinal cousins. Nevertheless she is at the same time to some extent kin, and it follows that she is less clearly and unambiguously an affine than the mother's brother. If we then suppose, as will be confirmed, that affinal relatives are in charge of ceremonial functions, we may expect the mother's brother to precede the father's sister in those functions.

The picture is quite different for the matrilineal, patrilocal Kondaiyam Kottai Maravar. With them descent and locality work in opposite directions, with the result that individual kinship relationships are not backed by corresponding relationships between groups. Here the sons of two brothers on the one hand and of two sisters on the other are recognized as 'brothers' in two different ways and the two kinds of relationship are stressed in quite different conditions, the first in a context of locality and the second in a context of alliance or of special ceremonial circumstances. On one side, a remote relationship between patrilocal brothers does not in general exclude alliance, so that the category in the long run is stripped of any kin content, being mainly a matter of socio-economic neighbourliness. On the other side, it is between sisters (and not brothers) and their descendants that the matrilineal kin relationship endures. The descent group has no tangible reality. What is stressed here is a matriline scattered in different localities, shifting from place to place and from house to house in each generation. In every locality a number of matrilineal exogamous units are represented, and a man may marry into any of them, except his own. In one's own village the terminological categories are fully realized only for three kinds of people: a smaller or larger circle of patrilocal brothers, a number of matrilineal brothers, and the affines of the first two. At the same time, a great number of people are undifferentiated: they may be at the same time brothers in a loose, merely local sense, and virtual affines, and it is only the nexus of individual alliances and their classificatory extensions which decides the question.

The opposition between father and mother's brother is seen here in different ways. From the matrilineal point of view the situation would be reversed, the mother's brother could be considered as kin and the father as an affine, but nevertheless the mother's brother's children will be terminological affines. We see that it is the mother's brother who receives the ambiguous character which attaches to the father's sister among Pramalai Kallar. In contradistinction to them, the foremost affine here is the father's sister, because locality is not exclusive of alliance and because matrilineality stresses the kin link with the mother. This will be confirmed later, when we study the ceremonial functions.

If the two preceding examples are compared, the difference in the affinal value of the mother's brother and of the father's sister can perhaps be summed up by saying that when paternal features (authority, locality) are present, the foremost affinal relative in the upper generation is the affine of the lineally-stressed parent, i.e. the mother's brother in patrilineality and the father's sister in matrilineality. This is only another expression of harmony and disharmony (Figure 3). It is hoped that this brief comparison has shown how we may speak of a common underlying alliance pattern which, when combined with different institutions, assumes different concrete forms.

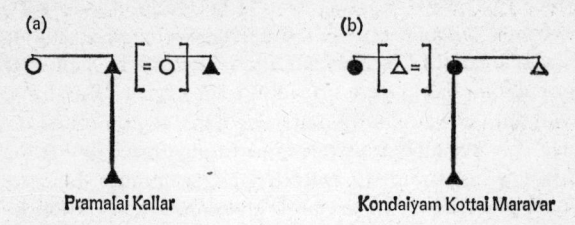

Figure 3 Stress on one affine in relation to descent: Pramalai Kallar and Kondaiyam Kottai Maravar

Inheritance and gifts

The most conspicuous feature of alliance as an enduring marriage institution that defines and links the two kinds of relatives consists in ceremonial gifts and functions. This perspective can be indirectly justified. If ceremonial gifts are essentially affinal and if they are important, it should follow that, in societies with male predominance, property is transmitted from one generation to the next under two forms: by inheritance in the male line and also by gifts to in-laws, namely from father-in-law to son-in-law. This is precisely what happens. In the groups with which we are immediately concerned, apart from the Nangudi Vellalar among whom female property is important, daughters have no formal share in their father's property, but they are entitled to maintenance and to the expenses necessary for their marriage and establishment.

Moreover, this is a case for generalization. The same rule, if it is not absolute and universal, has a widespread validity in Indian customary law, where it makes itself felt even when it is contradicted (Jolly, 1896, p. 83; Mayne, 1938, paragraphs 436, 421, 431, 488, etc.). The marriage expenses should not be taken as including only the cost of the necessary feasting and display, but also that of gifts to the in-laws on the occasion of marriage itself and later on as well. If the details vary, the broad institution is general, at least in the Tamil country, even among well-to-do people. This double transmission of property confirms the opposition between kin and alliance. It indicates that a review of ceremonial gifts must begin with marriage.

Marriage gifts

What is the most salient feature of the marriage ceremonies among the groups referred to? Sacramental acts like uniting hands or circumambulating the fire are not found. The tying of a string, with or without the well-known marriage badge or *tāli*, round the bride's neck has certainly a sacramental value, especially for the bride. But it is not witnessed by all relatives, because the ceremonies take place partly in the bride's and partly in the bridegroom's house, and only a few people go from one to the other. This explains why the tying of the *tāli* was sometimes repeated (Pramalai Kallar). A common meeting of the relatives of both sides is conspicuously absent. As a sign of union between the two families, I think we may say that it is replaced by the long series of alternate shiftings of the couple from one place to the other and back and again, which takes place from the marriage onwards and is accompanied by gifts in one direction and increased gifts in return. This chain of gifts, or 'prestations' and 'counter-prestations'[2] symbolizes the alliance tie and is the most important feature of marriage ceremonies from the point of view of the relation between the two families.

The Pramalai Kallar state with particular emphasis that 'gifts sent to the bride's house return increased twofold or threefold'. Among them, the man's family (which I shall designate as M) gives first a sum of money, *pariçam*, to the woman's family (designated as F) which has to spend at least twice as much for the bride's jewels. Then with the ceremony proper begins the series of visits to and stays with F, the couple being every time accompanied by a number of baskets (*çīr*), containing foodstuffs and other

2. Prestation, 'the action of paying, in money or service, what is due by law or custom, or feudally; a payment or the performance of a service so imposed or exacted, also, the performance of something promised' (*Shorter Oxford Dictionary*).

articles for consumption, from M to F and, increased, back from F to M. Prestations from F dominate more and more as time goes on until finally – it may be two or three years after the marriage ceremony – the young couple establish a separate household near M, and receive the necessary pots and pans from F without any return gift. This is the '*çīr* of going apart'.

Such are the main prestations, which I call external prestations in order to distinguish them from the following. During the marriage ceremony, in both houses, money is collected among the the bridegroom's relatives on the one hand and the bride's relatives on the other. This is called *moy*; its effect is to make the relatives contribute to the expenses of the family; it may be called an internal prestation. These two kinds of prestations are found in most other groups, internal prestations being likewise called *moy*, whereas there is no general term for external prestations, sometimes called *çuruḷ* if they consist of gifts in money and *çīr* if in kind. Linguistically, while *moy* indicates a mere collection ('crowd', 'multitude'), *çuruḷ* connotes a circular movement, a rolling up, perhaps a circular accumulation. Among the Nangudi all prestations are external, and people say that the *moy* has been replaced by collections where the two groups of relatives are mixed (*iNām*, a solemn word for 'gift'). The *moy* is not found in connection with marriage in Mudukkulattur, where it is known on other ceremonial occasions, i.e. girl's puberty and funerals. In Paganeri, internal prestations comprise a contribution in rice brought by all taking part in the feast (which may well be more widespread) and also a collection of money similar to the *moy*, bearing the name of *rēvei* or *rēgei*, 'list', and accompanied by small gifts of thanks in return. Among the Arupangu, the two *moy* are associated with a series of small external gifts.

In considering the external prestations, it is necessary to single out the matrilineal and matrilocal Nangudi who do not make reciprocal gifts. The pattern is definitely different: M's prestations are very slight on a ceremonial level; there is no *pariçam*, no gift of *tāli* or sari; the idea of competition is absent; the cost of the feast is shared afterwards between the two families. The parents of the bride make a point of providing everything except a foodstuff allowance, the same in all cases, which has to be regularly delivered by M to the new household. Moreover, the emphasis is here on the dowry, strictly the wife's property. In Paganeri also the reciprocity in gifts is weaker, but there a part of the usual prestations from M is found.

Otherwise the comparison shows that, while there are all possible variations for each element in particular, the whole is more uniform than its parts, and still more so is the form of small cycles inside the whole cycle. Leaving aside once for all the Nangudi Vellalar, we see that the *tāli* is everywhere paid by M. The gift of one or two saris to the bride by M is lacking among the Pramalai, so is the *pariçam* in Paganeri and among the Arupangu, while it is present in Mudukkulattur, and present but small among the Ambalakkarar. As a counterpart, the importance of jewels and dowry varies. Land is given among the Ambalakkarar and in Paganeri. Jewels are important in those two groups, but on the contrary their value is hardly mentioned at all in Mudukkulattur. This is obviously related to the economic situation, for the Maravar of Mudukkulattur are very poor and the Arupangu occupy an intermediary position between them and Paganeri or the Nangudi.

The masculine *çīr* brought for the ceremony is found everywhere, Nangudi excepted. Among the Arupangu, it is like that of the Pramalai, with one sari added. In Mudukkulattur, where it is preceded by another one for the betrothal, it includes rice. This also is seen, with more rice, in Paganeri and among the Ambalakkarar. In return the gift is multiplied thrice in Mudukkulattur, while in Paganeri the increase is marked in a different way, by the additions of pots and pans. The return gift is lacking among the Ambalakkarar and the Arupangu. In the latter group, it is probably only delayed on the one hand (*çīr* of the first visit to F) and, on the other, there is another form of reciprocity, that of *çuruḷ*, as will be seen below.

Regarding subsequent *çīr* gifts, the difference between the groups bears on the choice of the most important dates. The household equipment will be offered, here on the Pongal festival (in January), there on the first visit to F; the gifts of the month of *āḍi* will be more or less important, etc. The *çuruḷ* or external gifts in money are found among the Arupangu (1) from F to M as a return for clothes, (2) from F to M and back (individualized, as in Paganeri, where the *çuruḷ* is a small gift from the wife's father to the husband and from the husband's mother to the wife).

The common mechanism of the gifts appears clearly if one isolates small cycles based on reciprocity. There are three types. In the first of these, there is an exact reciprocity, as in Paganeri when clothes are given by M to F and then equivalent clothes by F to M; among the Arupangu the clothes presented by M to F are compensated for by a reverse gift in money (*çuruḷ*) which must be at least equal to their value. In a second type, the initial gift is not only reciprocated, but multiplied in return, as among the Pramalai. A third type has a reduced reciprocity, marked sometimes by a mere symbolical counter-gift. This is true among the Pramalai and in Paganeri for the *moy*; among the Arupangu the *çuruḷ* which has just been mentioned is in its turn followed by a symbolical return. It can also be shown how one given object receives a particular ceremonial value from its situation in the whole. This is so with rice among the Pramalai, where it does not occur in internal prestations nor in the masculine, but only in the feminine *çīr* as a sign of their substantial importance, i.e. of the 'increase' which characterizes them. On the contrary, rice is to be found everywhere in Paganeri and, to express the pre-eminence of the feminine *çīr*, one resorts to another element, namely the pots and pans which elsewhere appear only later.

The foregoing comparison will have shown how much stress is laid on the chain of prestations in all its details, and also in what sense it may be said to be common in spite of all variations. It is clearly impossible to single out one of the marriage 'payments', the *pariçam*, and to call it 'bride-price'.[3] It represents, at least in the examples cited here, the contribution of the husband's family to the buying of jewels which will be worn by the wife but normally become the property of the household, as can be ascertained from their treatment in case of divorce. That terms like 'bride-price' are inaccurate here is also obvious if one considers that, on the whole, and to varying degrees, it is the wife's family that gives more. The *pariçam* appears rather as a kind of earnest-money which is destined to come back increased. It would be almost

3. For a contrary view see Srinivas (1942, ch. 2), but the prestations are not analysed. Mousset and Dupuis (1928) wisely translate *pariçam* by the French *arrhes*. An exchange of gifts similar to those found here, but with mercantile features, has been described among the Nattukkottai Chettiar (Thurston and Rangachari, 1909, vol. 5, pp. 265 ff.).

equally misleading to reduce the whole to 'dowry', in cases when something of the kind actually appears. These are rather extreme cases among the rich and when patrilateral marriage promises a return in the next generation. The transfer of meaning of the classical word for dowry (Sanskrit *strīdhana*, 'wife's property') among the Pramalai Kallar is characteristic, since they call *çṛidaNam*, *çidaNam* all gifts due by the wife's family, including the future gifts of her brother to his sister's children. Obviously the meaning of the protracted exchange of gifts with which we are dealing, if it includes the final result in terms of plus and minus, goes far beyond this. On the whole, the final result is a gift which accompanies the gift of the girl. A relevant question here would be to ask why a transaction which finally amounts to a gift has to take the form of an exchange. I would say that it corresponds to the individual marriage's (i.e. gift's) being conceived of as a part of the whole nexus of intermarriages and their consequences as seen from the point of view of a single family (i.e. exchange). When the Pramalai Kallar state that 'gifts sent to the bride's house return increased', this is roughly true of one individual present, but it is still truer of the whole series, or rather it is true in the sense that it accounts for each exchange as seen in the light of the whole. There is certainty about increase, because increase is the law of the whole cycle. One knows very well that masculine gifts will decrease as time goes on, while feminine gifts will increase; the latter are substantial, the former initiatory and provocative. Generosity lies on the girl's side, but it has to be set in motion; a pledge to protracted, manifold, and mainly unilateral gifts is obtained by a formal exchange.

Indeed, this may be taken as a formula of Kallar marriage if one accepts the view that these prestations – and not the 'ritual' elements on which attention has been mainly focused – constitute the main part of marriage ceremonies. In favour of this view, the first argument is that prestations in fact do not stop at the point we have somewhat arbitrarily chosen. Those which follow may be called 'alliance prestations' and I shall trace them in all ceremonial circumstances of the individual's life. Marriage does not consist only in the consecration of conjugal union and the establishment of a new family, for this family is as inseparable from the alliance prestations as it is from the local lineage affiliation.

The alliance prestations are of two kinds: some are symmetrical or reversible and some are asymmetrical or oriented. If, after the marriage has been celebrated, a death occurs in the bride's family, the bridegroom's family, together with the other affines, will bring food presents. These I call 'reversible' gifts because, the bride's family would do the same if a death occurred in the bridegroom's. This reversible relationship we find reflected in the transport of gifts which accompany the young couple both ways after marriage. It is the most general and undifferentiated expression of alliance in gifts. The birth of a child in the new family will create a different situation which has no counterpart in the bride's family. This is an 'oriented' situation, where the Kallar will stress the gifts and functions of the maternal uncle. It should be added that one and the same ceremonial occasion calls for the two kinds of responses and gifts from different people. Whereas many people come and give the ordinary, reversible, affinal gift, one particular relative, who may be the maternal uncle, is singled out with particular, oriented gifts and functions: the oriented relationship stands against a background of reversible relationships. Both kinds of relationships are initiated (or renewed) in marriage, and this corresponds to the double aspect of exchange and gift in the marriage prestations: 'gifts sent to the bride's house return increased'.

That affinal ceremonial prestations in general constitute something like the core of family ceremonies is shown not only by their description, but also by the fact that it is possible for the people to dissociate what might be called the mere rite and the accompaniment of prestations which overshadow it. This is true of marriage among the Maravar (Thurston and Rangachari, 1909, pp. 37–8) and of funerals, on which occasions the prestations may be postponed. It is true also of circumcision, as two striking instances will show. Among the Pramalai Kallar, the circumcision of a boy is a source of income for the family. Therefore, two brothers are never circumcised together when their age would permit it. Further, old parents who are said to be anxious to see the circumcision while they are alive may have the ceremony performed several years in advance, but the operation itself will take place later and without any ceremony. The Ambalakkarar had for girls a ceremony parallel to the circumcision of boys, but with no technical counterpart. This had nothing to do with the common girls' puberty ceremony, although the two have been sometimes confused (Francis, 1914, p. 94). An informant states that this ceremony originated because parents who had no sons but only daughters wished to celebrate it as well as the others.

References

AIYAPPAN, A. (1944), 'Iravas and culture change', *Bull. Madras Govt. Mus.*, General Section, vol. 5, no. 1.

BRIFFAULT, R. (1927), *The Mothers*, vol. 1, Allen & Unwin.

DUMONT, L. (1953a), 'The Dravidian kinship terminology as an expression of marriage', *Man*, vol. 53, art. 54.

DUMONT, L. (1953b), 'Dravidian kinship terminology', *Man*, vol. 53, art. 224.

FRANCIS, W. (1914), 'Madura', *Madras District Gazetteers*, vol. 1, Madras Government Press.

JOLLY, J. (1896), 'Recht und Sitte (einschliesslich der einheimischen Literatur)', *Grundriss Indo-Arischen Philolog. Altertumskunde*, vol. 11, no. 8.

MAYNE, J. D. (1938), *A Treatise on Hindu Law and Usage*, 10th edn., Higginbotham, Madras.

MOUSSET, A., and DUPUIS, B. (1928), *Dictionnaire tamoul-francais*, Pondichéry, Société des Missions Etrangères.

RADCLIFFE-BROWN, A. R. (1953), 'Dravidian kinship terminology', *Man*, vol. 53, art. 169.

SRINIVAS, M. N. (1942), *Marriage and Family in Mysore*, Bombay New Book Co.

THURSTON, E., and RANGACHARI, K. (1909), *Castes and Tribes of Southern India*, Madras Government Press.

14 D. Maybury-Lewis

Prescriptive Marriage Systems[1]

D. Maybury-Lewis, 'Prescriptive marriage systems', *Southwestern Journal of Anthropology*, vol. 21, 1965, pp. 207–30.

This paper attempts to clarify some basic issues in the study of prescriptive marriage systems. It might seem presumptuous of me to offer a clarification of points which have already been thoroughly and vigorously discussed. I do so only because it seems to me that the discussions have lately, and inevitably, become enmeshed in their own dialectic of critique and rejoinder and are therefore no longer followed by many anthropologists whose attitudes, expressed informally, vary from 'A plague on all their houses' to 'What is the importance of it all anyway?' I believe that the issues are important and that a summary of them at this stage would serve a useful purpose, if only perhaps that of avoiding future disputes based on misunderstandings. At the same time I am, with a group of colleagues and students from Harvard and Rio de Janeiro, engaged on the study of a number of central Brazilian societies possessing two-section systems and/or exogamous moieties. The issues with which I deal here are of direct relevance to that enquiry.

The systems which I shall discuss are those which Needham has termed 'prescriptive'. In so doing I say nothing about the desirability of treating prescriptive and preferential marriage systems together or separately. I maintain only that an analytical distinction must be made between them. The justification for this distinction follows from the discussion of what in fact is meant by a prescriptive marriage system.

Previous discussions have dealt with three types of prescriptive marriage system:

---

1. I would like to express my gratitude to Dr Rodney Needham of Oxford University, whose critical comments on a draft of this paper have been most helpful.

1. Prescriptive matrilateral cross-cousin marriage (also known as MBD[2] marriage).
2. Prescriptive patrilateral cross-cousin marriage (also known as FZD marriage).
3. Prescriptive bilateral cross-cousin marriage (also known as marriage with the MBD/FZD).

This terminology dates at least from the time of Rivers (1914) and has been the source of much confusion. It has long been realized that the terms are unsatisfactory or even misleading (see, for example, Dumont, 1953, 1957a; Löffler, 1964). Yet anthropologists have continued to use them with the mental proviso, sometimes (though not always) made explicit, that when they wrote, for example, of marriage with the MBD, they really meant something else. It is therefore important at the outset to give a summary statement of what this 'something else' is.

Let us first take note of what it is not. A system of prescriptive cross-cousin marriage does not, in the usage adopted here, denote a system where marriage is prescribed with an individual in a specific genealogical relationship to Ego. Nor is it a system where Ego must marry a certain cross-cousin 'real or classificatory'. The notion of 'marrying a cross-cousin' is an analytical one, introduced by anthropologists and purporting to describe what happens in such systems. It is important to remember, however, that the rule in societies which practise 'cross-cousin marriage' is not phrased in terms of cross-cousins at all. Thus, as Needham pointed out (1962, p. 9), the Batak do not prescribe marriage with the MBD but rather with a woman of the category *boru ni tulang*, one of the specifications of which is MBD. Dumont has argued, lucidly and convincingly, that 'cross-cousin marriage' is a misnomer (1957a, pp. 24–5) and that '... "marrying a cross-cousin" is nothing but marrying an affine.' Ideally then we should couch a discussion of prescriptive marriage systems in terms which avoid genealogical specifications in general and the notion of cross-cousin in particular. Indeed this is what Needham has been doing where he speaks of matrilateral cross-cousin marriage

2. I shall throughout use the notation where relationship terms are represented by their initial letter, with the exception of Z = sister to distinguish it from S = son.

systems as systems of asymmetric alliance. Sooner or later, however, the genealogical specification comes back to plague the discussion. It will be necessary for me to make use of genealogical specifications, but I shall try to avoid misunderstanding by setting out in each instance, and at the risk of repetition, exactly what the function of the genealogical referent is. Finally, like the $\sqrt{-1}$ I shall elide it altogether in my final formulation.

In general, then, prescriptive marriage systems are here taken as being those in which there is a rule of marriage with a prescribed category of relative. The implications of such prescriptions are discussed in the following sections which deal with each type of prescription in turn.

Prescriptive matrilateral cross-cousin marriage

A minimal characterization of such a system is that a man must marry a woman whom he addresses by a relationship term which denotes a category of relatives that includes his MBD and excludes his FZD. This rule has certain consequences. The work of

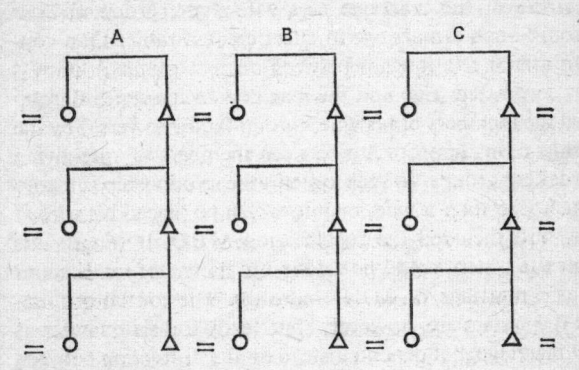

Figure 1 A formal model of asymmetric alliance

Dutch scholars (e.g. Van Wouden, 1935)[3] and the classic study of prescriptive marriage systems by Lévi-Strauss (1949) demonstrated that one result of it could be the establishment of enduring

3. I wish to acknowledge my debt to Dr Rodney Needham, who not only instructed me in the study of prescriptive marriage systems but also introduced me to the work of the Dutch anthropologists.

affinal relationships between descent groups. Group A gives women to group B, group B to group C, and so on until finally one group gives women to A and thereby closes the cycle (as in Figure 1).

Prescriptive matrilateral cross-cousin marriage was therefore held to produce cycles of marriage transactions, or *connubium* as the Dutch called it.

Such a model of the system contains the implicit assumption that a given male Ego in a patrilineal society would always take a woman from the descent group of his MBD even though he need not marry the MBD herself. Subsequent studies by Leach (1954) and Needham (1958a)[4] served to modify this thesis in at least one important respect. They showed that in certain patrilineal societies a man could marry in conformity with a rule of prescriptive matrilateral cross-cousin marriage even though he did not take a wife from the descent group of his MBD, provided that the wife he did take came from a descent group which (1) was not already thought of as taking women from Ego's group, and (2) was classified by virtue of the marriage as a wife-giving group *vis-à-vis* Ego's group. Such a marriage in effect created rather than continued an affinal relationship between descent groups.[5] Once it had been contracted, Ego and the members of his descent group addressed the members of his wife's group (and vice versa) by the relationship terms appropriate between members of wife-giving and wife-taking groups. In such systems the relationship category from which Ego took a wife, or into which he placed his wife at marriage, also included the specification MBD. It was in this sense that the system could be referred to as one of matrilateral cross-cousin marriage or MBD marriage. The formal requirements of the system are, however, imperfectly translated in terms of MBD marriage, but depend instead on the distinction between wife-giving and wife-taking groups and the rule that a spouse

4. Also by Dumont (1957a and b), considered later in connection with bilateral systems.

5. It is not essential that descent groups should be the wife-giving and wife-taking units, although they frequently are. In certain societies each marriage establishes mutually exclusive categories of wife-givers and wife-takers which do not correspond to descent groups. I couch my discussion here in terms of descent groups so that the exposition may be as simple and as clear as possible.

may not be taken from a group which is already in a wife-taking relationship to Ego's.

It could be argued that such societies cannot usefully be considered as instances of matrilateral cross-cousin marriage. Coult did in fact use such an argument in an exchange with Leach concerning the Kachin. He wrote:

the usual notion of cross-cousin marriage entails that a person marry a woman who is related to himself in one or another of a limited number of ways. If, for example, matrilateral cross-cousin marriage is practised among patrilineal descent groups, then this means that a man will marry his MBD, or MBSD, or MBSSD, or MFBSD, or MFBSSD, etc. Marriage with the MBD is regarded as true cross-cousin marriage; marriage with any of the remaining kin types as marriage with the classificatory cross-cousin (1963, p. 162).

He therefore insisted that if his theory of cross-cousin marriage (Coult, 1962a) did not apply to the Kachin, it was because the Kachin did not practise cross-cousin marriage (Coult, 1963, p. 163).

There is more to this divergence of views than mere disagreement over the use of a term. It is important to realize that Coult and Leach are writing about two quite different types of inquiry. Before we consider these, however, a preliminary contradiction in Coult's statement must be dealt with. The theory of cross-cousin marriage to which he refers above (Coult, 1962a) is an attempt to discover a formula which will explain why, in societies where men may marry their cross-cousins genealogically defined, they sometimes prefer the MBD to the FZD, sometimes the FZD to the MBD, and sometimes marry both indiscriminately. His paper thus derives explicitly from Homans and Schneider (1955). He apparently considers it irrelevant, for the purposes of his argument, whether these marriages are prescribed or preferred, since he tests his hypotheses by referring to Murdock's table showing the relationship of preferential marriage to descent (1957, p. 687), where all such systems are categorized as 'preferred'. However, Murdock's table includes the Kachin (Jinghpaw), which had previously been listed (Murdock, 1957, p. 680) as having patrilineal descent and matrilateral cross-cousin marriage preferred asymmetrically. Coult therefore accepts the Kachin as an instance of a society practising cross-cousin marriage when in

1962 he uses Murdock's table to test his hypotheses but denies that they do when in 1963 he is in argument with Leach.

A clue to this contradiction may lie in the last sentence of Coult (1963a). Commenting on Leach's assertion that 'A Kachin for example must marry a *nam*, that is a girl junior to Ego who is a member of any *mayu* (wife-giving) lineage with respect to Ego' (1963, p. 77), Coult replies that 'In the final analysis no theory can be a match for the awesome and far-ranging memories of individual ethnographers' (1963a, p. 163). The rejoinder, with its insinuation that Leach 'remembered' the evidence in order to controvert Coult, is in poor taste. It is also poor scholarship. The evidence which Leach is supposed to have remembered is set forth in *Political Systems of Highland Burma* (Leach, 1954, p. 74) and should certainly have been familiar to any anthropologist who seriously proposed to discuss the characterization of the Kachin.[6]

The implications of Coult's rejoinder transcend the Kachin, however. As I have already indicated, he is advocating a different type of inquiry from that which Leach pursued. If cross-cousin marriage systems are held to be only those where a man must marry his actual or classificatory cross-cousin, *genealogically defined*, then the study of such systems becomes an *etic* investigation which seeks to make statements about how particular genealogical specifications become the foci of marriage rules and what the consequences of this are.

Leach's study of the Kachin (1954) is, on the other hand, an *emic* investigation which seeks, among other things, to examine the social consequences of a marriage rule such that a bride must always belong to a specific relationship category. He therefore analyses Kachin categories in general and the categories of their relationship system in particular and in so doing elucidates the defining criteria of that category which must contain a man's wife/MBD. This approach is also common to the work of Dumont and Needham, who have emphasized that the study of

6. This appears to be another melancholy example of the type of mistake made by anthropologists who work with cross-cultural compilations without referring to the sources. The *World Ethnographic Sample* is certainly valuable, but it should be used as a starting point for comparative work, not as an isolated universe of data.

systems of social classification is an integral part of their investigation of prescriptive marriage.

Both Coult's approach and what I have here dubbed as Leach's approach are, of course, perfectly legitimate. It is only possible to choose between them by seeing how they account for particular cases or classes of cases. In dealing with prescriptive marriage systems Coult's approach suffers from a major disadvantage. We have already seen that societies do not in fact prescribe marriage with a cross-cousin. They prescribe marriage with categories such as *boru ni tulang* (Batak), *nam* (Kachin), and so on. An analysis based on genealogical specifications will therefore hold only for these societies where, e.g. *boru ni tulang* = MBD. We can state this as a general proposition by letting x be the vernacular term for any relationship category which includes the specification MBD and excludes FZD. Let y similarly symbolize the term for a category including FZD and excluding MBD. Let z be the term for a category which includes both MBD and FZD. A genealogical approach will only hold for prescriptive marriage systems where x = MBD, y = FZD, and z = MBD/FZD. A category approach deals with x, y and z and therefore holds not only in the cases where x = MBD, y = FZD and z = MBD/FZD but also in the cases where x > MBD, y > FZD and z > MBD/FZD.

It could nevertheless still be held that a genealogical theory was an adequate theory of 'prescriptive marriage systems' if it could be shown that all cases where MBD was part of x could be derived from x = MBD and so on. This was perhaps an implicit assumption of Homans and Schneider's *Marriage, Authority and Final Causes* (1955). To my knowledge, however, it has not yet been shown that this assumption is correct. On the contrary, I have argued elsewhere (Maybury-Lewis, in preparation) that we have no grounds for assuming that relationship terms refer to categories which are invariably derived (or 'extended') from genealogical specifications contained in them. Instead I suggest that we are not yet in a position to make statements about the general content of such categories. They may on occasion be genealogically derived, but it has also been shown that frequently they are not.

To sum up, then, the approach to prescriptive marriage systems here outlined takes as its point of departure the rule in certain societies that a man's wife must belong to a specific relationship category. Prescriptive matrilateral cross-cousin marriage has been so called because one of the specifications in that category is MBD. The formal requirements of the system are that, if a male Ego's descent group is in a wife-taking relationship with another one, it must:

(a) refrain from giving women in marriage to that other (wife-giving) group except after a certain conventional interval;[7]

(b) use to members of that group the relationship terms which are applied to wife-giving groups.

These terms will also be the ones applied to the members of any group which contains a woman who is MBD to any man of Ego's descent group.

In such a system the rule of marriage serves to define the relations between descent groups.[8] If a society is patrilineal, then the affinal ties of its constituent descent groups are maintained by the marriages of successive generations of males. Figure 2 shows the various marriage choices open to a male Ego in a patrilineal society with a rule of prescriptive matrilateral cross-cousin marriage. He may take a woman from his MB's descent group (P), thereby repeating his F's marriage and possibly (though not necessarily) marrying his actual MBD. He may take a woman from a descent group which has in the past given women to his own (Q) or he may take a woman from some other descent group (R) which henceforward become wife-givers. The only descent groups he may not take from are those such as Y and Z, which are taking women from his own.

In a matrilineal society the affinal ties of descent groups are maintained by the marriages of successive generations of females. If such a society had a rule of prescriptive matrilateral cross-cousin marriage, then women would always place their husbands in the category of FZS. The marriage choices open to a female Ego in such a society are analogous to those open to a male Ego in a patrilineal society, the husband invariably being classed in the same category as the FZD. In fact this type of society appears to

7. Wife-givers may then become wife-takers and vice versa, but they must be distinguished at any one time. See Needham (1960, p. 501) for a discussion of this point.

8. Except where it serves, as noted before, to distinguish categories of wife-givers and wife-takers.

be exceedingly rare.[9] I do not propose here to attempt to explain this. I merely point out that in matrilineal, as in patrilineal societies, prescriptive matrilateral cross-cousin marriage precisely defines the relation between affinally related descent groups or categories. This is not the case in a system of patrilateral cross-cousin marriage, to which we now turn.

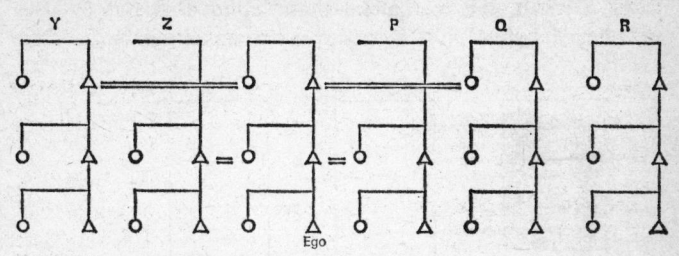

Figure 2 Types of marriage choices open to a male Ego with asymmetric alliance

Prescriptive patrilateral cross-cousin marriage

The minimal characteristic of such a system is that a man must marry a woman whom he addresses by a relationship term which denotes a category of relatives that includes his FZD and excludes his MBD. The consequences of such a rule are different from the matrilateral case, as has been amply demonstrated by Lévi-Strauss (1949). One possible outcome would be as in Figure 3. It will be seen from that figure that a descent group A which gives women to another descent group B in one generation will receive women from B in the next. Lévi-Strauss referred to this as discontinuous exchange and contrasted it with the generalized exchange effected by matrilateral cross-cousin marriage. He suggested that discontinuous exchange effected a series of short marriage cycles, whereas generalized exchange brought about a single unifying cycle in the society which practised it (Lévi-Strauss, 1949, p. 562). Homans and Schneider pointed out, however, that patrilateral cross-cousin marriage systems require a cycle of descent groups linked by marriage in the same way as with

9. Needham has argued that the Sirionó are such a society (1961). If he is correct, then they are the only known instance. I myself do not find his argument convincing, since I do not accept his inference from the structure of relationship terminology to the ordering of the marriage system.

matrilateral cross-cousin marriage (1955, p. 13). The difference between the two lies not in the length of the cycle but in the fact that a matrilateral prescription ensures a unidirectional flow of marriages from group to group in successive generations, whereas the patrilateral one results in a change of direction of this flow with each generation.[10]

As a result, the patrilateral prescription does not by itself define the relationship between descent groups. It can be seen from

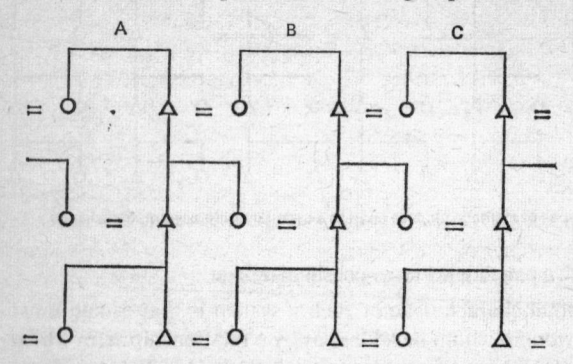

Figure 3 A formal model of prescriptive patrilateral cross-cousin marriage

Figure 3 that A and C are both wife-giving and wife-taking groups with respect to B. Consider the effect of this on the marriage choices open to a male Ego in a patrilateral society with this form of marriage prescription. He may, as we have already seen in the matrilateral case, marry a woman of a descent group which is neither wife-giver nor wife-taker to his own. In this case his marriage would create an affinal link between groups and would not contradict any previous relationship. But if he takes a wife from a descent group which already has an affinal link with his own, then there is some ambiguity. The group from which he proposes to take his wife is both wife-giving and wife-taking with respect to his own. In a prescriptive marriage system he could not take a wife from a wife-taking group. Such a marriage would be regarded

10. I have sometimes found it helpful to conceive of the difference in terms of an electrical circuit with direct current in the first (matrilateral) case, alternating current in the second (patrilateral) case. The length of the circuit remains constant, but the type of flow changes.

208 Marriage and Alliance

as incestuous. There must, therefore, be some institutional distinction between those women of his affinal descent group who were in the prescribed category and those who were forbidden to him. It would appear from Figure 3 that an age-set system or section system which effected a rigid demarcation between the generations in each descent group would make such a system workable. In this hypothetical situation a man would know which descent groups were givers and which takers *vis-à-vis* his own *in a particular generation*.

Nevertheless Needham has consistently maintained that a system of prescriptive patrilateral cross-cousin marriage cannot exist in theory and does not exist in fact (1958b; 1960; 1962; 1963a). A number of writers have expressed a contrary view (Livingstone, 1959; Coult, 1962b; Lane, 1962; and Salisbury, 1964). Let us consider their arguments first.

Coult suggests that '... the only necessary requirement is that a person marry his father's sister's daughter, or a classificatory father's sister's daughter, and the system could work perfectly,[11] (1962b, p. 330). But could it? A system where every man was obliged to marry his actual FZD would be unworkable for simple demographic reasons. If, on the other hand, he may marry his classificatory FZD, then how is this category to be defined?

One obvious possibility, already mentioned, is that it be defined in terms of a section system. Indeed this is the suggestion which has been advanced by most writers arguing for the feasibility of patrilateral cross-cousin marriage. Livingstone (1959) proposed that a variation on the eight-section system of the Arunta might be the solution. Hammel (1960) suggested that formally both a six-section and an eight-section system could provide an institutional matrix for this type of marriage prescription. Lane (1962) likewise proposed a form of eight-section system, and Coult (1962b) has argued, like Hammel, that both six and eight-section systems would satisfy the formal requirements of a patrilateral prescription.

These suggestions do not controvert Needham's contention, for he was not arguing that such a system was inconceivable, which would be absurd, nor even that its formal properties could not be

11. This simplistic assertion in itself is enough to make one wonder whether Coult has considered the matter very deeply.

described. He was claiming that the rules entailed by the system were unworkable. This is still a formal argument in the sense that he did not state that the rules did not or would not work in particular instances but that they could not work as a general principle. The issue then is not whether it is possible to suggest a formal model for a patrilateral prescriptive marriage system but whether such a model could be translated into actuality in a given society and by what rules.

Needham's central objection to the workability of the suggested models may be paraphrased as follows. The systems are cumbersome, but even if they were found to exist they would produce marriage with a bilateral cross-cousin (Needham, 1960, pp. 210–12; 1963, p. 203). This seemingly straightforward proposition is in fact rather complex, and its logical status similarly so.[12] Nor have Needham's attempts to demonstrate it, by showing that in a society with a patrilateral prescription FZD = MMBDD and is therefore a bilateral relative, served to clarify matters. On the contrary they appear to have caused some bewilderment (Coult, 1962, p. 328; Lane, 1962, p. 469–70). The difficulty stems, I believe, from the sudden introduction of genealogical terminology into a discussion of categories. If I may presume to try to restate Needham's argument without the genealogical reference, it appears to rest on the principle that a patrilateral prescriptive system effects exchanges of women between descent groups such that if group A gives women to group B in one generation, group B gives women to group A in the next. If we look at marriages *from the point of view of the descent group*, then it can be seen that they are not unilateral. To the men of group A (Figure 3) the women of B are matrilateral in one generation and patrilateral in the next. The system thus becomes a variation of bilateral cross-cousin marriage. If I have understood this argument correctly, it maintains that prescriptive patrilateral cross-cousin marriage must be a form of prescriptive bilateral cross-cousin marriage and cannot therefore be distinguished as a form of prescription in its own right.

It follows from this that even if a society were found which has

12. It could be taken as a statement to the effect that prescriptive patrilateral cross-cousin marriage cannot exist because, if it did, it would be prescriptive bilateral cross-cousin marriage. Such a proposition is clearly absurd. I shall rephrase it in the following paragraph.

an eight-section system such as the one postulated by Livingstone (1959, p. 370) with FZD marriage, Needham would argue that it was not a case of a distinct type of prescriptive marriage system but rather a form of bilateral cross-cousin marriage.[13]

It should by now be clear that an argument as to 'whether a prescriptive FZD marriage system can exist' is too loosely phrased to be useful. It seems to me that if Livingstone wished to call his hypothetical construct a system of prescriptive FZD marriage, he would be entitled to do so, and I can see no reason why such a system could not work. But the name used to designate the system is not the point at issue. Needham is in fact arguing that such a prescription cannot be distinguised *in terms of laterality* from other systems.

This is where the conventional glosses MBD and FZD are particularly misleading. What we refer to as a prescriptive MBD marriage system is in fact a system where there is a unilateral transfer of spouses from one descent group to another. What we refer to as prescriptive MBD/FZD marriage is a system where there is a bilateral exchange of spouses between descent groups. In terms of laterality there are no other possibilities open, and prescriptive FZD marriage thus becomes a sub-class of prescriptive MBD/FZD marriage.

It was for this reason that Needham considered the possibility of a six-section system as a matrix for patrilateral prescriptive marriage (1962, p. 112). It was not, as Coult supposed (1962, p. 331), because there are three lines in the conventional model of a patrilateral prescriptive system, but because such a system had to be asymmetric in order to be distinguished from bilateral prescription. Two, four, and eight-section systems effect a bilateral prescription and thus do not serve.

Lane (1962) nevertheless accepts the implied challenge in Needham's claim that there can be no system of prescriptive patrilateral cross-cousin marriage and argues that on the contrary there can and that the Pende have it. Similarly Salisbury, though he does not specifically mention Needham, presents the Siane as another society practising patrilateral cross-cousin marriage and feels obliged to restate his position 'in view of some theorists' failure

13. I would agree with Needham here as will become clear later in my discussion of the Siane case and of bilateral cross-cousin marriage systems.

to consider the ethnographical evidence when they assert that an obligatory patrilateral cross-cousin-marriage rule is impossible' (1964, pp. 168-9).

There are some problems in the Pende material, however, which Lane does not mention.[14] The Pende are reportedly divided into matrilineal clans, and a man will try to take a wife from his father's matriclan 'so that he may return to it the semen which was lost in engendering him' (Lane, 1962, p. 489).

Now, since the Pende are matrilineal, it is the women who provide the continuity of the descent groups. We should therefore consider Pende marriage arrangements from their point of view. A man tries to take a woman from his father's clan, and he is forbidden to marry his MBD. It therefore follows that a woman is sought by a man from her MBW's clan and is forbidden to marry her FZS. If the marriage rule is prescriptive, then she is faced with the problem we have already mentioned: how is she to know which of her MBW's clan are marriageable? Those of her mother's generation were presumably FZS to her mother and therefore forbidden. Yet we are not told how the Pende make this distinction, which is precisely the problem with a patrilateral prescription.

We are not told either what the boundaries of the kinship categories are which Lane cites. Do they include all members of Pende society, so that if a man may not marry his *tata* (some of the specifications of which are MBD, S, D) he must marry his *isoni* (one of the specifications of which is FZD)? Or do these terms refer to certain genealogical specifications? In the latter case how do the Pende operate a *prescriptive* marriage system in terms of genealogical relationships, which may be vacant for any given Ego?

Furthermore, Lane notes the provisions which the Pende make for cases where 'the preferred marriage with the FZD cannot be arranged' (1962, p. 485). This would seem to indicate then that the Pende have an ideology of FZD marriage but that this is not a prescription, for, as we have seen, it is characteristic of a prescriptive system that all marriages are treated as if they fall into the correct category.

14. I have unfortunately been unable to consult de Sousberghe's report (1955), which is unavailable here.

Finally, and perhaps conclusively, de Sousberghe, the ethnographer on whose report Lane based his contention, has in connection with the issue of prescriptive marriage among the Pende allowed himself to be quoted to the following effect: 'Marriage with the patrilateral cross-cousin among the Pende is not prescribed: it is merely preferential' (Needham, 1963b, p. 58).

Salisbury specifically states, on the other hand, that the rule of marriage for the Siane 'should not be called "prescriptive" as nothing is "prescribed"' (1964, p. 169). Yet he appears to be in two minds as to whether or not the rule is obligatory. Thus he states that 'there is definitely no obligatory marriage rule in Siane' (1956, p. 646) and later 'The marriage rule is obligatory as all men, when they marry, must be and are (with modern exceptions of those marrying foreign women) marrying a "father's sister's daughter"' (1964, p. 169). I shall not dwell on these fine distinctions. Instead I shall try to describe what appear to be the salient features of the Siane material in so far as they bear on the issue of patrilateral cross-cousin marriage.

The Siane are patrilineal, and they forbid the marriage of a man with a woman of his mother's clan. Nor may a man marry his true father's sister's child (Salisbury, 1956, p. 646). Instead he must marry a classificatory father's sister's daughter, since 'all the children of the other[15] clans are the children of father's sisters' husbands and Ego can, if he so desires, call them *novonefo* or "my cross-cousin"' (Salisbury, 1956, p. 647).

Now the term *novonefo* is presumably the same as *nofonefo*,[16] which Salisbury shows elsewhere (1962:19) to apply to at least the following: males and females of a male Ego's FZ clan in the same generation as Ego and in the next descending generation, *and* males and females of a male Ego's MB's clan in the same generation as Ego and the next descending generation. MBD is not therefore terminologically distinguished from FZD.[17]

15. Other than mother's clan.

16. Salisbury gives the translation 'cross-cousin' for *novonefo* (1956, p. 647), *nofonefo* (1962, p. 19), and *hovorafo* (1964, p. 169).

17. Although there is an alternate term *komonefo*, which may be applied to FZD but not to MBD. One of the specifications of this term is ZD. Salisbury gives its translation as 'My sister's son'. This is presumably a slip for 'My sister's child'.

It would seem then that the Siane have a category of bilateral cross-cousins from which a man must take a wife. Within the category there are certain prohibited unions; i.e. a man may not marry a cross-cousin of his MB's clan or a cross-cousin who is his actual FZD. This is not prescriptive patrilateral cross-cousin marriage in the sense that I have been using the term in this paper. A Siane man must marry in the category *novonefo*, but this is not a unilateral category in the sense that it may be contrasted with another category of prohibited women on the opposite side. Indeed the whole notion of unilaterality is only meaningful if two sides are contrasted. It is precisely the difficulty of doing this that renders a system of prescriptive patrilateral cross-cousin marriage so anomalous.

I would find it more useful to maintain that the Siane practised a form of bilateral cross-cousin marriage. They have an ideology of symmetric exchanges of women between clans (Salisbury, 1956, pp. 641, 642), they do not distinguish terminologically between the MBD and the FZD, and a man marries into a category which on the evidence Salisbury presents is bilateral rather than unilateral. Salisbury has presumably called this system patrilateral cross-cousin marriage because of a certain asymmetric feature of it. He discovered that there was a tendency for women in Siane country to pass from the south and west towards the north and east, while valuables moved in the opposite direction (1956, p. 646).

This discovery and Salisbury's discussion of it is extremely interesting, but it should not be permitted to confuse the issue of characterizing Siane marriage rules. When we refer to unilateral cross-cousin marriage as an asymmetric system, we are referring to an asymmetry in the rule, not in its social consequences. The consequences are perhaps likely to be asymmetric but they need not necessarily be so. Similarly it is possible for a society to have a symmetric marriage rule and for the application of the rule to result in asymmetry.

If Salisbury, and Livingstone who recently came out in support of his position (1964), wish to call the Siane a system of prescriptive patrilateral cross-cousin marriage, they are of course at liberty to do so. It seems to me that there is no profit in arguing about whether it is or is not. It is more important to understand in what sense Salisbury and Livingstone use the term and the reasons why others might reject their classification.

Prescriptive bilateral cross-cousin marriage

I have tried to show in the preceding section why, in my view, a discussion of prescriptive patrilateral cross-cousin marriage inevitably leads to a discussion of prescriptive bilateral cross-cousin marriage. By corollary with my previous characterizations I would suggest that a working definition of a bilateral prescriptive system is that a man must marry a woman whom he addresses by a relationship term denoting a category of relatives which includes the joint specification MBD/FZD.

The genealogical referent is here more than ever misleading. It may cause little difficulty in the consideration of systems such as those described by Dumont for South India (1957a; 1957b), where patrilineal descent groups enter into affinal relations with each other, predicated on the exchange of women. The relationship terminologies of these societies are of the type known as two-section systems. Ego thus applies the terms for 'own section' (kinsmen) to his own descent group and the terms for 'other section' (affines) to any group related to his own by marriage. Such specifications as MB and FZH therefore fall into a single category, that of male affine of the first ascending generation. Similarly MBD and FZD are subsumed under a single term which denotes female affine of own generation.

The inadequacy of the genealogical definition is brought out more clearly when we consider a society divided into exogamous moieties. Such a society may have a two-section system of relationship terminology, in which case the terms for own section/kinsmen are applied within Ego's moiety and the terms for other section/affines to the opposite moiety. But it need not have a two-section system (Maybury-Lewis, 1960, p. 210; Keesing, 1964, p. 297; Needham, 1964, p. 303). Alternatively it may have an explicitly asymmetrical relationship terminology of the Crow or Omaha type[18] adapted nevertheless to a two-section system.

18. I do not agree with Needham (1964, p. 312, n. 28) that either he or I was mistaken concerning the existence of cases of symmetric alliance with a Crow or Omaha relationship terminology. The instances I cited in my paper (1960, p. 210) seem to me, with the exception of the Eastern Timbira, to be still valid. I discuss the Sherente case in the next paragraph.

The Sherente of Central Brazil are such a society. They had patrilineal exogamous moieties, each subdivided into four patriclans, in conjunction with an Omaha type terminology (Nimuendajú, 1942). I studied them in 1955–6 and 1963 and discovered that the moiety system had fallen into desuetude. The terminology was still used, however, and applied as follows.[19] A male Ego uses one set of terms for members of those clans which would originally have been in his own moiety and another for members of those clans which would have belonged to the opposite moiety. For example, men of Ego's 'own moiety' in the first ascending generation are referred to by a single term, some of the specifications of which are F and FB. There are two terms (distinguishing between those older and younger than Ego) for all members of Ego's generation in Ego's 'own moiety' irrespective of sex. There is another term for all members of Ego's 'own moiety' irrespective of sex in the first descending generation.

In the 'opposite moiety' there must be some distinctions, since the terminology is of the Omaha type. All women of Ego's mother's patriclan are referred to by a single term ($\tilde{\imath}$-natkξ), some of the specifications of which are M, MZ, MBD. All men of the same patriclan are similarly classed together as nõkliekwa, and some of the specifications of that term are MB, MBS. All women of the 'opposite moiety' not in Ego's mother's clan are classed in a single category ($\tilde{\imath}$-tbe) if they are of first ascending generation or in another category (kremzú) if they are of Ego's or the first descending generation.

The rule of marriage was until recently that a man had to marry a kremzú.[20] Sherente would not normally express it that way. They would say instead that they married Wairí or Doí, the names of the moieties. But they will also explain that a man may not marry a girl who is $\tilde{\imath}$-natkξ (from his mother's clan). He must marry a kremzú, which in this context refers to any woman of the opposite moiety not in his mother's clan.

I would not follow Salisbury and call this a system of patrilateral cross-cousin marriage. In a sense it is, in so far as the actual

19. I give the broad outlines of the terminology without discussing its particular features.
20. Sherente say that this is still the rule, but go on to add that nowadays nobody pays any attention to it.

MBD is prohibited and the actual FZD falls into the prescribed category. In fact it gives a poor understanding of the *kremzú* category if we label it as 'patrilateral'. After all, Ego's mother refers to all members of her 'own moiety' in her own generation by a sibling term. Therefore male members of the Ego's 'opposite moiety' not in his mother's clan are classificatory MB as well as FZH. Similarly the specification MBD (in a classificatory sense) is as correct as the specification FZD for the category *kremzú*. Formally, then, the Sherente system could be said to prescribe marriage with a bilateral cross-cousin, although a sector of that category was prohibited.

We encounter similar difficulties when we progress from two-section systems to four and eight-section systems. Here it must be borne in mind that just as there is a difference between a two-section system and a system of exogamous moieties, so a four-section system does not entail marriage rules of the Kariera type, nor an eight-section system rules of the Arunta type. I refer specifically to the Arunta here as an example, not a prototype of an eight-section system.

Spencer and Gillen showed how the eight-section system had the effect of allocating the patrilineal Arunta groups into four categories (1927, p. 64). The model of the system thus required four categories, but each category actually embraced a number of local groups (there were seventy-three in all). This analysis is an important early demonstration, for which Spencer and Gillen are not often given credit nowadays, of an issue which has been taken up by other writers (e.g. Lévi-Strauss, 1949; Leach, 1951; Romney and Epling, 1958) and which is fundamental to the understanding of prescriptive marriage systems.

Seen from the point of view of a male Arunta these four categories may be distinguished as follows. Category 1 included his own local group, and the men in these groups were addressed by terms which included such specifications as F, B, S. Category 2 were groups unlike his own (defined by membership in different marriage-sections) but nevertheless of his own moiety. The men in them were addressed by terms which included such specifications as MMB, MMBS. Ego might not marry into either of these. Category 3 included groups of the opposite moiety, and the men in them were addressed by terms which included such specifications as MB/FZH and MBS/FZS. Yet Ego could not marry women of these groups, which included his actual MBD/FZD and other girls classified as such. He had instead to marry a girl of category 4 whom he addressed by a term, one of the specifications of which was MMBDD.

Lévi-Strauss has amply demonstrated that such a system was a development of a Kariera type four-section system where the bilateral cross-cousin category was further subdivided and marriage permitted with only half of its incumbents (1949, pp. 210–15). Yet according to our working definition of prescriptive bilateral cross-cousin marriage, the prescribed spouse must fall in the same category as the MBZ/FZD. Are we then to argue that a two-section system and a Kariera type four-section system may be classed as bilateral cross-cousin marriage, but an Arunta type eight-section system may not? This would be a *reductio ad absurdum*. Indeed the point of my argument is that if we perpetually orient our discussions of prescriptive marriage systems by means of genealogical referents, then sooner or later we are led to absurdities.

Conclusions

Let me therefore try and rephrase my conclusions without genealogical specifications. It is characteristic of prescriptive marriage systems that they prescribe marriage for a given Ego within a certain relationship category. All marriages which take place in such societies are therefore treated as being marriages within the prescribed category. There are two main varieties of such systems. The first, which I call symmetric alliance, divides Ego's conceptual universe into two parts. There are groups like Ego's and groups unlike Ego's. In a system of exogamous moieties there may be only one group like Ego's and one unlike Ego's, but this is not essential. Ego's wife must be classed in a certain category of the 'unlike' part of this dyadic model. Such a model can be described in terms of exchange between these two types of groups.

The second variety of prescriptive marriage system is the one I call, following Needham, asymmetric alliance. In such a system Ego's conceptual universe is divided into three parts. There are groups like Ego's and two classes of group unlike Ego's. These two 'unlike' classes are defined in terms of each other as opposites.

Ego's wife must be subsumed under a certain category of one 'unlike' class in the model. Let us call that class U_1. Let the other 'unlike' class be U_2. If the descent groups in this society are patrilineal, then certain marriages, either Ego's or that of previous men in his group, will bring certain other groups into a U_1 relationship with Ego's group. Ego's group will be U_2 to such other groups. Such a model may be described in terms of a unilateral passage of women from U_1 groups to groups like Ego's to U_2 groups.

This is in fact what writers have meant when they wrote of the radical distinction between wife-givers (U_1) and wife-takers (U_2), and argued that it was only in terms of this distinction that asymmetric alliance systems could be understood. I have tried to show that it is only in terms of this distinction that such systems can even be properly described. Much of the argument concerning 'prescriptive marriage systems' thus derives from the fact that different writers have understood 'cross-cousin marriage systems' to mean different things. The formulation proposed here derives from the work of Lévi-Strauss, Leach, Dumont and Needham. I am not suggesting that it should be universally adopted or even that it is the only way of tackling the problems which I have raised. I hope only that this statement of it is sufficiently explicit for the approach to be understood even by those who have no wish to use it.

It can be seen why there must be a distinction maintained between prescriptive and preferential marriage systems. A prescriptive marriage rule entails the social consequences already mentioned: the division of Ego's conceptual universe in a determined fashion, irrespective of the percentage of people who marry their actual MBD or into their MB's descent group.[21] These percentages may be of considerable interest in the handling of certain problems. They do not affect the prescription as here defined or its minimum social entailments.

On the other hand a preference for marriage with a certain relative, however defined, does not have such entailments. Here the percentages of people who actually marry according to the preference are more significant. A stated preference which is

21. It was partly a failure to appreciate this point which led Ackerman to his erroneous analysis of the Purum material (1964).

rarely acted upon is unlikely to produce social alignments predicated upon a 100 per cent compliance with it. The extent to which a preference for a certain type of marriage will influence the institutions of a society thus depends in large measure on the number of people who marry according to it. Nor is the argument that a society may order its institutions as if there were 100 per cent compliance with a marriage preference acceptable. Such a preference would be a prescription in terms of my definition. I suppose there must be a theoretical limiting case where a society may be said, for example, to prefer marriage with a woman of MB's clan and where 100 per cent of all marriages conformed to this preference. The institutions of that society might then be congruent with this fact, and it would be a nice point as to whether it was a case of preferential or prescriptive marriage. I would still argue that it would be preferential, on the grounds that a sudden change in people's marrying habits would presumably alter any institutional alignments based on statistical trends, whereas in a prescriptive system this would be irrelevant.

One final problem remains to be dealt with: the problem of 'choice'. Needham has written that if a system is prescriptive '... the emphasis is on the very lack of choice; the category of type of person to be married is precisely determined, and this marriage is obligatory' (1962, p. 9). Schneider has recently taken him to task, for using the word 'choice' in this context and from his use of the word has derived an argument which purports to show that prescriptive systems cannot be distinguished in this way from preferential ones. Now the word 'choice' may or may not be a good one to use here, yet it seems to me that Needham's meaning is quite clear. He does *not* mean that in a prescriptive marriage system Ego is told which individual to marry, but, as he says, that the category of person to be married is precisely determined. Schneider notes, as we have done, that this category cannot be determined by genealogical referents (1965, pp. 65-6) and thus poses the problem with which this paper has attempted to deal: i.e., how then *is* the prescribed category determined? In other words, what are the characteristics of a prescriptive marriage system?

Schneider concludes that the gloss for this category has to be 'marriageable woman'. He then asks how such a category could be defined in terms of choice or lack of it. After all, the opposite of 'marriageable woman' is 'unmarriageable woman'. He continues:

> Can we say that a prescriptive system is one in which ego is obliged to marry a woman whom he is permitted to marry and a preferential system one in which ego is permitted to marry a woman who is prohibited? This seems sheer nonsense, but it is to such sheer nonsense that one is led if one starts with a structural problem and tries to define it in terms of individual action (Needham, 1962) on a choice versus no choice basis (Schneider, 1965, p. 66).

It seems to me that this argument is fallacious on a number of counts. In the first place, as Schneider himself points out, every known system prescribes marriage with a marriageable woman. His gloss which purports to characterize prescriptive marriage systems is thus vacuous. To argue that prescriptive marriage systems cannot be distinguished on the basis of it is to knock down a straw man. In fact Needham's formulation does not lead to such a characterization. It could be taken as a statement of my contention in this paper that the distinction between a prescriptive and preferential marriage system is that in the former all marriages are treated as being of the prescribed category whereas in the latter not all marriages are treated as being of the preferred category.

It seems to me that these propositions may be phrased in terms of individual action if the phraser feels there is any advantage to be gained by so doing. Unlike Schneider I do not feel that the level of structural statements and the level of individual actions are mutually exclusive. On the contrary, I would argue that structural propositions are intimately linked with propositions about individual actions and if so desired may be expressed in terms of them. I do not feel that Needham's formulation is the most felicitous one, but I do not feel either that it leads to the sort of tautology which Schneider suggests. It is clear that in prescriptive marriage systems there is only one type of marriage by definition. In preferential marriage systems there are a number of possibilities. We may argue about how best to describe this state of affairs, but a repudiation of the word 'choice' cannot be made into a grounds for assuming that there is no valid distinction to be made or that Needham had not made it.

The implications of these arguments transcend what Murphy described – I hope and assume humorously – as 'whether one can be (or should be) forced to marry his patrilateral cross-cousin' (1963, p. 18). As Schneider indicated (1965), there are fundamental theoretical and methodological issues at stake. For example, the approach to the study of prescriptive marriage systems outlined here lays great emphasis on understanding through the analysis of social rules. It can be claimed, and the contention is implicit in many of the arguments which have been advanced against this approach, that such an emphasis is unwarranted and that an investigation along behaviourist lines would yield better results. Similarly we have seen that at least two radically different types of enquiry, which I have dubbed respectively as *emic* and *etic*, have been undertaken by students of prescriptive marriage systems. Much of the controversy which has surrounded the interpretation of these systems stems from the fact that the implications of this difference do not appear to have been fully appreciated. Here are two central issues in anthropology which have been brought out in the debate over prescriptive marriage systems and for which indeed the debate is perhaps a crucial instance.

Furthermore the discussions have resulted in a substantial rethinking of the function of anthropological terminology. Concepts such as *social structure*, *descent* and *alliance* are being continually revised or at least re-argued in the light of the work which Lévi-Strauss, Leach, Dumont and Needham have been doing. This is not 'merely' a matter of definition. The actual terms used are in a sense immaterial. It is the assumptions which lead to this or that use of them which have been called into question, the theoretical biases of the terminology which are being explored. In fact the whole question of models in social anthropology is really being debated, their use, their implications and whether and under what circumstances they have the explanatory power which Braithwaite indicated as a property of scientific models (1953, p. 108). The crux of the matter is the nature of explanation in social anthropology or, in other words, the nature of the subject itself, for a discipline is characterized by the sorts of questions it asks and the sorts of answers it is prepared to accept. It seems to me that these issues are broad enough, and I am therefore frequently surprised to learn that some anthropologists consider the debate concerning the analysis of prescriptive marriage systems to be a dispute over narrow technicalities. To paraphrase Dr Johnson, a man who is tired of issues such as these is tired of social anthropology.

References

ACKERMAN, C. (1964), 'Structure and Statistics: the Purum case', *Amer. Anthropol.* vol. 66, pp. 53–6.

BRAITHWAITE, R. B. (1953), *Scientific Explanation*, Cambridge University Press.

COULT, A. D. (1962a), 'The determinants of differential cross-cousin marriage', *Man*, vol. 62, art. 47.

COULT, A. D. (1962b), 'An analysis of Needham's critique of the Homans and Schneider theory', *Southwestern J. Anthropol.*, vol. 18, pp. 317–35.

COULT, A. D. (1963), 'The determinants of differential cross-cousin marriage', (letter), *Man*, vol. 63, art. 199.

DUMONT, L. (1953), 'The Dravidian kinship terminology as an expression of marriage', *Man*, vol. 53, art. 54.

DUMONT, L. (1957a), *Hierarchy and Marriage Alliance in South Indian Kinship*, Occ. Papers: roy. anthropol. Inst., no. 12.

DUMONT, L. (1957b), *Une Sous-caste de l'Inde du Sud: Organisation Sociale et Religion des Pramalai Kallar*, Mouton.

HAMMEL, E. A. (1960), 'Some models for the analysis of marriage-section systems', *Oceania*, vol. 31, pp. 14–30.

HOMANS, G. C., and SCHNEIDER, D. M. (1955), *Marriage, Authority and Final Causes*, Free Press.

KEESING, R. (1964), 'Mota kinship terminology and marriage: a re-examination', *J. Polynesian Soc.* vol. 73, pp. 294–301.

LANE, R. B. (1962), 'Patrilateral cross-cousin marriage: structural analysis and ethnographic cases', *Ethnol.*, vol. 1, pp. 467–99.

LEACH, E. R. (1951), 'The structural implications of matrilateral cross-cousin marriage', *J. roy. anthropol. Inst.*, vol. 81, pp. 23–55.

LEACH, E. R. (1954), *Political Systems of Highland Burma*, Bell & Sons.

LEACH, E. R. (1963), 'The determinants of differential cross-cousin marriage', (letter), *Man*, vol. 63, art. 87.

LÉVI-STRAUSS, C. (1949), *Les Structures Élémentaires de la Parenté*, Presses Universitaires de France.

LIVINGSTONE, F. B. (1959), 'A formal analysis of prescriptive marriage systems among the Australian aborigines', *Southwestern J. Anthropol.*, vol. 15, 361–72.

LIVINGSTONE, F. B. (1964), 'Prescriptive patrilateral cross-cousin marriage', (letter), *Man*, vol. 64, art. 59.

LÖFFLER, L. G. (1964), 'Prescriptive matrilateral cross-cousin marriage in asymmetric alliance systems: a fallacy', *Southwestern J. Anthropol.*, vol. 20, pp. 218–27.

MAYBURY-LEWIS, D. (1960), 'Parallel descent and the Apinayé anomaly', *Southwestern J. Anthropol.*, vol. 16, pp. 191–216.

MAYBURY-LEWIS, D., 'Relationship systems', n.d.

MURDOCK, G. P. (1957), 'World ethnographic sample', *Amer. Anthropol.*, vol. 59, pp. 664–87.

MURPHY, R. F. (1963), 'On Zen Marxism: filiation and alliance', *Man*, vol. 63, art. 21.

NEEDHAM, R. (1958a), 'A structural analysis of Purum society', *Amer. Anthropol.*, vol. 60, pp. 75–101.

NEEDHAM, R. (1958b), 'The formal analysis of prescriptive patrilateral cross-cousin marriage', *Southwestern J. Anthropol.* vol. 14, pp. 199–219.

NEEDHAM, R. (1960), 'Structure and change in asymmetric alliance: comments on Livingstone's further analysis of Purum society', *Amer. Anthropol.*. vol. 62, pp. 499–503.

NEEDHAM, R. (1961), 'An analytical note on the structure of Sirionó society', *Southwestern J. Anthropol.*, vol. 17, pp. 231–55.

NEEDHAM, R. (1962), *Stucture and Sentiment*, University of Chicago Press.

NEEDHAM, R. (1963a), 'Some disputed points in the study of prescriptive alliance', *Southwestern J. Anthropol.*, vol. 19, pp. 186–207.

NEEDHAM, R. (1963b), 'Prescriptive alliance and the Pende', (letter), *Man*, vol. 63, art. 62.

NEEDHAM, R. (1964), 'The Mota problem and its lessons', *J. Polynesian Soc.*, vol. 73, pp. 302–13.

NIMUENDAJÚ, C. (1942), *The Šerente*, Frederick Webb Hodge Anniversary Publication, no. 4.

RIVERS, W. H. R. (1914), *Kinship and Social Organization*, Constable.

ROMNEY, A. K., and EPLING, P. J. (1958), 'A simplified model of Kariera kinship', *Amer. Anthropol.*, vol. 60, pp. 59–74.

SALISBURY, R. F. (1956), 'Asymmetrical marriage systems', *Amer. Anthropol.*, vol. 58, pp. 639–55.

SALISBURY, R. F. (1962), *From Stone to Steel*, Melbourne University Press.

SALISBURY, R. F. (1964), 'New Guinea highland models and descent theory', *Man*, vol. 64, art. 213.

SCHNEIDER, D. M. (1965), 'Some muddles in the models, or how the system really works', in M. Banton (ed.), *The Relevance of Models for Social Anthropology*, Association of Social Anthropologists Monographs, no. 1, pp. 25–79.

SPENCER, B. and GILLEN, F. J. (1927), *The Arunta*, Macmillan.

DE SOUSBERGHE, L. (1953), *Structures de Parenté et d'Alliance d'après les Formules Pende*. Mémoires, Académie Royale des Sciences Coloniales: Classe des Sciences Morales et Politiques, vol. 4, no. 1.

VAN WOUDEN, F. A. E. (1935), *Sociale Structuurtypen in de Groote Oost*, J. Ginsberg.

Part Eight Divorce and Marriage Stability

The study of divorce has been important in kinship studies, firstly because of its bearing on the position of women and the nature of the kin groups to which they belong (or between which they are exchanged) and, secondly, because increasing divorce has sometimes been taken as an index of the effects of social change. The direction of recent studies of divorce in pre-industrial societies has been set by Gluckman's comparison of the Lozi of Zambia and the Zulu of South Africa. In Reading 15 he shows the link between frequent divorce and the bilateral kin groups of the Lozi, and rare divorce and the 'strong' patrilineal descent groups of the Zulu. His work has been elaborated and criticized by subsequent writers. Mitchell developed the argument in his study of divorce in the changing situation of urban Africa, where he points to the new types of conjugal union now emerging (Reading 16).

15 M. Gluckman

Marriage Payments and Social Structure among the Lozi and Zulu

Excerpt from M. Gluckman, 'Kinship and marriage among the Lozi of Northern Rhodesia and the Zulu of Natal', in A. R. Radcliffe-Brown and D. Forde (eds.), *African Systems of Kinship and Marriage*, Oxford University Press for the International African Institute, 1950, pp. 166–203. Revised for this edition by the author with a *Postscript*.

The evidence from the Lozi and Zulu indicates that we may have to distinguish different types of marriage payments. There are several aspects of marriage. It breaks or modifies certain existing social relationships and creates new social relationships: the union of a man and his wife, and an alliance between the kinsfolk of the two spouses. It unites men and women to produce children to occupy specific positions in the kinship system, since normally it is through the marriage of their parents that children acquire their kinsfolk on both sides. But clearly the structure of the kinship system primarily determines the consequences of marriage in the affiliation of children and therefore the attributes of the marriage payment.

Marriage in most societies transfers to the husband a certain common minimum of rights: almost always an exclusive right to the wife's sexual services, or to the lending of them, certain powers over her person, rights to the produce of her economic activity balanced by economic obligations to her, and a prima facie right to be pater to her children. The extent and duration of these rights varies greatly. We have seen that Lozi marriage payment is low, considering their wealth in cattle, and that even then it dates from a recent enactment. It does not transfer the woman's fertility altogether to her husband, let alone to her husband's kindred. Comparative data show that in general marriage payments fall with the decreasing dominance of patrilineal descent until very little is given in purely matrilineal societies. In Central Africa a son-in-law may give some years of service, but it is in uxorilocal marriage. The matrilineal Ovambo are rich cattle-owners, but a husband gives for his wife only a present to her mother, and it is killed for the wedding feast. That is, when children are not dominantly joined to the husband's line he tends to give but little for his wife, whose economic and sexual services alone are transferred to him. In almost every African tribe he does give something to get these rights and prima facie rights in relation to her children. On the other hand, in patrilineal societies of the Zulu type the marriage payment permanently transfers the woman's procreative capacity to her husband's lineage. Therefore, relative to the society's wealth, the payment tends to be large.

I suggest that it may no longer be wise to name the common institution of transferring goods by a single term (marriage payment, bridewealth, bride-price). This leads to disputes about whether the attributes ascribed to it, e.g. by Evans-Pritchard in East Africa, apply to the transfer of goods among the Yakö or Lozi or some other tribe. The Lozi institution, on the surface a similar transfer of property, is not the Nuer or the Zulu institution when we come to examine their structural relations. For the common element, the rights transferred in all societies, we may follow Radcliffe-Brown's use of the term marriage payment, but it may be necessary to distinguish at least marriage payment Type A, Type B, etc. I have analysed two types, and there are likely to be more. Certainly my crude categories will not cover every variation, and further analysis requires to be done in many tribes.

I consider that the data we have indicate that the basis of the variation in the complexes is probably the different affiliation of the children. Zulu society is chiefly distinguished from Lozi by its structure of unilineal agnatic groups, which are exogamous, and which are associated with a marriage rule by which the giving of cattle to a woman's father transfers her fertility for all her lifetime to the agnatic group of her husband, who may indeed have been dead before she was married to his name, or who may be a woman or an impotent man. If the wife goes off in adultery, the children are her husband's; if he dies, she continues to bear for him; if she is barren, or dies before bearing, a younger sister should replace her. The outstanding fact is the extreme endurance of the husband's rights and their passing on his death to his agnatic heirs. Legal marriage and the domestic unit it establishes are thus very stable, though there may be frequent adultery. The legal emphasis is the same among the Nuer, even though they have frequent changes in the constitution of households. Marriage is stable in that wherever the woman is her husband accompanies her, even after his death, to be pater of her children, for whoever their genitors are, they belong to the man or group which gave cattle for her. The husband or his heirs may let his wife go and not reclaim the marriage payment, since they get the children even though they lose her other services as wife. In these tribes marriage payment thus binds the woman's reproductive capacity to the perpetuation of the extended agnatic lineage. Each such group loses its daughters, but insists on its rights to the fertility of its daughters-in-law.

Moreover, rights of inheritance vest in children exclusively from the agnatic lineage of their pater. They have no rights in their mother's family unless they are unredeemed illegitimate children, when they rank as if they were members of her agnatic lineage. Therefore economic and other interests pull the children almost entirely to the home of their pater and his agnatic lineage.

The Lozi have no extended unilineal kin groups. Among them the corporate groups which endure in time are the cognates in family villages or in sections of a royal village, based on the mounds which dot the plain and which are centres of surrounding gardens, fishing-sites and pastures. Lozi's relatives in the patrilateral and matrilateral lines may be scattered at many places far over the surface of the great flood-plain. Because their productive activities are varied, and many fall in distant places in the same month, they require cooperation and help from many people. Kinship provides the framework for getting this help, but since neighbours in the various parts where they have economic resources are linked to them by patrilineal, matrilineal and mixed ties, they emphasize relationship in all of their lines of descent. For them it is not important to fix an individual's relationship to a single line, but to emphasize his links with many lines; therefore marriage does not tie a woman's procreative power to one line. She produces for many lines. Among the Zulu economic and other interests coincide with the pull of agnatic lineage ties; among the Lozi, with their limited resources centred in restricted dwelling-mounds, economic interests may pull a man to settle with his mother's kindred, in either of her lines of descent. As a woman's productive capacity is not tied to a single lineage group, the child goes to its genitor, not to the legal husband of the woman. This removes the main buttress of marriage; since the children can shift their allegiance and emphasize that relationship which most pleases or profits them, the family as a whole is an unstable association. I am not here referring only to the instability of households: this is also marked among the Nuer, but among them lineage ties always draw the family together about the woman's husband. Among the Lozi, too, a large proportion of children grow up elsewhere as foster children and not in the villages where they will ultimately settle. There is no dominant pressure of interests and law to induce them to return to their father's home, though most do. They may go to the home of any of their near ancestors. Adulterers can claim their children, and adultery is very frequent. Men divorce their wives easily and at personal will; women are always straining to be released. Marriage, as well as domestic association, is unstable. I have suggested that the reason for this is to be sought in Lozi kinship structure, which is of a pattern common in Central Africa, but which here is directly related to their modes of production and settlement in their physical environment.

We see then that in these societies the types of marriage and the forms of the family, with inheritance of property, rights of children in father's and mother's lines and the rights of these lines to claim them, laws of betrothal, destination of widows, rates of divorce, status of wives in their husband's homes, are all consistent with certain types of kinship system. In some societies the household group which is usually designated as the family may be unstable. The structural stability of the society rests in the extended kinship lines, one of which may be the nuclear framework on which local communities are organized as corporate groups. These reach back into the history of the tribe through all changes of personnel, while the domestic family itself is always an ephemeral, and often an unstable, association.[1]

I have presented my argument more strongly than I myself feel is justified at present, in order to make clear the type of data and analysis I consider likely to be most fruitful. I should have preferred to do further comparative research before publishing it, had it not been for the opportunity of presenting it in this symposium. I am fully aware of the difficulties of establishing the validity of the hypothesis, but even if it is wrong it may be useful. Some of the

1. See references on p. 166, n.1 of my original article, especially Evans-Pritchard (1938, pp. 64–5).

difficulties are inherent in sociological analysis, since in this there are always complicating variables. Others arise from the vague and embracing use of categories and concepts (of which I too am guilty) such as patrilineal, lineage, marriage, divorce, etc. When is a marriage complete, and when can we class the separation of a cohabiting couple as divorce?[2] Are the Bena patrilineal and the Ila matrilineal, and have they lineages? The literature is generally confused and imprecise, and the posing of problems may help to clarify descriptions.

I am myself uncertain whether it is the stability of people's attachment to specific areas, or patriliny or father-right itself, or the agnatic lineage, or all of these together, which, whatever the other variables are, tend to be associated with a strong marriage tie. That any or all of these are significant seems definite to me. Evans-Pritchard has stated that the Azande, organized on father-right but without the agnatic lineage, had rare divorce in the past. He has not reported on the problem fully, but it might be that the State power prevented women from leaving their husbands if they wanted to, i.e. there was instituted authority to compel them to remain in marriage. When that authority was restricted by British occupation divorce became rife.[3] On the other hand, despite European support for women against men in Zululand, something there, I suggest the agnatic lineage, has maintained the stability of marriage; while in Loziland the marriage tie has become looser and looser, even though tribal ethics approve of firm unions, while not condemning divorce. However, as we have seen, the code of the Zulu age-set regiments, backed by the State, punished severely unchastity and infidelity: perhaps

2. For example, on the difficulty of establishing when there is a marriage and when divorce, see Richards (1940). It is difficult to tell what Fortes means by divorce (1937). He speaks of a high divorce rate but divorce from a 'proper' marriage is obviously a most serious ritual and social step (Fortes, 1945). In Dahomey (Herskovits, 1938) the divorce rate varies according to which of the thirteen types of marriage is contracted, but it seems to vary according to my postulate. Bohannan (1949) appears to confirm the assessment in my essay.

3. I would now (1971) stress that at the time when Evans-Pritchard studied the Azande of the Anglo-Egyptian Sudan they had been moved out of their indigenous pattern of settlement and made to live in different kinds of neighbourly relationships along watersheds to escape sleeping-sickness.

these codes are still the main sanctions on marriage despite all structural changes. Yet the ban on prenuptial conception does not seem to have retained similar force. Illegitimate births are frequent while divorces are rare. According to old records and modern field-workers this seems to be the position among all Southern Bantu tribes who had tribal initiation into age-regiments (Kuper, 1947; Read, 1938; Casalis, 1859, pp. 231–2; Ellenberger and Macgregor, 1912, p. 273; Ashton, 1952; Harries, 1929, p. 36; Stayt, 1931, p. 152; Schapera, 1940, p. 294), save for the Thonga of Portuguese East Africa. In his book Junod (1927) implies that divorce is frequent, though this seems to contradict an earlier article on another group of Thonga, and Clerc states explicitly of the related Ronga that divorce is impossible once the wife has borne a child: 'she is forever bound to her husband's village' (1938, p. 89) (see also Junod, 1905, pp. 258–9; Harries, 1929).

Postscript, January 1971

The above attempt to correlate the contrasting patterns of marriage among the Lozi and the Zulu, and to relate these to other institutions, in the background of a wider comparative summary for other peoples, was written in 1947 and published in 1950. One of the hypotheses I advanced, at least, inspired much further research and both supporting and critical argument.[1] It is clear that that part of my argument which attempted to relate rates of divorce to the kinship structure, requires now, not surprisingly, twenty-four years after it was written, both clarification and emendation. But parts of the core of my analysis still stand; and in presenting a summary statement of my views in the light of over two decades of later research, I emphasize the mode in which I first formulated the hypotheses in order to eliminate what has been considerable misunderstanding of my argument. I do so to make clear on what lines I think future research might profitably proceed.

The section reproduced in this book of Readings is the final summary of an argument contrasting the patterns of marriage rules among the Lozi and the Zulu, supplemented for the Zulu by the very similar pattern among the Nuer far, to the north, as

1. I cite in the text of the original essay and in footnotes, earlier statements of parts of the hypothesis.

reported by Evans-Pritchard. I had studied the Zulu before studying the Lozi: and immediately I began work among the Lozi I was almost bewildered by the 'instability' of their marital associations, with very frequent divorce, either at the will of the husband or by suit in court of the wife on many grounds, when compared with the Zulu, among whom I did not record a single divorce. The historical records and the genealogies I collected showed that the Zulu had always had at most a very low rate of divorce, while similar sources of information on the Lozi showed that divorce had always been frequent among them. Hence it seemed to me that, following the arguments advanced by Durkheim about suicide, marriage and birth rates, these widely contrasting rates of divorce would have to be accounted for by reference to their respective social *milieux*, and that they could not be accounted for by the circumstances leading to the break-up of each individual marriage. Moreover, I judged that within the general pattern of high specialization and segregation of sexual and conjugal roles, which marks subsistence or tribal societies,[2] the relationships between Zulu and Lozi spouses respectively were not sufficiently different to account for the very great difference in divorce rates. I stress this point because D. M. Schneider pointed out in a comment on work on this theme that 'instability' of marriage can refer to several different types of phenomena, and I had thought I had made it clear that I was speaking of the breaking up of marriage as a legal or jural relationship.

As stated in the summary section reproduced above, I was at work on a full comparative study of the problem, centring on the Lozi and the Zulu, but covering data on all the peoples reported on in books and articles available to me in Livingstone and Johannesburg, when the invitation to participate in the symposium on *African Systems of Kinship and Marriage* (published eventually in 1950) led me to present an abstract of my analysis in a preliminary essay. As my researches in the ethnographic literature, as well as my own attempt to formulate hypotheses, had shown me how

2. See Gluckman (1955, ch. 3). For an account of this high segregation of roles in at least enclaves in industrial society, and a most illuminating hypothesis on factors leading to high segregation of conjugal roles, see Bott (1971), in which she discusses later work on her hypothesis (1957); and I comment on it in my 'Preface' to this edition.

imprecise were many of the statements on the rate of divorce, and how unclear were reports on whether a widow remained married under the true levirate to her dead husband while cohabiting with one of his kinsmen, or was married by his kinsman in a new marital union, and so forth, I suspended work on the fuller comparison. This I did in the hope that my strong statement of the general hypothesis set out above might encourage research which would produce better data on the whole problem of divorce rates in tribal societies, as well as on the other institutions associated with marriage, and lead to the formulating of hypotheses with firmer foundations. In this respect my essay has been very fruitful.

A comparison of Zulu and Lozi, with no divorces and with a large number respectively, was effective, as would be a testing of a new fertilizer producing radical improvements in yields on two pieces of ground, and not on a checkerboard of plots. But clearly for more refined work and for the comparing of divorce rates in different societies, it is essential to have more refined measurements. My essay immediately drew from my colleague, J. A. Barnes, suggestions for measuring divorce rates in tribal societies which he later refined (Barnes, 1949; 1967). Many of the problems discussed by Barnes arise from sampling difficulties. Others are caused by the fact that any still extant marriage may be terminated either by divorce or by death of a spouse; and so forth. All I have space to bring out here is that Barnes stressed the importance of trying to investigate at what points in its life a marriage in a particular society is most likely to break up, and he proposed that the best way of presenting the rates of divorce is in the form of life-tables of predictions of the chances of marriages surviving or not. Clearly in the end this type of analysis is crucial. For example, we are told that among the patrilineal Tallensi marriages are at high risk in their first year, and thereafter are likely to survive. On the other hand in many matrilineal, and in some bilateral, societies, a woman after living with a husband (or series of husbands) after her menopause may leave the husband to live with her brother, with whom her children, particularly her sons, may have settled. This is, for example, well described by Esther Goody for the Gonja of Ghana, whose marital institutions are very similar to those of the Lozi, where divorce may occur at any time during the marriage (Goody, 1962)[3]. Thus, obviously, a full study would have to take into account the variable points at which divorce is likely to occur. Some studies have followed Barnes's formulae, but on the whole we have still to discuss divorce rates stated in general terms.

Later work has concentrated on the problem of divorce rates and not on the very general difference between Zulu-type and Lozi-type rules of marriages, in terms of which I formulated my whole hypothesis. I consider that failure to deal with the whole hypothesis has led to certain major logical errors in hypotheses formulated by most of my commentators. We may anticipate that my argument could be wrong or right in a certain progression:

1. It may be right in its main outlines, but I may have formulated it incorrectly (I believe I did).

2. It may be that either I, or my commentators, have confused the internal consistency of marriage rules within a pattern, by explaining the occurrence of a pattern by one of the rules logically contained therein, and not by an independent principle having explanatory power. (I consider this is what Ackerman (1963), Fallers (1957) and Leach (1957), cited later, have done, and what I myself to some extent did.)

3. It may be that the stability of marriage, including a low divorce rate, as against instability including a high divorce rate, are related to some external variable, quite different from the one on which I laid emphasis.

4. It may be that the stability of marriage and rate of divorce are controlled by so many variables that we shall never work out interconnections, or the varying stability may be quite haphazard: this conclusion we can only accept at the end of a considerable amount of research, since accepting it now would entail ceasing inquiry.

5. It may be that when we apply hypotheses to a range of societies the hypotheses will cover most, but not all. Then we have to look for special variables in the exceptional cases; for as Durkheim said, '... to invalidate the proof, it is not sufficient to show that it is contradicted by a few particular applications of the method of

---

3. Since the Gonja are so distant from the Lozi, and yet their marriage rules are so similar, it is a pity that Goody did not refer to this general similarity or point up certain differences in her article. I lack space to do so.

agreement or difference ... certainly we must not abandon hastily the results of a methodically conducted demonstration' (1938, p. 131).

Bearing these considerations in mind, what I demonstrated was that there was a clear internal consistency between the patterns of rules of marriage of Zulu-type societies, and Lozi-type bilateral (or better, omnilateral) societies and matrilineal societies, of the form shown in Table 1.

Table 1

Zulu	Lozi
Very rare divorce	Frequent divorce
Marriage endures beyond death of spouse, in true levirate,[a] or sororate (deceased still married to relict, but pro-husband or pro-wife)	No endurance of marriage beyond death
Marriage contractable by dead man, or by woman to woman, or by group to woman	No such marriage contractable
Sororal polygyny encouraged	Marriage to near kin of spouse forbidden
Adulterine children to wife's husband	Adulterine children to their genitor
If goods available, high marriage payment	Even if goods available, high marriage payment is unusual

[a] Levirate: the institution by which a widow continues to produce children to her dead husband.

The work done since my comparison was published, either in new ethnographic studies, or arising from comparative studies of records not available to me, shows that my preliminary data were inadequate when they indicated to me a general correlation of patriliny itself, or what I tentatively called father-right, with stable marriage, levirate, low divorce rate, etc., and of the opposite situation with bilateral or omnilateral, and matrilineal societies. I know of only a few reports on matrilineal societies with very stable marriages, and I think in all of these special variables can be found to account for what is clearly an exceptional situation statistically (but see Jacobson, 1967). This is confirmed by Ackerman's conclusion, from a survey of more than 150 societies in the Human Relations Area Files, that '... in matrilineal societies marital instability is widespread ...' (1963, p. 19).

But the later work clearly shows that there are two very different types both of patrilineal societies and of bilateral societies, i.e. as against my straightforward formulation, there are some patrilineal societies which have a highish rate of divorce (Mitchell, 1963), and some bilateral societies with a low rate of divorce (and associated institutions). I begin my discussion of explanations advanced to explain these differences with the last, the two types of bilateral societies. The thesis I start with is that advanced by Ackerman (1963).

Ackerman made a laudable attempt to go beyond my own modest effort to explain patterns of marriage in tribal societies alone: he set out to try to bring together the work on tribal marriage with work done on the occurrence of particular divorces in modern American societies. The general thesis on which he bases his analysis is that it has been shown in America that the crucially important factors in determining whether or not a marriage will survive or break up are: (a) homogeneity or heterogeneity in the background and interests of the spouses; (b) homogeneity or heterogeneity in the network of affective affiliations surrounding the married pair; and (c) how far a family shares traits with the families of close friends. Wherever these are positive, they tend to stabilize marriage. Ackerman sums up:

... it is clear that when the affiliations of both spouses are *conjunctive*, that is, overlapping or identical, the behaviour and expectations of both spouses are affected by the same norm or value sets. The affiliations of the spouses can, on the other hand, be *disjunctive*: that is, each spouse may maintain membership in different collectivities. In such a situation, the behaviour and expectations of the spouses are affected by different norms and value sets.[4]

4. In terms of Bott's hypothesis (1971) referred to on p. 231, what she calls a close-knit network around the family – particularly where the networks of the two spouses overlap – tends to be associated with high segregation of conjugal roles; and this situation according to the works cited by Ackerman should produce stability in marriage. The two sets of findings require to be brought together: unfortunately I have not space in this Postcript to attempt it. Ackerman does not cite Bott's hypothesis, which was first published in 1954.

To test whether these findings could be applied *in general terms* to tribal societies (since there is no information on the situation of particular marriages in tribal societies), Ackerman selected some 150 tribes. For those like the Lozi, who are bilateral (i.e. where succession and inheritance can pass in any line of descent), he examined whether people could or could not marry close relatives; and he found indeed *statistically* that where there could be marriage between close relatives, the divorce rate tended to be described as low, but where such marriages were prohibited (as among the Lozi), the divorce rate was described as high. Hence he argued that 'as the network of conjunctive affiliations "tightens" around the spouses, marital stability increases'.[5]

Unfortunately other work has prevented me looking into the structure of the two types of bilateral societies, classified in terms of whether they have or have not stable marriage. But what we can say is that Ackerman's findings demonstrate that under my logical possibility (2) (p. 235), there are two types of marriage patterns in bilateral *milieux*: where persons marry close relatives, the divorce rate is low; where, as among the Lozi, such marriages are prohibited, the divorce rate is high. Ackerman might have cited here from my own article, that if two young Lozi who are related insist on marrying against their elders' wishes, the latter curse the marriage: 'You have chosen to marry, only death may now divorce you; you may not separate from each other' (p. 173 of my original article). I argued that these marriages were cursed in this way because they began to weave new ties of kinship and affinity in a neighbourhood, or between previously distantly related people, and hence such marriages were full of important social implications.

Unhappily Ackerman found that for the societies recognizing one main line of descent, there was 'no association ... between the assessed divorce rate and any kind or combination of kinds of endogamy in lineal societies'. But he suggests that if we go below the surface, we would find that the endogamous lineal community is not strictly analogous to the endogamous bilateral community, since organization on a unilineal basis introduces a new criterion of conjunctive affiliations. He postulates two mechanisms: (a)

5. For lack of space Ackerman's argument has to be stated in very bare terms.

the affiliations of each spouse may be extended to include those of the other; and (b) the prior affiliations of one spouse may be severed and she/he may be incorporated into those of the other. He then tests this by taking the levirate and he finds that 'the levirate is a sufficient condition for a low divorce rate' (p. 18). But in my formulation both the levirate and a low divorce rate were aspects of durable marriage: they are not, in my opinion, independent variables, and hence one cannot be the cause of the other. They show consistency in the pattern of marriage rules, and this pattern should be referred to some external variable. It is noteworthy that all the societies shown by Ackerman as having the true levirate are patrilineal, though some patrilineal societies have no levirate and a low divorce rate.

Ackerman's argument is that the levirate shows the radical severing of the wife from her group and hence her incorporation into the affiliations of her husband. Here he explicitly endorses a proposition of L. F. Fallers (1957).[6] The Soga of Uganda are patrilineal but Fallers' figures show that they have a high rate of divorce. (Curiously, when Fallers compared the rate of divorces among Soga in two different areas, he found that the rate was higher in that area where patrilineal lineages were more concentrated.) Hence he suggests (p. 116) that for the Soga my formulation would have to be reversed: the 'stronger' the patrilineal descent groups, the less stable is marriage. He concludes: 'It is, on the face of it, unlikely that Gluckman is simply wrong, for he presents convincing evidence that in some societies the relationship which he suggests does in fact hold. Rather, one suspects, there are some societies in which patrilineal institutions act to stabilize marriage and others in which patrilineal institutions, perhaps of a rather different sort, have the opposite effect.' Fallers then draws attention to the way in which marriage among the Zulu and the Nuer (as typical respectively of Southern Bantu and of many Northeastern African peoples) transfer all 'a woman's child-bearing properties to her husband's lineage' so that once the marriage payment is handed over, all children go to the husband, whosoever the genitor.[7] With this, he says, go the institutions listed by me

6. Fallers' argument is very compressed in my presentation.

7. Shown most strikingly in a Kipsigis rule that if a woman who has borne children to her husband is divorced and then remarried with marriage payment, the children of the first marriage go to the second husband.

(p. 236), such as the true levirate, institutions not found among the Soga save for approval of sororal polygyny. Among the Soga he argues that the patrilineal lineages act to pull the spouses apart because the wife remains a member of her natal lineage and is not *absorbed* into her husband's lineage as among Zulu and Nuer.

Before I consider to what external factors Fallers relates this difference, I note that Leach (1957)[8] reported a similar distinction among three Burma patrilineal peoples, who are culturally very similar. These three peoples (Ordinary Jingphaw, Gauri Kachins and Lakher) differ from the African peoples discussed in that they have what Leach calls 'class hypogamy', with girls marrying from lineages of higher status into those of lower status. The lineages here, like those of Soga, do not form a segmentary system. I set out the difference in marriage rules in Table 2.

Table 2

Jingphaw	Gauri	Lakher
Formal religious marriage, indissoluble unless lineage sister replaces wife	Divorce not common but possible, most easily by provision of lineage sister to replace wife, but marriage payment returnable	No religious element in marriage, divorce easy and apparently frequent
Widow inheritance, possibly leviratic	Widow inheritance, or marriage payment partially returned	Widows can remarry
Marriage payment high, transfers wife and children	Marriage payment high, transfers only children not wife	Marriage payment high, very complicated, transfers children only, not wife

Leach (1957) argues that since there is no difference in the system

8. Presumably in press at the same time as Fallers's article.

of descent, the differences are to be found in the institution of marriage itself. Starting with the assumption, which I accept, that it is 'arguable that it is in the general nature of kinship that a sibling link is "intrinsically" more durable than a marriage tie' (p. 120), he states that in the Jingphaw system the institutions operate so that 'the fragility is located in the sibling link between the bride and her lineage brothers; in the Lakher case the fragility is in the marriage relationship itself. ... It may be observed that the fact that the Lakher and Gauri are more sharply stratified – more class conscious – than the "Ordinary Jingphaw", also fits with the pattern ... described. Jingphaw aristocrats "sell" their daughters outright; Gauri and Lakher disdain to do so, they merely permit their inferiors to have sexual access conditional on the long continued payment of tribute fees', and in return the inferiors get the children. Leach then argues, as Fallers does, that one cannot explain the differences in terms of patriliny, since in these easy-divorce patrilineal systems the patrilineal tie of a woman to her lineage is asserted. He is therefore equally, and rightly, critical of my ascribing the difference to 'strong father-right'. He proceeds to propose that the factors controlling the differences may have to be sought in a difference between two types of unilineal descent systems: those where 'the ongoing structure is defined by descent alone and marriage serves merely to create "a complex scheme of individuation" within that structure ... [and] In contrast ... the category of those societies in which unilineal descent is linked with a strongly defined rule of "preferred marriage".' Here one would have to look at the economic and political significance of the chain of debts established by marriages, and running from generation to generation.[9]

Fallers summarized his argument most generally by postulating that 'common corporate group memberships [of the spouses] tend to reinforce the marriage bond, different corporate group memberships to work against it' (p. 121). Here is a formulation which seems consistent with Ackerman's (though Ackerman followed on Fallers and he generalized more widely). It seems also consistent with Leach's formulation, in so far as it deals with the

---

9. This argument is of course compressed, but I think it fairly presents the gist of Leach's paper.

pattern of marriage rules. But Fallers seeks for the difference, not in the balance of the lineal and the affinal ties in the ongoing structure, but in the role of lineal groups in the political system. He considers that among the Nuer and Zulu, lineages are the building blocks of the political structure, with patriliny directly determining citizenship; in contrast among the Soga though some important political roles are patrilineally inherited, others quite as important are acquired through citizenship. Hence in the Zulu-type system, he argues, since 'patrilineal descent is crucial to political status and, since her children are thus tied to her husband's lineage, [the wife] is also, through them, firmly tied to it.' She becomes 'absorbed' into her husband's lineage.

I consider that on the whole Leach, as he himself says, is defining variables contained within the patterns of marriage rules, and I am not attracted by Fallers' search in the political structure for the external factor in lineage organization which determines the absorption or not of the wife into the husband's lineage. I do not think that we can see either Zulu or Nuer polities as built out of lineages directly, since territorial units in both are occupied by many persons not related to one another by agnatic ties. While clearly marriages of high political importance may thereby be stabilized (see Marx, 1967, pp. 147 ff.), I still feel strongly that the clue to the general stability of marriage is to be sought, as I sought it, in the system of kinship relationships. Unfortunately in some of my phrasings I wrote as if the kinship system might be summarized simply in terms of descent rules and the rights of ascendants: as patriliny or matriliny, and father-right. But even the summary final section reproduced here indicates that in the text of my argument I examined the kinship relationships of Zulu and Lozi as these operated through links to property and to the transmission of property. Clearly it is not possession of lineage property alone which can stabilize marriage, as is shown by the high rate of divorce among Ashanti and other matrilineal peoples who are strongly attached to valuable areas of arable land. What I emphasized as between the Zulu and Lozi was that among the Zulu a man transmits property to his sons through his wife or wives: this mode of transmission, which I named the 'house-property complex', appears most clearly where a man has more than one wife. Throughout the Southern Bantu, up to the Limpopo River (i.e. stopping short of the Shona), and again in North-eastern Africa, in the house-property complex a man allocates land and/or cattle to each wife, and when he dies that wife retains right in those cattle and/or that land which pass to her own sons, as against her husband's sons by his other wives. In short, each wife becomes the nucleus of a set of patrimonial property for her sons, and they have claims on the marriage payments of their own sisters. As each wife forms thus a patrimonial nucleus she is very firmly attached to her husband: if he dies, she and that property remain nucleated for her sons and her future children, who are begotten by a pro-husband in the name of her dead husband; i.e. there is the true levirate – if the wife dies, the patrimonial nucleus endures, and she may be replaced in the sororate. The very low rate of divorce and the endurance of marriages beyond death in tribes with this system of descent and transmission of property thus keeps clear the structure of patrimonial estates in relation to one another.

On the other hand I found that among the Lozi, when a man dies, the land which his wives had worked is pooled after his death and passes back into the control of his heir, who may be a brother, son, uterine nephew, *aut alius*. And similarly it appears to me that among the Soga, the Shona and a number of other patrilineal tribes reported to have a highish or high (Soga) rate of divorce and no levirate, succession and inheritance are adelphic and not filial – i.e. they may go to brothers before passing to the filial generation. In these systems wives are not, then, nuclei of patrimonial estates, and are not as fully absorbed in the husband's lineage – perhaps in consequence.[10]

My early analysis laid stress on the affiliation of children, which, in agnatic systems, I thought pulled their mother to their father, i.e. the woman's husband could claim her children. Hence I spoke of

10. In my Marett Lectures for 1965–66 I suggested that this is why in house-property systems wives are suspected of witchcraft, since struggles over position and property within agnatic groups focuses on them, as against the situation in patrilineal societies where there is adelphic succession and men are the focus of such struggles. See Gluckman (1971) and also the statement by J. Middleton and E. H. Winter (1963, p. 161) that in East African tribes, among those who ascribe misfortune to witchcraft, it is where each wife is the centre of a separate estate within her husband's property, in house-property systems, that women are accused of this inherent evil.

'father-right' to cover this claim. But as I noted in a letter quoted by Leach in his article (1957), I had by 1957 decided that this term was incorrect: I had begun to realize that it would be better to characterize Zulu-type systems as dominated by 'wife/son-right', rather than by 'father-right', by filial inheritance rather than by patriliny. It would be interesting to see how this works outside of Africa: certainly the 'Ordinary Jingphaw', insofar as I can identify them in Leach (1954, p. 165), appear to have a ranking of wives akin to the Zulu.

I argue thus that the situation of virtually no divorce and of the true levirate and sororate will be found with house-property filial inheritance, but there will be some divorce at least in patrilineal systems with adelphic succession and inheritance. Mitchell found that in a small number of African societies where divorce rates had been calculated on Barnes's formulae, on the whole, save for the Soga, even adelphic succession systems had more stable marriage than matrilineal systems. He suggested (1963) that where the rights over a bride are transferred to a group of men, rather than to her husband alone, marriage will be stabilized. I believe this to be so, but consider that this rule itself appears most strongly in house-property systems, though as Mitchell says it may act to stabilize marriage in matrilineal systems, within their overall relatively high instability of marriage. If there is anything in my argument, it may have to be validated by a closer scrutiny of the relationship between women and property nucleations within matrilineal societies. I would also like, given time, to attempt to investigate whether similar variations in the disposition of property rights underlie the two types of bilateral societies distinguished by Ackerman: i.e. to investigate whether differences in property arrangements underlie the occurrence of endogamy or exogamy in bilateral systems.

I am encouraged by Jacobson (1967) to feel that my hunch here is correct. She examines the relation between marriage payments and marital stability in all the tribes of the Congo-Gabon region, an area of great cultural admixture. She finds that independently of the usual classification of societies as matrilineal, bilateral or patrilineal, a careful study of attitudes to divorce shows that the very many tribes of the region manifest two attitudes to marital stability: the first, a relative indifference; the second, a strongly positive conception of marital stability as such.[11] Relative indifference involves an elaborate specification of 'grounds' on which there can be divorce, ascription of guilt and liability to economic sanctions, absence of institutionalized obligatory mediation in divorce cases. High valuation of stability is marked by absence of specification of grounds, divorce being granted only when parties can no longer live together, there are no specific economic sanctions save return of marriage payment independently of blame, and repeated and compulsory attempts at mediation to save the marriage.

The differing attitudes appear in proverbs: in one set of peoples these stress the importance of details of marriage for its durability, while in the other they stress the overlooking of similar trifles. The rate of divorce correlates positively with the two attitudes. Jacobson's tables show the levirate as occurring among almost all the tribes considered, but she does not discuss whether she means true levirate or the possibility of widow-inheritance or remarriage of the widow within the husband's kin.

With what institutions does the distribution of these attitudes correlate? Jacobson found that in tribes with 'strict matrilineal descent and in tribes with strict patrilineal descent' alone there is the attitude linked with high divorce rates. But where the mother's agnatic group is also important, and in matrilineal societies where the father's group is important, marriage is valued highly and the divorce rate is low. She argues that as we find peoples which tend to fall between the two, the rate becomes intermediate. Her hypothesis is that where ego can satisfy all his wants within one group, there can be little interest of the groups in the stability of the marriage. Where there are complementary descent groups or complementary kin groups, the children will constitute a focus of common interests and create an interest in marital stability, i.e. where ego 'is dependent on both his father's and his mother's group to provide for the sum total of his political, economic, social, legal, religious and affective rights and needs, seeing that the two groups complement each other in these respects.' This

11. I reported that the Lozi and other tribes with high rates of divorce spoke as if they valued stable marriages, and they do; Jacobson, as will be seen, is concerned with the rules by which valuations of stability are in practice achieved.

M. Gluckman 245

suggests to me that it may be in relation to rights to property of children that factors stabilizing marriage in tribal societies will be found. But though it is clear that rates of stability of marriage in tribal societies are influenced by institutional milieux and patterns of marriage rules even more obviously show internal consistencies, more probably the degree of stability depends on more than one type of factor.

References

ACKERMAN, A. (1963), 'Affiliations: structural determinants of differential divorce rates', *Amer. J. Sociol.*, vol. 69, pp. 13–20.

ASHTON, E. H. (1952), *The Basuto*, Oxford University Press.

BARNES, J. A. (1949), 'Measures of divorce frequency in simple societies', *J. roy. anthrop. Inst.*, vol. 79, pp. 37–62.

BARNES, J. A. (1967), 'The frequency of divorce', in A. L. Epstein (ed.), *The Craft of Social Anthropology*, Tavistock, pp. 47–100.

BOHANNAN, L. (1949), 'Dahomean marriage: a revaluation', *Africa*, vol. 19, pp. 273–83.

BOTT, E. (1971), *Family and Social Network*, Tavistock, 2nd edn.

CASALIS, J. E. (1859), *Les Bassotos*, Société des Missions Evangeliques.

CLERC, A. (1938), 'The marriage laws of the Ronga tribe', *Bantu Studies*, vol. 12, pp. 75–104.

DURKHEIM, E. (1938), *The Rules of Sociological Method*, Free Press. Translated by S. A. Solvay and J. H. Mueller from *Les Règles de la Méthode Sociologique*, 1895.

ELLENBERGER, D. F., and MACGREGOR, A. (1912), *History of the Basuto*, Caxton Publishing Co.

EVANS-PRITCHARD, E. E. (1938), *Some Aspects of Marriage and Family among the Nuer*. Republished 1945 as Rhodes-Livingstone Paper, no. 11.

FALLER, L. A. (1957), 'Some determinants of marriage stability in Busoga: a reformulation of Gluckman's hypothesis', *Africa*, vol. 27, pp. 106–23.

FORTES, M. (1937), *Marriage Law among the Tallensi*, Accra, Government Printing Office.

FORTES, M. (1945), *The Dynamics of Clanship among the Tallensi*, Oxford University Press.

GLUCKMAN, M. et al. (1953–4), 'Bridewealth and the stability of marriage', correspondence in *Man*, arts. 75, 122, 223, 279; 96, 97, 153.

GLUCKMAN, M. (1955), *Custom and Conflict in Africa*, Blackwell.

GLUCKMAN, M. (1971), 'Moral crises: magical and secular solutions', in M. Gluckman (ed.), *The Allocation of Responsibility*, Manchester University Press.

GOODY, E. (1962), 'Conjugal separation and divorce among the Gonja of northern Ghana', in M. Fortes (ed.), *Marriage in Tribal Societies*, Cambridge University Press, pp. 14–54.

HARRIES, C. L. (1929), *The Laws and Customs of the BaPedi and Cognate Tribes*, Hortors.

HERSKOVITS, M. (1938), *Dahomey, An Ancient West African Kingdom*, J. J. Augustin.

JACOBSON, M. (1967), 'Marriage and Money', *Studia Ethnographica Upsaliensia*. vol. 28.

JUNOD, H. (1905), 'The Bathonga of the Transvaal', *Addresses & Papers: Brit. South African Ass. Advancement Sci.*, vol. 3, pp. 222–62.

JUNOD, H. (1927), *The Life of a South African Tribe*, vol. 1, Macmillan.

KUPER, H. (1947), *An African Aristocracy*, Oxford University Press.

KUPER, H. (1950), 'Kinship among the Swazi', in A. R. Radcliffe-Brown, and D. Forde (eds.), *African Systems of Kinship and Marriage*, Oxford University Press.

LEACH, E. R. (1954), *Political Systems of Highland Burma*, Athlone Press.

LEACH, E. R. (1957), 'Aspects of bridewealth and marriage stability among Kachin and Lakher', *Man*, vol. 57. Reprinted in *Rethinking Anthropology*, 1961, Athlone Presss, pp. 114–23.

MARX, E. (1967), *Bedouin of the Negev*, Manchester University Press.

MIDDLETON, J., and WINTER, E. H. (eds.), (1963), *Witchcraft and Sorcery in East Africa*, Routledge & Kegan Paul.

MITCHELL, J. C. (1963), 'Marriage stability and social structure in Bantu Africa', *Pro. internat. Union for the study of population*, vol. 2, pp. 255–63.

READ, M. (1938), 'Moral code of the Ngoni', *Africa*, vol. 11, pp. 1–24.

RICHARDS, A. I. (1940), *Bemba Marriage and Modern Economic Conditions*, Rhodes-Livingstone Paper, no. 4.

SCHAPERA, I. (1940), *Married Life in an African Tribe*, Faber & Faber.

STAYT, H. (1931), *The Bavenda*, Oxford University Press.

16 J. C. Mitchell

Social Change and the Stability of Marriage
in Northern Rhodesia

J. C. Mitchell, 'Social change and the stability of marriage in Northern Rhodesia', in A. Southall (ed.), *Social Change in Modern Africa*, Oxford University Press, pp. 316–29.

Measures of marriage stability

It is possible using appropriate statistical devices, to predict how long a given marriage will last. These statistical devices are analogous to those used in the life table and with suitable material a marriage duration table can be prepared (Barnes, 1949). In these tables divorce is analogous to death and the tables are constructed from an analysis of the periods marriages have survived before being dissolved by divorce or death, in the same way that life tables are constructed from the analysis of the ages at which people die. In this Reading I am not concerned with the termination of marriage by the death of one of the spouses, so that when I discuss the duration of marriage I mean the duration of marriage before it is ended by divorce or legal separation.

Failing measures of this sort, which are the only true comparative statistics we can work with, we must use the divorce ratios of the sort we have suggested elsewhere (Mitchell and Barnes, 1950), but we must appreciate that these measures may be seriously disturbed by differences in the average age of first marriage or in the age distribution of the population.

Eventually when the standard of collecting divorce statistics has advanced sufficiently we will be able to compare the stability of marriage from one society to another, as Barnes has started to do. He has been able to say, on the basis of his analysis, that the average Ngoni marriage will last for 15·5 years while among the Americans it will last 20·4 years.

This figure, like the life expectancy, is a general average arrived at purely empirically. It is obvious that the causes of death are numerous but the overall operation of these causes results in an expectancy of life which does not vary much from one year to another in the same community. The life expectancy, however, differs widely from one society to another. Demographers look beyond the life curve itself and are able to isolate from the myriad causes of death several significant factors and use these to explain the differences between societies. The high infantile mortality rate, for example, in non-literate societies, is instrumental in reducing the general life expectancy.

We may approach the analysis of the stability of marriage in the same way. There is no doubt that whether the marriage breaks up or not depends on a variety of factors, economic, social and personal, and that these factors operating simultaneously give rise to an overall divorce rate which does not differ much within the same society from one year to the next. The multiplicity of factors, therefore, operate adventitiously and not systematically, in the same way that random factors affect the trajectory of a missile to give rise to a cone of fire and not to a constant error. But from one society to another certain major determinants of the divorce rate can be isolated. In other words we may adopt the same type of reasoning as used by Durkheim in his analysis of suicide. A variety of factors he argues affect the *incidence* of suicide but the *rate* is determined in different countries, and at different times in the same country, by a few major sociological variables.

Kinship as the major determinant of marriage stability

Therefore, in trying to assess the probability of divorce in any particular marriage we should take into account a wide range of relevant factors, but if we are interested in trying to understand, say, the trend in divorce rates in general, then we need to be able to assess the influence of the major determinants, and, knowing these trends so deduce the trend in the divorce rate.

There have been many attempts to do this for Western European society but these studies are not directly relevant to the situation in Africa. Here we need to take account of the fact that tribal societies are organized on a different basis, and indeed we should make this the starting point of our analysis.

Marriage is essentially a relationship between two persons which fits into a larger pattern of social relationships. Marriage, therefore, operates within a social system and being itself part of it we should expect that the social system would determine its nature. In tribal societies in Africa, as in other parts of the world, the kinship system is a dominant feature of the social structure so that it is reasonable to suppose, as Gluckman (1950) has done, that the major determinants of marriage stability in tribal societies lie in the kinship system.

Basically Gluckman's argument is that in societies which are organized on the basis of corporate patrilineages marriage becomes the institutionalized means whereby new members are recruited to the patrilineages. Given rules of incest and exogamy, the patrilineal groups can survive only by securing rights over the reproductive powers of women from other groups. This they do by marriage, involving as it does the payment of bridewealth and the performance of appropriate ceremonies. These rights over the reproductive powers of the women are transferred permanently to the husband's group so that the marriage cannot easily be dissolved. On the specific reason why the rights should be transferred permanently Gluckman is not clear, but I would suggest that it is related to the prolonged infancy of the human child and the fact that in general the child needs its mother for several years before it can safely be separated from her. Before this stage is reached the woman is usually pregnant again and therefore will not easily be released by her husband's group.

In societies in which there are corporate matrilineages the woman produces children for her own descent group. Her reproductive powers are therefore not transferred and the duration of the marriage does not affect the welfare of the child, nor the rights of its matrilineal kinsmen over it. The duration of marriage here is therefore determined mainly by the personalities of the spouses and divorces usually are relatively frequent.

In bilateral societies kinship alone cannot be the basis of corporate kin groups, and therefore the possession of rights over a woman's reproductive powers is not a live issue. Marriage therefore, as in matrilineal societies, is brittle and of short duration.

In general these hypotheses have been upheld and we are able to use them in interpreting the trends in societies where the kinship systems are changing. In order to do this we need to emphasize some general features of kinship systems.

Marriage, we have argued, will assume different forms within different kinship systems. We may approach the analysis of the role marriage plays in different kinship systems by considering the sorts of rights and obligations which the formal act of marriage confers upon the contracting parties. Bohannan (1949) on the basis of her analysis of Dahomean marriage has suggested that we can approach the problem from the point of view of the rights a man or his kinsmen acquire over a woman through marriage. One set of rights are those held in her as a *wife*. These are the rights to her services both domestic and sexual and they may be termed *uxorial* rights. The other set of rights are the rights in the woman as a *mother* and refer particularly to the ownership of the child. These are the *genetricial* rights.

Now it follows that where there are corporate agnatic descent groups the patrilineage as a whole acquires the genetricial rights in the woman while the uxorial rights are usually held by one of their number. In this situation, as Gluckman has argued, divorce is rare and difficult. In matrilineal societies the uxorial rights are acquired by a man who is not a member of the matrilineal descent group while the genetricial rights in the woman are permanently held by the woman's mother's brother, or her own brothers. As Gluckman points out the uxorial rights may easily be transferred from husband to husband without affecting the genetricial rights in her so that divorce here is easy and frequent.

In bilateral societies recruitment to corporate groups is not by kinship alone, so that the genetricial rights in women are not relevant. Here uxorial rights as in matrilineal societies are easily transferred from husband to husband and divorce is consequently easy and frequent.

In order to appreciate fully the significance of genetricial rights as rights over the reproductive powers of the woman, we should consider the rights and obligations which the possession of these rights confers over the children born to the woman. In a society where corporate groups exist the possession of genetricial rights over a woman implies that her children will belong to the group which possesses these rights. The children, therefore, may expect the succour and protection from the other members of the group and they in turn must be loyal to their fellows. As Bohannan points out, the acquisition of genetricial rights confers jural authority over the child. The word 'jural' here presumably means that the sanctions behind the implementation of the obligations of the child to its group lie in force either through the mechanism of the courts or through the feud. In other words genetricial rights, being linked particularly to corporate relationships, operate in a political field.

Where corporate groups exist, the genetricial rights are held, as I have pointed out, by the group as a whole. But some genetricial rights may also be held by an individual as, for example, among the Bemba of Northern Rhodesia. The Bemba are a people amongst whom succession to office and membership of the non-corporate association of clanship is determined by matrilineal descent. The most important political unit is the village. Villages are built up on the basis of matrilocal extended families (Richards, 1950, p. 227), i.e. they are made up of the village headman and his married daughters. There may also be several of the headman's sisters and their daughters in the village. The Bemba practise shifting cultivation of a slash-and-burn type in rather poor soils and the size to which each village may grow is limited by this ecological factor. As the trees become exhausted in its vicinity each village must shift its locale approximately once in every five years and this is the time, as Richards points out, at which villages are particularly liable to fragment. The economy of villages is based upon the cultivation of eleusine in ash patches prepared from the burning of branches lopped from the trees by the young men of the village. The labour of the young men is crucial in the ecological balance between the Bemba and their somewhat inhospitable agricultural environment because pollarding the trees as against cutting them down completely, allows a much more rapid regeneration of the trees, and thus ultimately a higher carrying capacity of the land. The prosperity of a Bemba man, therefore, in a land where the margin between subsistence and starvation is narrow, is counted in food, and the labour of young men is essential to the production of food. This labour is provided by the husbands of the man's daughters. A man, therefore, is heavily dependent on his daughters' husbands for economic security, or as Richards (1956, p. 46) graphically puts it: 'Wealth consists of the power to command service.'

A Bemba man's dependence on his daughters' husbands is limited not to economic relationships only: it extends also into the social and political field. Within the social field, prestige in Bemba society is associated with the economic independence of the man. As Richards points out (1956, p. 42) a man can eventually acquire status and prestige as head of his own extended family with sons-in-law working for him whether he moves to one of his own relatives or stays where he is. But if he wishes to increase his renown he must try to become a village headman. Among the Bemba as amongst other Central Bantu, the ambition of every man is to become a village headman. In order to do this he must have the right to remove his wife and her children from her village. With his daughters' husbands then, provided that he has the permission of the chief, he will be able to set up his own village.

Genetricial rights amongst the Bemba therefore centre on a man's jural authority over his daughters and their husbands.

In Bemba marriage three payments are made (Richards, 1940). The first, a trifling amount of say 12½p, called *nsalamu*, confers uxorial rights upon the man. The second payment, called *chisungu*, is made during the girls' initiation and is made once only in respect of each girl. We can look upon it as a ritual payment which releases the mystical sexual powers of the girl. The third payment, *mpango*, formerly made up of barkcloth, hoes or arrows, conferred genetricial rights upon the husband. It was through this payment that the man established his rights to remove his daughter from his wife's village and thereby established his rights to the services of his sons-in-law. As Richards (1956, p. 44) puts it: 'The *mpango* gave the father those limited rights he secured over his children although it did not, in this matrilineal society, give him complete control over his wife's reproductive power as does the cattle *lobola* among the Southern Bantu.'

But these rights the Bemba man held personally: his brothers, for example, could not enforce them on his behalf, and from this point of view they differ from the genetricial rights acquired by a man in a patrilineal society with corporate kin groups. Divorce was easy and apparently frequent among the Bemba during the early years of marriage (Richards, 1940, p. 101) but less frequent and more difficult after children had been born (Wilson, 1941, p. 42). It was when the children were born that the man's ambitions became capable of being realized and it was to his advantage therefore not to seek a divorce at this stage: he could only build a village with the assistance of his daughters' husbands. The genetricial rights a Bemba man acquired over his wife, therefore, only became effective when his daughters were old enough to form the nucleus of a village, and the divorce apparently became more difficult and less frequent as this stage was reached.

This argument links the stability of marriage with a man's realization of the genetricial rights he acquires in his wife, whether this is in a society organized in corporate patrilineages or in a matrilineal society in which a man may personally acquire genetricial rights over his wife. In societies organized in corporate matrilineages such as among the Yao and Chewa a husband never acquires genetricial rights over his wife and therefore marriage is never stabilized by this factor. In bilateral societies also, as amongst the Lozi, genetricial rights are not involved so that we would expect the divorce rate to be higher than say amongst the Bemba. The rights which are disputed amongst the Yao and the Lozi are uxorial rights – particularly adultery – and not the rights over children. Among the Bemba, while adultery cases clearly figure prominently, the rights of a man to the portion of the marriage payment made for his daughter and the rights to the children are also involved. Note for example Richards's record (1940, p. 57) of the case where a woman screamed: 'We shall take the baby. . . . That is no father that! He paid us no *mpango*.'

Amongst bilateral peoples, in fact, the kinship system may operate to increase the instability of marriage. Gluckman (1950, p. 201) in fact describes how the Lozi system encourages the wide ramification of cognatic and affinal ties and how a person uses these ties to exploit the resources at its command. He writes:

Because their productive activities are varied and many fall in distant places in the same month, they require cooperation and help from many people. Kinship provides the framework for getting this help, but since neighbours in the various parts where they have economic resources are linked to them by patrilineal, matrilineal and mixed ties, they emphasize his links with many lines: therefore marriage does not tie a woman's procreative power to one line. She produces for many lines.

It follows from this that from the point of view of any one individual the less his kinship links coincide with another's the better his chances of operating these links to his personal advantage.

In other words in bilateral systems the emphasis is on filiation while in matrilineal or patrilineal societies the emphasis is more likely to be on corporate relations. Where the emphasis is on filiation we expect to find high divorce rates.

To summarize we should expect:

1. In patrilineal societies with corporate groups, i.e. genetricial rights acquired by *groups* – marriage duration is *long*.

2. In patrilineal or matrilineal societies where genetricial rights are acquired by *individuals* – marriage duration is *medium*.

3. In matrilineal societies with corporate groups, i.e. where genetricial rights are never transferred or bilateral societies where genetricial rights are not relevant – marriage duration is *short*.

In order to test this hypothesis we need detailed information on the duration of marriage such as to enable us to compute expectancies of marriage duration and this we cannot yet do.

Marriage stability and modern conditions

In broad terms we have tried to relate marriage stability in tribal areas to social structure: in particular, following Gluckman's lead, we have tried to relate it to the kinship system and the rights which marriage confers within these kinship systems. Therefore when we turn to modern conditions we must try to relate changes in marriage stability to changes in the kinship system whether through time (historically) or from place to place (situationally). Richards's (1940) study of Bemba marriage and Barnes's (1951) study of Ngoni marriage are studies of the historical sort. I intend, however, to try to consider marriage stability not in historical but in situational change, i.e. to look at marriage stability where the kinship system is altered fundamentally by the social situation in which it is set. The most striking examples we have are in the newly created industrial towns.

In these towns we may isolate two main types of related variables, i.e. the demographic and the sociological. Demographic factors influencing marriage would be such factors as the disproportion of sexes which Wilson (1941) emphasized so much. Another is the tribal heterogeneity of the towns and a third is the relatively high mobility of the town dwellers. All of these demographic characteristics have their influence on marriage stability as such, but the social structure, itself influenced by demographic variables, also affects marriage stability. Fortes (1953, p. 24) has pointed out that there is evidence that 'unilineal descent groups break down when a modern economic framework with occupational differentiation linked to a wide range of specialized skills, to productive capital and to monetary media of exchange, is introduced.' The unilineal descent groups under these conditions tend to become reorganized in nuclear families and the descent tends to be reckoned bilaterally (Gough, 1950, p. 85). This is particularly true in the industrial towns where the demographic and social conditions militate strongly against unilineal corporate group activity. As Fortes (1953, p. 36) remarks: 'A lineage cannot easily act as a corporate group if its members can never get together for the conduct of their affairs.' In these towns where the emphasis is on heterogeneity and on mobility the conditions prevent the daily participation of unilineal kinsmen in joint activities. There are no cattle, there is no land to focus the activities of say a patrilineage, and the working hours and conditions preclude their participating in joint ritual and ceremonies for protracted periods. The emphasis in town is on individual success in a competitive environment and this emphasis cuts across the ideology of corporate descent groups.

Kinship instead remains important in the form of filiation – as an ever-ramifying network of personal relationship which links any given person to others in haphazard fashion across the township. Kinsmen, who in tribal conditions played an unimportant part in the life of a person, assume a new importance in town where the overwhelming majority of contacts are with strangers. A person may call on distant kinsmen for help in town whom he would not consider approaching in his tribal home (Wilson, 1941, p. 53; Epstein, 1953, p. 11; Mitchell, 1957, p. 27). Though kinship is still important in the new industrial towns it possesses qualities different from kinship in tribal areas. Wilson (1941, p. 51) has drawn attention to an example of the way in which the relationships between kinsmen must inevitably alter in the urban situation. He points out that in the tribal areas the economic bond between Bemba men and their daughter's husband was particularly important. We have seen that the Bemba men acquire rights to the services of their daughters' husbands through the *mpango* payments. He writes:

the wife's parents were the skilled foremen, the young couple were the relatively skilled labourers of those times, and both couples alike benefited from their cooperation.... The domestic group formed by the old couple and a number of daughters and sons-in-law was the main factory of Bemba wealth and their living depended upon it.

But in towns, of course, this essential link between a man and his daughters' husbands cannot exist because 'the main productive relationship in which the urban Bemba are involved is that between European capital and skill on the one hand, and African unskilled labour on the other; it is on getting a job, not on getting married that a young man's living now depends.' We must therefore look at marriage and marriage stability in the matrix of urban social relationships of which it is a part.

In this situation genetricial rights in a woman fade in favour of uxorial rights. The rights by means of which kin groups are able to recruit new members are not significant where these groups cannot exist nor are the rights viable where the essential economic and political bond between a Bemba man and his daughters' husbands cannot exist. Instead where men are involved in wage-earning all day and individual households, as against joint households of the tribal type, are the pattern, the personal domestic services of the women achieve new importance. The emphasis on the personal services of the women is increased by what Wilson calls 'disequilibrium' or 'disproportion' (1941, p. 40), i.e. an unbalanced sex ratio. The adult sex ratio in the towns of Northern Rhodesia does not depart from equality as much as it does say in Southern Rhodesia or South Africa. On the Copperbelt, for example, there are 142 adult men per 100 adult women. Yet this is enough to give rise to a certain amount of competition among the men for the sexual and domestic services of the women.

It is not surprising, therefore, that the question of the custody of children or of a man's rights in them are seldom raised in court. Instead the emphasis is rather on adultery or from the woman's point of view, on her husband's neglect of her. The uxorial rights appear to be most significant in urban areas, and this accords with the different forms that kinship in towns has taken there.

As we may expect in towns the significance of the marriage payment differs from that in tribal areas. The initiating gift (*nsalamu*) and the 'virginity' (*chisungu*) payments are substantially the same but the *mpango* payment understandably appears to have lost its tribal function of fixing a man's right to the services of his daughters' husbands. Instead the *mpango* payment has become, as I have expressed it before as 'a sort of insurance policy against the possible dissolution of marriage' (Mitchell, 1957, p. 25). An aggrieved husband is able to sue for the return of his *mpango* payment if his uxorial rights have been transgressed. Those kinsmen who accept a marriage payment on the Copperbelt, therefore, do so in the full knowledge that they may be called upon to refund the amount if a divorce takes place. They will therefore become guardians of the husband's uxorial rights and will bring pressure to bear upon their kinswoman, the wife, if she deviates from the norms of accepted behaviour. This is the point made by a Lala man, quoted in an earlier paper (Mitchell, 1957, p. 25), who paid six times as much in marriage payment as he would have done in his rural home. He said his wife would not be as 'proud and cheeky' as she would have been had he only paid the usual amount. It is significant that three of four kinsmen who accepted the marriage payments were in fact living on the Copperbelt. They were themselves part of the social system in which the norms operated and were able to take a personal interest in the marriage.

We are, also, thus able to interpret the fact that even tribes which traditionally make no marriage payments, such as the Bisa and the Yao, fall into line on the Copperbelt and make substantial *mpango* payments. In the urban situation uxorial rights are as significant to them as other tribes and they endeavour to protect these rights both with their wives' kinsmen and in the courts by making the formal payments (Mitchell, 1957, p. 27).

Marriage stability in towns

We are now able to turn to the question of marriage stability in towns. Wilson was convinced that 'the instability of marriage is greater in town than in the country' (1941, p. 41). This he relates to the lack of traditional restraints, in town, the idleness of the women making them 'all the more ready for sexual adventures', the disproportion of men and women and to the number of inter-tribal marriages.

When Wilson wrote it was not generally realized that marriage was unstable among the matrilineal and bilateral peoples of Northern Rhodesia even in the rural areas. It seems likely that this had been so even before the advent of the Europeans. Richards had just published her figures (1940, p. 120) on Bemba divorce in the rural areas but Wilson was not able to collect comparable figures in Broken Hill. Since 1946 we have been able to make considerable advances in collecting the quantitative material on marriage stability and we have been able to clarify the methods of using this data to best advantage (Barnes, 1949; Mitchell and Barnes, 1950). The collection of data still lags a long way behind the sophistication of analysis Barnes has proposed but we are still in a better position to get at least a first estimate of the relative frequency of divorce in tribal and in urban areas. I have published some information (1957, p. 10) which suggests that urban marriages may be more stable than tribal in Northern Rhodesia. The figures, however, are not strictly comparable because of the possible effects of differing age structures in the samples. More refined work is necessary.

Nevertheless on the basis of our general analysis we might well have predicted this. Our argument, following Gluckman, has been that the main stabilizing influence in marriage is the legal transfer of genetricial rights to the husband. We would expect, therefore, that in the towns where corporate groups cannot operate as they do in tribal areas marriage duration will be shorter and the divorce rate will be higher. On the same reasoning since the legal transfer of rights over the services of the daughters' husbands is not significant in town we would expect the probability of divorce among urban Bemba couples to increase in the later years of marriage as against tribal couples. The overall duration of marriage may possibly be slightly shorter and the overall divorce rate will then be larger.

We would expect the duration of marriage in town to be longer, however, than among the strongly matrilineal people and the bilateral. Here the very assaults on the stability of marriage which Wilson emphasized have generated their own stabilizing reaction in the form of substantial marriage payments which protect the uxorial rights of the men. The result will be increasing reluctance to face divorce and a consequent lowering of the divorce rates.

These predictions are derivations from the hypothesis we have built up on the basis of viewing marriage as an element in a total social system in which certain clear-cut rights and obligations are involved. The next step is to proceed to test these by the use of refined quantitative techniques. I am able to do this for the urban side on the basis of social survey material from the Copperbelt but, except for material on the Ngoni, we are not yet in a position to compare this with measures in the rural areas.

References

BARNES, J. A. (1949), 'Measures of divorce frequency in simple societies', *J. roy. anthropol. Inst.*, vol. 79, pp. 37–62.

BARNES, J. A. (1951), *Marriage in a Changing Society*, Rhodes-Livingstone Paper, no. 20.

BOHANNAN, L. (1949), 'Dahomean marriage: a revaluation', *Africa*, vol. 19, pp. 273–87.

EPSTEIN, A. L. (1953), 'The role of African courts in the urban communities of the Northern Rhodesian Copperbelt', *Rhodes-Livingstone J.*, no. 13, pp. 1–17.

FORTES, M. (1953), 'The structure of unilineal descent groups', *Amer. Anthropol.*, vol. 55, pp. 17–41.

GLUCKMAN, M. (1950), 'Kinship and marriage among the Lozi of Northern Rhodesia and the Zulu of Natal', in A. R. Radcliffe-Brown and D. Forde (eds.), *African Systems of Kinship and Marriage*, Oxford University Press.

GOUGH, E. K. (1950), 'Changing kinship usage in the setting of political and economic change among the Nayars of Malabar', *J. roy. anthropol. Inst.*, vol. 82, pp. 71–87.

MITCHELL, J. C. (1957), 'Aspects of African marriage on the Copperbelt of Northern Rhodesia', *Rhodes-Livingstone J.*, no. 22, pp. 1–30.

MITCHELL, J. C., and BARNES, J. A. (1950), *The Lamba Village: A Report of a Social Survey*, Commun. School African Stud., University of Cape Town, no. 24.

RICHARDS, A. I. (1940), *Bemba Marriage and Present Economic Conditions*, Rhodes-Livingstone Paper, no. 4.

RICHARDS, A. I. (1950), 'Some types of family structure among the Central Bantu', in A. R. Radcliffe-Brown and D. Forde (eds.), *African Systems of Kinship and Marriage*, Oxford University Press.

RICHARDS, A. I. (1956), *Chisungu: A Girls' Initiation Ceremony among the Bemba of Northern Rhodesia*, Faber & Faber.

WILSON, G. (1941), *An Essay on the Economics of Detribalization in Northern Rhodesia*, Rhodes-Livingstone Paper, no. 6.

Part Nine **Kin Groups**

In most pre-industrial societies, kinship is important not merely as a way of defining a range of relatives but as providing a system of exclusive groups, or overlapping groupings, within and between which many significant aspects of social life are organized. These latter may include not only the transmission of property but also arrangements for dealing with marriage, defence, offence, religious action, and so on. Such groups may be unilineal descent groups (clans and lineages), bilateral kindreds of the kind reported for Anglo-Saxon England, or a range of intermediary types found most commonly in Polynesia. Unilineal descent groups may be recruited by patrilineal or matrilineal descent; in some societies (double descent systems), both types of descent group are found side by side.

The distribution, classification and characteristics of these groups, groupings and ranges of kin have been subject to much discussion and controversy.

Fortes' paper on the structure of unilineal descent groups attempted to summarize developments in the study of clans and lineages, groups that were widespread in Africa, where they often played a particularly important role in societies that lacked complex political institutions (i.e. 'acephalous' or 'segmentary' societies) (Reading 17).

Richards' analysis of the 'matrilineal puzzle' in Africa, based upon her own fieldwork among the Bemba, upon that of her teacher, Malinowski, among the Trobriands, and upon a comparative study of the Central Bantu, is a landmark in clarifying some of the main features of a system which has been so misunderstood by writers in many fields (Reading 18).

The kinship systems of societies without unilineal descent groups, western and non-western, have received much greater emphasis in recent years especially in the work of Firth, Freeman, Goodenough and Davenport. Pehrson's article (Reading 19) attempts to sum up some of the general characteristics.

17 M. Fortes

The Structure of Unilineal Descent Groups

Excerpts from M. Fortes, 'The structure of unilineal descent groups', *American Anthropologist*, vol. 55, 1953, pp. 17–41. Reprinted in M. Fortes, *Time and Social Structure and Other Essays*, Athlone Press, 1970, pp. 67–95.

What is the main methodological contribution of the study of unilineal descent groups? In my view it is the approach from the angle of political organization to what are traditionally thought of as kinship groups and institutions that has been specially fruitful. By regarding lineages and statuses from the point of view of the total social system and not from that of an hypothetical Ego we realize that consanguinity and affinity, real or putative, are not sufficient in themselves to bring about these structural arrangements. We see that descent is fundamentally a jural concept as Radcliffe-Brown argued in one of his most important papers (1935); we see its significance, as the connecting link between the external, that is political and legal, aspect of what we have called unilineal descent groups, and the internal or domestic aspect. It is in the latter context that kinship carries maximum weight, first, as the source of title to membership of the groups or to specific jural status, with all that this means in rights over and towards persons and property; and second as the basis of the social relations among the persons who are identified with one another in the corporate group. In theory, membership of a corporate legal or political group need not stem from kinship, as Weber has made clear. In primitive society, however, if it is not based on kinship it seems generally to presume some formal procedure of incorporation with ritual initiation. So-called secret societies in West Africa seem to be corporate organizations of this nature. Why descent rather than locality or some other principle forms the basis of these corporate groups is a question that needs more study. It will be remembered that Radcliffe-Brown (1935) related succession rules to the need for unequivocal discrimination of rights *in rem* and *in personam*. Perhaps it is most closely connected with the fact that rights over the reproductive powers of women are easily regulated by a descent group system. But I believe that something deeper than this is involved; for in a homogeneous society there is nothing which could so precisely and incontrovertibly fix one's place in society as one's parentage.

Looking at it from without, we ignore the internal structure of the unilineal group. But African lineages are not monolithic units; and knowledge of their internal differentiation has been much advanced by the researches I have mentioned. The dynamic character of lineage structure can be seen most easily in the balance that is reached between its external relations and its internal structure. Ideally, in most lineage-based societies the lineage tends to be thought of as a perpetual unit, expanding like a balloon but never growing new parts. In fact, of course, as Forde (1938) and Evans-Pritchard (1940) have so clearly shown, fission and accretion are processes inherent in lineage structure. However, it is a common experience to find an informant who refuses to admit that his lineage or even his branch of a greater lineage did not at one time exist. Myth and legend, believed, naturally, to be true history, are quickly cited to prove the contrary. But investigation shows that the stretch of time, or rather of duration, with which perpetuity is equated varies according to the count of generations needed to conceptualize the internal structure of the lineage and link it on to an absolute, usually mythological origin for the whole social system in a first founder.

This is connected with the fact than an African lineage is never, according to our present knowledge, internally undifferentiated. It is always segmented and is in process of continuous further segmentation at any given time. Among some peoples (e.g. the Tallensi and probably the Ibo) the internal segmentation of a lineage is quite rigorous and the process of further segmentation has an almost mechanical precision. The general rule is that every segment is, in form, a replica of every other segment and of the whole lineage. But the segments are, as a rule, hierarchically organized by fixed steps of greater and greater inclusiveness, each step being defined by genealogical reference. It is perhaps hardly necessary to mention that when we talk of lineage structure we are really concerned, from a particular analytical angle, with the organization of jural, economic and ritual activities. The point here is that lineage segmentation corresponds to gradation in the institutional norms and activities in which the total lineage organization is actualized. So we find that the greater the time depth that is attributed to the lineage system as a whole, the more elaborate is its internal segmentation. As I have already mentioned, lineage systems in Africa, when most elaborate, seem to have a maximal time depth of around fourteen putative generations. More common, though, is a count of five or six generations of named ancestors between living adults and a quasi-mythological founder. We can as yet only guess at the conditions that lie behind these limits of genealogical depth in lineage structure. The facts themselves are nevertheless of great comparative interest. These genealogies obviously do not represent a true record of all the ancestors of a group. To explain this by the limitations and fallibility of oral tradition is merely to evade the problem. In structural terms the answer seems to lie in the spread or span (Fortes, 1945) of internal segmentation of the lineage, and this apparently has inherent limits. As I interpret the evidence we have, these limits are set by the condition of stability in the social structure which it is one of the chief functions of lineage systems to maintain. The segmentary spread found in a given lineage system is that which makes for maximum stability; and in a stable social system it is kept at a particular spread by continual internal adjustments which are conceptualized by clipping, patching and telescoping genealogies to fit. Just what the optimum spread of lineage segmentation in a particular society tends to be depends presumably on extra-lineage factors of political and economic organization of the kind referred to by Forde (1947).

It is when we consider the lineage from within that kinship becomes decisive. For lineage segmentation follows a model laid down in the parental family. It is indeed generally thought of as the perpetuation, through the rule of the jural unity of the descent line and of the sibling group (cf. Radcliffe-Brown, 1950), of the social relations that constitute the parental family. So we find a lineage segment conceptualized as a sibling group in symmetrical relationship with segments of a like order. It will be a paternal sibling group where descent is patrilineal and a maternal one where it is matrilineal. Progressive orders of inclusiveness are formulated as a succession of generations; and the actual process of segmentation is seen as the equivalent of the division between siblings in the parental family. With this goes the use of kinship terminology and the application of kinship norms in the regulation of intra-lineage affairs.

As a corporate group, a lineage exhibits a structure of authority, and it is obvious from what I have said why this is aligned with the generation ladder. We find, as a general rule, that not only the lineage but also every segment of it has a head, by succession or election, who manages its affairs with the advice of his co-members. He may not have legal sanction by means of which to enforce his authority in internal affairs; but he holds his position by consent of all his fellow members, and he is backed by moral sanctions commonly couched in religious concepts. He is the trustee for the whole group of the property and other productive resources vested in it. He has a decisive jural role also in the disposal of rights over the fertility of the women in the group. He is likely to be the representative of the whole group in political and legal relations with other groups, with political authorities and in communal ritual. The effect may be to make him put the interests of his lineage above those of the community if there is conflict with the latter. This is quite clearly recognized by some peoples. Among the Ashanti for instance, every chiefship is vested in a matrilineal lineage. But once a chief has been installed his constitutional position is defined as holding an office that belongs to the whole community not to any one lineage. The man is, ideally, so merged in the office that he virtually ceases to be a member of his lineage, which always has an independent head for its corporate affairs (cf. Busia, 1951).

Thus lineage segmentation as a process in time links the lineage with the parental family; for it is through the family that the lineage (and therefore the society) is replenished by successive generations; and it is on the basis of the ties and cleavages between husband and wife, between polygynous wives, between siblings, and between generations that growth and segmentation take place in the lineage. Study of this process has added much to our understanding of well known aspects of family and kinship structure.

I suppose that we all now take it for granted that filiation – by contrast with descent – is universally bilateral. But we have also been taught, perhaps most graphically by Malinowski, that this does not imply equality of social weighting for the two sides of kin connection. Correctly stated, the rule should read that filiation is always complementary, unless the husband in a matrilineal society (like the Nayar) or the wife in a patrilineal society, as perhaps in ancient Rome, is given no parental status or is legally severed from his or her kin. The latter is the usual situation of a slave spouse in Africa.

Complementary filiation appears to be the principal mechanism by which segmentation in the lineage is brought about. This is very clear in patrilineal descent groups, and has been found to hold for societies as far apart as the Tallensi in West Africa and the Gusii in East Africa. What is a single lineage in relation to a male founder is divided into segments of a lower order by reference to their respective female founders on the model of the division of a polygynous family into separate matricentral 'houses'. In matrilineal lineage systems, however, the position is different. Segmentation does not follow the lines of different paternal origin, for obvious reasons; it follows the lines of differentiation between sisters. There is a connection between this and the weakness in law and in sentiment of the marriage tie in matrilineal societies, though it is usual for political and legal power to be vested in men as Kroeber (1938) and others have remarked. More study of this problem is needed.

Since the bilateral family is the focal element in the web of kinship, complementary filiation provides the essential link between a sibling group and the kin of the parent who does not determine descent. So a sibling group is not merely differentiated within a lineage but is further distinguished by reference to its kin ties outside the corporate unit. This structural device allows of degrees of individuation depending on the extent to which filiation on the non-corporate side is elaborated. The Tiv, for example, recognize five degrees of matrilateral filiation by which a sibling group is linked with lineages other than its own. These and other ties of a similar nature arising out of marriage exchanges result in a complex scheme of individuation for distinguishing both sibling groups and persons within a single lineage (L. Bohannan, 1951). This, of course, is not unique and has long been recognized, as everyone familiar with Australian kinship systems knows. Its more general significance can be brought out however by an example. A Tiv may claim to be living with a particular group of relatives for purely personal reasons of convenience or affection. Investigation shows that he has in fact made a choice of where to live within a strictly limited range of non-lineage kin. What purports to be a voluntary act freely motivated in fact presupposes a structural scheme of individuation. This is one of the instances which show how it is possible and feasible to move from the structural frame of reference to another, here that of the social psychologist, without confusing data and aims.

Most far-reaching in its effects on lineage structure is the use of the rule of complementary filiation to build double unilineal systems and some striking instances of this are found in Africa. One of the most developed systems of this type is that of the Yakö; and Forde's excellent analysis of how this works (Forde, 1950) shows that it is much more than a device for classifying kin. It is a principle of social organization that enters into all social relations and is expressed in all important institutions. There is the division of property, for instance, into the kind that is tied to the patrilineal lineage and the kind that passes to matrilineal kin. The division is between fixed and, in theory, perpetual productive resources, in this case farm land, with which go residence rights on the one hand, and on the other movable and consumable property like livestock and cash. There is a similar polarity in religious cult and in the political office and authority linked with cult, the legally somewhat weaker matrilineal line being ritually somewhat stronger than the patrilineal line. This balance between ritual and secular control is extended to the fertility of the women. An analogous double descent system has been described for some Nuba Hill tribes by Nadel (1950) and its occurrence among the Herero is now classical in ethnology. The arrangement works the other way round, too, in Africa, as among the Ashanti, though in their case the balance is far more heavily weighted on the side of the matrilineal lineage than on that of the jurally inferior and non-corporate paternal line.

These and other instances lead to the generalization that complementary filiation is not merely a constant element in the pattern of family relationships but comes into action at all levels of social structure in African societies. It appears that there is a tendency for interests, rights and loyalties to be divided on broadly complementary lines, into those that have the sanction of law or other public institutions for the enforcement of good conduct, and those that rely on religion, morality, conscience and sentiment for due observance. Where corporate descent groups exist the former seem to be generally tied to the descent group, the latter to the complementary line of filiation.

If we ask where this principle of social structure springs from we must look to the tensions inherent in the structure of the parental family. These tensions are the result of the direction given to individual lives by the total social structure but they also provide the models for the working of that structure. We now have plenty of evidence to show how the tensions that seem normally to arise between spouses, between successive generations and between siblings find expression in custom and belief. In a homogeneous society they are apt to be generalized over wide areas of the social structure. They then evoke controls like the Nyakyusa separation of successive generations of males in age villages that are built into the total social structure by the device of handing over political power to each successive generation as it reaches maturity (Wilson, 1951). Or this problem may be dealt with on the level of ritual and moral symbolism by separating parent and first born child of the same sex by taboos that eliminate open rivalry, as among the Tallensi, the Nuer, the Hausa and other peoples.

Thus by viewing the descent group as a continuing process through time we see how it binds the parental family, its growing point, by a series of steps into the widest framework of social structure. This enables us to visualize a social system as an integrated unity at a given time and over a stretch of time in relation to the process of social reproduction and in a more rigorous way than does a global concept of culture.

I do want to make clear, though, that we do not think of a lineage as being just a collection of people held together by the accident of birth. A descent group is an arrangement of persons that serves the attainment of legitimate social and personal ends. These include the gaining of a livelihood, the setting up of a family and the preservation of health and well-being as among the most important. I have several times remarked on the connection generally found between lineage structure and the ownership of the most valued productive property of the society, whether it be land or cattle or even the monopoly of a craft like blacksmithing. It is of great interest, for instance, to find Dr Richards attributing the absence of a lineage organization among the Bemba to their lack of heritable right in land or livestock (Richards, 1950). A similar connection is found between lineage organization and the control over reproductive resources and relations as is evident from the common occurrence of exogamy as a criterion of lineage differentiation. And since citizenship is derived from lineage membership and legal status depends on it, political and religious office of necessity vests in lineages. We must expect to find and we do find that the most important religious and magical concepts and institutions of a lineage-based society are tied into the lineage structure, serving both as the necessary symbolical representation of the social system and as its regulating values. This is a complicated subject about which much more needs to be known. Cults of gods and of ancestors, beliefs of a totemic nature and purely magical customs and practices, some or all are associated with lineage organization among the peoples previously quoted. What appears to happen is that every significant structural differentiation has its specific ritual symbolism, so that one can, as it were, read off from the scheme of ritual differentiation the pattern of structural differentiation and the configuration of norms of conduct that go with it. There is, to put it simply, a segmentation of ritual allegiance corresponding to the segmentation of genealogical grouping. Locality, filiation, descent, individuation, are thus symbolized.

Reference to locality reminds us of Kroeber's careful argument (1938) in favour of the priority of the local relationships of residence over those of descent in determining the line that is legally superior. A lineage cannot easily act as a corporate group if its members can never get together for the conduct of their affairs. It is not surprising therefore to find that the lineage in African societies is generally locally anchored; but it is not necessarily territorially compact or exclusive. A compact nucleus may be enough to act as the local centre for a group that is widely dispersed. I think it would be agreed that lineage and locality are independently variable and how they interact depends on other factors in the social structure. As I interpret the evidence, local ties are of secondary significance, *pace* Kroeber, for local ties do not appear to give rise to structural bonds in and of themselves. There must be common political or kinship or economic or ritual interests for structural bonds to emerge. Again spatial dispersion does not immediately put an end to lineage ties or to the ramifying kin ties found in cognatic systems like that of the Lozi. For legal status, property, office and cult act centripetally to hold dispersed lineages together and to bind scattered kindred. This is important in the dynamic pattern of lineage organization for it contains within itself the springs of disintegration, at the corporate level in the rule of segmentation, at the individual level in the rule of complementary filiation.

As I have suggested before, it seems that corporate descent groups can exist only in more or less homogeneous societies. Just what we mean by a homogeneous society is still rather vague though we all use the term lavishly. The working definition I make use of is that a homogeneous society is ideally one in which any person in the sense given to this term by Radcliffe-Brown in his recent (1950) essay, can be substituted for any other person of the same category without bringing about changes in the social structure. This implies that any two persons of the same category have the same body of customary usages and beliefs. I relate this tentative definition to the rule of sibling equivalence, so that I would say that, considered with respect to their achievable life histories, in a homogeneous society all men are brothers and all women sisters.

Societies based on unilineal descent groups are not the best in which to see what the notion of social substitutability means. For that it is better to consider societies in which descent still takes primacy over all other criteria of association and classification of persons in the regulation of social life but does not serve as the constitutive principle of corporate group organization. Central Africa provides some admirable instances (cf. Richards, 1950; Gluckman, 1951). Among the Bemba, the Tonga, the Lozi and many of their neighbours, as I have already remarked, the social structure must be thought of as a system of interconnected politico-legal statuses symbolized and sanctioned by ritual and not as a collection of people organized in self-perpetuating descent units. The stability of the society over time is preserved by perpetuating the status system. Thus when a person dies his status is kept alive by being taken up by an heir; and this heir is selected on the basis of descent rules. At any given time an individual may be the holder of a cluster of statuses; but these may be distributed among several persons on his death in a manner analogous to the widespread African custom by which a man's inherited estate goes to his lineage heir and his self-acquired property to his personal heir. Ideally, therefore, the network of statuses remains stable and perpetual though their holders come and go. Ritual symbols define and sanction the key positions in the system. What it represents, in fact, is the generalization throughout a whole society of the notion of the corporation sole as tied to descent but not to a corporate group. Descent and filiation have the function of selecting individuals for social positions and roles – in other words, for the exercise of particular rights and obligations – just as in cross-cousin marriage they serve to select ego's spouse.

The concept of the 'person' as an assemblage of statuses has been the starting point of some interesting enquiries. A generalization of long standing is that a married person always has two mutually antagonistic kinship statuses, that of spouse and parent in one family context and that of child and sibling in another (cf. Warner, 1958). This is very conspicuous in an exogamous lineage system; and the tensions resulting from this condition, connected as they are with the rule of complementary filiation, have wide consequences. A common rule of social structure reflected in avoidance customs is that these two statuses must not be confounded. Furthermore, each status can be regarded as a compound of separable rights and obligations. Thus a problem that has to be solved in every matrilineal society is how to reconcile the rights over a woman's procreative powers (rights *in genetricem* as Laura Bohannan (1949) has called them) which remain vested in her brother or her lineage, with those over her domestic and sexual services (rights *in uxorem*, cf. L. Bohannan, *loc. cit.*) which pass to her husband. Among the Yao of Nyasaland, as Dr Clyde Mitchell has shown (1956), this problem underlies the process of lineage segmentation. Brothers struggle against one another (or sisters' sons against mothers' brothers) for the control of their sisters' procreative powers and this leads to fission in the minimal lineage. It is of great significance that such a split is commonly precipitated by accusations of witchcraft against the brother from whose control the sisters are withdrawn. By contrast, where rights over a woman's child-bearing powers are held by her husband's patrilineal lineage the conflicts related to this critical interest occur between the wives of a lineage segment; and among the Zulu and Xhosa speaking tribes of South Africa these lead to witchcraft accusations between co-wives (cf. Hunter, 1961). As Laura Bohannan's paper shows, many widespread customs and institutions connected with marriage and parenthood, such as the levirate and the sororate, wife-taking by women, exchange marriage as practised by the Tiv, and ghost marriage as found among the Nuer (Evans-Pritchard, 1951) have structural significance not hitherto appreciated if they are regarded from the point of view I have indicated.

But one thing must be emphasized. This method of analysis does not explain why in one society certain kinds of interpersonal conflict are socially projected in witchcraft beliefs whereas in another they may be projected in terms of a belief in punitive spirits. It makes clear why a funeral ceremony is necessary and why it is organized in a particular way in the interest of maintaining a stable and coherent social system. It does not explain why the ritual performed in the funeral ceremonies of one people uses materials, ideas and dramatizations of a different kind from those used by another people. In short, it brings us nearer than we were thirty years ago to understanding the machinery by which norms are made effective, not only in a particular primitive society but in a type of primitive society. It does not explain how the norms come to be what they in fact are in a particular society.

In this connection, however, it is worth drawing attention to certain norms that have long been recognized to have a critical value in social organization. Marriage regulations, incest prohibitions and the laws of homicide and warfare are the most important. Analysis of lineage structure has revealed an aspect of these norms which is of great theoretical interest. It is now fairly evident that these are not absolute rules of conduct which men are apt to break through an outburst of unruly instinct or rebellious self-assertion, as has commonly been thought. They are *relatively* obligatory in accordance with the structural relations of the parties. The Beduin of Cyrenaica regard homicide within the minimal agnatic lineage, even under extreme provocation, as a grave sin, whereas slaying a member of a different tribal segment is an admirable deed of valour. The Tallensi consider sex relations with a near sister of the same lineage as incest but tacitly ignore the act if the parties are very distant lineage kin. Among the Tiv, the Nuer, the Gusii and other tribes the lineage range within which the rule of exogamy holds is variable and can be changed by a ceremony that makes formally prohibited marriages legitimate and so brings marriage prohibitions into line with changes in the segmentary structure of the lineage. In this way previously exogamous units are split into intermarrying units. In all the societies mentioned, and others as well, an act of self-help that leads to negotiations if the parties belong to closely related lineages might lead to war if they are members of independent – though not necessarily geographically far apart – lineages. Such observations are indications of the flexibility of primitive social structures. They give a clue to the way in which internal adjustments are made from time to time in those structures, either in response to changing pressures from without or through the momentum of their own development. They suggest how such societies can remain stable in the long run without being rigid. But this verges on speculation. [. . .]

What I wish to convey by the example of current studies of unilineal descent group structure is that we have, in my belief, got to a point where a number of connected generalizations of wide validity can be made about this type of social group. This is an advance I associate with the structural frame of reference. I wish to suggest that this frame of reference gives us procedures of investigation and analysis by which a social system can be apprehended as a unity made of parts and processes that are linked to one another by a limited number of principles of wide validity in homogeneous and relatively stable societies. It has enabled us to set up hypotheses about the nature of these principles that have the merit of being related directly to the ethnographic material now so abundantly at hand and of being susceptible of testing by further field observation. It cannot be denied, I think, that we have here a number of positive contributions of real importance to social science.

References

BOHANNAN, L. (1949), 'Dahomean marriage: a revaluation', *Africa*, vol. 19, pp. 273–87.
BOHANNAN, L. (1951), *A Comparative Study of Social Differentiation in Primitive Society*, D. Phil. thesis, University of Oxford.

BUSIA, K. A. (1951), *The Position of the Chief in the Modern Political System of Ashanti*, Oxford University Press.

EVANS-PRITCHARD, E. E. (1940), *The Nuer*, Clarendon Press.

EVANS-PRITCHARD, E. E. (1951), *Kinship and Marriage among the Nuer*, Clarendon Press.

FORDE, C. D. (1938), 'Fission and accretion in the patrilineal clans of a semi-Bantu community', *J. roy. anthrop. Inst.*, vol. 68, pp. 311–38.

FORDE, C. D. (1947), 'The anthropological approach in social science'. *The Advancement of Science*, vol. 4, pp. 213–24.

FORDE, C. D. (1950), 'Double descent among the Yakö', in A. R. Radcliffe-Brown and C. D. Forde (eds.), *African Systems of Kinship and Marriage*, Oxford University Press.

FORTES, M. (1945), *The Dynamics of Clanship among the Tallensi*, Oxford University Press.

GLUCKMAN, M. (1951), 'The Lozi of Barotseland in North Western Rhodesia', in E. Colson and M. Gluckman (eds.), *Seven Tribes of British Central Africa*, Oxford University Press.

HUNTER, M. (1961), *Reaction to Conquest*, Oxford University Press.

KROEBER, A. L. (1938), 'Basic and secondary patterns of social structure *J. roy. anthrop. Inst.*, vol. 68, pp. 299–309.

MAYER, P. P. (1949), 'The lineage principle in Gusii society', International African Institute, Memorandum 24.

MITCHELL, J. C. (1956), *The Yao Village*, Manchester University Press.

NADEL, S. F. (1950), 'Dual descent in the Nuba Hills', in A. R. Radcliffe-Brown and C. D. Forde (eds.), *African Systems of Kinship and Marriage*, Oxford University Press.

PETERS, E. L. (1951), *The Sociology of the Beduin of Cyrenaica*, D. Phil. thesis, University of Oxford.

RADCLIFFE-BROWN, A. R. (1935), 'Patrilineal and matrilineal succession', *Iowa Law Rev.*, vol. 20, pp. 286–303.

RADCLIFFE-BROWN, A. R. (1950), 'Introduction', *African Systems of Kinship and Marriage*, Oxford University Press.

RICHARDS, A. I. (1950), 'Some types of family structure among the Central Bantu', in A. R. Radcliffe-Brown and C. D. Forde (eds.), *African Systems of Kinship and Marriage*, Oxford University Press.

WARNER, W. L. (1958), *A Black Civilization*, Harper & Row.

WILSON, M. (1951), 'Nyakyusa age villages', *J. roy. anthrop. Inst.*, vol. 79, pp. 21–5.

18 A. I. Richards

Matrilineal Systems

Excerpts from A. I. Richards, 'Some types of family structure amongst the Central Bantu', in A. R. Radcliffe-Brown and D. Forde (eds.), *African Systems of Kinship and Marriage*, Oxford University Press for the International African Institute, 1950, pp. 207–51.

Characteristics of matrilineal kinship organizations in Central Africa

Most of the Bantu peoples of Central Africa reckon descent in the matrilineal rather than the patrilineal line, and many of them practise some form of what is usually known as matrilocal marriage. In fact, it is the matrilineal character of their kinship organization which distinguishes them so clearly from the Bantu of East and South Africa, and for this reason the territory stretching from the west and central districts of the Belgian Congo to the north-eastern plateau of Northern Rhodesia and the highlands of Nyasaland is sometimes referred to as the 'matrilineal belt'.[1]

Within this group of 'matrilineal' tribes there is a remarkable degree of uniformity as to the principles governing descent and succession and the various ideologies by which people explain their adherence to the mother's rather than to the father's line, and stress their community of interests with their maternal relatives.[2] Blood is believed to be passed through the woman and not through the man. The metaphors of kinship stress the ties between people 'born from the same womb' or 'suckled at the

1. There are, of course, a number of patrilineal or mainly patrilineal tribes in the Belgian Congo, including most of the Luba (as distinguished from the Luba-Hemba), the Songe and the Nkundo.

2. Matrilineal is used here in inverted commas because it is generally recognized that no society is entirely matrilineal or patrilineal as regards descent, inheritance, succession and authority, but that the family system provides a balance of interests and rights between the two sides of the family with a predominant emphasis on one side or the other, and it is in this sense that I shall use the term in this article. See Richards (1934) for a description of Bemba kinship from this point of view.

same breast', and in some tribes the physical role of the father is believed to be limited to the quickening of the foetus already formed in the uterus. The duty of the woman to produce children for her lineage is emphasized, and descent is traced from an original ancestress or a series of ancestresses known as 'mothers' of the lineage or clan, and also in some cases from the brothers of these founding ancestresses. The ancestral cult centres round the worship of matrilineal rather than patrilineal ancestors, although spirits of the father's line are sometimes the subject of subsidiary rites.

A child belongs to his mother's clan or lineage, and succession to office follows the common matrilineal rule, that is to say, authority passes to the dead man's brothers or to his sisters' sons, or to the sons of his maternal nieces. Among some of the Central Bantu women succeed to the titles of royal ancestresses, or hold positions as chieftainesses, with special ritual functions.

But with these principles of descent and succession the similarity ends. The Central African people differ in a rather striking way as to their family structure, and in particular as to the various forms of domestic and local grouping based on the family.

These variations in the family structure depend largely on the nature of the marriage contract and the extent to which the husband is able to gain control over his wife, who belongs, by virtue of matrilineal descent, to the lineage and clan of her mother and of her brothers and sisters; and also on the extent to which he manages to achieve a position of authority over the children she bears. In matrilineal societies the man's control over his wife and her children can never be complete, except in the case of a union with a slave woman, but he can gain considerable power over his wife's labour, her property and her child-bearing powers, as well as rights over his children's work and their marriages, by virtue of the service or payments he makes to his father- or brother-in-law. Moreover, the ways in which domestic authority is divided between a man and the head of his wife's kinship group are surprisingly varied. In some cases there is a formal allocation of rights and privileges between father and mother's brother in return for service and payments. In other cases the balance is less well defined, and every marriage produces what can only be described as a constant pull-father-pull-mother's-brother, in which the personality, wealth and social status of the two individuals or their respective kinsmen give the advantage to one side or the other, and a number of alternative solutions are reached within the same tribe.

In this balance of privileges and duties between the patrikin and the matrikin the crucial point is obviously the husband's right to determine the residence of the bride. If she and her children live in the same homestead or village as his kinsmen, his domestic authority is likely to be greater than where they remain with the wife's relatives.

Throughout this area, at any rate, the rule of residence at marriage seems to me to be the most important index of the husband's status. It also provides the most convenient basis for the classification of these different forms of matrilineal family. In Central Africa we find every gradation from the marriage in which the husband has the right to remove his bride immediately to his own village, to varieties of trial marriage, temporary unions or customs by which the husband takes up more or less permanent residence in the wife's group.

For this reason I have found the old terms 'matrilocal' and 'patrilocal' of little use for comparative purposes. Many writers have pointed out that the words are in themselves confusing, since there are two parties to a marriage and what is 'residence with the mother' for the one is 'residence with the mother-in-law' for the other. If the terms are to be retained for purposes of classification it would be necessary to adopt a convention by which, for instance, they were always used with relation to one sex. Firth (1936, p. 596) and Adam (1948, p. 12) suggest as an alternative the use of the words 'virilocal' and 'uxorilocal' to meet this difficulty,[3] and I shall use these terms from time to time.

Another difficulty with regard to the Central African area is the variety of forms of marriage relationship which could reasonably be included under the title 'matrilocal'. In societies practising matrilineal descent a man may live with his wife's people because

3. N. W. Thomas, who suggested the terms patrilocal and matrilocal, put them forward 'not as being specifically appropriate but as being parallel to patrilineal and matrilineal, denoting descent in the female or male line respectively' (1906, p. 108), thus showing that he realized from the start the ambiguity of the terms.

the marriage is on trial; because he is fulfilling a marriage contract by service instead of the payment of goods; or because he means to settle permanently in his wife's group.[4] He may have sex access to his wife at night and work in her fields, but act as head of his sister's house and spend a large part of his day with the latter. This is the practice of the matrilineal Menangkabau of the Padang highlands of Sumatra and the kindred peoples of Negri Sembilan (Verkerk-Pistorius, 1871; Cole, 1945).[5] A similar position holds good among the Hopi of Arizona. Alternatively a husband may live at his wife's village but often be away visiting his own relatives, as amongst the Yao; or he may spend alternate years in his own and his wife's village, as in Dobu Island. In any of these cases there will be some years, some months, or some hours in which the marriage may reasonably be called matrilocal. The term gives no indication of the length of time a man spends in his wife's village, or the degree to which he is incorporated with her matrikin, or isolated from his own family.[6] For this reason I have found it better to use the phrases 'marriage with immediate right of bride removal' or 'marriage with delayed right of bride removal' or 'marriage without bride removal' in describing the family systems of the Central Bantu.

The terms 'matrilocal' or 'patrilocal' are similarly lacking in precision when used as a means of classifying types of family and domestic unit. According to the terminology adopted in this book [i.e. *African Systems of Kinship and Marriage*], a parental family is a household or homestead composed of a man, his wife or wives, and their children. Such a unit naturally grows in size in societies where it is customary for either the sons or the daughters to live with their parents after marriage. This wider group, usually based on the principle of unilineal descent and composed of members

4. Rivers points out (1908), that marriage by service 'passes insensibly into the matrilocal form of marriage' and trial marriages 'shade insensibly into trials before marriage on the one hand and into ease and frequency of divorce on the other'.

5. Quoted also by Taylor (1896, p. 96) where he describes the 'Chassez Croisez' which takes place at dusk when each man leaves his sister's house where he has been by day, to join his wife and children at night.

6. R. Linton stresses the importance of the propinquity of the two settlements in determining the character of the descent system (1936, p. 168).

of three generations, is here described as an extended family.[7] Members of extended families of this kind usually live in a separate kraal or homestead or they may form the nucleus or core of a village or a section of a village. They tend to cooperate in economic affairs, to exercise some common rights over property, to accept their genealogical senior as a common authority and to practise some joint ritual. Where it is a common practice for a man who has married sons to separate off from his father's homestead to start a new community, and where the land situation makes this possible, a three-generation extended family of this kind becomes the normal pattern of residence as it is, for instance, amongst the Zulu. Where, however, the villages are more permanent and the splitting off of new extended families is not so easy, the residential pattern is naturally much less uniform. The eldest brother of a group of siblings may succeed to the position of his father in a patrilineal society or to that of his mother's brother in a matrilineal society, and various other changes of this kind may take place. Thus in the more or less permanent villages there may be two or three extended families or remains of extended families. There may also be two or three alternative types of marriage in the same community, and a number of principles of residence. Such larger residential units, usually based on a nuclear extended family but with a number of additions, I have called local kin groups, specifying whether they are predominantly matrilineal or patrilineal in composition.

In such extended families or local kin groups extension takes place on the basis of certain nuclear or pivotal relationships. For instance, according to the rules of residence at marriage, the children of one sex marry out of the homestead, whereas those of the other remain within it. Rules of succession and inheritance similarly determine the incidence of authority and economic privilege within the local community. Property rights and authority may go from father to son, from mother to daughter, from brother to sister's son, and so forth. I find it convenient to classify the different types of extended family by means of these nuclear

---

7. I have found it useful to employ the term 'grand-family' suggested to me by R. Firth to indicate a three-generation family descended in the direct line, patrilineal or matrilineal, when it is necessary to distinguish between this and other forms of extended family.

relationships, even though the categories constantly overlap. Thus I use the term 'father-son extended family' for a Zulu homestead; or the 'mother-son extended family' for a local unit which is a common pattern amongst the Swazi, where the woman leaves her husband's kraal at the time of her son's marriage and lives with him in a position of authority to the end of her life. Parent-daughter extended families of one kind or another exist where uxorilocal marriage is practised. These include the mother-daughter family of the Hopi, where property in land or houses is passed through the woman; the sororal family, where a group of married sisters and their daughters live together, usually under the care of an elder brother; or the sibling family found amongst the Nayar of Malabar, where a man lived with his sisters and the latter were visited by their husbands at night; or a father-daughter family, where married daughters live with their parents, but their father is very much the head of the group and may determine residence instead of the mother. Other types of extended family include the matrilineal fraternal family, where a group of brothers live with their wives and their sisters' sons.

It is obvious that in the case of residential units such as these the nuclear relationships vary from one type of extended family to the other; that is to say, one homestead is based on the close relationship of a group of the men of the family, as in the case of the patrilineal father-son family or the matrilineal fraternal family; while another is founded on the kinship of women, as in the mother-daughter family of the Hopi. The interests of brother and brother, brother and sister, or mother and daughter may be identified by one marriage system or the other, while the extended families so formed may attract to themselves additional households of kinsfolk or slaves, according to fixed rule or more casual association.

Conclusions

Among the Central Bantu the matrilineal system makes for certain elements of conflict for which some kind of solution has to be found. The problem in all such matrilineal societies is similar. It is the difficulty of combining recognition of descent through the woman with the rule of exogamous marriage. Descent is reckoned through the mother, but by the rule of exogamy a woman who has to produce children for her matrikin must marry a man from another group. If she leaves her own group to join that of her husband, her matrikin have to contrive in some way or other to keep control of the children, who are legally identified with them. The brothers must divide authority with the husband who is living elsewhere. If, on the other hand, the woman remains with her parents and her husband joins her there, she and her children remain under the control of her family, but her brothers are lost to the group since they marry brides elsewhere and they are separated from the village where they have rights of succession.

There is the further difficulty that in most societies authority over a household, or a group of households, is usually in the hands of men, not women, as are also the most important political offices. Thus any form of uxorilocal marriage means that an individual of the dominant sex is, initially at any rate, in a position of subjection in his spouse's village, and this is a situation which he tends to find irksome and tries to escape from.

There are, of course, a number of solutions to the matrilineal puzzle. The first of these may be described as the matriarchal solution, in that property, and particularly houses and lands, pass through the woman as well as the line of descent. The eldest brother usually acts as manager of the estate. This is achieved either by the institution of the visiting husband or by that of the visiting brother. The women of the *taravad* or matrilineal joint family of the Nayar of Malabar live with their brother or brothers and are visited by their husbands at night. In the case of the Menangkabau the men were members of their sisters' joint household (*rumah*) and spent much of the day there, but they returned to their wives' households at night (Cole, 1945, pp. 253, 266). Among the Hopi the situation is slightly different, in that a group of married women live together and own land and houses jointly, but each husband acts as manager of his wife's land and chief worker on it, while the brother acts as spokesman and ritual officiant for his sisters and as host in their houses.[8]

Such solutions only seem to me to be possible in big settlements with permanent housing, where a man can walk easily from his own household to that of his sisters and perform his two functions without clash. This is the case amongst the Nayar and something similar occurs in the large towns of Ashanti Province in the Gold

8. Verbal communication from Mrs Aitken; see also Forde (1931).

Coast where a woman visits her husband at night. But Central Africa is much less closely settled. In Northern Rhodesia shifting cultivation is practised, and villages not only move, but are more sparsely distributed, often at a distance of seventeen to thirty miles apart. In these circumstances either the wife or the husband may have to live some distance away from the group to which they are legally affiliated. The more densely occupied Yao area allows husbands to be away visiting their own relatives more easily and it appears that they often do so.[9]

The second solution is that of the fraternal extended family with sisters and children 'loaned away'. This is the solution adopted by the Trobriand islanders and the western Congo people. Here virilocal marriage makes it possible for a group of brothers to live together and to exercise full male authority over the community, while their sisters are loaned out to men in other communities and the children of the matrilineage are reclaimed at puberty.

The third solution might be said to be that of the borrowed husband. These are the various forms of uxorilocal marriage described in this area. The conflict of interests in these societies is probably the most extreme, since all the men of a community cannot at the same time act as mother's brothers with authority over their own local descent group and also as husbands living in their own wives' villages, as the rule of uxorilocal marriage demands. Amongst the Cewa and Yao it seems that the majority of marriages are uxorilocal but that marriages are easily broken. A man who cannot stand the situation in his wife's village leaves and goes elsewhere. This might in fact be described as the solution of the detachable husband. Added to this certain senior men have a right from the start to practise virilocal marriage since they are selected as heads of villages or inherit such positions. They thus escape from the difficult position in which their younger brothers are placed. In other words, there is here a stress on primogeniture with virilocal marriage as one of the privileges of the first born. The Bemba deal with this difficulty by the transfer or removal

9. Daryll Forde suggests to me that the necessary factor is not the size of the settlement but its compact and endogamous character. A man can act simultaneously as husband and manager-brother where he has married within the same community. Both the size and the endogamous character of the local unit seem to me to be relevant factors.

marriage, by which the young man is dependent on his father-in-law in youth but gains authority as the head of a father-daughter grand-family in his old age; this is a solution which is possible in areas where land is plentiful and the setting up of new homesteads and villages is easy, and where the political system allows of the constant creation of new units.

Still another way out of the difficulty is the solution of the selected heir, which allows the head of the matrilineage to choose one or more of his sisters' children to succeed him and to transfer these boys to his own village while the remaining children are allowed to stop with their father. This seems to be the practice among the Mayombe, according to Van Reeth. Kirchoff quotes the similar custom of the Tlingit by which one or two sons of a woman marry their cross-cousins and go to live with their mother's brother, whereas the rest of the children marry virilocally. The Nuba often adopt one or two sisters' sons to be brought up as their own sons in the same way (Kirchoff, 1932; Nadel, 1948, p. 31).[10]

In every case there are constitutionally recognized alleviations for the socially childless father in these matrilineal societies. Slavery allows him to gain control over the children of slave wives who thus join his clan, and Torday (1925, p. 103) speaks of Kongo fathers choosing slave wives for preference for this reason. Cross-cousin marriages may give the father control over some of his grandchildren that he cannot maintain over his children, or bring into his village members of his clan. By the mother's brother's daughter marriage of the Yao the son of one of the married sisters belonging to the sororal family marries the daughter of the manager-brother and therefore contracts what is virtually a virilocal marriage.

Polygyny and the marriage of widows also allow men to contract at least some virilocal marriages in most of the Central African tribes, and, whatever the rule of descent, a man who has succeeded in becoming the head of a polygynous household is in fact a patriarch over his wives and young children. Lastly men of wealth and distinction are able to reverse the usual rules of residence.

10. This list does not of course exhaust the logical possibilities. The solution of alternating residence among the Dobu has been mentioned already. There is also the separate men's and women's houses of the Ga of the Gold Coast.

Authority over the children of a marriage consists of a series of rights and privileges, and many kinship systems allow for the exercise of different types of authority by different members of the patrikin or matrikin. In Central Africa there may be a fairly complete severance between domestic authority exerted over the children brought up in their father's homestead and rights over their persons and the marriages they contract. These latter may be exerted by a man who lives some distance away. Domestic authority is a treasured asset in an area where local communities grow up round the core of the extended family and the head of such a family is actually or potentially the head of a village, and hence of the unit that is the basis of the whole political structure. On the other hand, this is an area in which slavery was formerly a very prominent institution, and, therefore, whatever hold the father may have gained over his children, the power of the mother's brother to sell them into slavery must have remained as a potential threat to be constantly feared. Even amongst the Ila, where the father is a patriarch ruling over a large polygynous homestead very similar to that found amongst the patriarchal Bantu, Smith and Dale (1920) describe the woman's brother as having 'power of life and death' over her children. The right to sell into slavery is apparently the power described.

A balance of rights and duties between the patrikin and the matrikin tends to produce secondary forms of descent. While it would be true to say that in every matrilineal society a man must know his father's clan and get some privileges from his patrikin, there are tribes in which both patrilineal and matrilineal relatives are organized in definite descent groups with names and corporate functions as amongst the Yakö. In Central Africa the existence of such double descent groups does not seem to be proved, but there is a secondary reckoning of descent in those tribes in which the patrilineal-matrilineal balance is most even. Amongst the Kongo the father's matrikin are known by a separate name and a man has sentimental ties with the men of his father's village in which he was brought up, and these informal ties seem to have led to the suggestion that the Kongo practise dual descent.

Ancestor worship also reflects the duality of the reckoning of descent. The Bemba commoner can inherit a guardian spirit from his father's side as well as his mother's, and will pray to his maternal grandfather as well as to his maternal uncle, although this would not be the case in the royal clan. The Ila pray to the ancestors both of the father and of the mother, and Kongo ceremonies honouring the father's ancestors have also been mentioned.

In all these forms of family structure the crucial point, I have suggested, is the question of residence at marriage, and the determining factor in this regard is the marriage payment or the type of goods and services which the bridegroom gives. In Central Africa the tribes which give large amounts of goods or money in bridewealth, as do the Mayombe and the Ila, seem invariably to practise virilocal marriage; whereas those who give service or token payments, like the Bemba or Bisa, do not. The importance of the marriage payment is shown by the fact that even amongst the western Congo peoples, where the avunculate is most pronounced, a man who gives an unusually large sum to his bride's family is able to gain permanent possession of his wife and to keep her children with him instead of returning them to their maternal uncle at puberty. The passage of cattle as *chiko* amongst the matrilineal Ila is an equally important determinant. The *chiko* gives the father permanent possession of his children and enables him to keep his married sons with him to form the basic residential unit, the *mukwashi*. The division of cattle among his sons and his daughters sets up what seem to be a number of three or four-generation patrilineages as well as similar groups united through rights of inheritance of cattle from their mother. In Northern Rhodesia there are no high marriage payments and a man cannot remove his wife and children to his village immediately. He may earn the permission to do so through service or joint residence, but he will never acquire complete possession of his wife and children.

As regards the stability of marriage in these different types of family, we have hints and impressions of various kinds but very little accurate quantitative data. The payment of bridewealth is assumed to encourage a stable marriage since the wife's family is pledged to return cattle or goods received in this way if she breaks her contract. If this assumption is correct, divorce should be rare in the western Congo, where the marriage payments are considerable, but I have no figures to show whether this actually is the case or not. The divorce rate should also be low amongst the Ila, but as a matter of fact Smith and Dale say that it is frequent. It seems clear to me that the size of the bridewealth and the way in which it is contributed are determining factors but by no means the only ones. Where the avunculate is strong the mother's brother usually has the power to take his sister's daughter away from the husband to whom she has been 'loaned' and give her to another man, and this must be reckoned as at least one of the causes of instability in marriage. It occurs amongst the Mayombe, the Ila and the Bemba, and probably elsewhere. Moreover, where the residential units are based on ties of kinship through the woman rather than the man, the link between mother and daughter, or sister and sister, may become so strong that it can threaten the marriage of one of these women. Divorces sometimes occur in Bemba society at the time of the conversion of a marriage, that is to say when the husband has won the right to take his wife back to his own village. The woman may refuse to go with him because she wants to stay with her mother and sisters.

There are also positive inducements to permanent marriage. Bemba give token presents not bridewealth, but a man stands to gain by a stable union because only by this means is he able to build up the basic domestic unit which puts him in a position of authority over several households and enables him to set up house where he wishes and ultimately to build his own village if he pleases. A stable marriage for a Bemba is the first step on the road to a headmanship. It is interesting to correlate different forms of family structure with greater or less stability in marriage in this way, but conclusive answers will have to wait until we have even some rough approximation to the differential divorce rates in these and contiguous areas.

Various economic and social determinants of family structure have been suggested in these pages, though fuller details of the economic organization of all the selected tribes would be required to test the hypotheses made. The presence or absence of inheritable possessions in the form of land, trees, cattle, or money have been correlated with the type of marriage, and the position of the father as against that of the mother's brother. It has also been associated with the corporate nature of a unit like the western Congo matrilineage, as against the dispersed descent groups of the peoples of Northern Rhodesia. It would no doubt be possible to start from the same set of facts and reach very different conclusions. Is it, for instance, the shortage of land and the value of the permanent palm-trees that make members of a matrilineage willing to live together in one closely organized group? Or is it the system of corporate matrilineages which makes them anxious to develop their land together instead of doing so alone, and encourages them to accept the rule of their genealogical head? No doubt there is something to be said from both points of view. Where the type of marriage makes it possible for a group of brothers to live together, an economic situation such as that of the western Congo increases their economic interdependence and counteracts centrifugal tendencies. Where, on the other hand, the family structure provides no basis for a group of cooperating men, and where the land supply is so ample that it is possible for men to set up new settlements easily, they do so and the matrilineage loses its corporate function. Detailed studies of contiguous people living in rather similar economic conditions are needed before we can generalize usefully on such questions. At present the variables are too numerous to permit more than likely guesses.

This article merely attempts to make some crude comparisons between four types of family structure associated with the rule of matrilineal descent in Central Africa, and to suggest some possible correlations between marriage type, residential grouping, economic and political organization.

References

ADAM, L. (1948), '"Virilocal" and "uxorilocal"', *Man*, vol. 48, art. 13.
COLE, F. C. (1945), *The Peoples of Malaysia*, Van Nostrand.
FIRTH, R. (1936), *We the Tikopia*, Allen & Unwin.
FORDE, D. (1931), 'Hopi agriculture and land ownership', *J. roy. anthropol. Inst.*, vol. 61, pp. 357-99.
KIRCHHOFF, P. (1932), 'Kinship organisation', *Africa*, vol. 2, pp. 184-91.
LINTON, R. (1936), *The Study of Man*, Appleton-Century-Crofts.
NADEL, S. F. (1948), *The Nuba*, Oxford University Press.
RICHARDS, A. I. (1934), 'Mother right in central Africa', in E. E. Evans-Pritchard *et al.*, *Essays Presented to C. G. Seligman*, Routledge & Kegan Paul.
RIVERS, W. H. R. (1908), 'Marriage', in J. Hastings (ed.), *Encyclopedia of Religion and Ethics*, T. & T. Clark.
SMITH, E. W, and DALE, A.M. (1920), *The Ila-Speaking Peoples of Northern Rhodesia*, Macmillan.

TAYLOR, A. (1896), 'Matriarchal family system', *The Nineteenth Century*, vol. 40, pp. 81–96.

THOMAS, N. W. (1906), *Kinship Organization and Group Marriage in Australia*, Cambridge University Press.

TORDAY, E. (1925), *Causeries Congolaises*, Vromant, Brussels.

VERERK-PISTORIUS, A. (1871), *Studien over de inlandische Houshouding in de Padangische Bovenlander*, Holland.

19 R. N. Pehrson

Bilateral Kin Groupings[1]

R. N. Pehrson, 'Bilateral kin groupings as a structural type: a preliminary statement', *University of Manila Journal of East Asiatic Studies*, vol. 3, 1964, pp. 199–202.

A good deal of anthropological theory concerning social organization is derived from investigations of societies based upon unilineal descent groups. The lineage looms large in our picture of non-Western societies. It is frequently assumed that societies based upon the bilateral principle of descent are 'amorphous', 'unstructured', 'loosely organized' or 'infinitely complex'. I wish to examine the local group organization and marriage residence patterns of one bilaterally organized society in order to suggest that there is structure to this type of society but that the structure may be obscured by approaching it from a unilineal viewpoint.

My model of bilateral organization derives from research among the North Lapp reindeer nomads who migrate near Karesuando in Sweden, Enontekio in Finland and Kautokeino in Norway. The fundamental bilateralism of Lapp society first becomes apparent in the reindeer nomads' inheritance rules and kinship nomenclature.

Among the Lapps, property is owned individually. Wealth is determined by the number of reindeer possessed and these are inherited and transmitted equally through the male and female lines. The reindeer are herded collectively by the migratory local group on pasturelands allocated according to customary rights of usage.

Neither is there any unilineal emphasis in the kinship terminology as shown by the complete bilaterality and symmetry of Lapp consanguineal kinship terms and by the rigid differentiation into

1. This paper was originally presented to the annual meeting of the Central States Anthropological Society at Urbana, Illinois, in May 1953. I am grateful for suggestions on the paper made by Professor E. Adamson Hoebel, University of Utah, and Mr McKim Marriott, University of Chicago.

generations. A third significant feature is the equivalence of siblings, terminologically expressed by classifying cousins with siblings (in Ego's generation, the term of cousin is derived from the sibling term). This equivalence of siblings also occurs in the affinal terminology; Ego classes together his or her spouse's sister and female cousin and brother and male cousin and brother's wife and male cousin's wife.

These terminological features are paralleled in local group organization which, among the Lapps, takes the form of migratory units or bands. Within the band, each generation has its own sphere of activities, rights and obligations. Band members of the same generational level are unified by the classification of cousins with siblings. The principle of the equivalence of siblings also acts to increase the number of band members available for economic activities. In examining kinship behavioural patterns, I came to the conclusion that sibling solidarity is the fundamental kinship bond of Lapp society.

A cursory glance at Lapp band genealogies does not, at first, reveal any clear organizational pattern. The reason for this, I believe, is that a Lapp migratory unit is not a corporate body as such is generally conceived in social anthropology. That is, it lacks such corporate attributes of unilineal kin groupings as perpetuity through time, collective ownership of property and unified activity as a legal individual. Instead of thinking of the Lapp band as a corporate body, we must think of it as a series of alliances between sibling groups. Since these alliances have varying degrees of permanence, a Lapp may be a member of several bands during his life. Within the band, every person is related by blood or marriage to every other person either directly or through a third person. However, the Lapp band is not an 'extended family' but, to repeat, an alliance between sibling groups, one of which is dominant. The dominant sibling group provides a nucleus to the genealogical structure of the band since it is the basic point of reference of that structure. The dominant sibling group also gives continuity to leadership since the leader is one of the dominant siblings and his successor is chosen from his sons or sons-in-law.

One of the problems involved in analysing local group organization is the problem of marriage residence patterns. (I might add that this is not the only problem involved in local group organization as some social anthropologists have assumed. It is also necessary to account for the presence of such unmarried adults as the hired herders found in many Lapp bands.) In analysing marriage residence, I found no clear-cut matrilocal or patrilocal rules. I also found that the bands are not exclusively exogamic or endogamic. The concepts of complete exogamy or endogamy in relation to local groups may be useful in dealings with societies based on unilineal descent. However, where the local group is neither exclusively exogamic or endogamic (and this seems to be true of many bilateral societies in addition to the north Lapps), the problem becomes one of determining effective range of relationship covered by incest taboos. This is so because the Lapp band is not a corporate entity. By analysing Lapp sociological concepts, it becomes apparent that the Lapp conceives of himself as a point in a network of kinship relations and not as a member of any corporate entity greater than the sibling group. In selecting a spouse, the Lapp must determine his position on this network of kinship ties in relation to the position of his prospective mate rather than whether or not she belongs to his local group. Thus, if two people in the same band are not directly related or if they are not too closely related, then they may marry. Ideally, incest taboos extend to third cousins but I found in analysing genealogical connections between spouses that there is a certain amount of cousin marriage. Here there was a discrepancy between the statements of informants and a statistical analysis of the actual situation.

I noted the same discrepancy in statements as to change of residence upon marriage. The Lapps invariably state that at marriage, the woman should join her husband's band but an analysis of all marriages shows that about equally often, the man joins his wife's band and remains there. Occasionally, the spouse who moves brings his or her parents and parental siblings and families into the new band. Thus, it became apparent that the Lapps have no simple rules of residence, that the matrilocal and patrilocal characterizations do not apply to a society where parents change residence upon the marriage of their children and that each case of residence change has to be investigated to determine the sociological factors at work.

Such an investigation reveals the following factors underlying marriage residence patterns (although not necessarily in the following order of importance):

Relative wealth. The spouse with less reindeer often moves to the band of the richer spouse. Rich Lapps frequently consider it desirable to marry off their children to poorer Lapps since, by so doing, they gain an addition to their labour force and do not lose their children's reindeer.

Relative status of the spouses' parents or siblings. Status is not determined exclusively by the individual's wealth. It may also derive from membership in the dominant sibling group of a particular band.

Relative labour convenience. A person who has several siblings may join his spouse's band if the latter lacks sufficient manpower to herd efficiently.

Relative age considerations. These are of two sorts. First, one must consider the age of the partners relative to their respective siblings. The eldest son tends to remain at home upon marriage if he is the son of a band leader or wealthy man. In poor families where the mother is widowed, the youngest son often remains at home upon marriage so that he may herd his family's reindeer while the elder siblings are employed as servants in other bands. One must also consider the age of husband and wife relative to each other. If there is a great age difference, the younger spouse may join the band of the elder spouse since the latter has had more time to accumulate property.

Demographic factors are also important in determining residence after marriage. If a herding leader has only daughters, then most of the adult males in the band are liable to have come from other bands (as Mr Ian R. Whitaker has shown).

Finally, ecological factors help to determine marriage residence. For example, the son of a rich man may decide to join his wife's band if his father and his own siblings have too many reindeer in relation to the available pastureland.

Now, throughout this consideration of factors determining residence, you may have noted that people may move in relation to their siblings instead of in relation to their parents. This may be correlated with the tendency for Lapps to marry at a relatively late age or when they have attained enough reindeer to set up their own household. By the time a Lapp is ready to marry, band and family leadership may reside in the person of a sibling or cousin rather than in a member of the parental generation. In other words, a

Lapp's relation to his siblings may be as important as his relation to his parents in determining local group membership. Therefore, the terms 'matrilocalism' and 'patrilocalism' do not correctly characterize the whole situation. The terms 'virilocal' and 'uxorilocal' are more useful here. Virilocalism means that the married couple lives at the locality of the husband's kinsmen, uxorilocalism that the married couple lives at the locality of the wife's kinsmen. The uxorilocal-virilocal characterization emphasize relationships within one generation, a relationship shown in Figure 1.

Figure 1

This relationship I believe to be crucial in bilateral society. The matrilocal and patrilocal characterizations emphasize the relationship over several generations, a relationship important in unilineal societies shown in Figure 2.

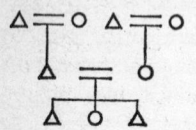

Figure 2

Thus, when dealing with a bilaterally organized society which emphasizes sibling solidarity it seems apropos to use the terms 'virilocal' and 'uxorilocal' in place of the terms 'matrilocal' and 'patrilocal' with their implications of unilineality.

Leonhard Adam (1948, p. 12) suggests that virilocal and uxorilocal are preferable to matrilocal and patrilocal which he considers etymologically incorrect and logically misleading. I also found the former terms more helpful in analysing marriage residence patterns in a bilateral society. In using them to characterize all marriages, it became clear that Lappish marriage residence patterns are, in fact, bilocal, that there appears to be equal chances of uxorilocalism and virilocalism with the issue settled in each case by the various factors I have discussed before (as was suggested to me by Mr Ralph Bulmer).

The structural features of Lapp bilateral organization which emerge from these considerations of kinship, marriage and local group affiliation may be summarized as follows:

1. The society is horizontally separated into generations.

2. The sibling group is the fundamental structural unit of the society. The sibling group is the basic point of reference of Lapp social structure.

3. When the society must act as a unit, these sibling groups form alliances by bilaterally tracing relationship over a network of kinship ties. The temporary nature of these alliances gives flexibility to the structure.

I have not tried in this paper to trace all of the structural ramifications of bilateral organization. Rather, I have attempted to establish that bilateral organization has more structure than has been allowed and that this structure must be studied in its own terms.

References

ADAM, L. (1948), '"Virilocal" and "uxorilocal"', *Man*, vol. 48, art. 13, pp. 12 ff.

WHITAKER, I. R. (1955), *Social Relations in a Nomadic Lappish Community*, Utgit a Nors Folkemuseum.

Part Ten **Kin Terms**

In this section I begin with an extended introduction to try to clarify certain of the issues in the study of terminology, in particular the technical vocabulary itself. This essay is followed by an excerpt from Radcliffe-Brown (Reading 21) on the relationship between terminology and behaviour, a subject which continues to be of critical interest even with the development of more formal methods of analysing kin terms as a linguistic set. Componential analysis of this kind has been developed by W. H. Goodenough and F. G. Lounsbury, to whose papers the reader is referred for further information about aims and methods. In this selection I have included Hammel's introduction to a symposium on 'Formal semantic analysis' (1965), which included papers by both these authors.

20 J. Goody

The Analysis of Kin Terms

A paper specially written for this volume.

The subject of kinship terminologies has for long played a dominant part in the study of kinship. At the beginning of the eighteenth century Father Lafitau (1724, p. 552) described the matrilineal Iroquois and Hurons of North America, where 'all the children of a cabin regard their mother's sisters as their mothers'; this observation was the basis of L. H. Morgan's 'classificatory' system of terminology (1871, pp. 468, 470), which he distinguished from the 'descriptive' variety (i.e. Western European) which gave different terms to lineal and collateral relatives (e.g. father and father's brother).

Morgan's typology was criticized by A. L. Kroeber (1909) on logical grounds. He suggested an analysis of kinship nomenclatures by means of the following more specific criteria:

(a) the difference of generation;
(b) the difference between lineal and collateral kin;
(c) the difference of age within one generation;
(d) the sex of the relative;
(e) the sex of the speaker;
(f) the sex of the connecting relative;
(g) the difference between consanguinity and affinity;
(h) whether the connecting relative was alive or dead.

For comparative purposes these criteria were somewhat cumbrous and attention was directed at the way only two sets of relatives were grouped, those of a person's own generation and those of his parents. With regard to the senior generation, Robert Lowie (1921, p. 57) and Paul Kirchhoff (1931) developed a scheme which classified males into four categories as in Table 1.

Table 1

System	Relatives			Criterion
	Father	Father's brother	Mother's brother	
Generational	Father	Father	Father	One 'father' term
Bifurcate merging	Father	Father	Mother's brother	Two terms: partial merging
Bifurcate collateral	Father	Father's brother	Mother's brother	Three terms: no merging
Lineal	Father	Uncle	Uncle	Two terms: merging only of collaterals

Leslie Spier (1925) attempted a similar classification of relatives of a man's own generation, that is, 'cousin terms'. The system was developed by various writers, but especially by G. P. Murdock, whose latest classification in the *Ethnographic Atlas* (1967) I present below. In classifying cousins there are four main possibilities (a, b, c, d) which involve grouping the following five categories:

	1	2	3	4	5
EGO	FS, MS	FBS	MZS	FZS	MBS

2 and 3 are 'parallel cousins'; 4 and 5 are 'cross-cousins'. The possibilities taken care of in the code for the Atlas are:
(a) Same term for all, i.e. 1,2,3,4,5; this is the *Hawaiian* type.
(b) All differentiated by descriptive terms, i.e. 1/2/3/4/5[1]; this is *Descriptive*.
(c) A single term for all except 1 (parental siblings), i.e. 1/2,3,4,5; this is the *Eskimo* type.
(d) Cross-cousins differentiated from parallel cousins, i.e. either 1,2,3/4,5, or 1/2,3/4,5; these are the *Iroquois* types.

1. / shows the division in the named categories.

The terms for parallel cousins (2 and 3) are often the same as those for siblings or else constitute a separate pair. But those for cross-cousins are frequently differentiated from one another. Two of the common ways of doing this skew the terms with respect to the generation structure, since they identify persons of an individual's own generation with those of the adjacent generation. These methods are:

(e) FZS = F and/or MBS = S; this is the *Crow* type;
(f) the opposite to this is MBS = MB and/or FZS = S; this is the *Omaha* type.

These are the main types of kinship terminology for cousins distinguished by Murdock, though he also adds an entry for Sudanese terms and one for mixed or variant patterns.

Although whole sets of kinship terms are sometimes described by the same words (e.g. Crow, Omaha) as the features of the cousin terminologies listed above, there is only a limited correspondence between, say, the terminology for ego's own generation and that for the senior generation. However, some work is proceeding in defining the variations found in sets of Eskimo (Dole, 1960), Crow and Omaha terms (Lounsbury, 1964).

When a set of kin terms has been established for a particular group, there are several methods of analysing them.

1. One can relate them to aspects of the past. W. H. R. Rivers and other writers tried to deduce pre-existing systems of marriage and descent from the presence of certain kin-terms; much of this work was rightly described as pseudo-history. More important is the analysis of cognate systems in order to understand their genetic divergence or to reconstruct their ancestral forms, as for example, in the kind of work carried out by Hoijer on Athapascan terms (1956) or by Friedrich on proto-Indo-European (1966). Such reconstructions carry dangers when used to deduce facts about the earlier societies (see Goody, 1959). But equally, the study of kin terms within a given region, according to the principles of historical linguistics, can help to prevent the investigator, whether the original collector or a subsequent discussant, from drawing dubious conclusions about their usage; comparative or etymological analysis can indicate the possibility of homonyms. With regard to the lengthy discussion between Leach, Lounsbury and Powell about the meaning of the Trobriand kinship term, *tabu*, and its assumed

relationship with the Oceanic word 'taboo', Ann Chowning has recently written that if anthropologists, including the original investigator, Malinowski, had possessed a general knowledge of Oceanic languages, 'it would probably never have occurred to them that there might be anything "forbidden" about the Trobriand kinsmen called *tabu*, and they might have devoted more time and ingenuity to dealing with the actual rather than the imagined content of the kinship system' (1970, p. 310).

2. One can relate them to aspects of present behaviour. The functionalists, Malinowski and Radcliffe-Brown, rejected the doctrine of survivals implicit in some earlier approaches, because of both practical and theoretical difficulties. If kin terms are related to other social institutions, then we should look for present correlations, not evidence of past associations. Radcliffe-Brown (1930) saw Australian kin terms as related to the existing system of marriage; elsewhere he particularly emphasized the relationship between kin terms and the structure of unilineal descent groups (1941). Murdock and others have established a high correlation between terminologies that distinguish siblings from cousins (e.g. Eskimo) and the presence of an isolated elementary family and also of neolocal residence (1949, p. 153; see also Marsh, 1967, ch. 3). Such terminologies are found among the simple hunters as well as among the most complex industrial civilizations. So that this correlation supports the curvilinear relationship between economy and extensive kinship groups (especially unilineal descent groups) suggested by Radcliffe-Brown (1935), Forde (1947) and Fortes (1953), and examined cross-culturally by Nimkoff and Middleton (1960).[2]

Both these approaches have proved fruitful not only in several comparative studies but also in the analysis of specific social systems, for example, in F. Eggan's study of the Hopi and Pueblo kinship systems (1950). Indeed any study of kinship roles is bound to deal with the terms people use to address or refer to kin, and the way these terms relate to other aspects of social action.

3. There is the study of kin terms as a bounded set, delineating the

2. For an attempt to test a related hypothesis concerning the relationship of lineal terminologies to systems of inheritance that keep property within the elementary family, see Goody (1969; 1970).

principles behind their employment. Essentially this is what Kroeber set out to do (like McLennan, in the nineteenth century, he claimed there was no close correlation with other aspects of society, though this view he later abandoned) and it is the examination of internal coherence that forms the basis of the more systematic, linguistically-derived study of such sets, known as componential analysis.

Componential analysis is at present much in vogue in the United States, though some of its most distinguished practitioners warn against expecting too much from its use. The pioneering work in this field was done by W. H. Goodenough and F. G. Lounsbury. In an article on the formal analysis of Crow and Omaha-type kinship terminologies, Lounsbury (1964) raises the general question of the 'meaning' of kinship terms, discussed by many authors, which is seen as critical to the definition of a set and is related to the problem of homonyms, polysemy or metaphor (Wallace and Atkins, 1960; Greenberg, 1949; Goodenough, 1956; Edmonson, 1957). In particular he asks whether kinship words have as their primary referent categories of kin (i.e. members of a clan) of senior generation or more immediate, genealogically, defined roles (e.g. father). This problem touches upon another, that is, on the meaning of kinship (rather than of kinship terms), which again turns partly on the problem of the 'biological' or 'social' reference of terms and the status of notions of conception and procreation. Lounsbury's position leads him to oppose a lineage explanation of Crow terms (e.g. Radcliffe-Brown, 1941, who points to the relationship with matrilineal descent groups) to one in terms of inheritance which he assumes to occur between close kin. The latter position is more in keeping with his need to define a bounded set for the purpose of analysing the components. The former approach is more in keeping with Radcliffe-Brown's emphasis on the necessity of understanding the lineage context (and indeed the wider social context) of the terms in order to understand their 'meaning'. The argument is somewhat academic, since there is no way of testing primacy (unless we refer to the meaning a child learns first of all, and this is not necessarily a useful guide). Moreover, there is something suspicious about a controversy that leads those who start from a genealogical (or familial) basis to find the evidence supporting the 'extensionist' approach, while those who start from a group (or 'structural') basis find the evidence supporting the categorical view of kinship terms. As far as the alternative 'explanations' of Crow terms are concerned, it is difficult to see how one could separate the factor of lineage membership from that of inheritance.

The data which any investigator has to analyse consists of a whole range of usages, part of which is specifically metaphoric (that is, recognized by the actors as such), and part may be cryptophoric (e.g. dead metaphors). This range we have to understand as best we can. Lounsbury is possibly correct in seeing close rather than distant relationships as constituting the core set of meanings from an overall analytic standpoint; indeed this view may be entailed in the definition of the field of kinship itself. But the conclusions he draws, in terms of the right to neglect other meanings in defining specific kinship sets seems highly questionable; so too does his espousal of Malinowski's phylogenetic reductionism, which again 'fits' with his linguistic approach. Like Malinowski, he appears to confuse an analysis of the structure of a system (e.g. a kinship set) with the developmental process by which it is learned.

Each of these approaches, the historical, the structural-functional and the formal, has something to offer and no competent analyst will overlook their various insights. But from the sociological standpoint, the most important task must be the investigation of the relationship between kinship terms and other aspects of social action, both by the intensive study of particular societies and the extensive comparison of regional groups and world samples. Such analysis must begin at the stage of data collection; it is too often assumed that for every 'society' there is one kinship terminology;[3] or that for every relative there is one usage. It sometimes seems that kinship terminologies have played so prominent a part because people have regarded them as so simple to collect. For instance, L. H. Morgan sent his questionnaires around the world and produced his famous book on *Systems of Consanguinity* on the basis of the data so acquired. Something can certainly be done by this means; but it is important not to over emphasize the

3. On the class basis of some English kinship terms, see J. Goody (1962).

results of this and more sophisticated work by assuming that in the study of kinship terms one has the key to the 'social structure', either in the present or in the past.

References

CHOWNING, A. (1970), 'Taboo', letter in *Man*, vol. 5, pp. 309-10.
DOLE, G. E. (1960), 'The classification of Yankee nomenclature in the light of the evolution of kinship', in G. E. Dole and R. L. Carneiro (eds.), *Essays in the Science of Culture*, Crowell, pp. 162-77.
EDMONSON, M. S. (1957), 'Kinship terms and kinship concepts', *Amer. Anthropol.*, vol. 59, pp. 393-433.
EGGAN, F. (1950), *Social Organization of the Western Pueblos*, Chicago University Press.
FORDE, C. D. (1947), 'The anthropological approach in social science', *Advance Sci.*, vol. 4, pp. 213-24.
FORTES, M. (1953), 'The structure of unilineal descent groups', *Amer. Anthropol.*, vol. 55, pp. 17-41.
FRIEDRICH, P. (1966), 'Proto-Indo-European kinship', *Ethnol.*, vol. 15, pp. 1-36.
GOODENOUGH, W. H. (1956), 'Componential analysis and the study of meaning', *Language*, vol. 32, pp. 195-216.
GOODY, J. (1959), 'Indo-European society', *Past and Present*, vol. 15, pp. 88-92.
GOODY, J. (1962), 'On nannas and nannies', *Man*, vol. 62, art. 288.
GOODY, J. (1969), 'Inheritance, property and marriage in Africa and Eurasia', *Sociol.*, vol. 3, pp. 55-76.
GOODY, J. (1970), 'Cousin terms', *Southwestern J. Anthropol.*, vol. 26, pp. 125-42.
GREENBERG, J. H. (1949), 'The logical analysis of kinship', *Philos. Sci.*, vol. 16, pp. 58-64.
HOIJER, H. (1956), 'Athapascan kinship systems', *Amer. Anthropol.*, vol. 58, pp. 309-33.
KIRCHHOFF, P. (1931), 'Die Verwandtschaftsorganisation der Urwälstamme Sudamerikas', *Zeits. Ethnol.*, vol. 63, pp. 85-191.
KROEBER, A. L. (1909), 'Classificatory systems of relationship', *J. roy. anthropol. Inst.*, vol. 39, pp. 77-84.
LAFITAU, J. F. (1724), *Moeurs des Sauvages Ameriquains*, vol. 1, Paris.
LOUNSBURY, F. G. (1964), 'A formal account of the Crow- and Omaha-type kinship terminologies', in W. H. Goodenough (ed.) *Explorations in Cultural Anthropology*, McGraw-Hill.
LOWIE, R. H. (1921), *Primitive Society*, ?
MARSH, R. M. (1967), *Comparative Sociology*, Harcourt, Brace & World
MORGAN, L. H. (1871), *Systems of Consanguinity and Affinity of the Human Family*, Smithsonian Institution Contributions to Knowledge, No. 17.
MURDOCK, G. P. (1949), *Social Structure*, Macmillan Co.

MURDOCK, G. P. (1967), 'The ethnographic atlas: a summary', *Ethnol.*, vol. 6, pp. 109–236.

NIMKOFF, M. F., and MIDDLETON, R. (1960), 'Types of family and types of economy', *Amer. J. Sociol.*, vol. 46, pp. 215–25.

RADCLIFFE-BROWN, A. R. (1930), 'Social organization of Australian tribes', *Oceania*, vol. 1, pp. 34–63, 206–46, 322–41, 426–56.

RADCLIFFE-BROWN, A. R. (1935), 'Patrilineal and matrilineal succession', *Iowa Law Rev.*, vol. 20, pp. 286–303.

RADCLIFFE-BROWN, A. R. (1941), 'The study of kinship systems', *J. roy. anthrop. Inst.*, vol. 71, pp. 1–17.

SPIER, L. (1925), *Distribution of Kinship Systems in North America*, University of Washington Publications in Anthropology, vol. 1. pp. 69–88.

WALLACE, A. F. C. and ATKINS, J. (1960), 'The meaning of kinship terms', *Amer. Anthropol.*, vol. 62, pp. 58–80.

21 A. R. Radcliffe-Brown

Kin Terms and Kin Behaviour

Excerpt from A. R. Radcliffe-Brown, 'The social organization of Australian tribes', *Oceania*, vol. 1, 1930, pp. 426–56.

The social organization of Australian tribes affords material of capital importance for the science of comparative sociology. We find an organization of a single specialized type over the whole continent, and the type has been elaborated into a large number of different varieties. A comparative study of all the details of these variations affords an opportunity for sociological analysis which is perhaps not equalled in any other part of the world. This is one of the chief reasons why it is of such importance to science to obtain an adequate record of the Australian aborigines before they and their culture disappear.

It is not possible in the space here available to undertake a detailed sociological analysis of the Australian organization. But a brief discussion seems desirable in order to remove misconceptions that have arisen in theoretical discussions.[1]

The first question that requires to be dealt with is that of the relation between social organization and the terminology of kinship. There are two views on this subject that I wish to controvert. One is the view of Lewis Morgan, adopted from him by Howitt and Sir James Frazer, which is to the effect that the kinship terminology of Australian tribes is not correlated with the existing social organization but is correlated with and has its origin in a hypothetical condition in which individual marriage did not exist, but groups of men were united in some sort of marriage bond with groups of women. The second view is one which is held by Professor Kroeber, that there is in general no very close correlation

1. Practically all the theoretical discussion of Australian social organization has been directed towards providing hypothetical reconstructions of its history. Even Durkheim, though approaching the subject as a sociologist, devotes his attention to questions of historical development. The more modest but really more important task of trying to understand what the organization really is and how it works has been neglected.

between the kinship terminology of a people and their social institutions (1909; 1917).

So far as Australian tribes are concerned it can be laid down as definitely proved that the kinship terminology of a tribe is an integral and essential part of the social organization. At every moment of the life of a member of an Australian tribe his dealings with other individuals are regulated by the relationship in which he stands to them. His relatives, near and distant, are classified into certain large groups, and this classification is carried out by means of the terminology, and could apparently not be achieved in any other way. Thus in any part of the continent when a stranger comes to a camp the first thing to be done, before he can be admitted within the camp, is to determine his relationship to every man and woman in it, i.e. to determine what is the proper term of relationship for him to apply to each of them. As soon as he knows his relation to a given individual he knows how to behave towards him, what his duties are and what his rights.

The case against Professor Kroeber is, I think, proved conclusively by the fact that variations in the kinship terminology from tribe to tribe are directly correlated with variations in the social organization, including variations in the regulation of marriage.

As against Morgan and those who follow him it can be shown that there is a very thorough functional correlation between the kinship terminology of any tribe and the social organization of that tribe as it exists at present. If this is so there is no reason whatever to suppose that the kinship terminology is a survival from some very different form of social organization in a purely hypothetical past.[2]

2. The conclusive criticism of Morgan's theories and others of the same kind was stated forty years ago by Starcke (1889, p. 18) 'Many learned men are too much disposed to seek for the explanation of a given custom in conditions of former times which have now perhaps disappeared. It is certain that customs persist by the force of habit, even when the conditions which first gave birth to them have long ceased to exist, yet it is scarcely necessary to remark that this appeal to early times can only be effective when it has been shown to be impossible to discover the cause of such custom in the conditions under which they still continue. If this main principle is not accepted, we shall be led astray by every idle delusion. If we are able to trace the cause of a custom in existing circumstances, we must abide by that cause, and nothing but a definite historical account of the prior existence of the custom can induce us to seek for another explanation.'

I propose therefore to consider briefly some of the principles that are active in the Australian classification of kin. The most important of these principles is one which is present in all classificatory systems of kinship terminology. Morgan applied that term to all systems which apply the same term to lineal and collateral relatives by regarding two brothers as equivalent, so that if a man stands in a certain relationship to Ego his brother is regarded as standing in the same relationship. This principle may be spoken of as that of the equivalence of brothers. It applies, of course, equally to two sisters. Now this principle is universally applied in all Australian systems of terminology. Everywhere the brother of a father is called 'father', and therefore his children are called 'brother' and 'sister', and similarly the sister of a mother is called 'mother' and her children are also called 'brother' and 'sister'.

This principle is not merely a matter of terminology. It is a most important sociological principle which runs through the whole of Australian life. It depends on the fact that there is a very strong, intimate and permanent social bond between two brothers born and brought up in the same family.[3] This solidarity between brothers, which is itself an expression or result of family solidarity, is a very obvious thing to anyone who studies the aborigines at first hand. It shows itself moreover in certain institutions. The levirate is, I believe, universal in Australian tribes. By this custom, when a man dies, his wife or wives and his dependent children pass to his brother, in some tribes only to his younger brother. When possible it is the man's own brother who succeeds him, but if he has no brother of his own his place is taken by someone who stands in the classificatory relation of 'brother' to the deceased.

The function of this custom in terms of social integration is fairly obvious. A marriage and the birth of children sets up certain social relations, a certain structural arrangement. The wife and children are dependent on the husband and father and their position in the society is fixed by that dependence. The man's death causes a disruption of the social structure and the society needs to restore it with a minimum of alteration of the structure as a whole.

3. For an account of the relation between brothers see Warner (1930). This article gives the best account of the actual working of an Australian kinship system in the everyday life of the tribe.

This is done by replacing the dead individual by a person who is as nearly as possible his social equivalent. The substitution of one brother for another thus permits the social structure to be restored with a minimum of change after the death of an individual.

Professor Sapir (1916) has suggested that there is a correlation between the custom of the levirate and the general principle of classificatory systems of terminology. In that I think he is right, but I think he is in error in suggesting a direct causal relation between the two whereby the custom of classifying the father's brother with the father is regarded as the effect of the levirate. In general I believe that it is a false procedure to look for the cause of one social institution in another particular institution. In the present instance my own view is that both the levirate and the classificatory principle in terminology are the results of the action of a single sociological principle, namely that which I have called the principle of the social equivalence of brothers. This principle is at work, I believe, wherever we find the levirate and wherever we find a classificatory system of terminology. Its action is more effective in some societies than in others, and it is combined with the action of other principles. Thus in some societies we may find a classificatory system without the levirate, and in others we may find the latter without the former.

The principle is obviously far more effective in the simpler societies than in the more complex. In such a simple society as that of an Australian tribe the intimate and close relationship between brothers lasts right through life. Two brothers necessarily belong to the same social groups, the same horde, the same clan, etc. The only exception to this would be in age groups, when older and younger brothers might belong to different groups. Two brothers, therefore, occupy similar positions in the total social structure. Their social personalities are almost precisely the same. This is rarely the case in our own complex societies.

The principle of the equivalence of brothers as an active principle determining social structure may be regarded as a special example of a more general tendency the presence of which is readily discovered in the social structure of the simpler cultures. Wherever the structure includes small groups of strong solidarity and having important and varied functions, when an individual is brought into some close social relation with one member of the group, there is a tendency to bring him into close relation with all the other members of the group. An instance of this tendency is to be seen in the special close relation that is set up in many societies between a man and the group (family, clan, etc.) from which he obtains a wife. In terms of persons, if there is a strong, intimate and permanent bond between two persons A and B, then when a third person C is brought into an important social relation with B there is a tendency to bring him into close relation with A. The resulting relation between C and A will depend, of course, on the kind of relation that already exists between A and B.[4] In terms of the Australian social organization I am by the fact of birth and upbringing brought into a specific relation with my father. Since between him and his brother there is the special intimate relation that we have seen I am brought into a very close relation with my father's brother in which he becomes for me another 'father'. This would seem to be the essential principle of the classificatory system of terminology and of the Australian social organization.

A similar custom to the levirate is that known as the sororate. The form that this takes in Australia is that when a man marries the elder of two or more sisters he becomes entitled to marry the younger ones also. In many Australian tribes the ideal arrangement is considered to be that a man who marries the eldest of the sisters should also marry the second and that he should then transfer his right to the third and fourth to his younger brother. In this custom of the sororate we have sisters treated as being socially equivalent, just as with brothers in the levirate. The existence of this close bond between sisters is shown also in the custom of some tribes, for example the Yaralde, whereby a special, strong and intimate bond is set up between two men who marry two sisters. In the Yaralde tribe there is a special term of relationship for two men thus connected.

Without considering in any way how the Australian social organization may have arisen in a distant past about which we shall never obtain any direct knowledge, we may say that as it exists at

4. Thus it can be shown, I think, that it is this tendency which in the instance of a man and his wife's mother finally results in the custom, universal in Australia, whereby the man must avoid all social contact with the woman while still regarding her, in the phrase of a native, as his 'best friend in the world'.

present an analysis of it reveals this important active principle of the solidarity of brothers, and we may say that on this principle the existing system is built. By applying the principle the father's brother comes to be regarded for social purposes as similar to the father, and the two are classified under a single kinship term, without, however, any confusion between the real father and his brother. Similarly the mother's sister and the father's brother's wife are classified as 'mother' and the behaviour towards them is modelled on that towards the mother. Carrying forward to the descending generation a man treats the children of his brother in a similar way to that in which he treats his own children, and calls them 'son' and 'daughter', just as they call him 'father'. Passing to more distant relationships the brother of the father's father is classified with the latter, both in terminology and for social purposes, and his son is therefore in turn classified with the father.

In this way the Australian native creates a stable social structure by which all the details of social intercourse between one person and another are regulated. Since relationships are traced without any limit an individual stands in some definite relationship to every person whom he meets in the course of his life.

Within a single class of relatives some are near and some are distant and the degrees of nearness, though not usually expressed in the terminology, are of course recognized for social purposes and such recognition is an integral and essential part of the system. Thus a man cannot marry, or show any familiarity towards the daughter of any man he calls 'father'. He could not fight with his own father, nor, I think, with his father's brothers or any of his nearer 'fathers', but he may quite well on occasion fight against a distant 'father', and indeed much more readily in some tribes than against a distant 'mother's brother'.

A second important principle of the Australian system is the distinction between the father and the mother, and therefore between relatives through the father and relatives through the mother. Father and mother are treated as two different kinds of relative, though it is difficult to give any simple statement as to what the difference consists in. Throughout Australia it seems that the personal bond between a child, even a son, and the mother, is regarded as stronger than that between child and father. By virtue of the act of suckling, if for no other reason, the personal relation of child and mother is a peculiarly intimate one, especially in the early years of life, and this creates a permanent bond of solidarity which has great importance in Australian life and in determining the social structure.

When we come to the brother of the mother and the sister of the father the classificatory principle takes a new form. Since there is a close bond between a child and its mother, and another bond between the mother and her brother the child is brought into a close personal bond with the mother's brother. The latter is not treated in any way as similar to the father or father's brother, but is treated as a sort of male 'mother'. Similarly the father's sister is treated as a sort of female 'father'. In all Australian tribes the actual mother's brother and the actual father's sister of an individual have important places in his life, and the whole system can only be understood when this is fully recognized. Thus the distinction in terminology between mother's brother and father and between father's sister and mother is correlated with social distinctions of the greatest importance. The tendency to treat the mother's brother as a sort of male 'mother' is the result of the action of the same principle that results in the father's brother being treated as a 'father'.[5]

Another important principle of the Australian system is connected with the relations between persons of different generations. The relationship of generation has its origin in the family in the relation of parents to children. It becomes of importance in general social life because social continuity requires that the body of tradition possessed by the society shall be handed on by one generation to the next, and this handing on of tradition entails a relation of superiority and subordination as between one generation and the next. The generation of parents must have authority over the generation of children. We find this in one form or another in every human society.

As between persons who are separated by an intervening generation a new situation arises. If we call the generations 1, 2 and 3, then those of generation 1 exercise authority over those of 2 and those of 2 over those of 3, but by a tendency which is apparent in many of the simpler societies and is perhaps really universal, persons of 1

5. The tendency can be seen in many classificatory systems in different parts of the world. See Radcliffe-Brown (1924).

and 3 are brought together into a different kind of relationship which, in spite of the difference of age, links them together on terms of familiarity and almost of equality. It is possible to demonstrate the reality of this tendency and its effectiveness in influencing the social structure in many parts of the world. It is certainly effective and important in Australian society. It shows itself in the terminology in two ways. In a few tribes the father's father is called 'elder brother' and the son's son is called 'younger brother', but this procedure is rare in Australia. More commonly a single reciprocal term is used between grandparents and grandchildren. Thus a father's father and his son's son address each other by the same term. Now it seems that very frequently in classificatory systems of terminology the use of a single self-reciprocal term between two relatives indicates that the social relation between them is symmetrical, whereas the use of two terms one reciprocal to the other implies that the social relationship is asymmetrical. By a symmetrical relationship is meant one in which, as between two relatives A and B, A behaves towards B in the same way as B towards A, whereas in an asymmetrical relationship A behaves in one way towards B and B behaves in a different but correlated way towards A. Thus the relation of father and son is a typical asymmetrical relationship in Australia and apparently everywhere. In Australia also the relationship between two brothers is always in some respects asymmetrical, and therefore in the terminology there is usually no word for brother but one term for elder brother and another for younger brother. Now in the case of grandparents and grandchildren, or at any rate in that of father's father and son's son, it does seem that the use of a single self-reciprocal term between them is associated with a tendency to group them together on terms of familiarity, and if not equality at any rate of social equivalence. This is borne out by the way in which, in certain kinship terminologies, a given individual applies the same term of relationship to two men who are father's father and son's son to one another. One of the significant features of the section system is that it brings together into the same position in the social structure the father's father and his son's son.

The principle that is here indicated enables us to understand a very strange feature of the terminology of some tribes. The father's father's father is called by the same term as 'son', and the son's son's son is called by the same term as 'father'. Since I include under a single relationship my father's father and my son's son, the sons of all relatives of that kind should fall together and can be called 'father', while the fathers of all of them should equally be classified together and may therefore be called 'son'.

Another most important principle in the Australian system is that of reciprocity in marriage. This is merely a special instance of a much wider principle of reciprocity. What underlies it is the fact that when a marriage takes place there is a change of social structure, certain existing social ties being broken or changed and other new ties created. The group from which the bride is taken, whether we regard the family only, or the horde, suffers a loss or damage. For this they must be compensated or indemnified. It is this aspect of marriage that affords the explanation of a great many of the ritual and other customs connected with marriage in all parts of the world. In Australia it results in a custom whereby marriage is normally an exchange in which each side loses a woman and gains one. In the majority of tribes this takes the form of sister exchange. A man receives a wife from a certain family and horde and his own sister goes in exchange to his wife's brother. Amongst the tribes of Gippsland, who have no moieties, the exchange of sisters is regarded (according to Howitt) as the only legitimate form of marriage. In the Yaralde and other tribes where the local patrilineal clan is a very important group the exchange is not between families but between clans. Where there is a system of moieties one of the functions of this is that every marriage, whether by exchange of sisters or not, is an exchange between one moiety and the other. So also, in the section system all marriages are parts of a continuous series of exchanges between the two sections or sub-sections of a pair.

Most Australian systems of terminology are dependent on this reciprocity in marriage. Where there is sister exchange the father's sister and the mother's brother's wife are classified together under a single term, and similarly the wife's brother is classified with the sister's husband. In the exceptional tribes in which sister exchange is not permitted these relatives are distinguished.

References

KROEBER, A. L. (1909), 'Classificatory systems of relationships', *J. roy. anthropol. Inst.*, vol. 39, pp. 77–84.

KROEBER, A. L. (1917), *Californian Kinship Systems*, University of California Publications.

RADCLIFFE-BROWN, A. R. (1924), 'The mother's brother in South Africa', *South African J. Sci.*, vol. 21, pp. 542–55.

SAPIR, E. (1916), 'Terms of relationship and the levirate', *Amer. Anthropol.* vol. 18, pp. 327–37.

STARCKE, C. N. (1889), *The Primitive Family*, Routledge & Kegan Paul.

WARNER, W. L. (1930), 'Morphology and functions of the Australian Murngin type of kinship', *Amer. Anthropol.*, vol. 32, pp. 207–56.

22 E. A. Hammel

Formal Semantic Analysis

Excerpt from 'Introduction', in E. A. Hammel (ed.), 'Formal semantic analysis', *American Anthropologist*, Special Issue, vol. 67, no. 5, pt 2, 1965, pp. 1–8. Revised for this edition by the author.

Formal analyses in anthropology are distinguished from others in two senses: the methodological and the theoretical. In the former sense they are characterized by particular attention to rigor and internal form, and in the latter by explicit recognition of one or more superordinate levels of analytic determinants in a given domain. This style of analysis has multiple and tangled historical roots, particularly because of its close connection with kinship studies on the one hand and with descriptive linguistics on the other. In one sense, it is but the most recent outgrowth of a long interest, in anthropology and philosophy, in the relationships between language and other aspects of culture, particularly perception and cognition. Wilhelm von Humboldt suggested such a connection as long ago as 1836, and Boas (1911) also suggested that the proper *entrée* into folk psychology was an appreciation of the internal form of language.

The contributions of Sapir, Whorf, Lee and others need not be summarized here. With respect to kinship studies, it is important to note that Kroeber (1909) took a Boasian view of the nature of kinship terminologies, insisting that internal form was indicative of a particular 'psychological' orientation toward the phenomena so described, although he later clarified his definition to include cognition in the broadest sense (1952).

A second current of explanation (in kinship studies) was manifested by Morgan (1871), Rivers (1914), Seligman (1917), Gifford (1916) and others in their ascription of facets of kinship terminologies to particular forms of marriage and in their use of terminologies to reconstruct sociological history. Similar weight was placed on sociological determinants by Radcliffe-Brown (1941), Tax (1937), Lowie (1930; 1932) and others with greater attention to total systems of prestations and statuses, and (by some) to sociological factors in reconstruction. Murdock's discussions (e.g. 1949) reject the particular sociological determinants employed by some of his predecessors, but return to the use of others in reconstruction. As different as all of these approaches seem, they are united in that they attempt explanation of terminological systems by reference to factors which do not seem, in our Western European or traditional anthropological ideology of kinship, internal to the terminological systems themselves. In contrast, most 'componential analyses' of kinship terminologies have been concerned with internal form and have specified as analytic determinants certain features of genealogical reckoning which the analysts felt in some way to be naturally 'inherent' in kinship. Whether genealogy is more or less relevant to kinship is moot, and we will consider the question further below.

Although the notion of 'components' and 'factors' was widespread in science, the evolution of a self-conscious methodology of formal semantic analysis seems to have taken place largely within descriptive linguistics, and almost all of the anthropologists who concern themselves with such analyses are linguists, or were trained by linguists, or were markedly influenced by linguistic theory. (Biological systematics also played a role, particularly in ethnoscience.) Bloomfield's insistence (1933) on the use of meaning only as a constant, in order to determine the variety of linguistic forms and the nature of phonological and morphological redundancy, obstructed the analysis of meaning until relatively recently. Three kinds of developments seem to have stimulated removal of the obstruction. First, out of the pioneering work of Jakobson in distinctive feature analysis (1928), of Hockett's concept of the portmanteau morph (1947; 1955), of Harris' analysis of a Hebrew paradigm (1948) and of Hjelmslev's hints at stratification (1943) there grew the employment of a hierarchy of superordinate and interacting analytic levels, populated by hypothetical constructs, and among which was a sememic stratum. Second, the notion of what we might loosely call 'syntactic control' was expanded from the simple utterance-matching procedures used in specifying minimal pairs in phonology, to include taxonomic specification of relationships of contrast and inclusion (Goodenough, 1956; Conklin, 1962; Frake, 1961) and eventually to include a wide range of social and cultural criteria (Gumperz, 1958; Hymes, 1962; Tyler, 1966). Neither of these concepts – that of higher levels in linguistic structure and interacting strata, now considerably elaborated in one way by Lamb (1964a; 1964b) and in another by Chomsky (1957) or the widened specification of syntactic control – is necessarily at variance with the basic analytic attitudes expressed by Boas, Bloomfield and other grandfathers of descriptive linguistics. The third factor in the evolution of formal semantic analysis was simply a reversal, but not a discard, of Bloomfield's dictum about meaning. Rather than holding a referential meaning constant and determining which linguistic forms may occur with it, we now also hold a linguistic form constant and determine which elements of referential meaning may occur with it.

The interweaving of linguistic developments with anthropological ones is complex, but we might say that the two were closely associated while linguistics and ethnology were themselves hardly separate, that is, for example, when Boas spoke of language and folk psychology (1911) and Kroeber of the nature of classificatory systems of relationship (1909). Anthropological emphasis until the early 1950s remained with 'external' analyses, while further methodological progress was made in linguistics itself. By that time, the influence of the linguistic development made itself felt in Goodenough's monograph on Truk (1951), his paper on componential analysis (1956) and Lounsbury's on the Pawnee system (1956). The two papers of 1956 were published as papers *in linguistics*.

From that point on, events are too numerous and complex to trace here. Nevertheless, it is worth pointing out that there are still two very strong trends evident within formal semantic analysis: one concerns itself with the rigorous analysis of seemingly internal form, and the other with the utility of such analyses in providing insight into other areas of behaviour. These two trends are themselves interrelated and cannot be separated from the three major issues raised by Gardin (1965): (1) delimitation of the corpus of phenomena to be investigated, (2) selection of the language of description and analysis, and (3) the relevance of the analysis.

The interrelationships of these three points can be seen more clearly if we admit that most formal analyses are grammars of correspondence between two languages, a target language (e.g. a kinship terminology) and a reference language (e.g. kin type designation) (cf. Hammel, 1964).[1] The first task, delimitation of the corpus in the target language, is usually achieved by syntactic control in the use of a superclass lexeme or phrase – for example, in the control question, 'Is your — a relative?' The difficulties attendant on this approach are pointed out by Schneider (1965), Bright and Bright (1965), and Burling (1964). When data from the literature are being analysed, one must often assume that some kind of control question was in fact used, so that, for example, all kin types reported would have fallen under some term for 'kinsman'. Control questions can be good for some purposes and bad for others. Delimitation of the corpus can also be attempted by referential control, for example, by insisting that 'kin terms' in the target language may only apply to persons genealogically linked, or to persons who live nearby, or to persons with whom Ego has social relationships of particular types, and so on. The essence of this procedure is that external factors are used in the delimitation. The essence of both procedures is that some rule of inclusion and exclusion must be used to define the corpus.

An analysis may proceed further in an essentially syntactic fashion in the target language, that is, solely on the grounds of internal form without reference (other than perhaps in delimitation) to any external descriptive grid. Burling's second analysis of Burmese (1965) follows this course, using internal lexical relationships. This internal approach, the search for intrinsic internal pattern without reference to an external descriptive grid or to sociological or psychological 'function', is characteristic of much research in ethnoscience and also of those analyses of kinship terminology that lean heavily on the process of enculturation (e.g. Burling, 1970) or the theory of information processing (Sanday, 1968). Most analyses, however, shift at this point to a reference

1. The term 'language' is used here in its most general sense. In using 'target language' to refer to a kinship terminology I mean not only the set of unit lexemes referring to kinsmen in a natural language but also the rules which govern their combinations as polylexemic utterances and those which describe their relationships of contrast and inclusion. In using 'reference language' to refer to a system of kin type designations, I mean not only the primitive 'lexical' elements F, M, B, Z, S, D, but also the rules which govern their combination into logically possible and nonredundant compounds, such as BS, MBD, etc.

language and continue within it. The reference language most commonly used for kinship studies is one of kin types (e.g. F, M, B and the relative products FB, MBS, etc.); the mapping of the target language onto the reference language is achieved by a listing of the 'lexemes' of the reference language which are included within the lexemes of the target language. It is worth noting that the reference language must be more primitive than the target language.[2] Some analyses such as those of Romney and D'Andrade (1964), Romney (1965), Hammel (1965a; 1965b) shift to a still more primitive reference language based on the logical genealogical definition of kin types.[3]

Up to this point, because the elements of the reference language are always equal to or more numerous than the corresponding elements of the target language, there is little in the analysis that can be called 'componential'. As the subsets in the reference language, which are externally delimited by their rules of inclusion under lexemes of the target language, come to be internally defined through their own distinctive features or through internal rules of inclusion and contrast, the componential character of the analysis emerges. It is at this point that the analysis shifts from its correlational focus, although the change may be only implicit. For example, in Lounsbury's analysis of Crow-Omaha systems (1964) or Hammel's of Comanche (1965a) there are defined certain rules of transformation which effect the reduction of the members of a subset of kin types to one such member and thereby define the nature of internal redundancies in the reference language. The basic member of each set (root, kernel) to which all other members are reduced (or from which they may be generated) can in fact be regarded as having a superordinate locus, the realizations of which constitute the members of the subset. If the class of *all* such super-

---

2. The use of a reference language which is more primitive than the target language simply allows one to examine a set of reference-language lexemes (simple or compound) which are grouped under a single target-language lexeme for the presence of distinctive features.

3. I have not included references to a number of studies, frequently much more abstract or mathematical, that discuss the theory of formal analysis or the comparative applications of formal analysis *per se*, without analysing *particular* terminologies as well. See for example Kay (1965; 1967; 1968), Tyler (1966a), as well as the comparative implications of Lounsbury (1964), Hammel (1965a; 1965b), Romney (1965).

ordinate units or 'archi-kin-types' is itself internally defined by the distinctive features of its separate member archi-kin-types, statement of and classification by those distinctive features constitute a componential analysis, and the distinctive features themselves can be regarded as components on a still higher level. Some transformational analyses are intended only as a statement of rules of redundancy; their purpose can be to make eventual specification of distinctive features easier and more rigorous. In many componential analyses, isolation of the components is accomplished by working out the rules of redundancy in the analyst's head instead of on paper, and 'proving' them by giving listings of correspondences between, say, kin types and features of genealogical reckoning like lineality, generation level, and so on.

Clearly, these procedures depend on the nature of the delimitation of the corpus in the target language and on the selection of the reference language(s). Up to this point, the analyses can be judged by criteria of accuracy, consistency and parsimony. Disputes about the worth of formal analyses, however, seldom rely on these criteria but relate to Gardin's third point (see p. 319) of 'what can the analysis teach us?' In my view, these questions are but a continuation of the earlier ones and pose a problem of the correspondence between one reference language and another. If our concern is the relevance of formal analyses (or indeed of any analyses), relevance must be taken to mean correspondence with a set of propositions or important questions in still another language of description. That language may concern itself with the nature of cognition independently assessed, with pragmatics, with residence, inheritance or succession rules, with the native ideology as independently expressed, or with a host of other matters. These are important questions if formal analyses are to be incorporated into the larger theoretical structure within which we think we are operating as social scientists. They determine, in fact, the rules according to which the lexical corpus of the target language is to be selected and those according to which the initial reference languages are to be specified. Each particular question allows us to determine whether, for it, the analytic domain is in fact a semantic domain or whether an analysis is a semantic analysis at all (cf. Gardin, 1965; Schneider, 1965) for an analysis can have meaning only with respect to some such question.

Up to this point in the history of the method there has been necessary and inevitable concern with technical detail, and the reference languages have been those which were easy to determine and profitable to use in an analytic sense. Thus, for example, analyses of kinship terminology have depended largely on genealogical criteria for several reasons: because of our own sanguine ideology of kinship, the detail of terminologies has most frequently been specified in genealogical terms, with only scattered information on other matters. Analyses often have tended to base themselves on genealogy for the same ideological reasons, as well as because of the nature of the data reported. Leach (1958), Beattie (1964), Schneider (1964) and others have taken issue with this genealogical and nuclear-family-based extensionist view of kinship, a view which underlies several of the analyses cited above and which is specifically espoused by Lounsbury (1964; 1965).

But we must observe that formal semantic analyses are not immediately concerned with the nature of 'kinship' as that word may be understood by social anthropologists, but rather with kinship terminologies as they may be found in ethnographic sources and data and delimited by their users. Further, 'kinship' is obviously many things, not only to many analysts but also to many as participants in their own social organization. True, we cannot assume that genealogy must underlie 'kinship', but by the same token we cannot reject all genealogical referents *a priori* or because incautious workers have made translation errors. A set of objects, such as the people grouped under a given kin term, can be defined simultaneously by rules based on very different characteristics; if these rules are in some way correlated, one kind of rule can be used as a diagnostic of the others and some superordinate rule may state their correspondence. So far, genealogically based analyses of kinship terminologies have provided the clearest and most elegant solutions. That regularity cannot be dismissed out of hand but must be justified, not only on the basis of formal closure but also on that of inclusion in a wider theoretical framework. Whether it exists because genealogically based criteria do underlie kinship, or because sociological, psychological, or other kinds of data were inconsistent or insufficient, or because there is some second-order correspondence between sociological and genealogical variables is at this juncture moot. Not enough comparisons have been made. There are of course some welcome exceptions, such as the paired analyses by Goodenough (1965) and Schneider (1965), Lounsbury's discussion of Leach's work (1965), Graburn (1964), Pospisil (1964), and Tyler (1966b). But the task of sociological analysis is clearly more difficult than that of the 'genealogical' analyst, largely because of the lack of adequate reference languages.

In this sense and for these purposes of semantic analysis of a terminological corpus, the dispute over whether kinship 'is' or 'is not' genealogical is no dispute at all but a statement of alternative strategies. If one is interested in the neatness, the closure, the sufficiency of an analysis in a formal sense, then genealogically based analyses clearly give the best results at this time. If one's concern lies in other areas, the reference language of analysis is determined by the theoretical question posed. The problems of formal analysis center now in improvement of the regularity of analyses, in construction of full parallel analyses using different reference languages, in expansion of the general method to other analytic domains, and most importantly in asking why the phenomena should exhibit particular regularities or indeed any regularity at all. The answer to this last question demands sensitivity to general theoretical issues, but it also demands one thing that formal analyses have been able to provide better than any others, regardless of the particular reference language involved – namely that the regularities are in fact demonstrable. The primary virtue of a formal analysis, whether on the grounds here outlined or any other, unlike those analyses that make vague appeals to theories of relevance, is that it may be subjected to the precise and public criticism that is the hallmark of scientific communication.

References

BEATTIE, J. (1964), 'Kinship and social anthropology', *Man*, vol. 64, art. 130.

BLOOMFIELD, L. (1933), *Language*, Holt, Rinehart & Winston.

BOAS, F. (1911), 'Introduction', *Handbook of American Indian Languages*, Bull. 40, The Smithsonian Institution: Bureau of American Ethnology, pt 1, pp. 1–83.

BRIGHT, W., and BRIGHT, J. (1965), 'Semantic structures in Northern California and the Sapir-Whorf hypothesis', in E. A. Hammel (ed.), 'Formal semantic analyses', *Amer. Anthrop.*, Special Issue, vol. 67, no. 5, pt. 2, 3249–57.

BURLING, R. (1964), 'Cognition and componential analysis: God's truth or hocus-pocus?', *Amer. Anthrop.*, vol. 66, pp. 20–8.

BURLING, R. (1965), 'Burmese kinship terminology', in E. A. Hammel (ed.), 'Formal semantic analysis', *Amer. Anthrop.*, Special Issue, vol. 67, no. 5, pt 2, pp. 106–17.

BURLING, R. (1970), 'American kinship terms once more', *Southwestern J. Anthrop.*, vol. 26, pp. 15–24.

CHOMSKY, N. (1957), *Syntactic Structures*, Mouton.

CONKLIN, H. C. (1962), 'Lexicographical treatment of folk taxonomies', in F. W. Householder and S. Saporta (eds.), *Problems in Lexicography*, Indiana University Research Center in Anthropology, Folklore, and Linguistics, publication no. 21.

FRAKE, C. O. (1961), 'The diagnosis of disease among the Subanun of Mindanao', *Amer. Anthrop.*, vol. 63, pp. 113–32.

GARDIN, J. C. (1965), 'On a possible interpretation of componential analysis in archaeology', in E. A. Hammel (ed.), 'Formal Semantic analysis', *Amer. Anthrop.*, Special Issue, vol. 67, no. 5, pt. 2, pp. 9–21.

GIFFORD, E. W. (1916), *Miwok moieties*, University of California Publications in American Archaeology and Ethnology, vol. 12, no. 4.

GOODENOUGH, W. H. (1951), *Property, kin and community of Truk*, Yale University Publications in Anthropology, no. 46.

GOODENOUGH, W. H. (1956), 'Componential analysis and the study of meaning', *Language*, vol. 32, pp. 195–216.

GOODENOUGH, W. H. (1965), 'Yankee kinship terminology: a problem in componential analysis', in E. A. Hammel (ed.), 'Formal semantic analysis', *Amer. Anthrop.*, Special Issue, vol. 67, no. 5, pt. 2, pp. 259–86.

GRABURN, N. H. H. (1964), *Taqagmiut Eskimo Kinship Terminology*, Northern Coordination and Research Centre, Department of Northern Affairs and Natural Resources, Ontario.

GUMPERZ, J. J. (1958), 'Dialect differences and social stratification in a north Indian village', *Amer. Anthrop.*, vol. 60, pp. 668–82.

HAMMEL, E. A. (ed.) (1964), 'Further comments on componential analysis', *Amer. Anthrop.*, vol. 66, pp. 1167–71.

HAMMEL, E. A. (1965a), 'Formal semantic analysis', *Amer. Anthrop.*, Special Issue, vol. 67, no. 5, pt. 2, pp. 1–7.

HAMMEL, E. A. (1965b), 'A transformational analysis of Comanche kinship terminology', in E. A. Hammel (ed.), 'Formal semantic analysis', *Amer. Anthrop.*, Special Issue, vol. 67, no. 5, pt. 2, pp. 65–105.

HAMMEL, E. A. (1965c), 'An algorithm for Crow-Omaha solutions', in E. A. Hammel (ed.), 'Formal semantic analysis', *Amer. Anthrop.*, Special Issue, vol. 67, no. 5, pt. 2, pp. 118–26.

HARRIS, Z. S. (1948), 'Componential analysis of a Hebrew paradigm', *Language*, vol. 24, pp. 87–91.

HJELMSLEV, L. (1961), *Prolegomena to a Theory of Language*, University of Wisconsin Press. Translated by F. J. Whitfield.

HOCKETT, C. F. (1947), 'Problems of morphemic analysis', *Language*, vol. 23, pp. 321–42.

HOCKETT, C. F. (1955), 'A manual of phonology', *Internat. J. Amer. Linguistics*, memoir 11.

VON HUMBOLDT, W. (1836), *Über die Kawisprache*, pt. 1, Berlin.

HYMES, D. H. (1962), 'The ethnography of speaking', in T. Gladwin and W. Sturtevant (eds.), *Anthropology and Human Behavior*, The Anthropological Society of Washington.

JAKOBSON, R. (1928), 'Quelles sont les méthodes les mieux appropriées à un exposé complet et practique de la phonologie d'une langue quelconque?', *Actes du Ier Congrès International de Linguistes*, Paris.

KROEBER, A. L. (1909), 'Classificatory systems of relationship', *J. roy. anthrop. Inst.*, vol. 39, pp. 77–84.

KROEBER, A. L. (1952), 'Introduction to "Classificatory systems of relationship"', *The Nature of Culture*, University of Chicago Press.

LAMB, S. M. (1964a), 'The sememic approach to structural semantics', *Amer. Anthrop.*, vol. 66, no. 3, pp. 57–78.

LAMB, S. M. (1964b), 'On alternation, transformation, realization and stratification', *Monogr. Lang. Ling.*, Georgetown University Institute of Languages and Linguistics, no. 17, pp. 105–22.

LEACH, E. R. (1958), 'Concerning Trobriand clans and the kinship category *tabu*', in J. Goody (ed.), *The Development Cycle of Domestic Groups*, Cambridge Papers soc. Anthrop., no. 1.

LOUNSBURY, F. (1956), 'A semantic analysis of the Pawnee kinship usage', *Language*, vol. 32, pp. 158–94.

LOUNSBURY, F. (1964), 'A formal account of the Crow- and Omaha-type kinship terminologies', in W. H. Goodenough (ed.), *Explorations in Cultural Anthropology*, McGraw-Hill.

LOUNSBURY, F. (1965), 'Another view of Trobriand kinship categories', in E. A. Hammel (ed.), 'Formal semantic analysis', *Amer. Anthrop.*, Special Issue, vol. 67, no. 5, pt. 2, pp. 142–82.

LOWIE, R. H. (1930), 'The Omaha and Crow kinship terminologies', in Grossman and A. B. Antze (eds.), *Verhandlungen des 24. Internationalen Amerikanisten Kongresses*, Friederichsen, De Gruyter, pp. 103–7.

LOWIE, R. H. (1932), 'Kinship', *Encyclopedia of the Social Sciences*, Macmillan, vol. 8, pp. 568–72.

MORGAN, L. H. (1871), *Systems of Consanguinity and Affinity of the Human Family*. Smithsonian Institution Contributions to Knowledge, no. 17.

MURDOCK, G. P. (1949), *Social Structure*, Macmillan Co.

POSPISIL, I. (1964), 'Law and societal structure among the Nunamiut Eskimo', in W. H. Goodenough (ed.), *Explorations in Cultural Anthropology*, McGraw-Hill.

RADCLIFFE-BROWN, A. R. (1941), 'The study of kinship systems', *J. roy. anthrop. Inst.*, vol. 71, pp. 1–18.

RIVERS, W. H. R. (1914), *Kinship and Social Organization*, London School of Economics.

ROMNEY, A. K. (1965), 'Kalmuk Mongol and the classification of lineal kinship terminologies', in E. A. Hammel (ed.), 'Formal semantic analysis', *Amer. Anthrop.*, Special Issue, vol. 67, no. 5, pt. 2, pp. 127–41.

ROMNEY, A. K., and D'ANDRADE, R. G. D. (1964), 'Cognitive aspects of English kin terms', *Amer. Anthrop.*, vol. 66, no. 3, pt. 2, pp. 146–70.

SANDAY, P. R. (1968), 'The "psychological reality" of American English kinship terms: an information-processing approach', *Amer. Anthrop.*, vol. 70, pp. 508–32.

SCHNEIDER, D. M. (1964), 'The nature of kinship', *Man*, vol. 64, art. 217.

SCHNEIDER, D. M. (1965), 'American kin terms and terms for kinsmen: a critique of Goodenough's componential analysis of Yankee kinship terminology', in E. H. Hammel (ed.), 'Formal semantic analysis', *Amer. Anthrop.*, Special Issue, vol. 67, no. 5, pt. 2.

SELIGMAN, B. Z. (1917), 'The relationship system of the Nandi, Masai and Thonga', *Man*, vol. 17, art. 46.

TAX, S. (1937), 'Some problems of social organization', in F. Eggan (ed.), *Social Anthropology of North American Tribes*, University of Chicago Press.

TYLER, S. A. (1966a), 'Parallel/cross: an evaluation of definitions', *Southwestern J. Anthrop.*, vol. 22, pp. 416–432.

TYLER, S. A. (1966b), 'Context and variation in Koya kinship terminology', *Amer. Anthrop.*, vol. 68, pp. 693–707.

Part Eleven **Fictive Kinship**

The study of kinship is not limited to biological relations, nor yet to those relationships that different societies define genealogically. In most societies there are a number of other relationships that are seen as approximating to kinship, but which stand somewhat apart from the main set. These relationships are seen either as a kind of sibling relation (e.g. blood-brotherhood) or as a kind of parent-child relation (e.g. adoption, fostering, ritual co-parenthood, step-parenthood, etc.). Such relationships are not only of widespread significance for particular societies, but are receiving increasing attention for theoretical reasons, since their study is seen to define 'the nature of kinship' itself. Esther Goody lays out a paradigm for the study of fictive kinship, in so far as parent-child relationships are concerned. Mintz and Wolf offer a historical and comparative analysis of ritual co-parenthood ('god-parents'), an institution that was widespread in Mediterranean Europe and has become of great significance in Latin America.

23 E. N. Goody

Forms of Pro-Parenthood: The Sharing and Substitution of Parental Roles

A paper specially written for this volume.

Parenthood is institutionalized in every known society. Parent-child relationships are thus among the most ubiquitous of all roles; every society has these to build on, and every society does so, albeit in widely differing ways. Broadly speaking, the parent-child relationship faces two ways. Looking inward, it constitutes one axis of the 'nuclear' family, i.e. a couple and their children. While a very few societies are so organized that the nuclear family is not at any time a residential unit, none exists without at least one parent-child dyad (usually mother-child) as a localized focus of kinship and domestic institutions. Extreme dependency and absolute power characterize child and parent respectively at the beginning. As the child matures the balance becomes less unequal, and may even invert if the parents reach old age. Intense, often ambivalent, feelings are also characteristic of the internal (and internalized) aspects of parent-child relations.

But every family is set in a nexus of other institutions: economic, political, religious and those arising from ties between neighbours. In its outward-facing aspect, parenthood serves to prepare the child for participation in these institutions, and more than this, the parents tend to mediate entry into the sphere of economic, religious and political activity. Initially it is as his father's son, or her mother's daughter, that the child acts and is perceived by others.

Given that parental roles are universally institutionalized and are central both to the internal, domestic system and in mediating between this and other institutions, it is hardly surprising that many societies use the parent-child dyad as a model for other relationships. I want here to discuss some of the main ways in which the peculiar characteristics of parenthood have been adapted to forge new links between people and to reinforce existing ones. I shall argue that there are several kinds of cement which together bind parent and child in this uniquely durable relationship. Of the various pro-parental institutions considered, some make use of one kind and some of another, and a few of more than one. But in each case, the choice of social cement is directly related to the functions which the institution serves.

The parent-child relationship is multi-bonded because of the many functions which it fulfils. Where the child grows to maturity with his biological parents, they fulfil all of the following role elements: genitor/genetrix; source of status identity (pater/mater); nurse; tutor in moral and technical skills; and sponsor in the assumption of adult status. The rights, obligations and experiences associated with each role element generate a characteristic bond between parent and child. The bond between a parent and his or her biological offspring is recognized in most, but not all, societies. This alone is not available for transfer or delegation, and hence only the biological parents can fill the full set of parent-child role elements.

In most societies the provision of status identity is based on birth to 'legally married' parents, and passes through one or other parent to the child. There are a few societies (e.g. the Lozi and the Gonja) where assumption of a full set of adult statuses is not linked to the marriage of the parents, so long as certain prohibitions are respected.[1] But however a given society defines the conditions

1. E. Kathleen Gough uses the concept of 'birth status rights' to mean '... all the social relationships, property-rights, etc. which a child acquires at birth by virtue of his legitimacy, whether through the father or through the mother' (1959, p. 32). Among the Gonja (E. Goody, 1962; 1970) and Lozi (Gluckman 1950), these rights are based on physiological paternity (i.e. no distinction is made between social and physical paternity) and they do not depend on marriage. They are, nonetheless, defined in terms of who the parents, father and mother, were. It is the designation of adult status rights in terms of the parents' identity that I refer to as 'birth status identity'. In some societies full birth status identity only accrues to children born in marriage. In other societies this is not the case.

Of course in matrilineal societies, like the Nayar, the major status reciprocities will link a child and his matrikin, and not involve the father. Typically, bestowal of birth status identity follows from the formal identification of the mother's genetricial powers with her lineage in an 'initiation' or 'puberty' rite and does not depend on the marriage of the parents.

under which it may be transmitted, full birth status identity carries with it rights and obligations (a share in, or management of property, worship of shrines, often burial of the previous status-holder) which may be termed *status reciprocities*.

Analytically separate from these are the *reciprocities of rearing*. These arise from the two phases of rearing: care and nurturance in infancy and early childhood, and education, both moral and technical, which characterizes later childhood and adolescence. Rearing reciprocities are based on the ambivalent affect which is generated by the dependency and discipline of the phases of nurturance and education. Characteristically, they depend for their strength on moral obligations, unlike the status reciprocities, which tend to be strongly sanctioned, and can fairly be classed as jural in nature.[2]

Sponsorship consists in the provision of a youth with the position and resources necessary for assumption of adult status. Just what is required varies widely from one society to another. Most often it is a spouse, and frequently this in turn entails the provision of bridewealth or dowry and often also the resources from which to support the new family. In rural Ireland a house and farmland must be available before the 'boy' can marry; a Yakö youth must have access to land for his yam farm; a Fulani husband cannot bring his wife and child to live with him until enough cattle are available to provide them with milk.

The protégé in return is usually expected to acknowledge himself subordinate to his sponsor, perhaps expressing this by living with him, or by contributing economic assistance. Or it may suffice that he serve his sponsor by granting him public respect, or as a political follower. As this suggests, the sponsor-protégé relationship not only provides for the transition between minority and adulthood, but extends the filial relationship into the adult world, into the external system. For the protégé enters the wider social system by making use of a share of his sponsor's resources and position in it.

2. Any definition of jural rights which is independent of the institutions of a concrete social system must be framed in extremely general terms. By jural rights and obligations are meant those which are accepted as the basis for claims in respect of ownership, inheritance and succession and membership in restricted groups, and to services based on membership in such groups.

It is very often the case that the status identity conveyed through the pater carries with it rights to position and resources needed to achieve full adulthood. Here the role of sponsor and pater are merged. But there are a number of societies where this is not so, usually because birth status is narrowly defined. In Euro-American society, for instance, the training received in adolescence determines to a large extent the position to be occupied in adulthood, and the intervention of a well-to-do sponsor who provides for a good education can completely transform the opportunities available to a working-class youth. This same phenomenon is seen in present-day Ashanti where either the father or the mother's brother pays for secondary schooling and university on the basis of which a man is enabled to enter the educated élite. Significantly, in Ashanti, the protégé incurs an obligation to support other members of the family later on. Or to take a somewhat different case, a Yakö youth who lives with his mother and her kin has the right to farmland which enables him to marry, despite the fact that land is usually reserved for agnates. But he may use this land only so long as he lives with and assists his matrikin (Forde, 1963). Perhaps the Tallensi case is the clearest of all. Here too a man can live with and farm on land belonging to his maternal kin. But so firmly is status identity tied to social paternity that he may never 'own' this land nor serve his mother's lineage ancestors. He has these rights only in patrilineal land and ancestors. Matrikin can sponsor him socially and economically, but they are unable to make him fully one of themselves (Fortes, 1949).

By far the most common situation that we find is for all five of these parental roles to be played by the same persons. When this happens the bond of begetting between genitor and biological offspring is combined with the status reciprocities linking pater and filius, with the reciprocities of rearing which unite nurse, and later tutor, and child, and finally, with the ongoing obligations of subordination and assistance required by the sponsor of his protégé. This is the 'ordinary' parent-child relationship, and it is very strongly cemented indeed.

It is, I suggest, the very over-determination of the ordinary parent-child relationship which accounts for the widespread occurrence of pro-parental institutions. For one or more elements of the total set can be split off and used to create a fictive parent-child tie without dissolving the remaining links between true parent and child. And indeed, in many of these institutions it is the continued existence of the links between true parent and child which give meaning to the reassignment of other parental roles. Which of the possible roles is transferred and which retained will determine the type of links between true parent and child, and between pro-parent and child. Together with other factors, such as their respective positions in the wider social system, the distribution of parental roles will also determine the relationship between true parent and pro-parent themselves. In order to illustrate how this works, three pro-parental institutions will be very briefly discussed: these are fosterage, ritual sponsorship and adrogation. Each will be shown to depend in a different way on the splitting of parental role elements between two sets of parents. Finally, we will consider the very different situation of adoption, where the substitution of one full set of parental roles for another, rather than the sharing of roles, is the object.

Fosterage

The verb 'to foster' is derived from the Old English root *fôd*, for food. To foster is 'to nourish, feed, or support; to cherish; to bring up with parental care' (*Shorter Oxford Dictionary*). In the present context fosterage can be defined as the institutionalized delegation of the nurturance and/or educational elements of the parental role. Thus we would expect the ties which link foster parent and foster child to be essentially affective and moral in character, based as they are on the reciprocities of rearing.

For some purposes it is also convenient to distinguish between fostering which is initiated of necessity, typically because the natal family of orientation has dispersed due to death or divorce, and fostering entered into voluntarily. Such a distinction has nothing to do with which parental role elements are delegated, but is only concerned with the basis on which the original decision to foster was made.[3]

3. A further distinction which I have developed elsewhere (E. Goody, 1968) turns on the difference in nurturance requirements of infants and young children on the one hand and older children and adolescents on the other. In the first case rearing means providing food and care and early socialization in control of impulses and bodily functions. This can con-

Equally important in defining fosterage is the designation of what it is not. As used here, fosterage does not effect the status identity of the child, nor the jural rights and obligations this entails. Fosterage concerns the *process* of rearing, not the jural definition of status or relationships.

The fostering of children by kin in Gonja

The Gonja of northern Ghana do not have the segmentary unilineal descent groups which characterize many African societies, and rights in children are held, and exercised, by kin of both parents. It is these joint rights in children which are made explicit in the institution of fosterage. Roughly one half of the adults in five samples had been reared during childhood and adolescence by kin other than their true parents.[4] A would-be foster parent may claim a sibling's child or a grandchild at its birth, or later during infancy or early childhood. The child remains with the biological parents until the age of five or six when it joins the foster parent in his or her home, sometimes in the same village, but often in a distant one, there to remain until ready to marry, except for visits home from time to time.

The Gonja do not think of physiological parenthood as separable from social parenthood. They do not distinguish between *pater* and *genitor*; both are determined by conception. Nor can either element be transferred by legal fiction. The act of begetting permanently fixes the status identity of the child, and with it his eventual eligibility for political and many ritual offices. Nor is the nurturance of the infant and young child delegated unless a crisis renders this unavoidable. It is the education of the older child and

---

veniently be termed nurturant fosterage. The older child also requires food and shelter, but the primary task of foster parents at this later period is training in adult role skills and the values of the society. Here the terms educational or apprenticeship fostering are appropriate, depending on the emphasis given to the institution in a given situation. The institution of the wet nurse in medieval Europe is a type-instance of nurturant fosterage, while apprenticeship as commonly practised in the same period provides an illustration of educational fosterage which merges in many cases with sponsorship as defined on p. 333.

4. The proportion in a sixth sample from a different part of the country was much lower. See E. Goody (1970), for an account of Gonja fostering.

adolescent that is transferred to kin, and the Gonja are quite explicit about this. 'It is so that the child will have a good character that we find another to rear (*belo*) him.' But it is also held to be important that every child knows both his mother's and his father's kin, and their respective home towns. This too is accomplished by the dispersal of the sibling group between true parents and their relatives in fosterage. The fostered child retains loyalty to and affection for his own parents and siblings, but adds to this a deep involvement with the kin of the foster home. In this way the sibling group, the members of which remain in close contact throughout their lives, includes persons who are literally at home with the different branches of the family. In the terms outlined above, respect for the genitor, status reciprocities and early rearing reciprocities are firmly anchored on natal kin, while the rearing reciprocities of the educational phase, and in some cases the obligations of protégé towards his sponsor, are located in the foster parent/foster child relationship.

It is characteristic of Gonja fosterage that foster parent and foster child often belong to different social estates, youths of the ruling group being, for instance, reared in commoner households, and vice versa. There is thus no clear pattern of using foster children to build up a following, perhaps in part because sons are expected always to return eventually to their own fathers' households. Nor was it possible to show that fostering provided a direct avenue of advancement in the acquisition of either traditional or modern office (E. Goody, 1970, p. 65 ff.). On the whole it seems best to accept the Gonja view of fostering as arising out of the joint claims kin have on one another's children, as serving several specific functions (companionship, domestic assistance, help with farm chores, and particularly character training) and as linking together socially and physically dispersed kin through their common bonds with children. That is, fostering here operates within a framework of fixed status identity and the jural reciprocities on which this is based. It is the affective and moral reciprocities of rearing which are manipulated, here shared between two sets of parents.

Ritual sponsorship

The historical development of ritual co-parenthood (*compadrazgo*) has been well documented by Mintz and Wolf (1950), who also consider the various functions of this institution in Europe and Latin America. They see co-parenthood as the creation (by ritual and legal fictions) of obligations similar to those imposed by parenthood. Essentially these involve the conversion of non-kin relationships into quasi-kin ties complete with constraints on marriage and sexual relations, the prohibition of quarrels and the obligation to provide economic assistance. Where ritual co-parents are selected from among existing kin this serves to impose specific obligations where previously diffuse ones obtained. Mintz and Wolf point out that co-parenthood can be based on lateral ties within a single social stratum in such a way that cohesion within the group is reinforced. But it can also be used to create a lien on a member of an adjacent stratum. The latter form allows the development of links between otherwise independent elements – farmer and shopkeeper, field-hand and foreman. Here an element of status imbalance is involved, deference being traded for social and economic advantage.

A second characteristic of ritual co-parenthood is that the effective ties are between parent and co-parent, with their common child a relatively passive member of the triad. This illustrates well the manipulative aspect of the institution. Ostensibly its purpose is to ensure the ritual well-being of a child. Yet repeatedly it has been socially elaborated in such a way that the child is the least important person involved. What element of the parental role complex is being used here? Clearly there is no alteration of the identity status of the child, and the central status reciprocities are not affected. Similarly, unless the parents cease for some reason to be able to care for the child, neither the nurse nor the tutor element is delegated. The child remains with the true parents who raise it, and with whom the affective and moral obligations of the rearing reciprocities are generated. There remains the role of sponsor. The special characteristic of this role is its mediation between the child and the external system. Originally meant to mediate between the child and the supernatural, there appears to be a recurrent tendency for the link between ritual co-parent, the child, and its own parents to be extended into other spheres. Economic cooperation is common between co-parents, and so also is the stating of claims to respect, importance and assistance. Here the prominence of the co-parents and the passivity of the child become more understandable, for children cannot operate effectively in the external system, although others can, and do so, on their behalf.

Like fosterage, co-parenthood seems designed for working in the gaps between the formal elements of the system. Neither institution affects jurally defined status identity, yet both make use of elements of the parental role to create reciprocities which form the basis of links between individuals and groups.

Ritual sponsorship in the Balkans: komstvo

A recent analysis of ritual sponsorship in the Balkans (*komstvo*) by Hammel (1968) provides an illustration of how the links based on sponsorship can be institutionalized to form continuing links between families. As Hammel describes it, *komstvo* has significance in determining the relative status of local descent groups, in that a sponsor is sought from an equal or higher status group, never one of lower position. Further, the 'giving' of *komstvo*, that is, the offering of the sponsorship role, conveys prestige, and this is acted out at each occasion on which the sponsor is present, for he is greatly deferred to and given precedence in ceremonies (especially in southern and eastern Serbia). Hammel is further able to show that *komstvo* links tend to be repeated in successive generations and are seen as affecting relations between kin groups in the same sort of way as ties of marriage and of descent. However, in *komstvo*, as with the *compadrazgo* complex, sponsorship, and indeed only *ritual* sponsorship, is the single parental role element to be transferred to the pro-parent; only by means of this link are joint interests created and maintained between the two sets of parents. And even more clearly than with *compadrazgo*, *komstvo* relations are extra-domestic, affecting as they do the relative statuses of local descent groups.

Adrogation

The final parental role element to be discussed is the provision of status identity. In order to avoid confusion, I suggest that the Roman term *adrogation* be used where the main purpose of creating fictive parenthood is the substitution of a new status identity for that which was acquired at birth. An extreme, and a very clear, example of this sort of re-allocation of the status-bestowing aspect of parenthood occurs in the adoptions by will which were accepted practice among the Roman nobility. It was in this way that Augustus became the 'son' of Julius Caesar. This may have been technically considered as 'inheritance on condition of taking the testator's name' (Crook, 1967, p. 112). But either way it illustrates how status identity can be altered without affecting the other parental role elements.

Roman 'adoption' and alliances based on adrogation

'Adoption' in Republican and Imperial Rome was basically a legal and ritual transaction by which a person passed from one *potestas* (legal authority) to another. 'It had nothing to do with the welfare of children' says J. A. Crook, but was 'the characteristic remedy for a family in danger of dying out' and '... those adopted were often adults' (1967, p. 111). Similarly, it has been argued that 'mainly the institution (adoption) was one whereby the great families provided themselves with heirs to their property and worship, successors to office or a political following' (J. Goody, 1969, p. 60).

The evidence for adoption in ancient Rome concerns the nobility almost exclusively. They had not only vast fortunes to transmit, but also the splendid reputations of their ancestors, whose wax effigies were celebrated at each new funeral and to whose descendants the consulship was effectively restricted. Under such circumstances it is hardly surprising that there were fathers willing to lose their sons in adoption. That it was a loss is indicated by the fact that the son ceased to be a legal member of his natal family, and should the other members all die, the adopted son could not return to save it from extinction.

Yet there were advantages. In a study of party politics at the end of the Republic, L. R. Taylor writes

To unite families, adoptions were as important as intermarriages ... By such adoptions the two (noble) houses were brought closely together, and the man adopted was thought to belong to both families. Thus the younger Scipio Africanus, son of Aemilius Paullus ... speaks of *both* his fathers, and is proud of the family tradition of both his houses (Taylor, 1966, p. 34).

There is an apparent contradiction in these accounts, for on the one hand both Taylor and Crook speak of the fact that the adopted son must renounce any legal or religious link with his natal family, and yet both also refer to the use of adoption to create an alliance between two noble houses. The key to the problem lies in the fact that, as both writers again note, adoption often concerned adult men rather than children. In terms of the distinctions we have been using, the reciprocities of rearing, and of course the bond of begetting, are already firmly forged between the son and his natal kin. There remains the transfer of status identity so explicitly arranged by the Romans, and in some cases the sponsorship of the young adult.[5] The bonds of parenthood are again split between two families, in this case in line with the distinction we have made between jural and moral reciprocities. Significantly, the adopting father did not seek an infant or young child with whom he might expect to fill an almost complete set of paternal roles. Instead he often appears to have preferred a son for whom, since he was already adult, the nurturant and educational aspects of parenthood were closed. Such a son combines in his person loyalties to two great families; his adoption secures the basis for a lasting alliance as well as an heir to name, traditions and estate.

The characteristic feature of Roman adoption, then, is the concern to substitute one legal status for another. Adoption of a jurally independent person, one whose father and father's father were dead, was referred to by the distinctive term, *adrogation*. For adrogation meant the disappearance of the separate identity of the adrogee and his descendants, and each instance apparently required a special law (Taylor, 1966, pp. 88, 91). There was not a direct correspondence between adrogation and the adult status of the new son in ancient Rome, since children might be orphaned, and adults remained in the *potestas* of their father until his death. However the term does correctly emphasize the substitution of status-identity independently of the reassignment of other parental roles. In addition, in Roman usage, it commonly *was* adults who were 'adopted', and their persisting ties of affection and duty towards their natal kin were utilized to forge alliances central to

---

5. The *peculium* was a sum of money placed by his pater at the disposal of the adult who was still under *potestas* and thus unable legally to own property on his own account. It fits exactly the functions we have indicated for sponsorship, allowing the young man to establish his own household, and thus gain a measure of independence even though legally a jural minor.

political life, while their recruitment to the adopting family insured the legal continuity of its reputation and estate.

Adoption

Adrogation is seldom institutionalized, as the special conditions which render it advantageous are relatively rare. It is far more often the case that where an heir to office, property or shrines is needed those concerned hope also to find a child whom they may rear and train, and who will love and respect them as well as observe the legal formalities of status reciprocities. While the bond of begetting is not transferable, we have seen that the remaining parental role functions may be filled by others besides the biological parents. I suggest it is where the complete set of available parental role elements is transferred from natal to pro-parents, that the term adoption is best employed. This has the advantage of consistency with popular usage. But more than that, it allows us to distinguish institutions which depend for their effectiveness on the *sharing* of parental role elements, from the case where 'total parenthood' is renounced by one couple and assumed by another, i.e. adoption.

Of course 'total parenthood' is not transferable. For the fact of physiological parenthood is not open to social manipulation. But the desire for a total transfer can be inferred in respect to adoption in western society from the efforts made to keep the identity of the real parents secret. Writing about contemporary America, V. Carroll remarks on the concern with secrecy lest the natural parents try to reclaim their child from its adoptive parents (1970, p. 4). But he goes on to speak of the lengthy jural processes which, once completed, render such an attempt illegal. The adoptive parents appear to fear that the bond of begetting may prove stronger than both the ties of affection and moral obligations arising out of child rearing and the legal claims of status reciprocities. Thus there is in adoption, as it is practised in our society, no basis for the *sharing* of parental role elements, just because adoptive parents are seeking to fill all these roles themselves. They want a whole child, not part of one.

Eskimo adoption provides another instance of institutionalized preference for total transfer of parental roles. For despite the difficulties of rearing an infant apart from its mother, adoptions were ideally arranged during the pregnancy and completed shortly after the child's birth. When, as sometimes happened, an older child was orphaned, even close relatives were reluctant to adopt it (Rousseau, 1970, pp. 5, 40). As with Western parents, the Eskimo make every effort to secure rights to nurse the adopted child in infancy, thus preventing the development of affective ties between natural parents and their child which might later weaken the attachment to the adoptive parents.

The care of orphans and destitute children

The definition of who is obligated to care for whom is a function of both legal and moral norms, and these in turn are based on rights in property and in persons. But inevitably, the definition of what should be done to care for deprived children is related to the existing modes of delegating parental roles. Thus, in Gonja, where fostering by kin is voluntarily arranged, fostering is also used as a way of caring for children if their natal family of orientation disperses. Kin who have a *right* to claim a child in voluntary fosterage, have a *duty* to accept the role of foster parent in a crisis.[6] But in both cases it is the roles of nurse and tutor which are assumed, with the identity of the sponsor more likely to be filled by the foster parent if the true parents are dead. Since these roles are separated from that of pater/genitor in voluntary fostering, there is no reason to redefine the child's jural identity when fostering is necessitated by family crisis. In Gonja, rearing children has no effect on *who* they are.

A similar situation typically obtains where one finds institutionalized co-parenthood. The privilege of being a ritual sponsor carries with it the obligation to provide assistance in crisis if this becomes necessary. Ordinarily the co-parent is concerned only with partial sponsorship, and not with either jural status or rearing. Should his protégé be orphaned the sponsor may take over his care and full sponsorship obligations if kin are not available to fill these roles. But the main function of the sponsor in crisis is to be an interested party, to see that suitable arrangements are made, and to ratify

6. Because moral and legal rights and obligations seldom coincide exactly, the individuals who act voluntarily and those who come forward in a crisis may not be identical. The degree of fit is a matter for investigation in any given society. In Gonja there is a high correspondence, and the institutional charter is the same for both voluntary and crisis fosterage.

these as being appropriate. Again there need be no question of redefining the jural identity of the orphan, although for other reasons (e.g. that the role of pater is vacant, and the sponsor would like to fill it) this may be done.

Adrogation, where jural status only is altered, does not serve to provide for the care and training of an orphaned child. Adrogation of an orphaned adult does, however, mean that there will be no persisting ties to parents to act as the basis for claims on the adrogated son.

We have defined adoption as the transfer of all available parental roles. As such it is clearly an effective way of providing for the various needs of destitute children. But there is a special sense in which adoption is appropriate in such cases. For by definition, where the parents are dead or have actively rejected the child, they present less of a threat to the adoptive parents' monopolization of parental roles. Adoption brings together those who need parents and those who need children. But more than this, adoption of orphans and illegitimate children brings together those who lack someone to fill key parental roles, and those who wish to pre-empt these roles completely. Potential conflict between natural and adoptive parent is thus eliminated or minimized. Such a rigid separation of natural and adoptive parents is the antithesis of the pattern found in the institutions of kinship fosterage, ritual sponsorship and adrogation.

Because in our own society all parental roles are concentrated within the nuclear family we tend to see this as both right and necessary. Yet these roles are potentially available for sharing among kin or even with unrelated neighbours or friends. To do so is one way of spreading the task of caring for deprived children. But it is also an effective way of forging links between adults – parent and pro-parent – and between generations – child/parent and child/pro-parent. Where sharing of parental roles is institutionalized, as in the giving of foster children and ritual sponsorship, such links are systematically created. To understand these as simply ways of coping with crisis situations, or of arranging to cope with them should they occur, is to fail to recognize the way in which many societies make use of the unique strength of the bonds between parent and child.

References

ARENSBERG, C. N., and KIMBALL, S. T. (1940), *Family and Community in Ireland*, Harvard University Press.

CARROLL, V. (ed.) (1970), *Adoption in Eastern Oceania*, Hawaii, Bishop Museum.

CROOK, J. A. (1967), *Law and Life in Rome*, Thames & Hudson.

FORDE, D. (1963), 'Unilineal fact or fiction: an analysis of the composition of kin groups among the Yakö', in I. Schapera (ed.), *Studies in Kinship and Marriage*, Royal Anthropological Institute.

FORTES, M. (1949), *The Web of Kinship among the Tallensi*, Oxford University Press.

GLUCKMAN, M. (1950), 'Kinship and marriage among the Lozi of northern Rhodesia and the Zulu of Natal', in A. R. Radcliffe-Brown and D. Forde (eds.), *African Systems of Kinship and Marriage*, Oxford University Press.

GOODY, E. (1962), 'Conjugal separation and divorce among the Gonja of northern Ghana', in M. Fortes (ed.), *Marriage in Tribal Societies*, Cambridge University Press.

GOODY, E. (1968), 'Paradigm for the analysis of pro-parental relationships', unpublished report submitted to the Social Science Research Council.

GOODY, E. (1970), 'Kinship fostering in Gonja: deprivation or advantage?', in P. Mayer (ed.), *Socialization: The Approach of Social Anthropology*, Tavistock.

GOODY, J. R. (1969), 'Adoption in cross-cultural perspective', *Comp. Stud. Soc. Hist.*, vol. 11, pp. 55–78.

GOUGH, E. K. (1959), 'The Nayars and the definition of marriage', *J. roy. anthropol. Inst.*, vol. 89, pp. 23–34.

HAMMEL, E. A. (1968), *Alternative Social Structures and Ritual Relations in the Balkans*, Prentice-Hall.

MINTZ, S. W., and WOLF, E. R. (1950), 'An analysis of ritual co-parenthood (*compadrazgo*)', *Southwestern J. Anthropol.*, vol. 6, pp. 341–65.

ROUSSEAU, J. (1970), *L'Adoption chez les Esquimeaux Tununermuit*, Centre d'Études Nordiques, Université Laval.

STENNING, D. J. (1958), 'Household viability among the pastoral Fulani', in J. Goody (ed.), *The Developmental Cycle in Domestic Groups*, Cambridge University Press.

TAYLOR, L. R. (1966), *Party Politics in the Age of Caesar*, University of California Press.

24 S. W. Mintz and E. R. Wolf

Ritual Co-Parenthood (*compadrazgo*)

Excerpts from S. W. Mintz and E. R. Wolf, 'An analysis of ritual co-parenthood (*compadrazgo*)', *Southwestern Journal of Anthropology*, vol. 6, no. 4, 1950, pp. 341–65.

As anthropologists have been drawn into the study of Latin American cultures, they have gathered increasing amounts of material on the characteristic cultural mechanisms of *compadrazgo*. This term designates the particular complex of relationships set up between individuals primarily, though not always, through participation in the ritual of Catholic baptism.

This rite involves, among its various aspects, three individuals or groups of individuals. These are: first, an initiate, usually a child; secondly, the parents of the initiate; third, the ceremonial sponsor or sponsors of the initiate. It thus involves three sets of relationships. The first links parents and child, and is set up within the confines of the immediate biological family. The second links the child and his ceremonial sponsor, a person outside the limits of his immediate biological family. This relation is familiar to most Americans as the relation between godfather or godmother and godchild. The third set of relationships links the parents of the child to the child's ceremonial sponsors. In Spanish, these call each other *compadres* (Latin *compater-commater*, Spanish *compadre-comadre*, Italian *compare-commare*, French *compère-commère*, German *Gevatter-Gevatterin*, Russian *kum-kuma*, etc.), literally co-parents of the same child. The old English form of this term, *godsib*, is so unfamiliar to most English-speaking people today that they even ignore its hidden survival in the noun 'gossip' and in the verb 'to gossip'. In English, as in the Ecuadorian *compadrear*, the meaning of the term has narrowed to encompass just one, if perhaps a notable characteristic of *compadre* relations. Most other aspects of this relationship have, however, fallen by the wayside. In contrast, in medieval Europe, the *compadre* mechanism was of considerable cultural importance, and in present-day Latin

America, its cultural role is attested by its frequent extensions beyond the boundaries of baptismal sponsorship. [...]

Functional analysis

The Catholic ceremonial complexes, when carried to the New World, were to develop under conditions very different from those of fifteenth-century Europe. Alienation of Indian lands through such devices as the *repartimiento* and the *encomienda* proceeded concurrently with the wholesale conversion of millions of native peoples to Catholicism. The functioning of such mechanisms as *compadrazgo* in Latin American communities is strongly colored by four hundred years of historical development within this new setting. Yet there is little material on the cultural significance and usages of the *compadre* mechanism during the colonial period. Certainly considerable research needs to be carried out on the processes of acculturation following early contact. Analysis of the social functioning of *compadrazgo* in its American beginnings is but a minor aspect.

Historical sources attest that baptism of natives had proceeded from the time of first contact. Fray Toribio de Benavente writes that in the fifty-five year period between 1521 and 1576 more than four million souls were brought to the baptismal font (Gonzalez, 1943, p. 193). The evidence is good that emphasis was not on prior instruction in the catechism, but rather on formal acceptance of the faith. Father Gante and an assistant, proselytizing in Mexico, claims to have baptized up to fourteen thousand Indians in a single day. In all, Gante and his companion stated that they baptized more than two hundred thousand souls in a single Mexican province (Bancroft, 1883, p. 174).

Baptism was a sacrament designed to remove the stigma of original sin. The acquisition of godparents purported to guarantee to the initiate religious guidance during the years following his baptism. Actually, Spaniards who were members of exploring parties frequently served as sponsors for Indian converts, and thus fulfilled but a formal ritual necessity (Espinosa, 1942, pp. 70 ff.). We can assume that most of the social implications of the *compadre* mechanism developed but slowly at first, if for no other reason than this.

Yet the baptismal ceremony established an individual in the

Catholic universe, and perhaps by virtue of its symbolic simplicity, it was readily accepted by many native populations. Redfield and Villa R (1934), Parsons (1936), Foster (1948) and Paul (1942, pp. 79 ff.), among others, have sought to differentiate between aboriginal and Catholic elements in the modern Latin American ritual. Parsons, Redfield and Paul have felt further that certain derivations of the modern godparental ritual have come from the adaptation of this ceremonial form to pre-Columbian ceremonies and social patterns. The Maya of Yucatan possessed a native baptism so like the Catholic ritual that, according to one authority,

> some of our Spaniards have taken occasion to persuade themselves and believe that in times past some of the apostles or successors to them passed over the West Indies and that ultimately those Indians were preached to (Lopez Medel, quoted in Landa, 1941, p. 227).

The Aztecs also had a kind of baptism, and in addition, godparents of sorts were chosen in an indigenous Aztec ear-piercing ceremonial, according to Sahagun (1932, pp. 34–5). Paul feels that there may even have been an aboriginal basis for the *compadre* aspect of the complex in the existence of various kinds of formal friendship among native peoples (1942, pp. 85–7).

But it is impossible to generalize about the ease with which aboriginal ceremonial procedure could be accommodated to the new sacrament, as endorsed by the Church. The most important modern social result of the baptismal ceremony in practice – the creation of a security network of ritual kin folk through ceremonial sponsorship – seems rather to be due to the institution's inherent flexibility and utility, than to any pre-existing pattern with which the new complex might be integrated. Present-day folklore concerning the fate of an unbaptized child (Redfield and Villa R, 1934, p. 169; Parsons, 1945, p. 44; Paul, 1942) suggests that a strong emphasis on the moral necessity for baptism was made from the start. In modern practice, however, whether the people in a given culture will feel that baptism requires the official approval and participation of representatives of the Church varies considerably. The evidence is that once the secular utility of this sacred institution was established, the native populations could count on the fulfilment of these reciprocal obligations which godparentage and *compadrazgo* entailed, the Church might not even be consulted. Makeshift ceremonies, consummated without orthodox clerical approval, became so widespread as to be illegalized by ecclesiastical ruling in 1947, except in cases where the child's death seemed imminent before official baptism.

The mechanism of godparenthood took shape originally as a means for guaranteeing religious education and guidance to the Catholic child. This aim was achieved through the ritual kinship established between the newborn infant, its parents, and its godparents, at the baptismal ceremony. The relationship frequently was reinforced, or extended with new sponsors, at other life crisis ceremonies, including confirmation and marriage.

From the original Catholic life crisis ceremonial sponsorship, godparenthood has been elaborated in various Latin American communities into the ceremonial sponsorship of houses, crosses, altars, or carnivals (Gillin, 1945, p. 105), circumcision (Beals, 1946, p. 102), the future crop (Parsons, 1936, p. 228, n. 96), commercial dealings (Zingg, 1938, pp. 717–18), and so on. Gillin lists fourteen forms of *compadrazgo* for a single community (1945). In certain cases, it cannot be said with any certainty whether the new adaptation was developed locally, or constitutes a carryover of some kind from some older European elaboration.

In general, ritual ties between contemporaries seem to have become more important than those between godparents and godchildren. This point is elaborated by Gillin in his discussion of the Peruvian community, Moche. He writes:

The essence of the system in Moche is an 'artificial bond', resembling a kinship relationship, which is established between persons by means of a ceremony. The ceremony usually involves a sponsorship of a person or material object by one or more of the persons involved, and the ceremony itself may be rather informal. However in Moche it seems to be placing the wrong emphasis to label the whole system ... 'ceremonial sponsorship.' ... The emphasis in Moche is upon the relations between sponsors of an individual or thing, and between them and other persons – in other words, relations between adults rather than between adults and children or things (1945, p. 104).

While the custom derives primarily from a conception of spiritual parenthood, modern Latin American emphasis seems to be rather on ritual co-parenthood; the *compadre-compadre* relationship outweighs the godparent-godchild relationship.

The ritual complex has been demonstrated to be of so flexible and adaptable a nature that a wide group of individuals can be bound together ceremonially. Paul makes the points that the mechanism of *compadrazgo* may be used either to enlarge numerically and spatially the number of ritually related kin on the one hand, or to reinforce already existing blood or ritual ties on the other. These contrasting motives he calls 'extension' and 'intensification' (Paul, 1942, p. 57). The authors of the present article feel that whether the *compadre* mechanism will be used prevailingly to extend or to intensify a given set of relationships will be determined in a specific functional-historical context.

In modern Latin American communities, there is clear patterning of choice. *Compadres* may be chosen exclusively from within one's own family, or perhaps blood kin will be preferred to outsiders. In other communities, on the other hand, one pair of godparents may serve for all of one's children, or *compadres* chosen from outside one's own family may be rigidly preferred. The present writers are convinced that the rare usages of *compadrazgo* in inheritance indicate the lack of utility of this mechanism in dynamically affecting prevailing patterns of ownership. It is a mechanism that can be used to strengthen existing patterns, but not to change them. In the two cases in which *compadrazgo* plays any role in determining land inheritance, land is held by the village community, and all that is inherited is temporary right of use (Wisdom, 1940; Villa R, 1945). Marital impediment under Canon Law, a factor of continuing importance in much of the New World (Herskovits, 1937, p. 98), and the selection of *compadres* within the kin group or outside it, are also factors bound together functionally and historically. This problem lies beyond the scope of the present article.

Compadrazgo, once accepted by a social grouping, can be moulded into the community way of life by many means. It is a two-way social system which sets up reciprocal relations of variable complexity and solemnity. By imposing automatically, and with a varying degree of sanctity, statuses and obligations of a fixed nature, on the people who participate, it makes the immediate social environment more stable, the participants more interdependent and more secure. In fact, it might be said that the baptismal rite (or corresponding event) may be the original basis for the mechanism, but no longer its sole motivating force. Some brief examples will demonstrate the institution's flexibility.

In Chimaltenango (Wagley, 1949, p. 19) two *compadres*

will lend each other maize or money ('as much as six dollars'). ... Two *comadres* should visit each other often and they may borrow small things readily from one another. When one is sick, or when one has just had another child, her *comadre* should come bringing tortillas for the family, and she should work in her *comadre's* house 'like a sister.'

In Peguche (Parsons, 1945, p. 45), 'white *compadres* are an asset for anyone who has business in Otovalo or Quito.'

In Tzintzuntzan (Foster, 1948, p. 264),

On the economic level, the *compadrazgo* system forms a kind of social insurance. Few are the families which can meet all emergencies without outside help. Often this means manual help at the time of a fiesta, or the responsibility of a *carguero*. Sometimes it means lending money, which near blood relatives do not like to do, because of the tendency never to repay a debt. But *compadres* feel obliged to lend, and no one would have respect for a man who refused to repay a *compadre*.

In San Pedro de Laguna (Paul, 1942, p. 92),

The practical purpose motivating the selection of Ladinas as *comadres* is the belief that they can cure infant illnesses and have access to the necessary medicines. The Indians store no medicine. But the Ladinas – by virtue of their cultural tradition and their greater income – customarily have on hand a number of drugstore preparations. The godparent bond imposes on the Ladina the responsibility of coming to the medical aid of her Indian godchild. The first year or two is correctly considered to be the most critical period of the infant's life. Hence the natives sacrifice long-run considerations in favor of providing a measure of medical protection during the infancy of the child. ...

Evidence from studies of two communities in Puerto Rico suggests that the *compadre* relation may be invoked to forestall sexual aggressions (Wolf, 1950; Manners, 1950). Cases are mentioned where a man concerned about the attentions of a family friend to his wife, sought to avoid trouble by making his friend his *compadre*. Thus a new and more sacred relationship was established.

Among the Huichol (Zingg, 1938, p. 57), the *compadre* relationship unquestionably strengthens Huichol social organization outside the family, which is not strong. Though *compadres* are not under economic bonds to each other, the injunction to be kind and friendly prevents drunken fights and brawls, which are the greatest source of weakness in Huichol society.

One form of *compadrazgo* is

specifically organized to avoid aggression between two *compadres*: '*el compadrazgo de voluntad*'. People say that where there are two bullies in the same *barrio*, they will conclude a 'non-aggression pact' and make themselves *compadres de voluntad*, which means that they can no longer fight each other (Wolf, 1950).

The persistence of *compadrazgo* in very secularized contexts, and its existence in such cases even without the sponsorship of a person, object or event, is evidence of its frequently high social and secular plasticity.

The formal basis for selecting godparents for one's children – religious guidance, and if necessary, the adoption of orphaned children – is sometimes carried out. Gamio mentions this traditional usage in the Valley of Teotihuacan (1922, vol. 2, p. 243), Redfield and Villa R for Chan Kom (1934, p. 250), Villa R for Tusik (1945, p. 90), Gonzales for the Mixe and Zoque (1943, pp. 204–5), and Wisdom for the Chorti (1940, pp. 293–4). Among the Chorti,

the godfather often acts in every way as the actual father in the event of the latter's death. He gives his ward advice, gets him out of difficulties, sometimes trains him in a man's work, and may act as his parent when he marries. The same is done by the godmother for her female godchild. If both parents die, and the godchild is young, the godparent may receive the portion of the property which the child inherited, and put it to his own use, in return for which he must bring up the child as one of his own family. As soon as the young man or woman becomes eighteen years of age, his inheritance is made up to him by his godfather. Where there is more than one minor child, each godfather receives his ward's share out of the total property, each child going to live in the home of its own godfather, leaving the adult children at home.

This usage is of particular interest because the *compadre* mechanism can be seen here as a link in the process of inheritance. Yet final property rights in this society are vested in the village, and not in the individual. A single case of the same kind of usage is mentioned by Villa R for the Maya Indian community of Tusik

(1945, p. 90). Yet *compadrazgo* cannot override the emphasis on group land tenure in either of these societies. The mechanism is flexible and adaptable specifically because it usually carries with it no legal obligations – particularly regarding inheritance. Paul makes this point clearly when he writes that,

> Unlike the involuntary ties of kinship those of ritual sponsorship are formed on the basis of choice. This enables godparenthood to serve as the social link connecting divergent income groups, disparate social strata, and separated localities. Affinity too may cut across class and locality through the practices of hypergamy and intermarriage. But the frequency with which such irregular forms of marriage occur throughout the world is sharply limited by strong social pressures operating to keep the unions within the class or community. This is understandable in view of the fact that marriage is the means by which the in-group perpetuates itself. Because no such considerations of social recruitment impede the formation of godparent bonds between persons of different social strata, godparenthood more readily serves as a mechanism for intergroup integration (1942, pp. 72–3).

It may be fruitful to examine cases of *compadrazgo* as examples of mechanisms cross-cutting socio-cultural or class affiliations, or as taking place within the socio-cultural confines of a single class. The authors believe such patternings will prove to be determined, not haphazard in character, nor determined solely along continuums of homogeneity-to-heterogeneity, or greater-to-lesser isolation. Rather they will depend on the amount of socio-cultural and economic mobility, *real and apparent*, available to an individual in a given situation. There is of course no clear-cut device for the measurement of such real or apparent mobility. Yet the utility of *compadrazgo* might profitably be examined in this light. The aim would be to assess whether the individual is seeking to strengthen his position in a homogeneous socio-cultural community with high stability and low mobility, or to strengthen certain cross-cutting ties by alignment with persons of a higher socio-cultural stratum, via reciprocal-exploitative relationships manipulated through *compadrazgo*. Some examples may illuminate the problem.

The Maya Indian people of Tusik (Villa R, 1945), a community in east central Quintana Roo, Yucatan, are homogeneous in a tribal sense, rather than having a mono-class structure. Says Villa R:

There are no classes here in the sense that different groups of people have different relations to the production and distribution of economic goods; in the sense that some people own land on which other people work, or that some people are engaged in producing goods while others are engaged in distributing them or in servicing the rest of the population. As we have already pointed out, everyone in the subtribe has the same relation to the land as everyone else; the land is commonly held by the subtribe, and a man's rights to a piece of land rests only on the right that he has put agricultural labor into the land and is entitled to the products of his labor. Every man makes *milpa* – even the sacred professionals earn their living as farmers – and since the secular division of labor is practically nonexistent, there are no merchants or artisans.

The economic life of the group centers about maize, and the people consume all that they produce. Labor for other men is rare, and when done, payment in kind prevails. The only cash commodity is chicle. Says Villa R:

Apparently all the people of the subtribe enjoy the same economic circumstances. Nothing one observes in their ordinary, daily behavior suggests the existence of differences in accumulated wealth. ... The acquisition of wealth is related directly to the personal ambition of the individual, for there are no differences in opportunity and no important differences in privilege. The principal source of wealth is the extraction of chicle, which is within the reach of all. ... This equality of opportunity is a recent matter, for some years ago when the chiefs had greater authority, the lands of the bush were distributed by them and the best portion preserved for their own use. In some cases men were thus able to enrich themselves through special advantage.

Regarding *compadrazgo*, the grandparents of the child to be born, preferably the paternal ones, are chosen. If they are not alive, chiefs or *maestros cantores*, as persons of prestige and good character, are selected. It is noteworthy that no mention is made of any choice of travelling merchants as *compadres*, although

the travelling merchants are the natives' main source of contact with the outer world. It is they who bring into the region ... the most important news from the city. ... The arrival of the merchant is the occasion for the people to gather together and excitedly discuss the events he relates to them, and in this atmosphere the merchant's own friendly ties with the natives are strengthened.

Chicle is sold, and commodities bought through these travellers, but apparently ritual kinship is not used to bind them with the community.

In marked contrast to the isolated, subsistence crop, tribal culture of Tusik, we may examine two communities which exhibit cultural homogeneity under completely different conditions. They are fully integrated economically, and to a great degree welded culturally into national cultures. The first of these is Poyal (Mintz, 1950).

Barrio Poyal is a rural community on the south coast of Puerto Rico, in an area of large-scale sugar cane production, with corporate ownership of land and mills. The lands are devoted exclusively to the production of the single cash crop. While the *barrio* working population forms what is practically a mono-class isolate, *compadres* could be selected among the foremen, administrators, public officials, store owners, and so forth. Instead, there is an overwhelming tendency to pick neighbors and fellow workers as *compadres*. A man who seeks a wealthy *compadre* in Poyal is held in some contempt by his fellows; a wealthy *compadre* would not visit him nor invite him to his house. People remember when the old hacienda owners were chosen as godparents to the workers' children, but this practice is totally outmoded now. A local landowning group no longer exists in Poyal.

Compadre relationships generally are treated reverentially; *compadres* are addressed with the polite *Usted*, even if they are family members, and the *compadre* relationship is utilized daily in getting help, borrowing money, dividing up available work opportunities, and so forth. However, as more and more Poyal workers migrate to the United States, the utility of many *compadre* ties is weakened.

Another example of the same category is Pascua (Spicer, 1940), a community of essentially landless, wage-earning Yaqui Indian immigrants who, with their descendants, form a village on the outskirts of Tucson, Arizona. The economic basis of Pascua life bears certain striking resemblances to *Barrio* Poyal: the almost total lack of subsistence activities, the emphasis on seasonal variation, the emphasis on wage-earning as opposed to payment in kind, and so on. Says Spicer:

Existence is wholly dependent on the establishment of relationships with individuals outside the village. If for any reason the economic relations of a Pascuan with outside persons are broken off for an extended period, it becomes necessary to depend upon other Pascuans who have maintained such relations.

While the economic linkages are exclusively with external sources of income and employment, the *compadre* structure is described

as an all-pervasive network of relationships which takes into its web every person in the village. Certain parts of the network, here and there about the village, are composed of strong and well-knit fibers. Here the relationships between *compadres* are functioning constantly and effectively. Elsewhere there are weaker threads representing relationships which have never been strengthened by daily recognition of reciprocal obligations. These threads nevertheless exist and may from time to time be the channels of temporarily re-established *compadre* relationships.

Spicer notes that:

sometimes in Pascua sponsors are sought outside the village in Libre or Marana, or even among the Mexican population of Tucson.

But everything suggests that the ritual kinship system here functions predominantly within the wage-earning, landless mono-class grouping of the Yaqui themselves. Spicer's description of *compadrazgo* is probably the most complete in the literature today, and the Pascua system appears to be primarily between contemporaries in emphasis, and as in *Barrio* Poyal horizontal in character.

These three cases, Tusik, *Barrio* Poyal, and Pascua, illustrate the selective character of *compadrazgo* and some of its functionings, within small 'homogeneous' groupings. The mechanism plainly has considerable importance and utility and is treated reverentially in all three places. Yet while Tusik is isolated and lacks a class-character, *Barrio* Poyal and Pascua are both involved in wage-earning, cash crop, world market productive arrangements where the homogeneity is one of class membership only, and isolation is not characteristic.

In Tusik, *compadrazgo* is correlated with great internal stability, low economic mobility, ownership of land by the village, and the lack of a cash economy and class stratification. In *Barrio* Poyal and Pascua *compadrazgo* correlates with homogeneous class membership, landlessness, wage-earning, and an apparent growing identity of class interest.

An interesting contrast is provided by Gillin's study of Moche. This is a Peruvian coastal community which, according to the Foreword,

is in the last stages of losing its identity as an Indian group and of being absorbed into Peruvian national life. ... Surrounded by large, modern haciendas, Moche is 'Indian' only in that its population is largely Indian in a racial sense, that it has retained much of its own lands, that it exists in a certain social isolation from surrounding peoples, retaining a community life organized on a modified kinship basis, mainly of Spanish derivation. ... Its lands, however, are now owned individually, and they are being alienated through sale and litigation. It is on a cash rather than subsistence basis economically. ... Many Mocheros even work outside the community for wages, and some are in professions. ... Formal aspects of native social organization have disappeared, and contacts with the outside world are increasing (Gillin, 1945).

In Moche, the *compadre* system would expectably be subject to the same stresses as those suffered by any other local social institution. Yet

the whole idea of this type of relationship has been carried to extremes in Moche. There are more types of *padrinazgo* [i.e. godfatherhood] in this community than in any other concerning which I have seen reports. This fact may be linked with the absence of spontaneous community organization and solidarity.

Gillin finds evidence for fourteen different kinds of *compadre* relations. As to the choice of *compadres*, Gillin says:

Godparents may be blood relatives, but usually the attempt is made to secure persons who are not relatives of either of the parents. Not only Mocheros, but in these days, trusted *forasteros* [i.e. outsiders] are chosen. From the point of view of the parents it is desirable to choose godparents who are financially responsible, if not rich, and also persons who have 'influence' and prestigeful social connections. The real function of godparents is to broaden, and, if possible, increase the social and economic resources of the child and his parents and by the same token to lower the anxieties of the parents on this score.

In a later section, however, Gillin states that he does not feel that socially defined classes as such exist in Moche (1945, pp. 107, 113).

It is extremely noteworthy that the mechanism of *compadrazgo* has maintained itself here in the face of what appears to be progressively accelerating social change. We wonder whether the elaborations of the mechanism's forms may be part of the community's unconscious effort to answer new problems. It must increasingly face the insecurity of growing incorporation into the national structure and increasing local wage-based, cash crop competition. This may call forth an increased emphasis on techniques for maintaining and strengthening face-to-face relationships. Eggan's study of Cheyenne kinship terminology (1937) suggests that the kinship structure is sensitive to rapid social change if the changing terminology reflects genuine structural modifications. Ritual kinship structures may react to the weakening of certain traditional obligations by spreading out to include new categories of contemporaries, and therefore potential competitors.

Other examples suggest that vertical phrasings of the *compadre* system may take place in situations where change has been slowed at some point, and relationships between two defined sociocultural strata, or classes, are solidified. San Jose is a highland coffee and minor crop-producing community of Puerto Rico (Wolf, 1950). The frequency distribution of land shows a considerable scatter, with 55 per cent of the landowners holding 10 per cent of the land at one extreme, and 5 per cent holding 45 per cent of the land at the other. Thus, while Tusik people hold their land communally, *Barrio* Poyal and Pascua people are landless, and Moche people are largely small landowners with no farm over four acres, San Jose people are in large part landowners with great variability in the size of holdings. While a large part of the agricultural population is landless, agricultural laborers in San Jose may be paid partly in kind, and frequently will be given in addition a small plot of land for subsistence farming. Production for wages is largely of the main cash crop, coffee.

In the rural zones of this community, a prevailing number of the *compadre* relations tie agricultural workers to their landholding employers, or small landholders to larger ones. Thus a large landowner may become *compadre* to twenty smaller landowners living around his farm. In isolated areas, where the 'community' is defined entirely in familial terms, most *compadre* relationships take place within the family. Yet it must be recognized that members of the same family, and brothers of the same filial generation, may be variously landowners, sharecroppers (*medianeros*), and laborers.

Compadrazgo in San Jose may help in the stabilization of productive relations between large and small landholders, or between landholders and their sharecropping employees and laborers. Interesting in this connection is the fact that the economic basis in San Jose is much less exclusively cash than in Tusik, *Barrio* Poyal, or Pascua. The land tenure pattern in San Jose does not appear to be changing rapidly. *Compadrazgo* relations are phrased vertically, so as to cross-cut class stratification, quite probably serving in this connection to solidify the relationships of people to the land. There is evidence of landowners getting free labor out of their laborer brothers who have been made *compadres*. Contrariwise, laborers bound by *compadrazgo* to their employers are accustomed to rely on this bond to secure them certain small privileges, such as the use of equipment, counsel and help, small loans, and so on.

The authors know of no fully documented study of *compadrazgo* in the context of an 'old-style' plantation or hacienda. Siegel's material on the Guatemalan plantation community of San Juan Acatan indicates that the Indians there often invite Ladinos with whom they come in contact to sponsor the baptisms of their children. But Siegel adds that the relationship in this community is 'virtually meaningless' (quoted in Paul, 1942, p. 72). The authors of the present article would in general predict that plantation laborers, either bound or very dependent on the plantation, with daily face-to-face contacts with the owner or *hacendado* would seek to establish a reciprocal coparental relationship with the owner. Historical material from old informants in *Barrio* Poyal offer evidence of this tradition, now markedly altered in the pure wage, absentee ownership context.

The mechanism may be contrasted, then, in several distinct contexts. In the first context are Tusik, *Barrio* Poyal and Pascua. These communities are alike in their 'homogeneity', and the horizontal structuring of the *compadre* system; yet they are markedly different in other respects. Tusik is tribal and essentially isolated from the world market, while *Barrio* Poyal and Pascua are incorporated into capitalistic world economies, and are fully formed working class strata.

In the second context is San Jose, with its varied land ownership pattern, its mixed (cash and subsistence) crop production and its several classes. Through the vertical phrasing of its *compadre* system, San Jose demonstrates a relatively stable reciprocity, economic and social, between the landed, large and small, and the sharecroppers and laborers.

In the third context is Moche. Land is held predominantly in small plots; the crops, as in San Jose, are both cash and subsistence, and while Gillin doubts the existence of classes, certainly the *compadre* system is described as a vertical structuring one. Here, too, the elaboration of face-to-face ceremonialism may help to slow the accelerated trend towards land concentration, a cash economy, and incorporation into the world market.

Conclusion

Thus in cases where the community is a self-contained class, or tribally homogeneous, *compadrazgo* is prevailingly horizontal (intra-class) in character. In cases where the community contains several interacting classes, *compadrazgo* will structure such relationships vertically (inter-class). Last, in a situation of rapid social change *compadre* mechanisms may multiply to meet the accelerated rate of change.

References
BANCROFT, H. H. (1883), *History of Mexico*, The History Society of San Francisco.
BEALS, R. L. (1946), *Cherán: A Sierra Tarascan Village*, Smithsonian Institution publication no. 2.
EGGAN, F. (1937), 'The Cheyenne and Arapaho kinship system', in F. Eggan (ed.), *Social Anthropology of North American Tribes*, Chicago University Press.
ESPINOSA, J. M. (1942), *Crusaders of the Rio Grande*, Chicago University Press.
FOSTER, G. N. (1948), *Empire's Children: The People of Tzintzuntzan*, Smithsonian Institution publication no. 6.
GAMIO, M. (1922), *La Población del Valle de Teotihuacán*, Secretaria de Agricultura y Fomento, Mexico.
GILLIN, J. (1945), *Moche: A Peruvian Coastal Community*, Smithsonian Institution publication no. 3.
HERSKOVITS, M. J. (1937), *Life in a Haitian Valley*, Knopf.
DE LANDA, D. (1941), Landa's Relación de las Cosas de Yucatan, in A. M. Tozzer (ed.), *Papers: Peabody Museum of American Archaeology and Ethnology*, Harvard University, vol. 18.
MANNERS, R. A. (1950), *A Tobacco and Minor Crop Community in Puerto Rico*, unpublished ms.

MINTZ, S. W. (1950), *A Sugar-Cane Community in Puerto Rico*, unpublished ms.

PARSONS, E. C. (1936), *Mitla: Town of the Souls*, Chicago University Press.

PARSONS, E. C. (1945), *Peguche: A Study of Andean Indians*, Chicago University Press.

PAUL, B. D. (1942), 'Ritual Kinship: With Special Reference to Godparenthood in Middle America', doctoral thesis, University of Chicago.

REDFIELD, R., and VILLA R, A. (1934), *Chan Kom: A Maya Village*, Carnegie Institution of Washington, publication no. 448.

ROJAS, G. F. (1943), 'La institución del compadrazgo entre los Indigenas de México', *Rev. Méxicana Sociol.*, vol. 5, no. 1.

DE SAHAGUN, B. (1932), *A History of Ancient Mexico*, Nashville.

SPICER, E. (1940), *Pascua: A Yaqui Village in Arizona*, Chicago University Press.

VILLA R, A. (1945), *The Maya of East Central Quintana Roo*, Carnegie Institution of Washington, publication no. 559.

WAGLEY, C. (1949), *The Social and Religious Life of a Guatemalan Village*, Memoir, American Anthropological Association, no. 71.

WISDOM, C. (1940), *A Chorti Village in Guatemala*, Chicago University Press.

WOLF, E. R. (1950), *A Coffee-Growing Community in Puerto Rico*, unpublished ms.

ZINGG, R. (1938), *Primitive Artists: the Huichols*, University of Denver Contributions to Ethnology.

Part Twelve **Changing Patterns of Kinship**

The kinship behaviour of simple hunters is clearly different
from that of groups practising irrigation agriculture. In the first
place, kinship is often used to channel the inheritance of
property, so that where the means of production change, kin
relationships are likely to do so as well. Equally, the industrial
process brings with it an individualization of the family income
and stress on spatial and social mobility, so that it is associated
with changes both of a demographic and of a structural kind.
It is particularly important to investigate these changes if we
are to understand kinship and family patterns in the developing
world; in many parts the kin groups of an earlier period are
being shattered by political, economic, religious and educational
changes, affecting a whole network of interpersonal behaviour
and patterns of dependence and co-operation. The classic work
on these changes is Goode's *World Revolution and Family
Patterns* (1963), from which our final Reading comes.

25 W. J. Goode

World Changes in Family Patterns

Excerpts from W. J. Goode, *World Revolution and Family Patterns*, Free Press, 1963, pp. 1–15.

For the first time in world history a common set of influences – the social forces of industrialization and urbanization – is affecting every known society. Even traditional family systems in such widely separate and diverse societies as Papua, Manus, China and Yugoslavia are reported to be changing as a result of these forces, although at different rates of speed. The alteration seems to be in the direction of some type of *conjugal* family pattern – that is, toward fewer kinship ties with distant relatives and a greater emphasis on the 'nuclear' family unit of couple and children. In the Western Culture Complex – the New World, Australia, New Zealand and Europe west of the Urals – where a conjugal family system has already been in operation to some extent, the direction of change seems to be toward its wider spread.

If it is true that the rough outlines of a conjugal system are beginning to emerge in such disparate cultures as China and the Arab world, we are witnessing a remarkable phenomenon: the development of similar family behavior and values among much of the world's population. This inquiry will try to ascertain whether, and why, this process is indeed occurring.

Such an investigation raises a host of complex theoretical problems. But important theoretical problems direct any fruitful study of the facts, just as facts in turn serve to sharpen theory. Therefore, an outline of the broad, relevant, theoretical issues should preface our analysis of family changes in six major world cultures.

1. Even if the family systems in diverse areas of the world are moving *toward* similar patterns, they *begin* from very different points, so that the trend in one family trait may differ from one

society to another – for example, the divorce or illegitimacy rate might be dropping in one society but rising in another.

2. The elements within a family system may each be altering at different rates of speed. While some were greatly strained under the traditional system, others were buttressed by many institutional supports; new influences, therefore, encounter more resistance at some points in the family system than at others.

3. Just *how* industrialization or urbanization affects the family system, or how the family system facilitates or hinders these processes, is not clear.

4. It is doubtful that the amount of change in family patterns is a simple function of industrialization; more likely, ideological and value changes, partially independent of industrialization, also have some effect on family action.

5. Some beliefs about how the traditional family system worked may be wrong. Even to measure change over the past half-century requires a knowledge of where these family systems started *from*. We may learn, for example, that although some family patterns are thought to be new, they have in fact always been part of the traditional system – for example, the reported breakup of the Indian joint family. Reports that the joint family system is breaking up have been prevalent for sixty years. It now seems likely that although most Indian families are 'joint' at some phase in their life cycle, they also go through a stage of breaking up when the married sons move away to found their own households. Thus, the 'breakup' is really one stage in the process of formation and growth of individual families, and has characterized the Indian family system for decades.

6. Correlatively, it is important to distinguish *ideal* family patterns from *real* family behavior and values, and it is especially necessary to differentiate the social habits of upper-class families from those of the majority of the society.

7. Finally, since the aim of research is precision and understanding, it is necessary to examine carefully whatever numbers and counts can be obtained in order to be sure that they are in fact descriptions of reality and not accidents of poor recording procedures. Especially when inquiring into the past, we must question the validity of the data.

Those involved in the process of social change often exaggerate its radical character. If public opinion polls had been taken in every important historical period, they would probably have revealed that the participants thought *all* the old traditions were dissolving, although from our perspective the alterations of each period seem minor. Western people, for example, tend to believe that morals have deteriorated greatly over the past hundred years. However, the illegitimacy rate has actually dropped slightly; and some evidence suggests that the percentage of women who are pregnant when they marry is about the same as it was in the past – although perhaps not so high as it was two centuries ago.

Unfortunately, the data are not yet available for most of the problems with which we are concerned here – a fact to be noted when considering the opinions of social analysts, who tend to assume that changes in economic or industrial systems are the primary cause of alterations in family systems. This relationship has been taken for granted, but has never been scientifically demonstrated.

Social science developed only one comprehensive theory of family change, one based on nineteenth-century evolutionary ideas. (The science has since evolved beyond that theory without developing a substitute.) Intended to explain both the observable differences among the world's family patterns and their history, the theory asserted that in the course of man's development the family had 'progressed' from the primitive sexual promiscuity of a semi-animal horde, through group marriage, matriarchy and patriarchy in some polygynous form, to culminate in the highest spiritual expression of the family, Victorian monogamy.[1] But growing philosophic doubts that the nineteenth-century family and religious systems were indeed the highest levels reached by man began to bring into question the validity of this sweeping theory. In addition, as knowledge about human societies over the world accumulated, the core of the evolutionary theory – that each advance in technology was accompanied by an advance in family patterns and religion – dissolved. No such correlation actually emerged.

E. B. Tylor, who was otherwise so shrewd in his understanding of

1. For a concise statement of nineteenth-century family theory see König (1955).

human societies, formulated the main technique being used in the nineteenth century, the interpretation of certain social patterns, such as 'marriage by capture' or the custom of doffing the hat as a greeting, as 'social survivals' or *social fossils* (Tylor, 1888). He claimed that just as we can ascertain what *Eohippus* was like from his fossil remains, so can we learn what Stone Age man was like from the survival of some of his social patterns – for example, the relic of marriage by capture appears in some primitive societies in the form of a mock fight between the kin of bride and groom before the bride is carried away. Thus, by looking at Australian aborigines or Polynesians, we can learn about Stone Age man; and the Hawaiian marriage patterns 'proved' for a while the former existence of group marriage.

Curiously, the determined anti-evolutionists never attacked this great reconstruction systematically. But the growing use of social research techniques at the end of the nineteenth century added to suspicions about the validity of such reconstructions of man's past. About the turn of the century the evolutionist approach was being labeled irrelevant, foolish, and amateur, and it became itself a 'survival' in the writings of *dilettanti* and Communist apologists through the succeeding half-century. It was seen that 'primitive' societies like those of the Australian aborigines might have very complex religious and kinship systems, and that modern stone-using societies do not all have the same social systems. Moreover, since all men presumably come from the same evolutionary line and are equally distant historically from Cro-Magnon men, all societies are *equally* old.

Social scientists came to see, then, that contemporary primitive societies were not necessarily 'primeval', nor necessarily closer to the social behavior of Neolithic man than to civilized societies. The family patterns of both Neolithic and Paleolithic man are forever lost to us. We cannot reconstruct them either from the behavior of the gorilla or chimpanzee (about which almost no valid information was available, in any event, at the turn of the century), or from the technologically least advanced societies still in existence.

Technological systems may be ranked as more or less advanced, and, with somewhat greater theoretical difficulty, so may economic systems; but no specific family forms seem to be correlated with the specific 'stages' of the economic and technological evolution. For example, the Eskimo types of kinship and that of the United States are very similar[2]. Both religious and family systems seem to vary independently of economic and technological systems[3]. This statement does not imply that family systems have not gone through any evolutionary sequence – that is, some determinate series of changes – or even that there is no set of determinate relations among family and economic or technological variables. At the present time, however, no such set of determinate sequences or relations has been *demonstrated* – although they are often assumed to be well known.

Marx did not aim at a comprehensive theory of family social change; but in explaining the origins of industrial England in the mid-nineteenth century he took the trouble to analyse the effects of the machine upon the working class family in a society that accepted rational calculation as the basis for economic decisions.

As Marx pointed out, the essence of the machine is not that it is driven by non-human power, but that it can perform the work of the human hand, and can thus be multiplied or speeded up. Consequently, women, children or unskilled men could be used in the labor force, causing the wages of skilled men to drop to the level of those paid to women or children. Furthermore, since *all* could now work, the wage level could be reduced to the point where a composite family income was needed to produce the wages formerly earned by one male household head. Consequently, either everyone worked or all starved. A manufacturer could pay higher wages only at the risk of being driven out of business by his less scrupulous, but more rational, competitors.

Women were forced into factories and thus separated from their children and households. The results were inevitable: infant and child mortality rates rose, the working day lengthened, children were kept out of school, young girls did not learn the necessary domestic arts and fathers sold their children's labor on harsh terms.[4] Thus, a century ago, did Marx document industrialization's

---

2. See Murdock (1949), p. 226–7. Not all Eskimo groups fall into the same kinship category: see Hughes (1959).

3. Attempting to locate underlying variables by scalogram analysis, Winch and Freeman found that two variables would not 'fit' into a scale of societal complexity (1957). Recently, Meyer F. Nimkoff has begun a cross-cultural attempt to fit different forms of the family with different economic and technological traits.

4. Marx's analysis of the process may be found in *Capital*, chapter 15.

destructive effect on the lower-class family, using the numerous research reports of his time. In fact, however, the processes were much more complex, as Smelser has indicated. In the earlier phases of the factory system, men were able to supervise their own children and thus maintain their authority as household heads. (Smelser, 1959).

But though Marx was able to show a few effects of the factory system on the family, his analysis was limited by his political commitment. One could not have predicted from Marxian theory all the changes in the family that have occurred since his time in both industrial and non-industrial cultures. Certainly, he failed to prove that particular forms of the family emerge when certain economic or technological stages are reached in the history of a given society.

William F. Ogburn also gave major attention to the process of social change, emphasizing technology's impact on the family. Although he is prominently identified with one version of Marxian theory – that the prime mover is technology ('material culture') and that after a period of time ('culture lag') the non-material elements of culture adjust to it – his analyses are actually eclectic, recognizing a wide range of innovations as sources of family change: ideologies, birth control, urbanism, steam engines, airplanes, etc.[5] Ogburn not only pointed out the probable effects of a given invention or social innovation on the family but also traced specific family changes – the increasing divorce rate, for example – to its various probable causes. According to his analysis, with economic production as well as education, religious training, and protection being taken away from the home, the family in the United States was 'losing its functions'. This opinion has been widely accepted by family analysts, although its precise meaning is unclear and, for the most part, simply incorrect. Ogburn's contribution was not theoretical, and in any event, our aim here is not to criticize large-scale theories of family change, which could only be premature. Ogburn was particularly effective in aggregating masses of empirical data, or in using his mastery of research techniques to test easy assumptions about some detail of behavior. For example, he shows that although the average United States household dropped from about 5·5 persons in 1850 to 3·5 in 1950, the large

5. Ogburn's earlier formulation may be found in *Social Change* (1922). See also his more mature analysis (1955, chs. 11 and 12; 1946, ch. 15).

household made up of many persons was not typical even a century ago (Ogburn, 1955).

Similarly, he was able to ferret out data to show that the 'labor-saving devices' in the United States home seem to have saved no labor at all, since housewives who owned them continued to work as many hours per week as those who did not (Ogburn, 1955). In his mature work, he no longer held that the machine was a primary factor in altering society, but rather that society was made up of intricately interwoven elements so that almost any part could be linked causally with any other.

Such technically careful summations of fact, however, constitute neither a theory of family change nor even a charting of the effects of industrialization on the family. Ogburn's later expositions are guided not so much by a theory as by a general orientation – that to understand family change it was most fruitful to examine the nexus between a specific technological innovation and its several possible effects on family relations (as evaluated by commonsense expectations). This examination proceeded under the assumption that the acceptance of an innovation was to be taken for granted on grounds of rationality. That the responses of different cultures to such innovations would vary did not constitute an inquiry of research for Ogburn. He saw the upward march of technology as both inevitable and theoretically unproblematic.

This has been a brief summary assault upon the attempts to show a simple correlation between economic or technological development and particular stages or forms of family systems. As against this necessary skepticism, one crude observation derived from modern events seems accurate enough: wherever the economic system expands through industrialization, family patterns change. Extended kinship ties weaken, lineage patterns dissolve, and a trend towards some form of the conjugal system generally begins to appear – that is, the nuclear family becomes a more independent kinship unit. Modern commentators have reported this process from many parts of the world, some interpreting it as one aspect of the 'Americanization' of Europe, or even of the world. [. . .]

The conjugal family as an ideal type

As now used by family analysts, the term 'conjugal family' is technically an *ideal type*; it also represents an ideal.[6] The concept was not developed from a summary or from the empirical study of actual United States urban family behavior; it is a *theoretical* construction, derived from intuition and observation, in which several crucial variables have been combined to form a hypothetical structural harmony. Such a conceptual structure may be used as a measure and model in examining real time trends or contemporary patterns. In the ensuing discussion, we shall try to separate the fundamental from the more derivative variables in this construction.

As a concept, the conjugal family is also an *ideal* in that when analysts refer to its spread they mean that an increasing number of people view some of its characteristics as *proper* and legitimate, no matter how reality may run counter to the ideal. Thus, although parents in the United States agree that they *should* not play an important role in their children's choice of spouse, they actually do. Relatives *should* not interfere in each other's family affairs, but in a large (if unknown) percentage of cases they do. Since, however, this ideal aspect of the conjugal family is also part of the total reality, significant for changes in family patterns, we shall comment on it later as an ideology.

The most important characteristic of the ideal typical construction of the conjugal family is the relative exclusion of a wide range of affinal and blood relatives from its everyday affairs: there is no great extension of the kin network.[7] Many other traits may be derived theoretically from this one variable. Thus, the couple cannot count on a large number of kinfolk for help, just as these kin cannot call upon the couple for services. Neither couple nor kinfolk have many *rights* with respect to the other, and so the reciprocal *obligations* are few. In turn, by an obvious sociological principle, the couple has few moral controls over their extended kin, and these have few controls over the couple.

The locality of the couple's household will no longer be greatly

6. It is an ideal type in the Weberian sense; see Weber (1949, pp. 88 *et seq.*) also a brief summary in Goode (1947, pp. 473–5).

7. For a list of additional variables for comparing family systems see Goode (1959, pp. 178–91).

determined by their kin since kinship ties are weak. The couple will have a 'neolocal' residence, i.e. they will establish a new household when they marry. This in turn reinforces their relative independence, because it lowers the frequency of social interaction with their kin.

The choice of mate is freer than in other systems, because the bases upon which marriage is built are different: the kin have no strong rights or financial interest in the matter. Adjustment is primarily between husband and wife, not between the incoming spouse and his or her in-law group. The courtship system is therefore ideally based, and, at the final decision stage, empirically as well, on the mutual attraction between the two youngsters.

All courtship systems are market or exchange systems. They differ from one another with respect to *who* does the buying and selling, which characteristics are more or less valuable in that market, and how open or explicit the bargaining is. In a conjugal family system mutual attraction in both courtship and marriage acquires a higher value. Nevertheless, the elders do not entirely lose control. Youngsters are likely to marry only those with whom they fall in love, and they fall in love only with the people they meet. Thus, the focus of parental controls is on who is allowed to meet whom at parties, in the school and neighbourhood, and so on.[8]

When such a system begins to emerge in a society, the age at marriage is likely to change because the goals of marriage change, but whether it will rise or fall cannot be predicted from the characteristics mentioned so far. In a conjugal system, the youngsters must now be old enough to take care of themselves, i.e. they must be as old as the economic system forces them to be in order to be independent at marriage. (Alternative solutions also arise: some middle-class youngsters may marry upon the promise of support from their parents, while they complete their education.[9]) Thus, if the economic system changes its base, e.g. from agriculture to industry, the age at marriage may change. The couple decides the number of children they will have on the basis of their own needs, not those of a large kin group, and contraception, abortion or

8. For an analysis of love-control in various societies see Goode (1959a, pp. 38–47).

9. Additional help patterns are described in Sussman (1953, pp. 18–22).

infanticide may be used to control this number. Whether fertility will be high or low cannot, however, be deduced from these conjugal traits. Under some economic systems – for example, frontier agriculture – the couple may actually need a large number of children.

This system is bilineal or, to use Max Gluckman's term, multilineal: the two kin lines are of nearly equal importance, because neither has great weight. Neolocality and the relative freedom from control by an extended kin network prevent the maintenance or formation of a powerful lineage system, which is necessary if one line is to be dominant over the other.[10]

Since the larger kin group can no longer be counted on for emotional sustenance, and since the marriage is based on mutual attraction, the small marital unit is the main place where the emotional input-output balance of the individual husband and wife is maintained, where their psychic wounds can be salved or healed. At least there is no other place where they can go. Thus, the emotions within this unit are likely to be intense, and the relationship between husband and wife may well be intrinsically unstable, depending as it does on affection. Consequently, the divorce rate is likely to be high. Remarriage is likely because there is no larger kin unit to absorb the children and no unit to prevent the spouses from re-entering the free marriage market.

Finally, the couple and children do recognize some extended kin, but the husband recognizes a somewhat different set of kindred than does his wife, since they began in different families. And the children view as important a somewhat different set of kindred than do their parents: the parents look back a generation greater in depth than do the children, and perhaps a greater distance outward because they have had an adult lifetime in which to come to know more kin. That is, each individual takes into account a somewhat different set of kindred, though most of them are the same for all within the same nuclear unit.

The foregoing sketch is an ideal typical construction and thus must be compared with the reality of both behavior *and* ideal in those societies which are thought to have conjugal family patterns. To my knowledge, no such test has been made. Very likely, the *ideals* of a large proportion of United States families fit this con-

10. For other kinship characteristics of this 'Eskimo' type see Murdock (1949, pp. 226–8).

struction very well. Some parts of the construction also fit the *behavior* of a considerable, but unknown, fraction of United States families – e.g. the emphasis on emotionality within the family, the free choice of spouse, and neolocality, bilineality and instability of the individual family. On the other hand, data from both England and the United States indicate that even in lower-class urban families, where the extension of kin ties might be thought to be shorter (following the ideal type), many kin ties are active. No one has measured the intensity and extensivenes of kin ties in a range of societies in order to ascertain how Western family patterns compare in these respects. It is quite possible that those countries thought to be closest to the conjugal pattern do in fact have a less extended kin network.

Nevertheless, the ideal type conflicts sharply with reality *and* theory in one important respect. Theoretical considerations suggest that, without the application of political pressure, the family *cannot* be as limited in its kin network as the ideal typical construction suggests. Both common observation and theory coincide to suggest that: (1) grandparent-grandchild ties are still relatively intense and (2) emotional ties among siblings are also strong. Consequently (3), parents-in-law interact relatively frequently with their children-in-law (see Sussman, 1953, pp. 22–8), and (4) married people have frequent contacts with their brothers- or sisters-in-law. It follows, then, that (5) children maintain contacts, at least during their earlier years, with their uncles and aunts, as well as with their first cousins. Without question, of all types of 'visiting' and 'social occasions', the most common, even in the urban United States, is 'visiting with relatives'.

If no active ties are maintained with the categories of kin mentioned above, the family feels that some explanation is called for, and pleads some excuse ('They live too far away,' or 'We've never got along well').

In addition, perhaps most families have *some* tie with one or more relatives still further away in the kin network. Those noted above seem to be linked to the nuclear family in an inescapable way; it is difficult to ignore or reject any of them without simultaneously rejecting a fellow member of *one's own* nuclear family. The child can not ignore his uncle without hurting one of his own parents, and reciprocally. A girl may not neglect her sister-in-law without impairing her relationship with her brother. Of course, brother and sister may combine against their own spouses, and social interaction may continue even under an impaired relationship. Cousins are dragged along by their parents, who are siblings and siblings-in-law to one another. The extension of the family network to this point, then, seems determined by the emotional ties within the nuclear family unit itself. To reduce the unit to the nuclear family would require coercive restriction of these ties between siblings or between parents, as the Chinese commune has attempted to do.

The 'fit' between the conjugal family and the modern industrial system

The argument as to whether political and economic variables, or the reverse, generally determine family patterns seems theoretically empty. Rather, we must establish any determinate relations (whichever direction the causal effect) among any particular family variables and the variables of other institutional orders – not a simple task. Even the relation between the conjugal family and industrialization is not yet entirely clear. The common hypothesis – that the conjugal form of the family emerges when a culture is invaded by industrialization and urbanization – is an undeveloped observation which neglects three issues: (1) the theoretical harmony or 'fit' between this ideal typical form of the family and industrialization; (2) the empirical harmony or fit between industrialization and any actual system; and (3) the effects upon the family of the modern (or recently past) organizational and industrial system, i.e. how the factors in the system influence the family.

At present, only the first of these can be treated adequately. The second has been dealt with primarily by researchers who have analysed a peasant or primitive culture with reference to the problem of labor supply, and who suggest that family systems *other* than the conjugal one do not adequately answer the demands of an expanding industrial system. Malinowski asserted, for example, that although young Trobriander men could earn more by working on plantations than by growing yams, they preferred to grow yams because this activity was defined as required for their family roles. Similarly, a head tax was necessary to force young men to leave their families to work in the South African mines.[11] Men's objections to women leaving the home for outside jobs have limited the labor supply in various parts of the world, especially in Islamic areas. On the other hand, within conjugal or quasi conjugal systems such as those in the West, the strains between family patterns and industrial requirements have only rarely been charted empirically (see, however, Smelser, 1959, chs. 9, 10, 11).

This last task would require far more ingenious research designs than have been so far utilized. It requires that the exact points of impact between family and industrial organization be located and the degree of impact measured. Succeeding chapters will devote some attention to this problem. Specific decisions or choices need to be analysed, in which both family and industrial variables are involved.

Nevertheless, if we are to achieve a better understanding of world changes in family systems, it may help if we can correct the theoretical analyses of the first problem, the fit between the ideal typical form of the conjugal family and industrialization. It seems possible to do this through some reference to common observations about both United States and European family patterns.

Let us consider first the demands of industrialization, which is the crucial element in the complex types of change now occurring in even remote parts of the world. Although bureaucratization may occur without industrialization (witness China), and so may urbanization (for example, Dahomey, Tokugawa, Japan), neither occurs without some rise in a society's technological level, and certainly the modern system of industry never occurs without *both* urbanization and bureaucratization.

The prime social characteristic of modern industrial enterprise is that the individual is ideally given a job on the basis of his ability to fulfill its demands, and that this achievement is evaluated universalistically; the same standards apply *to all who hold the same job*. His link with the job is functionally specific; in other words, the enterprise cannot require behavior of him which is not relevant to getting the job done.

Being achievement-based, an industrial society is necessarily

11. See also Moore's (1951, chs. 9, 10, 11) report on the relation between traditional family patterns and industrial demands in Mexico.

open-class, requiring both geographical and social mobility. Men must be permitted to rise or fall depending on their performance. Moreover, in the industrial system, jobs based on ownership and exploitation of land (and thus on inheritance) become numerically less significant, again permitting considerable geographical mobility so that individuals are free to move about in the labor market. The neolocality of the conjugal system correspondingly frees the individual from ties to the specific geographical location where his parental family lives.

The conjugal family's relationship to class mobility is rather complex. Current formulations, based on ancient wisdom, assert that by limiting the extensiveness of the kin network, the individual is less hampered by his family in rising upward in the job structure. Presumably, this means that he owes less to his kin and so can allocate his resources of money and time solely to further his career; perhaps he may also more freely change his style of life, his mode of dress and speech, in order to adjust to a new class position without criticism from his kin. On the other hand, an industrial system pays less attention to what the individual does off the job, so that family and job are structurally somewhat more separated than in other systems. Consequently, one might reason that differential social or occupational mobility (as among siblings or cousins) would not affect kin ties. Yet the emotional ties within the conjugal system are intense, compared to other systems, so that even though there are fewer relatives, the weight of kin relationships to be carried upward by the mobile individual might be equivalent to that in a system with more, but less intense, ties.[12]

An alternative view must also be considered. Under some circumstances the kin network actually contributes greatly to the individual's mobility, and 'social capillarity' as a process (that is, that individual rises highest who is burdened with least kin) moves fewer people upward than does a well-integrated kin network.[13] A brief theoretical sketch of this alternative view also

12. Parsons (1949, ch. 5) has analysed some parts of this relationship between role needs of job and family, and has particularly used the two pattern variables of ascription – achievement and universalism – particularism to differentiate among four types of societies.

13. For a good analysis of mobility rates in a kin-based society see Marsh (1961).

throws light on the supposed 'adjustment' between the needs of the small conjugal family and those of a modern industrial system.

First, in the modern industrial system, the middle and upper strata are by definition more 'successful' in the obvious sense that they own it, dominate it, occupy its highest positions and direct its future. One must concede that they are 'well adjusted' to the modern industrial society. Paradoxically, their kin pattern is in fact *less* close to the ideal typical form of the conjugal family than is the family behavior of the lower strata. The upper strata recognize the widest extension of kin, maintain most control over the courtship and marriage choices of their young, and are most likely to give and receive help from one another.

Consequently, the lower strata's freedom from kin is like their 'freedom' to sell their labor in an open market. They are less encumbered by the weight of kin when they are able to move upward, but they also get less help from their kin. Like English peasants, who from the sixteenth to eighteenth centuries were gradually 'freed' from the land by the enclosure movement, or nineteenth-century workers, who were 'freed' from their tools by the development of machinery, the lower strata have fewer family ties, less family stability and enjoy less family-based economic and material security. The lower-class family pattern is indeed most 'integrated' with the industrial system but mainly in the sense that the individual is forced to enter its labor market with far less family support – his family *does not prevent industry from using him for its own goals*. He may move where the system needs him, hopefully where his best opportunity lies, but he *must* also fit the demands of the system, since no extended kin network will interest itself greatly in his fate. The job demands of the industrial system move the individual about, making it difficult for him to keep his kin ties active; and because his kin are also in the lower strata he has little to lose by relinquishing those ties. In short, lower-strata families are most likely to be 'conjugal' and to serve the needs of the industrial system; this system may not, however, serve the needs of that family pattern. This means that when industrialization begins, it is the lower-class family that loses least by participating in it and that lower-class family patterns are the first to change in the society.

We might speculatively infer further that *now*, a century after the first great impact of industrialization on the lower-class family in the Western urban world, family patterns of Western middle and upper classes may be changing more rapidly than those of the lower. (Whether rural changes may not be occurring equally rapidly cannot be deduced from these inferences.) However, although this inference may be empirically correct, the available data demand a more cautious inference. Whether or not the middle and upper strata *are* now changing more rapidly in the Western world, they *do* have more resources with which to resist certain of the industrial system's undermining pressures (e.g. capital with which to support their youngsters through a long professional training) and a considerable interest in resisting them because their existing kin network is more active and useful. We would suppose, then, that in an industrializing process both the peasants and primitives are forced to adjust their family patterns to the demands of industrial enterprise more swiftly, and see less to lose in the adjustment. By contrast, the middle and upper strata are better able to utilize the new opportunities of industrialization by relinquishing their kin ties more slowly, so that these changes will occur only in a later phase of industrialization, such as the United States is now undergoing.

Continuing now with our analysis of the 'fit' of the conjugal family to industrial needs; the more limited conjugal kin network opens mobility channels somewhat by limiting the 'closure' of class strata. In general, rigid class boundaries can be maintained partly by the integration of kin bonds against the 'outsider' through family controls. When the network of each family is smaller, the families of an upper stratum are less integrated, the web of kin less tightly woven, and entrance into the stratum easier. Since the industrial system requires relatively free mobility, this characteristic of the conjugal pattern fits the needs of that system. This general principle also holds for classical China, where an empirically different system prevailed. A successful family would normally expand over generations, but thereby have insufficient resources to maintain so many at a high social rank. That is, the reciprocal exchanges necessary for tightness and closure of the kin system could be kept up only by a few individual families in the total network. If all the families in the network shared alike as kinsmen (which did not happen), the entire network would lose social rank. If the few well-to-do families helped their kin only minimally and maintained ties with other upper stratum families the integration of the stratum was kept intact and the stratification system was not threatened.

The modern technological system is psychologically burdensome on the individual because it demands an unremitting discipline. To the extent that evaluation is based on achievement and universalism, the individual gets little emotional security from his work. Some individuals, of course, obtain considerable pleasure from it, and every study of job satisfaction shows that in positions offering higher prestige and salaries a higher proportion of people are satisfied with their work and would choose that job if they had to do it again. Lower-level jobs give little pleasure to most people. However, in higher-level professional, managerial and creative positions the standards of performance are not only high but are often without clearly stated limits. The individual is under considerable pressure to perform better than he is able.

The conjugal family again integrates with such a system by its emphasis on emotionality, especially in the relationship of husband and wife. It has the task of restoring the input-output emotional balance of individualism in such a job structure. This is so even for lower-strata jobs where the demands for performance are kept within limits by an understood quota but where, by contrast with upper-strata jobs, there is less intrinsic job satisfaction. Of course, the family cannot fully succeed in this task, but at least the technological system has no moral responsibility for it and can generally ignore the problem in its work demands.

Bilateral in pattern, this family system does not maintain a lineage. It does not concentrate family land or wealth in the hands of one son through whom the property would descend, or even in the hands of one sex. Dispersal of inheritance keeps the class system fluid. Daughters as well as sons will share as heirs, and a common legal change in the West is towards equal inheritance by all children (as is already the situation generally in the United States). Relatively equal advantages are given to all the sons, and although even United States families do not invest so heavily in daughters as in sons (more boys than girls complete college), the differences in training the two sexes are much less than in other family systems. Consequently, a greater proportion of all children are given the opportunity to develop their talents to fit the manifold opportunities of a complex technological and bureaucratic structure.

The conjugal system also specifies the status obligations of each member in much less *detail* than does an extended family system, in which entrepreneurial, leadership or production tasks are assigned by family position. Consequently, wider individual variations in family role performance are permitted, to enable members to fit the range of possible demands by the industrial system as well as by other members of the family.

Since the young adult is ideally expected to make his own choice of spouse and the young couple is expected to be economically independent, the conjugal system by extending the adolescent phase of development, permits a long period of tutelage. For example, it is expected that the individual should be grown up before marrying. Note, however, that it is not the family itself that gives this extended tutelage, but public, impersonal agencies, such as schools, military units, and corporations, which ideally ignore family origin and measure the individual by his achievement and talent. This pattern permits the individual to obtain a longer period of training, to make a freer choice of his career, and to avoid the economic encumbrance of marriage until he has fitted himself into the industrial system. Thus, the needs of the industrial system are once more served by the conjugal family pattern.

References

GOODE, W. J. (1947), 'Note on the ideal type', *Amer. Sociol. Rev.*, vol. 12, pp. 473–5.

GOODE, W. J. (1959), 'The sociology of the family', in R. K. Merton, L. Broom and L. S. Cottrell (eds.), *Sociology Today*, Basic Books.

GOODE, W. J. (1959a), 'The theoretical importance of love', *Amer. Sociol. Rev.*, vol. 24, pp. 18–28.

HUGHES, C. C. (1959), 'An Eskimo deviant from the "Eskimo" type of social organisation', *Amer. Anthrop.*, vol. 60, pp. 1140–47.

KÖNIG, R. (1955), 'Familie und Familiensoziologie', in W. Bernsdorf and F. Bulow (eds.), *Worterbuch der Soziologie*, Stuttgart.

MARSH, R. (1961), *The Mandarins*, Free Press.

MARX, K. (1936), *Capital*, Modern Library.

MOORE, W. E. (1951), *Industrialization and Labor*, Cornell University Press

MURDOCK, G. P. (1949), *Social Structure*, Macmillan Co.

OGBURN, W. F. (1922), *Social Change*, Viking, rev. edn, 1952.

OGBURN, W. F. (1946), *The Social Effects of Aviation*, Houghton Mifflin.

OGBURN, W. F. (1955), *Technology and the Changing Family*, Houghton Mifflin.

PARSONS, T. (1949), *The Social System*, Free Press.

SMELSER, N. (1959), *Social Change in the Industrial Revolution*, University of Chicago Press.

SUSSMAN, M. B. (1953), 'The help pattern in the middle class family', *Amer. sociol. Rev.*, vol. 24, pp. 38–47.

TYLOR, E. B. (1888), 'On a method of investingating the development of institutions: applied to laws of marriage and descent', *J. anthrop. Inst.*, vol. 18, pp. 245–72.

WEBER, M. (1949), '"Objectivity" in social science and social policy', in *The Methodology of the Social Sciences*, Free Press. Translated by E. A. Shils and H. A. Finch.

WINCH, R. F., and FREEMAN, L. C. (1957), 'Societal complexity: an empirical test of a typology of sciences, *Amer. J. Sociol.*, vol. 62, pp. 461–6.

Further Reading

Introduction
The best introductory book on kinship is:
Fox, R., *Kinship and Marriage*, Penguin, 1967.
Radcliffe-Brown, A. R., 'Introduction' in *African Systems of Kinship and Marriage* (ed. A. R. Radcliffe-Brown and C. D. Forde), Oxford University Press, 1950, remains a most stimulating survey. So too, in a different vein, does:
Lévi-Strauss, C., *Les Structures élémentaires de la parenté*, 1949, translated into English as *The Elementary Structures of Kinship*, 1969, Eyre & Spottiswoode.
Another general work is:
Fortes, M., *Kinship and the Social Order: the Legacy of Lewis Henry Morgan*, Aldine Press, 1969.

The Family
Bott, E., *Family and Social Network*, Tavistock, 1971, 2nd edn.
Levy, M. J., and Fallers, L. A., 'The family; some comparative considerations', *American Anthropologist*, vol. 61, 1959, pp. 647–51.
Malinowski, B., 'Kinship', *Man*, vol. 30, 1930, pp. 19–29.
Parsons, T., and Bales, R. F., *Family, Socialization and Interaction Process*, Free Press, 1955.
Smith, R. T., *The Negro Family in British Guiana: Family Structure and Social Status in the Villages*, Routledge & Kegan Paul, 1956.
Smith, R. T., 'Culture and social structure in the Caribbean: some recent work on family and kinship studies', *Comparative Studies in Society and History*, vol. 6, 1963, pp. 24–46.
Spiro, M. E., 'Is the family universal?', *American Anthropologist*, vol. 56, 1954, pp. 839–46.
Spiro, M. E., *Children of the Kibbutz*, Harvard University Press, 1958.

Incest and Sex
Aberle, D. *et al.*, 'The incest taboo and the mating patterns of animals', *American Anthropologist*, vol. 65, 1963, pp. 253–65.
Davies, K., 'Intermarriage in caste societies', *American Anthropologist*, vol. 43, 1941, pp. 376–95.
Fox, J. R. 'Sibling incest', *British Journal of Sociology*, vol. 13, 1962, pp. 128–50.

Kortmulder, K., 'An ethnological theory of the incest taboo and exogamy', *Current Anthropology*, vol. 9, 1968, pp. 437–49.

Malinowski, B., *Sex and Repression in Savage Society*, Routledge & Kegan Paul, 1927.

Merton, R., 'Intermarriage and social structure; fact and theory', *Psychiatry*, vol. 4, 1941, pp. 361–74.

Middleton, R., 'Brother-sister and father-daughter marriage in Ancient Egypt', *American Sociological Review*, vol. 27, 1962, pp. 603–11.

Parsons, T., 'The incest taboo in relation to social structure and the socialization of the child', *British Journal of Sociology*, vol. 5, 1954, pp. 101–17.

Weinberg, S. K., *Incest Behaviour*, Citadel Press, 1955.

The Developmental Cycle

Collver, A., 'The family cycle in India and the United States', *American Sociological Review*, vol. 28, 1963, pp. 86–96.

Fortes, M., 'Introduction' in *The Developmental Cycle in Domestic Groups* (ed. J. Goody), Cambridge University Press, 1958.

Fortes, M., *Time and Social Structure*, Athlone Press, 1970.

Joking and Avoidance

Goody, J. 'The mother's brother and the sister's son in West Africa', *Journal of the Royal Anthropological Institute*, vol. 89, 1959, pp. 61–88. Reprinted in *Comparative Studies in Kinship*, Routledge & Kegan Paul, 1969.

Marshall, L., 'The kin terminology system of the !Kung Bushmen', *Africa*, vol. 27, 1957, pp. 1–25.

Marshall, L., 'Sharing, talking and giving: relief of social tensions among !Kung Bushmen', *Africa*, vol. 31, 1961, pp. 231–49.

Radcliffe-Brown, A. R., 'The mother's brother in South Africa', *South African Journal of Science*, vol. 21, 1924, pp. 542–55. Reprinted in *Structure and Function in Primitive Society*, Cohen & West, 1950.

Radcliffe-Brown, A. R., 'On joking relationships', *Africa*, vol. 13, 1940, pp. 195–210. Reprinted in *Structure and Function in Primitive Society*, Cohen & West, 1950.

Marriage Transactions

Bohannan, L., 'Dahomean marriage: a revaluation', *Africa*, vol. 29, 1949, pp. 273–87.

Evans-Pritchard, E. E., *Kinship and Marriage among the Nuer*, Clarendon Press, 1951.

Gray, R. R., 'Sonjo bride-price and the question of African "wife-purchase"', *American Anthropologist*, vol. 62, 1960, pp. 34–57.
Yalman, N., *Under the Bo Tree: Studies in Caste, Kinship and Marriage in the Interior of Ceylon*, University of California Press, 1967.

Plural Marriage
Clignet, R., *Many Wives, Many Powers: Authority and Power in Polygynous Families*, Northwestern University Press, 1970.
Gough, E. K., 'The Nayars and the definition of marriage', *Journal of the Royal Anthropological Institute*, vol. 89, 1959, pp. 23–34.
HRH Prince Peter of Greece and Denmark, *A Study of Polyandry*, Mouton, 1963.
Smith, M. G. ,'Secondary marriage in Northern Nigeria', *Africa*, vol. 23, 1953, pp. 298–323.

Marriage and Alliance
Ackerman, C., 'Structure and statistics: the Purum case', *American Anthropologist*, vol. 65, 1964, pp. 53–6.
Coult, A. D., 'An analysis of Needham's critique of the Homans-Schneider theory', *Southwestern Journal of Anthropology*, vol. 18, 1962, pp. 317–35.
Homans, G. C., and Schneider, D. M., *Marriage, Authority and Final Causes*, Free Press, 1955.
Leach, E. R., *Political Systems of Highland Burma*, Bell, 1954.
Needham, R., *Structure and Sentiment*, University of Chicago Press, 1962.
Schneider, D. M., 'Some muddles in the models', in *The Relevance of Models for Social Anthropology*, Tavistock, 1965.

Divorce and Marriage Stability
Ackerman, C., 'Affiliations: structural determinants of differential divorce rates', *American Journal of Sociology*, vol. 69, 1963, pp.13–20.
Ardener, E., *Divorce and Fertility: an African Study*, Oxford University Press, 1962.
Fallers, L. A. 'Some determinants of marriage instability in Busoga: a reformulation of Gluckman's thesis', *Africa*, vol. 27, 1957, pp. 106–21.
Goode, W. J.. 'Marital satisfaction and instability: a cross-cultural class analysis of divorce rates', *International Social Science Journal*, vol. 14, 1962, pp. 507–26.
Goody, E. N., 'Conjugal separation and divorce among the Gonja of Northern Ghana', in *Marriage in Tribal Societies* (ed. M. Fortes), Cambridge University Press, 1962.

Goody, J., and Goody, E., 'The circulation of women and children in Northern Ghana', *Man*, n.s., vol. 2, 1969, pp. 226–48. Reprinted in J. Goody, *Comparative Studies in Kinship*, Routledge & Kegan Paul, 1969.

Leach, E. R., 'Aspects of bridewealth and marriage stability among the Kachin and Lakher', *Man*, vol. 57, 1961, pp. 50–55. Reprinted in *Rethinking Anthropology*, Athlone Press, 1961.

Kin Groups

For a summary of recent work, see my article on 'Kinship: Descent Groups', in D. L. Sills (ed.), *Encyclopedia of the Social Sciences*, Macmillan Co. 1968.

For a discussion of basic concepts see: Schneider, D. M. 'Some muddles in the models: or, how the system really works', in M. Banton (ed.), *The Relevance of Models for Social Anthropology*, Association of Social Anthropologists, monograph no. 1, Tavistock, 1965.

For the discussion of particular types of kin groups, see:

Davenport, W., 'Nonunilinear descent and descent groups', *American Anthropologist*, vol. 61, 1959, pp. 557–72.

Firth, R., 'Bilateral descent groups: an operational viewpoint', in *Studies in Kinship and Marriage* (ed. I. Schapera), pp. 22–37, Royal Anthropological Institute, 1963.

Freeman, J. D., 'On the concept of the kindred', *Journal of the Royal Anthropological Institute*, vol. 91, 1961, pp. 192–220.

Goodenough, W. H., 'A problem in Malayo-Polynesian social organization', *American Anthropologist*, vol. 57, 1955, pp. 71–83.

Goody, J., 'The classification of double descent systems', *Current Anthropology*, vol. 2, 1961, pp. 3–25. Reprinted in J. Goody, *Comparative Studies in Kinship*, Routledge & Kegan Paul, 1969.

Scheffler, H. W., 'Ancestor worship in anthropology: or, Observations on descent and descent groups', *Current Anthropology*, vol. 7, 1966, pp. 541–51.

Schneider, D. M., and Gough, K., *Matrilineal Kinship*, University of California Press, 1961.

Smith, M. G., 'On segmentary lineage systems', *Journal of the Royal Anthropological Institute*, vol. 86, 1956, pp. 39–80.

For a comparison of systems of unilineal descent see:

Barnes, J. A., 'African models in the New Guinea highlands', *Man*, vol. 62, 1962, pp. 5–9.

Fried, M. H., 'The classification of corporate unilineal descent groups', *Journal of the Royal Anthropological Institute*, vol. 87, 1957, pp. 1–30.
Lewis, I. M., 'Problems in the comparative study of unilineal descent', in M. Banton (ed.), *The Relevance of Models for Social Anthropology*, pp. 87–112, Association of Social Anthropologists, monograph no. 1, Tavistock, 1965.

For studies of societies with descent groups see:

America
Eggan, F., *Social Organisation of the Western Pueblos*, University of Chicago Press, 1950.
Eggan, F. (ed.), *Social Anthropology of North American Tribes*, University of Chicago Press, 1962.
Fox, R., *The Keresan Bridge*, Athlone Press, 1967.

New Guinea
Glasse, R. M., and Meggitt, M. J. (eds.), *Pigs, Pearlshells, and Women: Marriage in the New Guinea Highlands*, Prentice-Hall, 1969.
Strathern, A., 'Descent and alliance in the New Guinea highlands: some problems of comparison', *Proceedings of the Royal Anthropological Institute*, 1968, pp. 37–52.

Australia
Warner, W. L., *A Black Civilization*, Harper & Row, 1937. Revised edn. 1958.
Meggitt, M. J., *Desert People*, Angus & Robertson, 1962.

Africa
Evans-Pritchard, E. E., *The Nuer*, Clarendon Press, 1940.
Evans-Pritchard, E. E., *Kinship and Marriage among the Nuer*, Clarendon Press, 1951.
Fortes, M., *The Dynamics of Clanship among the Tallensi*, Oxford University Press, 1945.
Fortes, M., *The Web of Kinship among the Tallensi*, Oxford University Press, 1949.

China
Freedman, M., *Lineage Organisation in South-eastern China*, Athlone Press, 1958.
Freedman, M., *Chinese Lineage and Society: Fukien and Kwangtung*, Athlone Press, 1966.

Oceania
Firth, R., *We, the Tikopia*, Allen & Unwin, 1936.

For non-unilineal systems see:
Arensberg, C. M. and Kimball, S. T., *Family and Community in Ireland*, Harvard University Press, 1940.
Barton, R. F., *The Kalingas*, University of Chicago Press, 1949.
Campbell, J. K., *Honour, Family and Patronage*, Clarendon Press, 1964.
Pehrson, R. N., 'The bilateral network of social relations in Könkämä Lapp district', *International Journal of American Linguistics*, vol. 23, 1957, part 2.
Schneider, D. M., *American Kinship: a Cultural Account*, Prentice-Hall, 1968.
Young, M. and Wilmott, P., *Family and Kinship in East London*, Routledge & Kegan Paul, 1957, Penguin, 1962.

Kin Terms
Goodenough, W. H., 'Componential analysis and the study of meaning', *Language*, vol. 32, 1956, pp. 195–216.
Hammel, E. A. (ed.), 'Formal semantic analysis', *American Anthropologist*, Special Issue, vol. 67, 1965.
Lounsbury, F. G., 'The structural analysis of kinship semantics', *Proceedings of the Ninth International Congress of Linguists*, Mouton, 1962.
Lounsbury, F. G., 'A formal account of the Crow- and Omaha-type kinship terminologies', in W. H. Goodenough (ed.), *Explorations in Cultural Anthropology: Essays in Honour of George Peter Murdock*, McGraw-Hill, 1964, pp. 351–93.
Lowie, R. F., and Eggan, F. R., 'Kinship terminology', *Encyclopaedia Britannica*, vol. 13, 1964, pp. 407–409.
Murdock, G. P., *Social Structure*, Macmillan, 1949.

Ritual and Fictive Kinship
Carroll, V. (ed.), *Adoption in Eastern Oceania*, Bishop Museum, Hawaii, 1970.
Goody, E. N., 'Kinship fostering in Gonja: deprivation or advantage?', in P. Mayer (ed.), *Socialisation: the Approach of Social Anthropology*, Tavistock, 1970.
Goody, J., 'Adoption in cross-cultural perspective', *Comparative Studies in Society and History*, vol. 11, 1969, pp. 55–78.

Hammel, E. A., *Alternative Social Structures and Ritual Relations in the Balkans*, Prentice-Hall, 1968.
Pitt-Rivers, J., 'Pseudo-kinship', *International Encyclopedia of the Social Sciences*, vol. 8, pp. 408–413, Macmillan, 1968.

Changing Patterns of Kinship
Goode, W. J., *World Revolution and Family Patterns*, Free Press, 1963.
Laslett, P., *The World We Have Lost*, Methuen, 1965.

Acknowledgements

Permission to reproduce the Readings in this volume is acknowledged to the following sources:

1 Thomas T. Crowell Co. Inc. and Richard N. Adams
2 George Allen & Unwin Ltd and the Macaulay Co.
3 Routledge & Kegan Paul Ltd and Humanities Press Inc.
4 Eyre & Spottiswoode (Publishers) Ltd and Beacon Press
5 Routledge & Kegan Paul Ltd and Stanford University Press
6 Cambridge University Press and Meyer Fortes
7 Routledge & Kegan Paul Ltd and Free Press
8 Oxford University Press for the International African Institute
9 Holt, Rinehart & Winston Inc. and Ernestine Friedl
10 Edward Arnold (Publishers) Ltd and J. Hajnal
11 Royal Anthropological Institute
12 Northwestern University Press
13 Royal Anthropological Institute
14 *Southwestern Journal of Anthropology* and D. Maybury-Lewis
15 Oxford University Press for the International African Institute and Max Gluckman
16 Oxford University Press for the International African Institute
17 Athlone Press, American Anthropological Association and Meyer Fortes
18 Oxford University Press for the International African Institute
19 University of Manila Press
21 Royal Anthropological Institute
22 American Anthropological Association and Eugene Hammel
23 Esther Goody
24 *Southwestern Journal of Anthropology* and Eric R. Wolf
25 Free Press and William Goode

Author Index

Ackerman, C., 219, 235, 236, 237, 238, 239, 241, 244
Adam, L., 278, 294
Adams, R. N., 17
Aiyappan, A., 159, 184

Bachofen, J. J., 11
Baker, T., 177
Banton, M., 176
Barnes, J. A., 234, 235, 244, 255, 259
Beattie, J., 323
Best, E., 51
Bird, M., 176, 177
Blake, J., 174
Bloomfield, L., 318, 319
Boas, F., 317, 319
Bohannan, L., 231, 251, 273
Bott, E., 233, 237
Braithwaite, R. B., 222
Brass, W., 165, 173
Briffault, R., 184
Burling, R., 320

Carneiro, R. L., 19
Caroll, V., 342
Chomsky, N., 319
Chowning, A., 302
Clement, P., 176
Clerc, A., 232
Clignet, R., 10, 149
Cohen, R., 173
Coult, A. D., 203, 204, 205, 209, 211
Crook, J. A., 340
Csoscán, J., 140, 141

D'Andrade, R. G. D., 321
Davenport, W., 262
Davis, K., 174
Dole, G. E., 19
Dorjahn, V., 164, 171, 173
Dumont, L., 181, 200, 202, 204, 215, 219, 222
Durkheim, E., 57, 181, 233, 235, 249, 307

Eggan, F., 101, 102, 302, 358
Engels, F., 10
Evans-Pritchard, E. E., 77, 114, 228, 230, 231, 233

Fallers, L. F., 235, 239, 240, 241, 242
Firth, R., 262, 278, 280
Fischer, H., 151, 152
Forde, D., 156, 265, 268, 282, 283, 302
Fortes, M., 26, 66, 70, 71, 78, 79, 83, 105, 115, 155, 231, 256, 261, 302
Fortune, R. F., 60, 76, 77, 79
Foster, G. N., 348
Frazer, J. G., 181, 307
Freeman, J., 262
Freud, S., 45, 76
Friedl, E., 9, 117, 149

Galton, F., 11
Gamble, D., 176
Gardin, J. C., 319, 322
Gautier, E., 141
Gifford, E. W., 317
Gillen, F. J., 217

Gillin, J., 349, 357
Ginsberg, M., 11
Gluckman, M., 225, 233, 239, 243, 250, 251, 254, 259, 374
Gonzales, R. F., 352
Goode, W. J., 9, 10, 363, 372, 373
Goodenough, W., 36, 88, 262, 297, 303, 319, 324
Goody, E., 234, 235, 329, 336
Goody, J., 45, 302, 304
Gough, E. K., 153, 332
Graburn, N. H. H., 324

Hajnal, J., 9, 10, 117
Hallam, H. E., 146
Hammel, E. A., 209, 297, 321, 339
Harris, Z. S., 318
Henry, L., 141
Hjelmslev, L., 318
Hobhouse, L. T., 11
Hockett, C. F., 318
Hoebel, E. A., 290
Hoijer, H., 301
Homans, G. C., 145, 203, 205, 207
Howitt, A. W., 307

Jacobson, A., 244, 245
Jakobson, R., 318
Junod, H., 102, 232

Kirchoff, P., 284, 299
Kroeber, A. L., 267, 270, 299, 303, 307, 308, 317, 319

LaBarre, W., 19
Labauret, H., 105, 113
Lamb, S. M., 319
Lane, R. B., 209, 211, 212, 213
Leach, E. R., 149, 202, 203, 204, 205, 219, 222, 235, 240, 241, 242, 244, 301, 323, 324
Le Play, P. G. F., 144
LeVine, R., 166
Levi-Strauss, C., 45, 76, 79, 181, 201, 207, 218, 219, 222
Levy, M. J., Jr, 20
Little, K., 176
Linton, R., 55, 279
Livingstone, F. B., 209, 211, 214
Lonsbury, F. G., 297, 301, 303, 304, 319, 321, 323, 324
Lowie, R., 29, 299, 317
Lubbock, J., 50

McLennan, J. F., 11, 50, 303
Maine, H., 11
Malinowski, B., 10, 12, 17, 45, 56, 57, 60, 65, 66, 69, 70, 76, 77, 261, 266, 302, 304, 376
Malthus, T. R., 140
Marriott, M., 290
Marsh, R., 378
Marx, K., 10, 369, 370
Mauss, M., 101, 181
Maybury-Lewis, D., 181, 205
Mead, M., 55, 56
Mercier, P., 176
Middleton, J., 243
Middleton, R., 302
Mintz, S. W., 329, 337
Mitchell, J. C., 225, 244, 272
Monteil, V., 175
Moore, F., 163
Moore, W. E., 377
Morgan, L. H., 10, 299, 304, 307, 308, 309, 317
Muhsam, H. V., 174
Murdock, G. P., 11, 19, 20, 24, 25, 26, 27, 28, 31, 34, 65, 66, 76, 163, 203, 204, 300, 301, 302, 318, 369, 374
Murphy, R. F., 222

Nadel, S. F., 268
Needham, R., 199, 200, 201, 202, 204, 206, 207, 209, 210, 211, 215, 218, 219, 220, 221, 222
Nimkoff, M. F., 302, 369

Ogburn, W. F., 370, 371

Parsons, E. C., 348
Parsons, T., 24, 25, 26, 27, 28, 31, 34, 76, 378
Paul, B. D., 348, 350, 353
Paulme, D., 102, 105, 113
Pedler, F. J., 104, 105
Pehrson, R., 262
Peter, H.R.H., Prince of Greece and Denmark, 151, 152, 153, 155, 157
Pospisil, I., 324
Powell, H., 301

Radcliffe-Brown, A. R., 12, 30, 31, 65, 66, 76, 99, 117, 152, 228, 263, 271, 297, 302, 303, 313, 317
Rathray, R. S., 66, 68, 69
Redfield, R., 348, 352
Richards, A. I., 231, 252, 253, 254, 255, 259, 261, 269
Rivers, W. H. R., 200, 279, 301, 317
Romney, A. K., 321

Salisbury, R. F., 211, 213, 214, 216
Sapir, E., 310, 317
Sawer, J., 159, 160, 166
Schneider, D. M., 203, 205, 207, 220, 221, 222, 233, 320, 323, 324
Seligman, B. Z., 54, 76, 79, 317

Smelser, N., 370
Smith, A., 121
Smith, R. T., 23, 24, 25, 26, 27, 31, 32, 33, 35
de Sonsberghe, L., 212, 213
Spencer, B., 217
Spicer, E., 355, 356
Spier, L., 300
Spiro, M. E., 20, 30
Srinivas, M. N., 195
Sussman, M. B., 373

Tardits, C., 176
Tax, S., 317
Taylor, L. R., 340
Thomas, N. W., 278
Thore, L., 176
Torday, E., 284
Tyler, S. A., 321, 324
Tylor, E. B., 9, 11, 45, 60, 76, 78, 99, 181, 367

Von Humboldt, W., 317
Villa R, A., 348, 352, 353, 354
Vinogradoff, P., 120

Warner, W. L., 309
Weber, M., 263, 372
Westermarck, E. A., 17
Wheeler, G. C., 11
Whiting, J., 174
Whorf, B. L., 317
Williams, F. E., 60
Wilson, G., 255, 256, 257, 258, 259
Winch, R. F., 170, 369
Winter, E. H., 243
Wisdom, C., 352
Wolf, E. R., 329, 337

Zelditch, M., Jr, 166

Subject Index

Adoption, 91, 342–4
  Roman, 340–41
Adrogation, 340–42
Adultery, 64–81, 128
  payment, 67
Alliance, 105, 106, 112–15, 129–32, 181, 183–98
  see also Marriage
Ancestors, 132
Avoidance relationships, 99, 102–15

Bilateral systems, 23, 290–95
Blood-brotherhood, 54–62, 112, 113
Bridewealth, 117, 119–32, 169, 250, 286

Child-rearing, 89–98, 331–44
Church, 121–32
Clans, 216, 277
Class, 379–82
Class hypogamy, 240
Complementary filiation, 267–74
Componential analysis, 9, 297, 303, 318
Conjugal family, 371–82 see also Family, Nuclear family
Corporate group, 229, 252, 270, 271
Cousin terms, 300
Cross cousin, 213, 300
  classificatory, 203
Cross-cousin marriage, 11, 53, 61, 104–15, 131–2, 157, 181, 183–98, 200–223, 284
  matrilateral, 184, 200, 201–23
  patrilateral, 200, 207–223
  bilateral, 211, 214, 214–23

Demographic factors, 10
Descent, 9, 11, 96–8, 181, 263–74, 281
Descent groups, 205–23, 263–76, 290–95
  matrilineal, 66–81, 227, 245, 252
  patrilineal, 66–81, 227, 267
Developmental cycle, 83, 85–98
Divorce, 149, 225, 231–46, 248–60
Domestic group, 85–98
Double unilineal descent, 156
Dowry, 117, 119–31, 134–9

Endogamy, 11, 48–62, 157
Evolutionary theories, 367
Exchange, 113–15, 129–32
Exogamy, 11, 42, 45, 48–62, 65, 69, 77–81, 90, 134–9, 250, 281–8
Extended family, 280, 283, 291

Family, 17, 19–36, 42–4, 64–81, 83, 86–98, 276–88
'Father-right', 241, 244
Fictive kinship, 329
Filiation, 181, 266, 272
Formal analysis, 317
Fosterage, 335–44
Fostering, 331–44
  voluntary, 343

Genetical rights, 251–60

Grand family, 280

Incest, 11, 45, 50, 51, 56–62, 64–81, 250, 274
Inheritance, 90, 134–9, 151–61, 191–8, 229, 271–4
Initiation, 44, 57, 94, 95, 119

Joking relations, 10, 99, 101–15
Jural authority, 96, 251

Kibbutz, 20, 30
Kin groups, 9, 123–32, 261–2
 bilateral, 254, 290–95
Kin network, 135–9, 336, 372, 380
Kin terms, 110–12, 297, 307–15, 320 *see* Kinship terminology
Kinship, 10, 11, 17, 38, 47–62, 52, 65, 78, 83, 183–91, 249–55 256, 323, 363
 categories, 212, 220
 classificatory, 90, 107, 216
 matrilineal, 255, 276–81
 patrilineal, 255
 system, 30, 42–4, 53, 106–10, 227–46, 254
Kinship terminology, 185–91, 290, 297, 317, 358
 Arunta type, 217, 218
 Australian type, 309
 Crow type, 215, 301, 303, 321
 Eskimo type, 309
 Hawaiian type, 300
 Iroquois type, 300
 Kariera type, 217, 218
 Omaha type, 215, 216, 301, 303, 321
Komstvo, 339

Land tenure, 134–9
Legitimacy, 38–41, 158
Levirate, 11, 165, 234, 236, 239, 243, 245, 310, 311

Lineage, 31, 91–3, 264, 265, 273, 277–88

Marriage, 9, 47–62, 88–9, 102–4, 119–32, 151–61, 181, 227, 368
 alliance, 47–62, 77, 183–98
 father's sister's daughter, 200–13
 gifts, 191–8
 see also Dowry
 mother's brother's daughter, 200–13
 patterns, 140–47
 payments, 10, 120–32, 177, 227–32, 240, 244, 258, 286
 plural, 76, 149, 163–78
 preferential, 203, 213, 221–3
 prescriptive systems, 181, 199–223
 prohibitions, 55–62, 65–6
 regulations, 183–5
 residence patterns, 134–9, 169–78, 227, 278–81, 290–95, 368, 373
 stability, 225, 228–32, 233–46, 248–60, 286
 transactions, 117, 119–32
 transfer of rights at, 227
Maternal dyad, 20–36
Matrilineal belt, 276

Nuclear family, 17, 19–36, 331–44

Oedipus complex, 17, 43
Orphans, 343–4

Parent–child relationship, 38–41, 329, 331–44
Polyandry, 149, 151–61
Polygyny, 10, 117, 149, 151–61, 163–78, 284
 sororal, 165, 166, 169

398 Subject Index

Polykoity, 151
  adelphic, 152, 157
Potestas, 128, 340–42
Prestations, 90, 124, 192–8
  see also Marriage gifts

Reciprocities of rearing, 333
Reciprocity, 60, 315
Residence patterns, 87–98
Rites de passage, 93, 94
Ritual co-parenthood
  (*compadrazgo*), 329, 346–60
Ritual sponsorship, 337–9
  see also Komstvo

Segmentation, 91, 264, 267
Sex ratio, 257
Sexual offences, 66–81
Sexual prohibitions, 45, 72–81
Sibling groups, 31, 96, 152, 267, 268, 291, 295
Slavery, 91, 284, 285
Social change, 85–98, 175–8, 284–60
Social structure (organization), 20, 29, 30, 38–41, 112–15, 119–32, 227–46, 307–15
Sororate, 11, 243, 311
Sponsorship, 333, 346
Status, 51, 167, 271, 272, 332, 333, 334, 339
Stem-family, 144
Structural approach, 26–8, 28
Succession, 90, 252, 276–88

Taboo, 45, 302
  incest, 65–6
  sexual, 174

Unilineal descent groups, 66–81, 90–98, 228, 261, 263–74
  see also Double unilineal descent
Uxorial rights, 251–60

Virginity payments, 258

Wedding, 120
Wido inheritance, 165, 240